Corporate Communication

SAGE was founded in 1965 by Sara Miller McCune to support the dissemination of usable knowledge by publishing innovative and high-quality research and teaching content. Today, we publish over 900 journals, including those of more than 400 learned societies, more than 800 new books per year, and a growing range of library products including archives, data, case studies, reports, and video. SAGE remains majority-owned by our founder, and after Sara's lifetime will become owned by a charitable trust that secures our continued independence.

Los Angeles | London | New Delhi | Singapore | Washington DC | Melbourne

Corporate Communication

5th edition

A Guide to Theory & Practice

Joep Cornelissen

Los Angeles | London | New Delhi
Singapore | Washington DC | Melbourne

Los Angeles | London | New Delhi
Singapore | Washington DC | Melbourne

SAGE Publications Ltd
1 Oliver's Yard
55 City Road
London EC1Y 1SP

SAGE Publications Inc.
2455 Teller Road
Thousand Oaks, California 91320

SAGE Publications India Pvt Ltd
B 1/I 1 Mohan Cooperative Industrial Area
Mathura Road
New Delhi 110 044

SAGE Publications Asia-Pacific Pte Ltd
3 Church Street
#10-04 Samsung Hub
Singapore 049483

Editor: Matthew Waters
Editorial assistant: Lyndsay Aitken
Production editor: Sarah Cooke
Copyeditor: Sharon Cawood
Proofreader: Tom Hickman
Indexer: Martin Hargreaves
Marketing manager: Alison Borg
Cover design: Francis Kenney
Typeset by: C&M Digitals (P) Ltd, Chennai, India
Printed in the UK

Library of Congress Control Number: 2016944938

British Library Cataloguing in Publication data

A catalogue record for this book is available from
the British Library

ISBN 978-1-4739-5369-7
ISBN 978-1-4739-5370-3 (pbk)

At SAGE we take sustainability seriously. Most of our products are printed in the UK using FSC papers and boards.
When we print overseas we ensure sustainable papers are used as measured by the PREPS grading system.
We undertake an annual audit to monitor our sustainability.

Summary of Contents

Contents

List of Figures

List of Tables

List of Case Studies

List of Case Examples

About the Author

 Joep Cornelissen is a Professor in Corporate Communication and Management at the Rotterdam School of Management, Erasmus University and a Visiting Professor at IE Business School in Madrid. In his day job, he teaches corporate communication and change management on executive and MBA programmes and actively writes on these topics for leading academic journals such as the *Academy of Management Review*, *Organization Science* and the *Journal of Management Studies*. He also frequently speaks at conferences and draws on his management and communication expertise to work with entrepreneurs and managers in private and public sector organizations.

Preface to the Fifth Edition

The world of business is constantly changing. Since the previous editions of the book, there have been a number of high-profile scandals in the corporate world and we have been through an economic downturn in most parts of the globe. These conditions have created a very difficult trading environment for many companies, and, equally, many organizations have had a rough time in communication and reputation terms. Companies that previously were the darling of the stock market or the preferred choice of customers may have seen the tables turned on them and may no longer enjoy strong reputations.

Stakeholders, for their part, also increasingly demand insight and information from companies in a quest for more transparency. The new media landscape has added further pressures in this respect, with citizens and customers blogging and tweeting about companies and with critical journalists zealously looking for gaps, contradictions and discrepancies in corporate messages. The decisions and actions of companies are increasingly put under the microscope.

Whilst the environment for companies is constantly changing and has perhaps become more challenging in recent years, the central message across these trends is clear: executives and practitioners within organizations need to be empowered with a way of thinking and with tools that can help them navigate the current corporate landscape in which reputations have become more fragile and stakeholders have become more demanding. The basic idea underlying the book, therefore, is to equip the reader with an understanding of the concepts and tools of corporate communication.

PURPOSE OF THE BOOK

This book is about corporate communication. Its chief aim is to provide a comprehensive and up-to-date treatment of the subject of corporate communication. The book incorporates current thinking and developments on the topic from both the academic and practitioner worlds, combining a comprehensive theoretical foundation with numerous practical guidelines and insights to assist managers in their day-to-day work and in their strategic and tactical communication decisions. Illustrative examples and case studies are based on companies in the USA, the UK, continental Europe, South-East Asia and elsewhere.

In other words, in a comprehensive and practical manner, the book aims to provide insights into the nature of corporate communication, the issues that define this critical area of practice, the strategies and activities that fall within its remit, and the ways in which it can be managed in companies. Specifically, the reader will learn about the following:

- the nature of corporate communication, its historical emergence and its role in contemporary companies
- the critical role of corporate communication in building and maintaining relationships with the stakeholders of a company
- the key issues – corporate social responsibility, reputation management, corporate branding, corporate identity, integrated communication – that define this area of practice and how to deal with them
- different approaches to developing corporate communication strategies and to implementing communication programmes and campaigns
- different approaches to measuring and monitoring the impact of communication on stakeholders' opinions and on the company's reputation
- the key activities and skills in specific disciplines and emerging areas of practice, including change communication, social media, issues management, crisis communication, employee communication and community relations.

APPROACH OF THE BOOK

For the fifth edition of the book, my aim again was to satisfy three key criteria by which any management text can be judged:

- Depth: the material in the book needs to be comprehensive in covering both the academic and practitioner literatures and the knowledge base of corporate communication.
- Breadth: the book covers the range of topics that define the field of corporate communication and that practising managers and students of corporate communication find important or of interest.
- Relevance: the book has to be well grounded in practice and easily relatable to practical examples and case studies.

Although a number of books on corporate communication exist in the market, it has been my belief that no book has really maximized these three dimensions to the best possible extent. Accordingly, this book sets out to fill that gap by accomplishing three things.

First, instead of being only based on practitioner experiences and anecdotes or case-based learning, the book provides an evidence-based account of corporate communication by drawing on theories, models and concepts from academic research.

Second, all the contemporary and important themes and topics within the remit of corporate communication, including 'corporate social responsibility', 'social media' and 'stakeholder management', are discussed in detail. Particular attention is paid to central topics such as the structuring of the communication function within organizations and the development of communication strategies and programmes – these have received little attention in other books.

Third, the book not only presents the latest academic thinking and research on the subject, but also features case studies and shorter case examples to illustrate the concepts and themes of the book and to meet the 'double hurdle' of academic rigour and practical relevance.

For the fifth edition, all the case studies and topics have been updated with more cases from the USA and South-East Asia added to the text. The text itself has also been revised and updated, and I have added new material and chapters on social media, employee communication, leadership communication and anti-corporate activism.

In summary, by combining theory with practical cases and examples, the fifth edition of the book provides a comprehensive, practically grounded and up-to-date overview of the state and playing field of corporate communication. All the major critical issues in managing communications are discussed, providing practising managers with appropriate concepts, theories and tools to enable them to make better management and communication decisions. And thus, after reading the book, readers will, I hope, have gained a greater appreciation and a more in-depth understanding of the range of topics covered in corporate communication, as well as a means to organize their thoughts on those topics.

READERSHIP OF THE BOOK

A wide range of people can benefit from reading this book, including the following groups:

- students at the graduate level enrolled on a business, management, marketing, corporate communication, public relations or business communication course, who are interested in increasing their understanding of the theory and practice of corporate communication
- managers and marketing and communication professionals with an interest in aspects of corporate communication (such as change or leadership communication), who are concerned with making informed decisions that will maximize their day-to-day performance
- senior executives looking for an understanding of corporate communication and what it can do for their business
- academics researching and reading in the areas of corporate communication, public relations, marketing and strategic management who are looking for a resource guide that contains all the major topics in corporate communication in a single volume.

ORGANIZATION OF THE BOOK

As mentioned, the aim of this book is to present an overview of the theory and practice of corporate communication. The distinction between the 'theory' and 'practice' of corporate communications is intentional and implies that the book aims to integrate theoretical concepts and frameworks on corporate communication with more hands-on, practice-based insights and skills from the profession. In the book, I also take the view that corporate communication is a field of management within organizations, and that not only our understanding of it but also the development of the field are best served by adopting a management perspective. This means that alternative sociological and critical perspectives on corporate communication are included in the book's ruminations on the field, yet are considered of secondary importance in view of the core management perspective of the book.

Adopting this management perspective, the book is laid out in five parts:

Part 1, Introduction to Corporate Communication, provides a characterization of the historical and practical roots of the field of corporate communication and defines the role and use of corporate communication in contemporary organizations and in a changing media environment.

Part 2, Conceptual Foundations, includes two chapters on key concepts such as stakeholders and corporate reputation and on communication models that provide the theoretical background to the practice of corporate communication.

Part 3, Corporate Communication in Practice, includes two chapters that focus on the development of a communication strategy, the planning and execution of communication programmes and campaigns, and on research and measurement of communication effects.

Part 4, Specialist Areas in Corporate Communication, covers important specialist areas within corporate communication: media relations, employee communication, issues management and crisis communication.

Part 5, New Developments in Corporate Communication, involves chapters on important emerging areas of practice within corporate communication: change and leadership communication and corporate social responsibility (CSR) and community relations.

The chapters in each part include case studies and case examples and a list of sources for further reading. At the tail end of the book, the reader will find a glossary of key communication terminology that may be useful as a quick reference to the key concepts in corporate communication.

Joep Cornelissen,
Amsterdam, June 2016

Acknowledgements

In writing, revising and editing this book, I have had a lot of help and encouragement from corporate communication colleagues and practitioners around Europe. I have also benefited from the wisdom of colleagues and graduate students at the various institutions with which I have been associated. I would also like to thank my reviewers as well as Karel Slootman (Motivaction), Betteke Van Ruler (University of Amsterdam) and Michael Etter (Copenhagen Business School) for useful suggestions. At Sage Publishing, Delia Martínez Alfonso has been a friend and supporter for years, and without her this book would never have been written. Thanks also go to Matthew Waters and Lyndsay Aitken at Sage who supported me for this fifth edition. Finally, Mirjam, Siri and Freya, as always, have offered me lots of cheerful respite from working on this latest edition of the book and have been really patient with me over the past couple of months as I put the finishing touches to the text.

Guided Tour

CHAPTER OVERVIEW

Recent years have witnessed the growing use of social media and Web 2.0 technologies to communicate with employees, customers, the news media and other stakeholders. The chapter categorizes these new media and discusses the challenges and opportunities around using these tools and technologies as part of corporate communication. Besides providing an overview of the changing media environment for corporate communication, the chapter also provides case examples and outlines the practical benefits associated with the use of social media and Web 2.0 technologies.

Chapter overview: A brief synopsis of each chapter is provided.

3.1 INTRODUCTION

Recent years have seen an explosion in the opportunities and use of 'new' media in society, including social media sites such as Facebook, Wikipedia and YouTube and other Web 2.0 applications such as blogs and wikis. These advances in media and web technology provide new challenges and opportunities for organizations to communicate and engage with their stakeholders, including their own employees, local communities, customers and the news media. The basic trend associated with the development of these new media is that it highlights the democratization of the production and dissemination of news on organizations, enabled by web technologies. Rather than the classic model of communication practitioners liaising with official news channels, blogs and social networking sites now also offer content on organizations, and indeed may influence stakeholders or the general public in their perceptions and subsequent behaviours. Equally, employees can nowadays distribute their own information about an organization electronically to outside stakeholders, often

Introduction: The introduction provides the overall framework of each chapter.

3.5 CHAPTER SUMMARY

In this chapter, we have provided an overview of the changing media environment of corporate communication. The chapter started by setting the scene for developments around social media. We then provided a classification of social media that puts the characteristics of each medium in perspective and highlights their potential use as part of corporate communication. The chapter ended by summarizing the practical benefits of using social media as part of corporate communication.

Chapter summary: We review the main concepts and issues to be sure that you are clear on what was covered, and why.

Case study: Each chapter contains an international case study, accompanied by questions designed for reflective learning and the reinforcement of key concepts.

Case example: Corporate communication topics are illustrated with full, real-life examples supported by useful reflective questions.

Discussion questions: Questions are provided at the end of each chapter to encourage you to explore what you have learnt.

Key terms: Each chapter's key terms are listed here and in the glossary at the end of the book, which covers all of the book's key concepts.

Further reading: Relevant articles and book chapters will enhance your understanding of each chapter.

Companion Website

Joep Cornelissen's *Corporate Communication*, 5th edition is supported by a companion website. Visit https://study.sagepub.com/cornelissen5e to take advantage of the learning resources for students and lecturers.

For students:

- Full-text journal articles: Access to a selection of free Sage journal articles provides students with a deeper understanding of the topics in each chapter.
- Glossary: A glossary of key terms and definitions is available online.
- Weblinks: Direct links to relevant websites for each chapter are provided.
- Author-selected videos: Students can link to a collection of videos relevant to the key themes and hot topics covered in the textbook directly from the site.
- Link to the author's blog: The blog includes contributions from other figures in the field which develop and provide further discussion around the book's topics and themes.
- Author video: Watch the author offer further insights on-screen.

For lecturers:

- Case study notes: These notes provide model answers to the 'questions for reflection' for each case study detailed in the book, to support lecturers' seminar and class teaching.
- PowerPoint slides: PowerPoint slides for each chapter for use in class are also provided.
- Additional case studies: These additional case studies will provide further teaching support.
- Multiple-choice questions: A test bank containing questions related to the key concepts in each chapter can be downloaded and used in class, as homework or for exams.

Introduction

1

In Part 1, we explore the historical development of communication within organizations, describe why corporate communication emerged and demonstrate the importance of corporate communication to contemporary organizations. The basic characteristics of corporate communication are described *vis-à-vis* related concepts such as marketing communication and public relations.

After reading Part 1, the reader should be familiar with the basic characteristics of corporate communication, its historical emergence and its relevance to contemporary organizations.

Defining Corporate Communication

1

⌐ **CHAPTER OVERVIEW** ⌐

This introductory chapter provides a definition of corporate communication and lays out the themes for the remainder of the book. The chapter starts with a brief discussion of the importance of corporate communication, defines key concepts and spotlights a number of important trends and developments in corporate communication.

1.1 INTRODUCTION

There is a widespread belief in the management world that in today's society the future of any company critically depends on how it is viewed by key stakeholders such as shareholders and investors, customers and consumers, employees, and members of the community in which the company operates. Globalization, corporate crises and the recent financial crisis have strengthened this belief even further. CEOs and senior executives of many large organizations and multinationals nowadays consider protecting their company's reputation to be 'critical' and as one of their most important strategic objectives.[1] This objective of building, maintaining and protecting the company's reputation is the core task of corporate communication practitioners. However, despite the importance attributed to a company's reputation, the role and contribution of corporate communication is still far from being fully understood in many companies. In such companies, communication practitioners feel undervalued, their strategic input into decision-making is compromised and senior managers and CEOs feel powerless because they simply do not understand the events that are taking place in the company's environment and how these events can affect the company's operations and profits. There is therefore a lot to gain when communication practitioners and senior managers are able to recognize and diagnose communication-related management problems and know about appropriate strategies and courses of action. Such an understanding is not only essential to an effective use of corporate communication, but it is also empowering. It allows communication practitioners and managers to understand and take charge of events that fall within the remit of corporate communication, to determine which events are outside their control and to identify opportunities for communicating and engaging with stakeholders of the organization.

The primary goal of this book, therefore, is to give readers a sense of how corporate communication is used and managed *strategically* as a way of guiding how organizations can communicate with their stakeholders. The book combines reflections and insights from academic research and professional practice in order to provide a comprehensive overview of strategies and tactics in corporate communication. In doing so, the book aims to provide a range of concepts, insights and tools to communication practitioners and senior managers to be used in their day-to-day practice.

In this introductory chapter, I will start by describing corporate communication and will introduce the strategic management perspective that underlies the rest of the book. This perspective suggests a particular way of looking at corporate communication and indicates a number of management areas and concerns that will be covered in the remaining chapters. As the book progresses, each of these areas will be explained in detail and the strategic management perspective as a whole will become clearer.

1.2 SCOPE AND DEFINITIONS

Perhaps the best way to define corporate communication is to look at the way in which the function has developed in companies. Until the 1970s, practitioners had used the term 'public relations' to describe communication with stakeholders. This 'public relations' function, which was tactical in most companies, largely consisted of communication with the press. When other stakeholders, internal and external to the company, started to demand more information from the company, practitioners subsequently started to look at communication as being more than just 'public relations'. This is when the roots of the new corporate communication function started to take hold. This new function came to incorporate a whole range of specialized disciplines, including corporate design, corporate advertising, internal communication to employees, issues and crisis management, media relations, investor relations, change communication and public affairs.[2] An important characteristic of the new function is that it focuses on the organization as a whole and on the important task of how an organization presents itself to all its key stakeholders, both internal and external.

This broad focus is also reflected in the word 'corporate' in *corporate communication*. The word, of course, refers to the business setting in which corporate communication emerged as a separate function (alongside other functions such as human resources and finance). There is also an important second sense with which the word is being used. 'Corporate' originally stems from the Latin words for 'body' (corpus) and for 'forming into a body' (corporare) which emphasize a unified way of looking at 'internal' and 'external' communication disciplines. That is, instead of looking at specialized disciplines or stakeholder groups separately, the corporate communication function starts from the perspective of the organization as a single embodied entity when communicating with internal and external stakeholders.[3]

Corporate communication, in other words, can be characterized as a management function that is responsible for overseeing and coordinating the work done by communication practitioners in different specialist disciplines such as media relations, public affairs and internal communication. Van Riel defines corporate communication as 'an instrument of management by means of which all consciously used forms of internal and external communication are harmonized as effectively and efficiently as possible', with the overall objective of creating 'a favorable basis for relationships with groups upon which the company is dependent'.[4] Defined in this way, corporate communication obviously involves a whole range of 'managerial' activities such as planning, coordinating and counselling the CEO and senior managers in the organization, as well as the 'tactical' skills involved in producing and disseminating content and messages to relevant stakeholder groups. Overall, if a definition of corporate communication is required, the following characteristics can provide a basis for one:

> Corporate communication is a management function that offers a framework for the effective coordination of all internal and external communication with the overall purpose of establishing and maintaining favourable reputations with stakeholder groups upon which the organization is dependent.

One consequence of these characteristics of corporate communication is that it is likely to be *complex in nature*. This is especially so in organizations with a wide geographical range, such as multinational corporations, or with a wide range of products or services, where the coordination of communication is often a balancing act between corporate headquarters and the various divisions and business units involved. However, there are other significant challenges in developing effective corporate communication strategies and programmes. Corporate communication demands an *integrated approach* to managing communication. Unlike a specialist frame of reference, corporate communication transcends the specialties of individual communication practitioners (e.g. branding, media relations, investor relations, public affairs, employee communication) and crosses these specialist boundaries to harness the *strategic interests of the organization at large*. Richard Edelman, CEO of Edelman, the world's largest independent PR agency, highlights the strategic role of corporate communication as follows: 'we used to be the tail on the dog, but now communication is the organizing principle behind many business decisions'.[5] The general idea is that the sustainability and success of a company depends on how it is viewed by key stakeholders, and communication is a critical part of building, maintaining and protecting such reputations.

A variety of concepts and terms is used in relation to corporate communication and reflects these characteristics. Here, the chapter briefly introduces these concepts but they will be discussed in more detail in the remainder of the book. Table 1.1 lists the

key concepts that readers will come across in this and other books on corporate communication and that form the vocabulary of the corporate communication practitioner.
Table 1.1 briefly defines the concepts and also shows how they relate to a specific
organization – in this case, British Airways.

Not all of these concepts are always used in corporate communication books.
Moreover, it may or may not be that mission, objectives, strategies and so on are
written down precisely and formally laid down within an organization. As will be
shown in Chapter 5, a mission or corporate identity, for instance, might sometimes
more sensibly be conceived as that which is implicit or can be deduced about an

TABLE 1.1 Key concepts in corporate communication

Concept	Definition	Example: British Airways*
Mission	Overriding purpose in line with the values and expectations of stakeholders	'British Airways is aiming to set new industry standards in customer service and innovation, deliver the best financial performance and evolve from being an airline to a world travel business with the flexibility to stretch its brand into new business areas'
Vision	Desired future state: the aspiration of the organization	'To become the undisputed leader in world travel by ensuring that BA is the customer's first choice through the delivery of an unbeatable travel experience'
Corporate objectives	Statement of overall aims in line with the overall purpose	'To be a good neighbour, concerned for the community and the environment', 'to provide overall superior service and good value for money in every market segment in which we compete', 'to excel in anticipating and quickly responding to customer needs and competitor activity'
Strategy	The ways or means in which the corporate objectives are to be achieved and put into effect	'Continuing emphasis on consistent quality of customer service and the delivery to the marketplace of value for money through customer-oriented initiatives (online booking service, strategic alliances) and to arrange all the elements of our service so that they collectively generate a particular experience... building trust with our shareholders, employees, customers, neighbours and with our critics, through commitment to good practice and societal reporting'
Corporate identity	The profile and values communicated by an organization	'The world's favourite airline' (this corporate identity with its associated brand values of service, quality, innovation, cosmopolitanism and Britishness is carried through in positioning, design, livery and communications)

Concept	Definition	Example: British Airways*
Corporate image	The immediate set of associations of an individual in response to one or more signals or messages from or about a particular organization at a single point in time	'Very recently I got a ticket booked to London, and when reporting at the airport I was shown the door by BA staff. I was flatly told that the said flight in which I was to travel was already full so my ticket was not valid and the airline would try to arrange for a seat on some other flight. You can just imagine how embarrassed I felt at that moment of time. To make matters worse, the concerned official of BA had not even a single word of apology to say' (customer of BA)
Corporate reputation	An individual's collective representation of past images of an organization (induced through either communication or past experiences) established over time	'Through the Executive Club programme, British Airways has developed a reputation as an innovator in developing direct relationships with its customers and in tailoring its services to enhance these relationships' (long-standing supplier of BA)
Stakeholder	Any group or individual who can affect or is affected by the achievement of the organization's objectives	'Employees, consumers, investors and shareholders, community, aviation business and suppliers, government, trade unions, NGOs, and society at large'
Market	A defined group for whom a product is or may be in demand (and for whom an organization creates and maintains products and services)	'The market for British Airways flights consists of passengers who search for a superior service over and beyond the basic transportation involved'
Communication	The tactics and media that are used to communicate with internal and external groups	'Newsletters, promotion packages, Facebook site, consultation forums, advertising campaigns, free publicity'
Integration	The act of coordinating all communication so that the corporate identity is effectively and consistently communicated to internal and external groups	'British Airways aims to communicate its brand values of service, quality, innovation, cosmopolitanism and Britishness through all its communications in a consistent and effective manner'

Note: *Extracted from British Airways annual reports and the web organization from what it is doing and communicating. However, as a general guide-line, the following concepts are often used in combination with one another.

A *mission* is a general expression of the overriding purpose of the organization, which, ideally, is in line with the values and expectations of major stakeholders and concerned with the scope and boundaries of the organization. It is often referred to with the simple question 'What business are we in?'. A *vision* is the desired future state of the organization. It is an aspirational view of the general direction that the organi-zation wants to go in, as formulated by senior management, and that requires the energies and commitment of members of the organization. *Objectives* are the more precise (short-term) statements of direction – in line with the formulated vision – which are to be achieved by strategic initiatives or strategies. A *strategy* involves actions and communications that are linked to objectives and are often specified in terms of specific organizational functions (e.g. finance, operations, human resources). Operations strategies for streamlining operations and human resource strategies for staff support and development are common to every organization as well as, increasingly, full-scale corporate communication strategies.

Key to having a corporate communication strategy is the notion of a *corporate identity*: the basic profile that an organization wants to project to all its important stakeholder groups and how it aims to be known by these various groups in terms of its *corporate image* and *reputation*. To ensure that different stakeholders indeed conceive of an organization in a favourable and broadly consistent manner, and also in line with the projected corporate identity, organizations need to go to great lengths to *integrate* all their *communication*, from brochures and advertising campaigns to websites, in tone, themes, visuals and logos.

The *stakeholder* concept takes centre stage within corporate communication rather than considering the organizational environment simply in terms of markets or the general public. Organizations are increasingly recognizing the need for an 'inclusive' and 'balanced' stakeholder management approach that involves actively communicating with *all* stakeholder groups on which the organization depends, and not just shareholders or customers. Such awareness stems from high-profile cases where undue attention to certain stakeholder groups has led to crises for and severe damage to the organizations concerned.

All these concepts will be discussed in detail in the remainder of the book, but it is worthwhile to emphasize already how some of them hang together. The essence of what matters in Table 1.1 is that corporate communication is geared towards establishing favourable corporate images and reputations with all of an organiza-tion's stakeholder groups, so that these groups act in a way that is conducive to the success of the organization. In other words, because of favourable images and reputa-tions, customers and prospects will purchase products and services, members of the community will appreciate the organization in its environment, investors will grant financial resources, and so on. It is the spectre of a damaged reputation – of having to make costly reversals in policies or practices as a result of stakeholder pressure, or, worse, as a consequence of self-inflicted wounds – that lies behind the urgency with which integrated stakeholder management now needs to be treated. The classic case example (1.1) of Barclays Bank illustrates this importance of managing communica-tions with stakeholders in an integrated manner.

CASE EXAMPLE 1.1

BARCLAYS BANK: HOW (NOT) TO COMMUNICATE WITH STAKEHOLDERS

In 2003, Barclays, a UK-based bank and financial services group, appointed a new advertising agency, Bartle Bogle Hegarty (BBH). BBH was hired to spearhead a 'more humane' campaign, after the bank was lambasted for its 'Big Bank' adverts in 2000 that featured the slogan 'a big world needs a big bank'. Barclays had spent £15 million on its 'Big' campaign, which featured celebrities such as Sir Anthony Hopkins and Tim Roth. The adverts were slick and had received good pre-publicity, but they turned into a communication disaster when they coincided with the news that Barclays was closing about 170 branches in the UK, many in rural areas. One of the earlier adverts featured Welsh-born Sir Anthony Hopkins talking from the comfort of a palatial home about the importance of chasing 'big' ideas and ambitions. The adverts provoked a national debate in the UK when a junior government minister, Chris Mullin, said that Barclays' customers should revolt and 'vote with their feet'. Barclays' image crisis worsened when communication executives announced that the new Chief Executive, Matthew Barrett, had been paid £1.3 million for just three months' work. At the time, competitors – including NatWest – quickly capitalized on the fall-out from the Big Bank campaign and were running adverts which trumpeted the fact that it had abolished branch closures.

Local communities that had lost their branch were particularly angry at the closures. The situation was further aggravated by the arrogance with which Barclays announced and justified the decision. Matthew Barrett had explained the branch closures by saying, 'We are an economic enterprise, not a government agency, and therefore have obligations to conduct our business in a way that provides a decent return to the owners of the business. We will continue to take value-maximizing decisions without sentimentality or excuses.' Barclays was openly admitting that its main focus was on shareholder returns and larger customers across its investment and retail businesses. Perhaps the most amusing story of the many that emerged during that period was of the fact that the village where Anthony Hopkins was born was one of the victims of the branch closures. He was seen as a traitor to his heritage, and the local Welsh Assembly Member wrote to him as part of her campaign about the closures. Hopkins was moved to write back to her, complaining about being used as a scapegoat when in fact he was just an actor and felt that he needed to set the record straight by pointing out that he did not run Barclays Bank. In an attempt to respond to the image crisis, Barclays extended opening hours at 84 per cent of its branches and recruited an extra 2,000 staff to service the extra hours. However, the damage to its reputation with some of its previously most loyal customers had already been done.

Questions for reflection

What are the main reasons for why Barclays ended up in a reputational crisis and what could the company have done to avoid the crisis? In your view, what broader lessons does the case imply for corporate communication?

Source: Garfield, A. (2000) 'Everything's big at Barclays: The chairman's pay has quadrupled just as 171 branches are closing', *The Independent*, 31 March; Wilson, B. (2003) 'Barclay chief's gaffe recalls Ratner howler', BBC News, 17 October.

These concepts together also mark the difference between corporate communication and other professional forms of communications within organizations including

business communications and management communications. Corporate communication focuses on the organization as a whole and the important task of how an
organization is presented to all of its key stakeholders, both internal and external.
Business communications and management communications are more technical and
applied[6] – focusing on writing, presentational and other communication skills – and
their focus is largely restricted to interpersonal situations such as dyads and small
groups *within* the organization. Business communication, for its part, tends to focus
almost exclusively on skills, especially writing, and looks towards the individual manager or professional, whilst corporate communication focuses on the entire company
and the entire function of management.[7]

With its focus on the entire organization, and broader corporate interests, it is perhaps not surprising that corporate communication is typically researched and taught in a
business school environment, although study programmes also exist in schools of communication and journalism. What this signifies is that corporate communication, as an
area of study and practice, benefits from direct access to research and ideas from areas
such as strategy, management and organizational theory.[8] Many concepts and frameworks
that are now commonplace, such as stakeholder management or corporate reputation
management, have in fact sprung from this connection. The advantage, as confirmed by
many practitioners, is that this linkage invigorates corporate communication not only
with new ideas but also with concepts and principles that are business-relevant. This does
not mean, however, that corporate communication should exclusively rely on business
school knowledge. There is in fact much to be gained from embedding a much greater
understanding of subjects such as framing, rhetoric and psychological processes of judgment formation into the discipline, with most of those ideas and concepts stemming from
fields such as communication science, psychology and the broader humanities. Whilst I
will draw primarily on the existing knowledge base on corporate communication in the
book, I will therefore also bring in ideas and principles from these other fields and in
ways that will benefit the practice of corporate communication.

1.3 TRENDS IN CORPORATE COMMUNICATION

To appreciate recent developments in corporate communication, it is useful to take
a look back at the period of the 1980s. That period saw a powerful restructuring
trend in many corporate organizations where every function in the organization
was assessed based on its accountability and contribution to the organization. This
led many organizations to restructure separate communication disciplines such as
media relations, advertising, sales promotions and product publicity, and bring these
together into more integrated departments or into specific working practices. At the
time, this proved productive in that it offered direct organizational and managerial
benefits. The consolidation of communication disciplines into one or a few departments enabled organizations, for example, to provide strategic direction to all of their
communication with different stakeholder groups and to derive guidance for communication efforts from the strategic interests of the organization as a whole. Many
organizations also recognized that the previous fragmentation of communication in
terms of separate disciplines and the spreading out of communication responsibilities

across the organization had often proved counterproductive. Fragmentation, it was realized, is likely to lead to a process of sub-optimization where each department optimizes its own performance 'instead of working for the organization as a whole'.[9] Many organizations therefore instead developed procedures (e.g. communication guidelines, house-style manuals) and implemented coordination mechanisms (e.g. council meetings, networking platforms) to overcome this kind of fragmentation and coordinate their communication on an organization-wide basis.

A further driver for integrating communication at the organizational level was the realization that communication generally had to be used more strategically to 'position' the organization in the minds of important stakeholder groups. Since the early 1990s and right up until the early 2000s, organizations became primarily concerned with ideas such as 'corporate identity', 'corporate reputation' and 'corporate branding', which emphasize the importance of this positioning. This primary focus, as already mentioned, was also created by the fact that it is a key outcome. A favourable reputational position in the minds of stakeholders drives whether stakeholders want to transact with an organization and effectively choose the organization over other rival firms.

Perhaps the key downside of this view was that, at times, it reinforced an assumption that the minds of stakeholders can, in a sense, be managed, and even controlled. Models of reputation management, for example, often link corporate messages to direct outcomes in terms of stakeholder awareness and attitude as well as broader reputational change. In other words, the assumption is that corporate communicators can strategically plan and design their messaging in order to, in effect, 'take up' a reputational 'position' in the minds of stakeholders. This obviously implies a somewhat linear model of communication that assumes a relatively uncomplicated process of sending and receiving messages, where any outcomes are already largely predetermined or given. This assumption also effectively starts with the communicator's intentions and their skill in framing a message but it neglects stakeholders as active agents. Instead, they are cast as a passive agent whose basic role is to respond (or not) to the communicator's message.[10] In other words, it suggests a linear, or what is sometimes labelled as a 'conduit', model of communication, as opposed to seeing communication as *a joint activity*.[11]

This view, in its strong form, has, to some extent, been overtaken by current events. Stakeholders have, in recent years, become much more active in voicing their expectations towards organizations and, empowered by new media technologies, have also started to expect more interactive and dialogue-based forms of communication. This in turn has led to some in the industry proclaiming that the old models of corporate communication are obsolete or 'dead', and that we are seeing a wholesale change towards interactive models of communication. A recent business book, for example, proclaims the virtues of interactive, conversational forms of corporate communication as, in effect, replacing 'the traditional one-way structure of corporate communication with a dynamic process in which leaders talk with employees and not just to them'.[12] It is no doubt true that more interactive forms of communication are enabled by new technologies and social media (in comparison to broadcast media), and such forms of communication are also increasingly expected by stakeholders. But proclaiming that there is a paradigm shift may be a rushed judgment, or at least too early to tell. Others in the industry have taken a more moderate view in suggesting

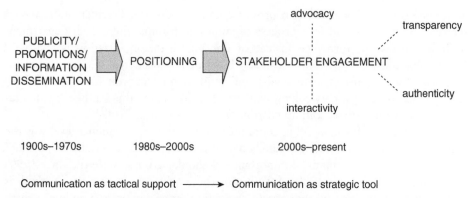

FIGURE 1.1   Trends and developments in corporate communication

that what we are seeing is a gradual change, in that individual stakeholders can now share experiences, opinions and ideas about organizations, and organize for action, at scale. Again, new media technologies are the enabling factor in this process. This situation offers challenges but also opportunities to organizations in terms of word-of-mouth and peer-to-peer influence when individuals self-organize and may become advocates for the organization. In other words, whilst the mechanics in a sense might have changed, the overriding principle is, to some extent, still the same – that is, when individuals hold an organization in esteem, value its reputation and decide to buy from, work for, invest in or otherwise decide in favour of that organization, they are more likely to become genuine advocates and supporters.[13]

In this view, the current state of corporate communication is one of gradual change, where there is change in terms of *how* organizations communicate with stakeholders, but also continuity in that the old principles of strategic messaging and reputation management still apply. Where the difference lies is in the outright dismissal of the view that stakeholders can be managed and controlled in their views – if there ever was such a thing. Another break with the 'positioning' model lies in the principle that organizations need to 'engage' individual stakeholders through different platforms, in addition to addressing broader audiences, publics or entire stakeholder groups. The focus with 'engagement' is not merely on shaping opinions or perceptions, but on the organization being 'transparent' and acting in character in order to bring across its distinctive identity and in a way that fosters individuals to become genuine advocates and act in their favour. The implication for corporate communicators is that they have an important organizational role to play in having the company con-sistently 'think like' and 'perform like' its character, or overall identity. If there are any outright discrepancies, or concerns about the organization not being true to its values, or not acting in character, this is picked up by the media and individual stake-holders, who will quickly organize for action and point out the lack of 'authenticity'.

Figure 1.1 displays these changes and sets them in a historical context. Communication was, up until the 1970s, largely used in a tactical support role for other functions such as finance and marketing in the organization, where its role was to announce corporate decisions, publicize corporate events or promote prod-ucts and services. The 1980s, as mentioned, saw a real shift in that communication became used in a more strategic sense to realize the organization's objectives and to build reputational capital with stakeholders upon whom the organization depends for its continued success and survival. The 'positioning' paradigm that emerged at that time is, however, gradually evolving into a new era of 'stakeholder engagement' which brings with it new points of emphasis around interactivity, authenticity, transparency and advocacy. One of the best cases to demonstrate the overall change in corporate communication that we are witnessing in recent years is Apple Inc.

CASE STUDY 1.1

APPLE INC: ACTING IN CHARACTER

The story of Apple and its phenomenal success since the early 2000s is intertwined with the visionary ability, determination and marketing acumen of one its co-founders, Steve Jobs. Jobs instilled a culture in the company that reflected his own entrepreneurial values. He fostered individuality and excellence, and combined this with a focus on perfectionism and accountability. This combination of entrepreneurial values and the workplace that it created was perhaps not for everyone, but it created a particular ethos in Apple that has spawned such great innovative products as the iPhone, the iPad and the iPod. One particularly strong asset of the company, particularly during Jobs' tenure, was its ability to come up with innovations that, in effect, created entirely new markets and cemented Apple's reputational position as operating at the cutting edge of innovations in consumer technology.

The development of the iPod perhaps best illustrates the entrepreneurial character that Jobs cultivated and that the company is now broadly known and appreciated for by its customers. In January 2001, Jobs unveiled iTunes, in a two-pronged response to the changing business model of the music industry and to meet the demand for Apple users to integrate their video and music devices as part of a single digital hub at work or at home. The rationale for the iPod, as a portable music player, pretty much grew out of the development of iTunes, the connection being that storing your music would naturally lead Apple to develop a playing device. But it also came about because of Jobs' fanatical love of music. This fanaticism suggested to Jobs that he needed to develop a *portable* music player, so that you could take your personal music collection with you wherever you went.

One would have thought that this path would pit the iPod directly against MP3 players, as well as evoke memories of the older stalwarts in the portable music category such as the Sony Walkman and Philips CD player. But Jobs judged that the music players that were already on the market 'truly sucked'. In a crucial internal meeting within the company in April 2001, Jobs also waved away the threat of other players in the market. 'Don't worry about Sony', he said, 'We know what we're doing, and they don't'. At that meeting, Jobs and his colleagues instead focused on the design and functionality of the iPod device, trying to think of how they could do something different from, and better than, their competitors. One outcome of this thought process was the famous trackwheel on the original iPod, which allows users to scroll through a collection of songs as opposed to repeatedly having to press the same button (which would be rather irksome). And as Jobs' biographer suggests, the 'most Zen of all simplicities was Jobs' decree, which astonished his colleagues, that the iPod would not have an on-off switch'.

Besides its design, the other element that determined the iPod's success was Jobs' rhetorical skill in framing the device as something completely 'new' that defied

(Continued)

(Continued)

the logic of existing market categories and as essentially a must-have product for customers. He positioned the iPod in such a way that, even if the device was similar in some respects to MP3 players, it was considered by technology critics and customers alike as unique and starkly different from (and thus allegedly superior to) competing products. The subsequent launch of the iPhone and the iPad by Apple followed the same script and helped reinforce the claimed position of Apple's 'cool' superiority over its competitors, which is a remarkable feat given that previous to its launch the company did not have a track record to speak of in mobile communications or handheld devices. Other technology companies have since tried to follow the same communication principles and grand rhetoric – most notably Microsoft claiming at the launch of Xbox One that it 'changes everything' – in positioning their technological products and firms, but in many cases with much less success. A key issue for Apple, however, is that the new CEO, Tim Cook, is a far less skilled communicator than Jobs and he may not embody Apple's corporate image the way Jobs, the quintessential entrepreneur and an obsessed perfectionist, did.

Its phenomenal success in recent years also means that Apple has been struggling to uphold its image of being the entrepreneurial outsider, who rails against the established powers in the industry. In many ways, the company is itself an industry giant and stakeholders increasingly expect the company to behave that way. Where Apple has often been secretive and not very open about many of its operations – a trait stemming from Jobs' focus on developing great new products in secret which then surprise everyone and break new ground – this level of openness and transparency is increasingly expected of Apple as a large corporate firm and as a 'corporate citizen' with social and environmental responsibilities. In 2011, for example, the company was accused by environmental groups in China of environmental pollution in its supply chain operations. The company has also now – post the Steve Jobs era – started to disclose information on the environmental performance of its products, something which customers had been requesting for ages. The risk that the company faces is that a continuing lack of transparency and engagement with customers and, indeed, other stakeholders in a number of areas may come to cost the company dearly.

A recent example of this involves the tax returns of the company and the lack of transparency over its financial affairs. In May 2013, US senators questioned the CEO Tim Cook over this issue and described a 'highly questionable' web of offshore entities that Apple uses to claim 'non-resident' status in the USA, and indeed elsewhere, which, in effect, exempts the company from paying its fair share of corporation tax. Another recent case in 2016 involves the public fight between Apple and the FBI. The FBI had asked Apple, through a court order, to assist in retrieving information from an iPhone that was used by one of the alleged terrorists in the San Bernardino shootings. In this instance, Apple realized that, rather than letting the conversation about the issue be controlled by others, it has proactively entered the fray. CEO Tim Cook wrote an open letter to customers, explaining why the case has wider repercussions for the safety and security of storing private information on iPhones. In the letter, Cook explains in detail the company's stance to its customers. He also made the case in a video and in an interview on national TV in the USA.

In this particular case, Apple has the difficult challenge of explaining its pro-privacy stance in the balance between privacy and national security without appearing uncooperative with law enforcement or unsympathetic to the San Bernardino victims and their families. However, by employing Tim Cook as its spokesperson and through using open, transparent communication that educates its customers and the general public about why it is unwilling to do what the FBI asks, the company is actively trying to manage and protect its reputation.

Questions for reflection

Discuss the communication challenges for Apple: will the company be able to ride out the recent storm of criticism and requests for more transparency on the back of its strong reputational position, or do you think it now needs to engage more systematically with its stakeholders on various issues and talking points?

Source: Cornelissen, J.P. (2013) 'Portrait of an entrepreneur: Vincent van Gogh, Steve Jobs and the entrepreneurial imagination', *Academy of Management Review*, 38 (4): 700–9; Gardise, Juliette (2013) 'Tim Cook defends Apple's use of tax loopholes', *The Guardian*, 29 May; and Vanian, Jonathan (2016) 'Cracked Apple iPhone by FBI puts spotlight on Apple security', *Fortune*, 28 March.

1.4 CHAPTER SUMMARY

All organizations, of all sizes and operating in different sectors and societies, must find ways to successfully establish and nurture relationships with the stakeholders on which they are economically and socially dependent. The management function that has emerged to deal with this task is corporate communication, and this chapter has made a start by outlining its importance and key characteristics. The next chapter describes in more detail how and why corporate communication historically emerged and how it has grown into the management function that it is today in many organizations.

 ——— DISCUSSION QUESTIONS ———————

Pick a company with which you are familiar or that you may have worked for in the past. Describe the company's corporate communication in terms of its reputation management and stakeholder engagement.

In your experience, how good is this company in communicating and engaging with its stakeholders? And how does the company compare on this with its direct competitors?

KEY TERMS	
Corporate communication	Market
Corporate identity	Mission
Corporate image	Stakeholder engagement
Corporate reputation	Transparency
Integration	Authenticity
Vision	Advocacy

 ───── FURTHER READING ──────────────────

Arthur W. Page Society (2012) *Building Belief: A New Model for Activating Corporate Character and Authentic Advocacy* [report]. www.awpagesociety.com/insights/building-belief/
Groysberg, Boris and Slind, Michael (2012) *Talk, Inc.: How Trusted Leaders Use Conversation to Power Their Organizations*. Boston, MA: Harvard Business School Press.

> Want to know more about this chapter? Visit the companion website at: https://study.sagepub.com/cornelissen5e to access videos, web links, a glossary and selected journal articles to further enhance your study.

NOTES

1. See, for example, PWC's 18th CEO survey (2015) and the Conference Board CEO Challenge 2016.
2. Argenti, P.A. (1996) 'Corporate communication as a discipline: Toward a definition', *Management Communication Quarterly,* 10 (1): 73–97.
3. See, for example, Christensen, L.T., Morsing, M. and Cheney, G. (2008) *Corporate Communications: Convention, Complexity and Critique.* London: Sage.
4. Van Riel, C.B.M. (1995) *Principles of Corporate Communication.* London: Prentice Hall, p. 26.
5. *The Economist* (2010) 'Public relations in the recession: Good news', *The Economist,* 14 January, p. 59.
6. Shelby, A.N. (1993) 'Organizational, business, management and corporate communication: An analysis of boundaries and relationships', *Journal of Business Communication,* 30 (3): 241–67.
7. Argenti, P.A. (1996) 'Corporate communication as a discipline: Toward a definition', *Management Communications Quarterly,* 10 (1): 73–97.
8. Argenti, P.A. (1996).
9. Gronstedt, A. (1996) 'Integrated communications at America's leading total quality management corporations', *Public Relations Review,* 22 (1): 25–42, quote on p. 26.
10. To illustrate this point, see, for example, Bavelas, J.B., Coates, L. and Johnson, T. (2000) 'Listeners as co-narrators', *Journal of Personality and Social Psychology,* 79: 941–52.
11. The classic reference on conduit models of communication is: Reddy, Michael J. (1979) 'The conduit metaphor – a case of frame conflict in our language about language', in Ortony, Andrew (ed.), *Metaphor and Thought.* Cambridge: Cambridge University Press, 284–97.
12. Groysberg, Boris and Slind, Michael (2012) *Talk, Inc.: How Trusted Leaders Use Conversation to Power their Organizations.* Boston, MA: Harvard Business School Press.
13. Arthur W. Page Society (2012) 'Building Belief: A New Model for Activating Corporate Character and Authentic Advocacy [report]'. (www.awpagesociety.com/insights/building-belief/); Scott, David Meerman (2013) *The New Rules of Marketing & PR: How to Use Social Media, Online Video, Mobile Applications, Blogs, News Releases and Viral Marketing to Reach Buyers Directly.* London: Wiley, 4th edition.

Corporate Communication in Contemporary Organizations

2

| CHAPTER OVERVIEW |

This chapter describes the development of the professional discipline of communication within organizations and the emergence of corporate communication. It starts with a brief discussion of the development of marketing communication and public relations, and moves on to explain why organizations have increasingly drawn these two disciplines together under the umbrella of corporate communication. The chapter concludes by discussing the ways in which contemporary organizations organize communication activities in order to strategically plan and coordinate the release of content and messages to different stakeholder groups.

2.1 INTRODUCTION

This chapter is about the changing definition, scope and organization of the professional discipline of communication in organizations, and about the societal and market dynamics that have shaped its evolution. A brief sketch will be provided of the development of the two main individual communication disciplines in each organization: marketing and public relations. The chapter will describe the development of both disciplines and will then move on to discuss why organizations have increasingly started to see these disciplines not in isolation but as part of an integrated effort to communicate with stakeholders. This integrated effort is directed and coordinated by the management function of corporate communication. As a result of this development, managers in most corporate organizations have realized that the most effective way of organizing communication consists of 'integrating' most, if not all, of an organization's communication disciplines and related activities such as media relations, issues management, advertising and direct marketing. The basic idea is that whereas communication had previously been organized and managed in a rather fragmented manner, a more effective organizational form is one that integrates or coordinates the work of various communication practitioners. At the same time, when communication practitioners are pulled together, the communication function as a whole is more likely to have an input into strategic decision-making at the highest corporate level of an organization. By the end of the chapter, the reader will have an overview of the historical development of corporate communication, of its strategic role and of the various ways in which communication is organized across companies and corporations.

2.2 INTEGRATED COMMUNICATION

Both marketing and public relations emerged as separate 'external' communication disciplines in the twentieth century when organizations realized that in order to prosper they needed to concern themselves with issues of public concern (i.e. public relations) as well as with ways of effectively bringing products to markets (i.e. marketing). Since those early days, both the marketing and public relations disciplines have gone through considerable professional development, yet largely in their own separate ways. Since the 1980s, however, organizations have increasingly started to bring these two disciplines together again under the umbrella of a new management function that we now know as corporate communication. This trend towards 'integrating' marketing and public relations was noted by many in the field, including Philip Kotler, one of the most influential marketing figures of modern times. Kotler commented in the early 1990s that 'there is a genuine need to develop a new paradigm in which these two subcultures [marketing and public relations] work most effectively in the best interest of the organization and the publics it serves'.[1]

In 1978, Kotler, together with William Mindak, highlighted the different ways of looking at the relationship between marketing and public relations. In their article, they had emphasized that the view of marketing and public relations as distinct disciplines had characterized much of the twentieth century, but they predicted that a view of an integrated paradigm would dominate the 1980s and beyond as 'new patterns of operation and interrelation can be expected to appear in these functions'.[2] Figure 2.1 outlines the different models that Kotler and Mindak described to characterize the relationship between marketing and public relations, including the integrated paradigm (model (e)) where marketing and public relations have merged into a single external communication function.

Until the 1980s, marketing and public relations were considered as rather distinct in their objectives and activities, with each discipline going through its own trajectory of professional development.[3] Central to this traditional view (model (a) in Figure 2.1) was the simple point that marketing deals with markets, whilst public relations deals with all the publics (excluding customers and consumers) of an organization. Markets, from this perspective, are created by the identification of a segment of the population for which a product or service is or could be in demand, and involves product or service-related communication. Publics, on the other hand, are seen as *actively* creating and mobilizing themselves whenever companies make decisions that affect a group of people adversely. These publics are also seen to concern themselves with more general

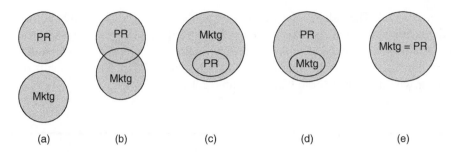

FIGURE 2.1 Models for the relationship between marketing and public relations

Reprinted with permission from *Journal of Marketing*, published by the American Marketing Association, Kotler, P. and Mindak, W., 1978, 42 (10): 13-20.

news related to the entire organization, rather than specific product-related information. Kotler and Mindak articulated this traditional position (model (a)) by saying that 'marketing exists to sense, serve, and satisfy customer needs at a profit', whilst 'public relations exists to produce goodwill with the company's various publics so that these publics do not interfere in the firm's profit-making ability'.[4]

Over time, however, cracks appeared in this view of marketing and public relations as two disciplines that are completely distinct in their objectives and tactics. Rather than seeing them as separate, marketing and public relations, it was recognized, actually shared some common ground (model (b) in Figure 2.1). Already in the 1980s, for instance, concern over the rising costs and decreasing impact of mass media advertising encouraged many companies to examine different means of promoting customer loyalty and of building brand awareness to increase sales. Companies started to make greater use of 'marketing public relations': the publicizing of news and events related to the launch and promotion of products or services. 'Marketing public relations' (MPR) involves the use of public relations techniques for marketing purposes which was found to be a cost-effective tool for generating awareness and brand favourability and to imbue communication about the organization's brands with credibility.[5] Companies such as Starbucks and The Body Shop have consistently used public relations techniques such as free publicity, features in general interest magazines and grassroots campaigning to attract attention and to establish a brand experience that is backed up by each of the Starbucks and The Body Shop stores.

In the 2010s, the emergence of 'branded content' drove a further wedge between marketing and public relations. The generation of 'content' for a corporation or a brand in the form of a press release, an opinion article, a keynote or a video has always been a part of public relations. The rise of social media, and the desire to feed all those channels with marketing content, has, however, also made content generation a clear marketing prerogative. 'Branded content' is, in effect, a bit of both; it involves the generation of content on an online marketed platform that features both product-related content as well as general interest content that speaks favourably to the corporation or brand in question. An example is the LEGO YouTube channel which involves content that features Lego products but is, first and foremost, focused on engaging children in play and building, rather than simply advertising its products in a direct manner to their parents. Fun videos, webisodes and movie tie-ins appear on the channel. The videos offer tips and tricks for building with LEGOs, informing and educating children on play as well as keeping them engaged with the product. Because of the quality of the content, the channel receives more than 1 billion visits every month. Another example of branded content is L'Oréal's ownership of the popular website makeup.com (Case Example 2.1).

 CASE EXAMPLE 2.1

MAKEUP.COM: AN ONLINE PLATFORM FOR BRANDED CONTENT FROM L'ORÉAL

The popular website makeup.com provides visitors with features and videos that provide beauty tips, make-up tricks and advertised products. The site sources content from an editorial staff and a network of vloggers. YouTube vloggers share the branded content on their own channel, resulting in an even broader reach for the site's content. But the website also has a sizeable fan base of its own, with, for example, 781,000 fans on Facebook. With almost daily updates, the site caters for an engaged and captive audience of women who are interested in finding educational and fun content that is useful to them. Features involve spotlighting particular beauty products or interviews with beauty experts and industry insiders giving tips on beauty treatments and their favourite products.

L'Oréal realized that many potential consumers nowadays rely on social media influencers and mobile apps to make their purchase decisions. The company recognized the real potential of a platform for branded content that does more than simply push or promote its products. The website is accordingly designed to offer targeted and interactive content that can be matched to the interests of the visitor, complementing L'Oréal's more generic and one-way inspirational adverts. It is in fact not immediately obvious to visitors that the website is run by L'Oréal; visitors often only realize the ownership when they scroll to the bottom of the site and see the brands from the L'Oréal family listed. But in this way, the website, as a non-explicitly branded content hub, gives L'Oreal the opportunity to show its products in videos and blogs without making it appear to be an overt advertisement.

Question for reflection

What role do you think the makeup.com website plays in promoting L'Oréal products and in influencing the purchase decisions of potential consumers?

'Marketing public relations' (MPR) and 'branded content' use public relations techniques but are directly or indirectly focused on the marketing of a company's products and services. As such, these forms of communication are distinct from 'corporate' activities within public relations. These corporate activities, that are sometimes labelled as 'corporate public relations' (CPR), involve communication with investors, communities, employees, the media and government. Figure 2.2 displays a number of core activities of both the public relations and marketing disciplines, and outlines a set of activities (including specific tools and techniques) that are shared, indicating the overlap between the two functions.[6]

Starting on the left of the figure, marketing of course involves a range of activities such as distribution, logistics, pricing and new product development (area 'C' in Figure 2.2)

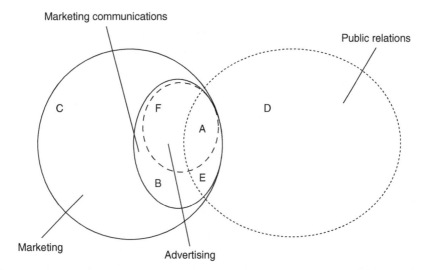

Key:

A = corporate advertising (advertising by a firm where the company, rather than its products or services, is emphasized).

B = direct marketing (direct communication via post, telephone, online or e-mail to customers and prospects) and sales promotions (tactics to engage the customer including discounting, coupons, guarantees, free gifts, competitions, vouchers, demonstrations and bonus commission).

C = distribution and logistics, pricing and development of products.

D = 'corporate' public relations (public relations activities towards 'corporate' stakeholders, which excludes customers and prospects in a market); includes issues management, community relations, investor relations, media relations, internal communication and public affairs.

E = 'marketing' public relations and 'branded content' (the use of what are traditionally seen as public relations tools for marketing purposes); includes product publicity and sponsorship.

F = mass media advertising (advertising aimed at increasing awareness, favour or sales of a company's products or services).

FIGURE 2.2 Marketing and public relations activities and their overlap

besides marketing communications. Marketing communications, in the middle of the figure, involves corporate advertising ('A') and mass media advertising ('F'), direct marketing and sales promotions ('B'), and product publicity and sponsorship ('E'). Two of these activities – corporate advertising ('A') and marketing public relations (product publicity and sponsorship) and branded content ('E') – overlap with public relations. Corporate advertising involves the use of radio, TV, cinema, poster or internet advertising to create or maintain a favourable image of the company and its management. Although it is a form of advertising, it deals with the 'corporate' image of the company and is as such distinct from mass media advertising ('F'), which is focused on the company's products or services to increase awareness or sales. Product publicity and sponsorship, as part of marketing public relations, involve activities that aim to promote and market the company's products and services. Both sets of activities draw on techniques and expertise from public relations. Publicity in particular is often achieved through coverage in the news media. Sponsorship of a cause or an event may also serve both marketing and corporate objectives. It can be tied into promotional programmes around products and services but can also be used to improve the company's image as a whole. In addition, branded content, as mentioned, involves the use of traditional public relations techniques (e.g. editorials, features, informational videos) for marketing purposes such as brand image management and the showcasing of products.

Besides the direct sharing of activities such as branded content and sponsorship, there are also a number of ways in which marketing and public relations activities can complement one another. For example, there is evidence that a company's image, created through public relations programmes, can positively reflect on its product brands, thereby increasing the awareness of the product brand as well as enhancing consumers' favourable impression of the brand. Another complementary relationship that exists is the guardian role of public relations as a 'watchdog' or 'corrective' for marketing in bringing other viewpoints and the expectations of other stakeholders besides customers to bear on strategic decision-making.

This overlap and complementarity between marketing and public relations suggested to organizations that it is useful to align both disciplines more closely or at least manage them in a more integrated manner. Not surprisingly, a lot of discussion and debate during the 1990s and 2000s took place on the importance of 'integration' and what such integration should look like within organizations. Back in 1978, Kotler and Mindak articulated three models of integration (models (c), (d) and (e) in Figure 2.1). Each of these models articulates a different view of the most effective form of integration.

Model (c) involves a view of marketing as the dominant function which subsumes public relations. In this model, public relations becomes essentially part of a wider marketing function for satisfying customers. An example of this perspective involves the notion of Integrated Marketing Communications (IMC) which is defined as a concept of marketing communication planning that recognizes the 'added value' of a comprehensive plan that evaluates the strategic role of a variety of disciplines (advertising, direct marketing, sales promotions and public relations) and combines these disciplines to provide clarity, consistency and maximum communication impact.[7]

Within IMC, public relations is reduced to activities of product publicity and sponsorship, ignoring its wider remit in communicating to employees, investors, communities, the media and government.

Model (d) suggests the alternative view that 'marketing should be put under public relations to make sure that the goodwill of all key publics is maintained'.[8] In this model, marketing's role of satisfying customers is seen as only part of a wider public relations effort to satisfy the multiple publics and stakeholders of an organization. An example of this perspective involves the notion of 'strategic public relations' which assumes that all 'communication programmes should be integrated or coordinated by a public relations department', including 'integrated marketing communication, advertising and marketing public relations' which should 'be coordinated through the broader public relations function'.[9]

Model (e), finally, favours a view of marketing and public relations as merged into one and the same 'external communication' function. In the view of Kotler and Mindak, 'the two functions might be easily merged under a Vice President of Marketing and Public Relations' who 'is in charge of planning and managing the external affairs of the company'.[10] Despite Kotler and Mindak's preference for this model, it is not a form of integration that is that common within organizations. Instead of merging the two disciplines into one and the same department, organizations often still want to keep them separate but then actively coordinate public relations and marketing communication programmes. In other words, most organizations appear to practise model (b) to coordinate marketing communications and public relations, although there is some emerging evidence of a number of organizations that are starting to embrace model (e).[11]

2.3 DRIVERS FOR INTEGRATED COMMUNICATION

In short, in most organizations the marketing and public relations disciplines are still not merged or reduced within those organizations to one and the same function. This may not be feasible in practice given the important differences in activities and audiences addressed by each (see Figure 2.1). However, both disciplines, whilst existing separately, are balanced against each other and managed together from within the overarching management framework of corporate communication. This management framework suggests a holistic way of viewing and practising communication management that cuts across the marketing and public relations disciplines (and activities such as advertising and media relations within them). According to Anders Gronstedt, a communication consultant, corporate communication 'inserts the various communication disciplines into a holistic perspective, drawing from the concepts, methodologies, crafts, experiences, and artistries of marketing communication and public relations'.[12]

The importance of integrating marketing communications and public relations in this way has resulted from a variety of factors, or 'drivers' as these can be more

TABLE 2.1 Drivers for integration

Market- and environment-based drivers
Stakeholder roles overlap
Internal communication *is* inseparable from external communication
Demands for greater transparency

Communication-based drivers
Greater amounts of message clutter
Increased message effectiveness through consistency and reinforcement of core messages
Complementarity of media and media cost inflation
Media multiplication requires control of communication channels

Organizational drivers
Improved efficiency
Increased accountability
Provision of strategic direction and purpose through consolidation
Commonalities and overlap between communication disciplines

aptly called. Generally, these 'drivers' can be grouped into three main categories: those drivers that are market- and environment-based; those that arise from the communication mix and communication technologies; and those that are driven by opportunities, changes and needs from within the organization itself. All these drivers are set out in Table 2.1.

Market- and environment-based drivers

The environment in which organizations operate has changed considerably over the past two decades. The demands of different stakeholders such as customers, investors, employees and activist groups have forced organizations to put considerable effort into integrating all their marketing and public relations efforts. This integration is also important when one considers the multiple stakeholder roles that any one individual may have, and the potential pitfalls that may occur when conflicting messages are sent out. Individuals may be employees of an organization, but also, at the same time, its customers or members of the local community in which the organization resides. As a result, *internal communication to employees cannot be divorced from external communication*, and vice versa. New technologies have also erased the dividing line between internal and external communication; smartphone and BlackBerry-wielding workers, for example, can broadcast corporate information in real time, with much corporate news nowadays coming from Twitter feeds. Organizations are also facing increased demands for *transparency* about their operations. In their efforts to respond to these social expectations and to present themselves as coherent, reliable and trustworthy institutions with nothing to hide, organizations across industries and sectors increasingly embrace measures of integration. Organizations often adapt to the growing demand for information and stakeholder insight through policies of consistency, that is, by formalizing all communications and pursuing uniformity in everything they say and do.

Communication-based drivers

In today's environment, it is also much more difficult for an organization to be heard and to stand out from its rivals. Media and communication experts have estimated that, on average, a person is hit by 13,000 commercial messages (including being exposed to company logos) a day. Integrated communication strategies are more likely to break through this *communication clutter* and make the company name or product brand heard and remembered than ill-coordinated attempts would. Through *consistent messages*, an organization is more likely to be known and remembered by key stakeholder groups. Organizations have therefore increasingly put considerable effort into managing their corporate image by rigorously aligning and controlling all communication campaigns and all other contact points with stakeholders.

Organizations also realized that *messages in various media can complement one another*, leading to a greater communication impact than any one single message can achieve. Because of the increasing costs of traditional mass media advertising and the opportunities afforded by the internet and social media, many organizations have therefore re-examined their *media presence and how to control it*. As a result of these two developments, organizations now tend to look at media in a much broader sense (see Chapter 3) and across the disciplines of marketing and public relations. Organizations have also become more creative in looking beyond corporate and product advertising to other media to communicate with stakeholders.[13] Many organizations today, for example, use a whole range of online media including corporate blogs, websites, banners and sponsored online communities (see Chapter 3).

Organizational drivers

One of the main organizational drivers for integration has been the need to *become more efficient*. By using management time more productively and by driving down the cost base (for example, as research and communication materials are more widely shared and used for more than one communication campaign), organizations have been able to substantially improve the productivity of their communications.

There is, in other words, an economic rationale behind bringing activities and disciplines together into consolidated departments. It is relatively expensive to have stand-alone units for different communication disciplines, as it raises the costs of coordinating tasks and responsibilities. In contrast, when disciplines are taken together into one or a few departments, it may not only enhance the functional expertise and skills base of communication professionals within those departments, but it may also ease coordination and minimize the necessity and cost associated with cross-department or cross-unit interaction. Greater integration, in other words, increases the *accountability* of the communication function in many organizations. An added organizational benefit is that with easier coordination across communication practitioners and disciplines, organizations were better able to *provide strategic direction* to all of their communication with different stakeholder groups and to guide communication efforts from the strategic interests of the organization as a whole.

A further driver for integration at the organizational level was the increasing realization that various communication disciplines, regardless of their internal or external focus, shared many *commonalities in expertise and tools*, and also overlapped to a large extent. Often, PR, marketing and internal communication professionals *share similar goals, skills or tasks*, or indeed are actively dependent on each other to realize their own objectives. As such, it made sense to organize these professionals in ways that bring together their joint expertise and harness the ability to channel their efforts into building strong reputations with stakeholders. The new digital age has even further eroded whatever boundaries one may have thought existed between these disciplines, with online PR tools serving marketing objectives and messages meant for an internal audience often quickly finding their way to external audiences.

2.4 THE ORGANIZATION OF CORPORATE COMMUNICATION

This chapter began with a description of the historical context of communication in organizations and reviewed different perspectives on the relationship between two main disciplines of communication: marketing and public relations. These different

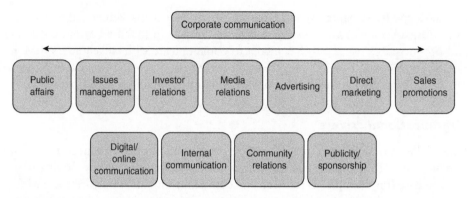

FIGURE 2.3 Corporate communication as an integrated framework for managing communication

perspectives on the relationship between marketing and public relations each present different views of how communication in organizations is managed and organized. The historical developments which led to a view of these two disciplines first as distinct then as complementary, and finally to a view that sees them as integrated, provide a stepping stone for understanding the emergence of corporate communication. Corporate communication is a management framework to guide and coordinate marketing communication and public relations. Figure 2.3 displays this integrated framework of corporate communication.

Within this framework, coordination and decision-making take place between practitioners from various public relations and marketing communication disciplines. The public relations disciplines are displayed towards the left in Figure 2.3, whereas marketing communication disciplines are aligned towards the right. Whilst each of these disciplines may be used separately and on their own for public relations or marketing purposes, organizations increasingly view and manage them together from a holistic organizational or corporate perspective with the company's reputation in mind. Many organizations have therefore promoted corporate communication practitioners to higher positions in the organization's hierarchical structure. In a growing number of organizations, senior communication practitioners are even members of their organization's management team (or support this management team in a direct reporting or advisory capacity). These higher positions in the organization's hierarchy enable corporate communication practitioners to coordinate communication from a strategic level in the organization in order to build, maintain and protect the company's reputation with its stakeholders.

Many organizations have also started to bring the range of communication disciplines together into a single department so that the knowledge and skills of practitioners are shared and corporate communication is seen as an autonomous and significant function within the organization. Some communication disciplines might still be organized as separate units or devolved to other functional areas (e.g. finance, human resources), but the general idea here is to consolidate most communication disciplines into a single department so that communication can be strategically

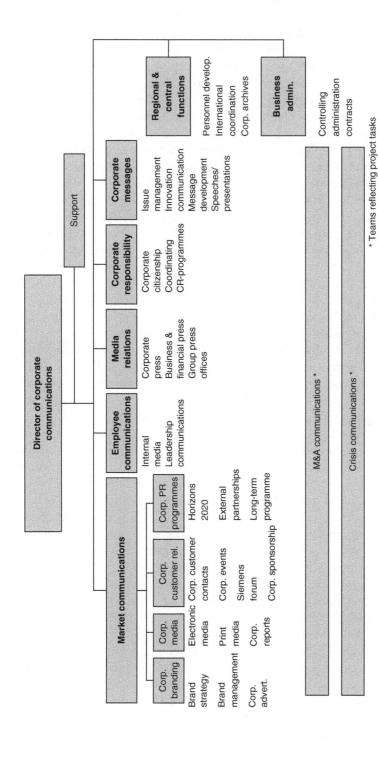

FIGURE 2.4 The organization of corporate communication within Siemens

managed from a central corporate perspective. Figure 2.4 illustrates this greater consolidation of communication disciplines in Siemens, one of the world's largest electrical engineering and electronics companies. Figure 2.4 highlights the different disciplines within the central corporate communication department, including media relations, corporate responsibility and employee communication. In addition, there are specific project teams for mergers and acquisitions (M&A) and crises, incorporating staff from these different areas within corporate communication. Interestingly, Siemens has organized market communications as part of the wider corporate communication function rather than as a separate department. The explanation for this may be that Siemens is mainly a business-to-business organization and does not market itself to end-consumers or end-users of its technology.

Larger organizations, such as multi-divisional companies and multinational corporations, often locate the corporate communication department at a high level, vertically, within the organization. The *vertical structure* refers to the way in which tasks and activities (and the disciplines that they represent) are divided and arranged into departments (defined as the departmental arrangement) and located in the hierarchy of authority within an organization. The solid vertical lines that connect the boxes on an organization chart depict this vertical structure and the authority relationships involved (see Figure 2.4). Within such vertical lines, the occupant of the higher position has the authority to direct and control the activities of the occupant of the lower position. A major role of the vertical lines of authority on the organization chart is thus to depict the way in which the work and output of specialized departments or units are coordinated *vertically*, that is by authority in reporting relationships. The location of the communication department close to senior management also means that staff of this department directly report to the CEO and executive team. Most multi-divisional and multinational corporations have a communication department linked to the CEO and executive team in an advisory capacity. In practice, this typically means that the communication department is a staff function at corporate headquarters from where it can advise the senior decision-making team, and that the most senior communication practitioner has a direct reporting or advisory relationship to the CEO or even a seat on the executive board or senior management team.

The vertical structure divides each organization's primary tasks into smaller tasks and activities, with each box on an organization chart representing a position assigned to undertake a unique, detailed portion of the organization's overall mission. Such vertical specialization, and the spreading out of tasks over different departments, however, requires some coordination or integration of work processes. This coordination or integration is achieved through so-called *horizontal structures*, which ensures that tasks and activities, whilst spread out over departments, are combined into the basic functions (e.g. managing employees, communicating internally and externally) that need to be fulfilled within the organization. Working across departments allows communication practitioners to coordinate their work with the human resources, finance, legal and marketing departments, as the main other functions with which corporate communication usually collaborates. For example, corporate communication practitioners often have a direct line into the human resources department, so as to ensure that employee communication supports the company's overall HRM policy and its mechanisms of attracting and retaining staff.

In the area of marketing and communication, horizontal structures are furthermore important as these enable companies to respond fast to emergent issues, provide control and ensure that consistent messages are being sent out through all the various corporate and marketing communication channels. A final point stressing the importance of horizontal structures is that these may offset the potential disadvantages (functional silos, compartmentalization and 'turf wars') of the vertical structure and allow for cross-functional teamwork and flexibility. Horizontal structures can take various forms, including multi-disciplinary task or project teams, standardized work processes and council meetings, and these are not normally displayed on an organization chart.

Multi-functional teams are an important mechanism in the coordination and integration of work of different communication disciplines. Teams can be further distinguished in terms of the natural work team, permanent teams that work together on an ongoing basis (e.g. a cross-company investor relations team) and the task force team, created on an ad hoc basis for specific projects (e.g. around a crisis or a corporate restructuring). Task force teams are also assembled when an issue or crisis emerges in the company's environment (Chapter 11) and an adequate response needs to be formulated and communicated to key stakeholders.

Organizations can also use various tools to document work processes across disciplines and departments in visual and standardized formats, such as flow charts, process maps and checklists. Such process documentation creates a shared understanding amongst all communication practitioners about the processes of integration. It institutionalizes processes of integration, thus making the organization less dependent on certain individuals, facilitates continuous improvements of the processes of integration, enables communication practitioners to benchmark their processes against other companies and creates opportunities for cycle-time reduction.

In addition to documented work processes that are explicit and formal, integration also occurs through more informal channels. Much of the interaction amongst communication practitioners in fact takes place informally, in the e-mail system, over the phone and in the hallways. Companies can facilitate such informal communications by placing communication professionals physically close to one another (in the same building), by reducing symbolic differences such as separate car parks and cafeterias, by establishing an infrastructure of e-mail, video conferences and other electronic communication channels, and by establishing open access to senior management. In large organizations, it is also important that communication practitioners from different disciplines (e.g. marketing communications, internal communications) frequently meet at internal conferences and meetings, where they can get to know one another, network and share ideas.

Council meetings are another horizontal structure often used in multinational corporations.[14] A council meeting usually consists of representatives of different communication disciplines (e.g. media relations, employee communication, marketing communications), who meet to discuss the strategic issues concerning communication and review their past performance. Typically, ideas for improved coordination between communication disciplines bubble up at such council meetings, and the council appoints a subcommittee or team to carry them out. Generally, communication councils support coordination by providing opportunities for communicators world-wide to develop personal relationships, to coordinate communication projects, to share best practices, to learn from each other's mistakes, to learn about the company, to provide professional training, to improve the status of communication in the company and to make communication professionals more committed to the organization as a whole. For all of this to happen, it is important that council meetings remain constructive and participative in their approach to the coordination of communication (instead of becoming a control forum or review board that strictly evaluates communication campaigns), so that communication professionals can learn about, debate and eventually decide on the strategic long-term view for communication that is in the interest of the organization as a whole.

A final mechanism for horizontally integrating the work processes of communication practitioners involves the use of communication guidelines. Such guidelines may range from agreed-on work procedures (whom to contact, formatting of messages, etc.) to more general design regulations on how to apply logo types and which PMS colours to use. Many organizations have a 'house style' book that includes such design regulations, but also specifies the core values of the corporate identity. For example, most multinational corporations have a 'global brand book' that distils the corporation's identity in a number of core values that communication practitioners are expected to adhere to and incorporate in all of their messages to stakeholders. Most of these corporations also convene workshops with communication practitioners across their organization to familiarize practitioners with the company's identity and the brand book.

A point that is worth mentioning on the subject of organizing communication is that in multinational corporations it is not always easy for practitioners to work across time zones, cultures and languages. Practitioners within the local setting of a business may not be in compatible time zones with practitioners located at the staff department in the corporate headquarters. Cultures and languages may also be different, affecting the ease with which coordination between practitioners at the corporate centre and different businesses takes place. Many multinational corporations have also increasingly adopted language policies across the corporation, typically using English as the common business language.[15] Whilst the rationale for such a common language is clear, it may create further difficulties for non-native communication practitioners to liaise with, and make themselves understood to, others internally. The reality of the multilingual environment of the multinational corporation offers yet further communication challenges to non-native communication practitioners who are tasked with fluently translating the common business idiom (such as website texts, speeches or corporate slogans in English) to the different local businesses of the multinational corporation around the world.

Case Study 2.1 illustrates how communication is organized in Siemens, a large multinational corporation. It shows the choices that were made within Siemens regarding the vertical and horizontal structuring of communication and how these relate to changes in the corporation's corporate strategy, the company's culture and the geographical complexity of its operations.

CASE STUDY 2.1

ORGANIZING COMMUNICATION IN SIEMENS

Siemens is a large multinational corporation focused on energy, mobility, medical and resource-saving technologies and equipment. The company has around 348,000 employees and operates in more than 200 countries. In 2015, the company decided to reorganize its communication and marketing functions, in line with a broader reorganization across the company and in pursuit of efficiency gains. Besides a step forward in efficiency, the move was also triggered by the increasingly significant role of social media within marketing and communications. The disruptive force of social media has led to a greater overlap, and convergence even, between marketing and communication functions and channels.

A leaner organizational structure

The reorganization of communication and marketing took place against the background of a company restructuring from 16 to 9 divisions and an elimination of the sector level (i.e. divisions had been previously bundled together into broader market sectors such as mobility, building technologies and energy management). The new organizational structure is expected to bring significant cost savings, including a reduction of staff in communication and marketing who previously worked at the sector level. In other words, the company is going for a leaner and simpler design where communication staff from across the corporation are pooled into a central communication department (the so-called communication and government affairs department – an update of the departmental arrangement shown in Figure 2.4), which includes market-focused communication and representatives for 30 lead countries (country heads). This central department provides the overall governance for marketing and communication, and is supported by two specific units: centres of expertise and functional shared services.

These units again involve a pooling of staff that were previously embedded in sectors and divisions, who will now work for the corporation as a whole. Centres of expertise in internal and external communication (including speeches, PR, employee communications, leadership communications, brands, product communications, online marketing and government affairs) involve 'know-how-oriented support', which, when bundled together, 'achieves quality improvement and specialization through economies of scope'. Functional shared services units (fairs and events, digital infrastructure and production) involve 'transaction-oriented support' and provide 'economies of scale' in support and execution. The main line of communication into the divisions across the world is the 'business partners' who are, at the same time, full members of centres of expertise, but are also embedded (with their teams) in the divisions and are the main point of call for connecting communication to the needs of a particular division.

(Continued)

(Continued)

Centralization and process survey tools

In other words, within Siemens, there is a move towards centralization, in part driven by efficiency motives to have central centres of expertise and service units service the different divisions. This centralization involves changing the position and role of communication staff to those of company-wide representatives, who are either skilled in content and expertise (centres of expertise) or execution (functional shared services). The centralization is also anticipated to bring further benefits in that it brings professionals together with different business backgrounds (i.e. greater diversity and creativity in the main centres and support services units) and encourages them to adopt a company-wide perspective besides their knowledge of, and links with, specific divisions.

Siemens is also horizontally formalizing the working relationships between professionals in the new design based on process survey tools. Various work processes (product launch campaign, trade events, etc.) have been documented, including the contribution of professionals from the different units as part of the process. Central to these process descriptions is the split between business, concept and execution competence. The business partners in the division, together with the communication department, bring in the required business-level knowledge and needs, whereas the centres of expertise work as teams on the concept (messaging) and functional shared services take care of the execution (production and channels). It is too early to tell how this arrangement and the new working relationships will work out on the ground, as this is only now being implemented.

On the whole, it seems that these changes to the organization of corporate communication are driven by considerations of efficiency and greater consolidation:

Efficiency: the first motive is to enhance efficiency through cost savings and a leaner structure that brings the central departments closer to the divisions and country operations (as clients). Siemens has simplified and streamlined its organization, saving costs and employing a leaner set-up at the corporate and aggregate group levels.

Consolidation: the second motive has been to strengthen the expertise in content and channels by pooling staff and resources into central departments and service units, and by reorganizing the work of communication into a clear split between concept (messaging) and execution, and between know-how-oriented and transaction-oriented support. Such pooling enhances expertise in each area (by bringing experts together and giving them a specific focus) and enhances the quality of the work through a basic division of labour.

To some extent, these motives and the changes in organization within Siemens appear to signal a new era in corporate communication – one in which design is less dictated by claimed areas of expertise (and 'turf wars' between marketing and communication) and more by strategic and efficiency gains. Such gains are prompted by the greater convergence between areas of marketing and communication, as well as by the need to drive down costs in support of company-wide financial goals. Whilst these motives are sound, it is also important to realize that whilst a new design brings certain benefits, it often brings other challenges as well. For example, the greater convergence between marketing and communication, and the pooling of expertise into separate departments or units may lead to economies of scale and greater control and consistency. It may, on the other hand, also lead to a leveling of subject-specific, specialist (communication or marketing) expertise in the long run – that is, it suggests a move away from subject specialists and to discipline generalists. Another potential trade-off involves the split between content and execution in Siemens. It again brings benefits in terms of focus and efficiency, but it also comes with some professional challenges. That is, for some professionals it will be difficult to focus on becoming either a content expert or a master of execution, but not both. This may affect the career path that they see for themselves within the organization and also the way in which they identify with the work at hand.

Questions for reflection

Consider the vertical and horizontal structuring of corporate communication within Siemens. Do you think that the new arrangement is sufficient, or would you change something else?

What do you see as the strengths and weaknesses of the new organizational set-up for corporate communication within Siemens?

Source: This case study is based on discussions with Hartmut Huebner, Head of Communications and Government Affairs, Siemens Financial Services.

2.5 CHAPTER SUMMARY

This chapter has discussed the historical development of communication in organizations, the emergence and significance of corporate communication and the ways in which communication is organized in contemporary corporate organizations. This discussion provides a context for understanding why corporate communication emerged and how it is useful for today's organizations. The chapter also described the variety of factors or 'drivers' that triggered the emergence of corporate communication and continue to drive its widespread use within companies around the globe. Corporate communication has brought a more strategic and integrated perspective on managing communication for the benefit of the entire organization. To give this shape, many corporate organizations have consolidated their communication activities into a single department with ready access to the executive decision-making team.

 ———— DISCUSSION QUESTIONS ————————

What are the main benefits of integrating communication? What in your view would be the optimal level of 'integration' between marketing and communication?

How important is the organizational structure in ensuring integration and avoiding a fragmentation in communication?

KEY TERMS

Marketing	Marketing public relations
Advertising	Markets
Audience fragmentation	Publicity
Communication clutter	Public relations
Corporate communication	Publics
Sponsorship	Sales promotions
Direct marketing	Team
Council meeting	Process documentation
Departmental arrangement	Reporting relationship
Horizontal structure	Vertical structure

 — FURTHER READING —

Marchand, Ronald (1998) *Creating the Corporate Soul: The Rise of Public Relations and Corporate Imagery*. Berkeley, CA: University of California Press.

Sheldrake, Philip (2011) *The Business of Influence: Reframing Marketing and PR for the Digital Age*. London: Wiley.

Want to know more about this chapter? Visit the companion website at: https://study.sagepub.com/cornelissen5e to access videos, web links, a glossary and selected journal articles to further enhance your study.

NOTES

1. Kotler (1989), cited in Grunig, J.E. and Grunig, L.A. (1991) 'Conceptual differences in public relations and marketing: The case of health-care organizations', *Public Relations Review*, 17 (3): 257–78, quote on p. 261.
2. Kotler, P. and Mindak, W. (1978) 'Marketing and public relations: Should they be partners or rivals?', *Journal of Marketing*, 42 (10): 13–20, quote on p. 20.
3. See, for example, Ehling, W.P., White, J. and Grunig, J.E. (1992) 'Public relations and marketing practices', in Grunig, J.E. (ed.), *Excellence in Public Relations and Communication Management*. Hillsdale, NJ: Lawrence Erlbaum, 357–83; and Ehling, W.P. (1989) 'Public relations management and marketing management: Different paradigms and different missions', paper presented at the meeting of the Public Relations Colloquium, San Diego.
4. Kotler and Mindak (1978), p. 17.
5. See, for example, Ries, A. and Ries, L. (2002) *The Fall of Advertising and the Rise of PR*. New York: HarperCollins; Sheldrake, Philip (2011) *The Business of Influence: Reframing Marketing and PR for the Digital Age*. London: Wiley; Scott, David Meerman (2013) *The New Rules of Marketing & PR: How to Use Social Media, Online Video, Mobile Applications, Blogs, News Releases and Viral Marketing to Reach Buyers Directly*. London: Wiley, 4th edition.
6. Based on Hutton, J.G. (1996) 'Integrated marketing communications and the evolution of marketing thought', *Journal of Business Research*, 37: 155–62.

7. Duncan, T. and Caywood, C. (1996) 'Concept, process, and evolution of IMC', in Thorson, E. and Moore, J. (eds), *Integrated Communication: Synergy of Persuasive Voices*. Mahwah, NJ: Lawrence Erlbaum, 13–34, quote on pp. 19–20.

8. Kotler and Mindak (1978), p. 18.

9. This perspective is associated with the IABC Excellence Study on strategic public relations. Work cited is Grunig, J.E. and Grunig, L.A. (1998) 'The relationship between public relations and marketing in excellent organizations: Evidence from the IABC study', *Journal of Marketing Communications*, 4 (3): 141–62, quote on p. 141. See also Grunig, J.E. (1992) *Excellence in Public Relations and Communication Management*. Hillsdale, NJ: Lawrence Erlbaum; and Grunig, L.A., Grunig, J.E. and Dozier, D.M. (2002) *Excellent Public Relations and Effective Organizations: A Study of Communication Management in Three Countries*. Mahwah, NJ: Lawrence Erlbaum.

10. Kotler and Mindak (1978), p. 18.

11. Weber Shandwick (2014) Convergence ahead: The integration of communications and marketing. www.webershandwick.com/uploads/news/files/convergence-ahead-the-integration-of-communications-and-marketing.pdf

12. Gronstedt, A. (1996) 'Integrating marketing communication and public relations: A stakeholder relations model', in Thorson, E. and Moore, J. (eds), *Integrated Communication: Synergy of Persuasive Voices*. Mahwah, NJ: Lawrence Erlbaum, 287–304, quote on p. 302.

13. Sheldrake, Philip (2011) *The Business of Influence: Reframing Marketing and PR for the Digital Age*. London: Wiley; Scott, David Meerman (2013) *The New Rules of Marketing & PR: How to Use Social Media, Online Video, Mobile Applications, Blogs, News Releases and Viral Marketing to Reach Buyers Directly*. London: Wiley, 4th edition.

14. See, for example, Gronstedt (1996); Fombrun, C. and Van Riel, C.B.M. (2004) *Fame and Fortune: How Successful Companies Build Winning Reputations*. London: FT Prentice Hall; and Argenti, P., Howell, R.A. and Beck, K.A. (2005) 'The strategic communication imperative', *MIT Sloan Management Review* (Spring): 83–9.

15. There is now an extensive literature on this subject, often abbreviated as BELF (Business English as Lingua Franca); see, for example, Louhiala-Salminen, L. and Charles, M. (2006) 'English as the lingua franca of international business communication: Whose English? What English?', in J.C. Palmer-Silveira, M.F. Ruiz-Garrido and I. Fortanet-Gomez (eds), *English for International and Intercultural Business Communication*. Bern: Peter Lang, 27–54.

Corporate Communication in a Changing Media Environment

3

| CHAPTER OVERVIEW |

Recent years have witnessed the growing use of social media and Web 2.0 technologies to communicate with employees, customers, the news media and other stakeholders. The chapter categorizes these new media and discusses the challenges and opportunities around using these tools and technologies as part of corporate communication. Besides providing an overview of the changing media environment for corporate communication, the chapter also provides case examples and outlines the practical benefits associated with the use of social media and Web 2.0 technologies.

3.1 INTRODUCTION

Recent years have seen an explosion in the opportunities and use of 'new' media in society, including social media sites such as Facebook, Wikipedia and YouTube and other Web 2.0 applications such as blogs and wikis. These advances in media and web technology provide new challenges and opportunities for organizations to communicate and engage with their stakeholders, including their own employees, local communities, customers and the news media. The basic trend associated with the development of these new media is that it highlights the democratization of the production and dissemination of news on organizations, enabled by web technologies. Rather than the classic model of communication practitioners liaising with official news channels, blogs and social networking sites now also offer content on organizations, and indeed may influence stakeholders or the general public in their perceptions and subsequent behaviours. Equally, employees can nowadays distribute their own information about an organization electronically to outside stakeholders, often without any gatekeeping or control from corporate communication practitioners. Indeed, with access to e-mail, blogs and social networking sites for sharing corporate information, many employees become corporate communicators themselves.

From a corporate communication perspective, these developments in new media and web-based technologies can be seen as both a challenge and an opportunity. It is seen as a challenge when practitioners take the view that the new media landscape blurs the boundaries between content providers and consumers and makes news gathering and dissemination increasingly fragmented, for themselves as well as for stakeholders. As a consequence, they may feel that these developments challenge them in managing or even controlling the corporate messages that go out of an organization and the way in which an organization is subsequently seen and understood. The developments around new media can also be seen as an opportunity. Involving the organization somehow in these developments may create new ways of reaching and engaging with stakeholders. For one, it provides an organization with the opportunity to engage in conversations, and to tell and elaborate on its story or key messages to stakeholders or the general public in an interactive manner – a real advance compared to the arm's-length messaging model associated with more traditional channels.

In this chapter, we outline the current use of new media technologies as part of corporate communication, discuss the opportunities and challenges, and provide a number of practical case examples. Besides this overview, the chapter also summarizes the practical benefits of new media as part of corporate communication. These benefits include companies being able to speak in an authentic voice, engaging stakeholders in an interactive manner and empowering them to become true advocates of the organization. Before we turn to these benefits and discuss them in more detail, the chapter starts by providing an overview of the current new media landscape.

3.2 THE NEW MEDIA LANDSCAPE

For some, the explosion of blogs, social networking sites, collaborative sites, Twitter and other digital communication platforms is a game-changer for corporate communication.[1] The basic idea behind this view is that where corporate communication used to follow a command-and-control model with messages being issued from the top of the organization, social media and Web 2.0 technologies foster more interactive and free-flowing conversations between members of an organization or between corporate communication practitioners and external stakeholders. As such, these media and their potential mark a clear break from traditional communication models and message flows. And thus these new media present both an opportunity and a challenge. The simultaneous challenge and opportunity is, to some extent, tied into the democratizing nature of these media. These media are generally less about control and more about proactive engagement within digital and web-based conversations and communities. The information scientist Komito describes this development as follows:

Where discussion previously focused on the consumption of digital information, as individuals accessed information provided by organizations, these
popular new Internet applications enable sharing of information amongst users
who are now individual information providers. [...] There is good empirical
evidence that the Internet is, decreasingly, a means by which corporate information is provided to users rather than a means by which user-generated information
is shared amongst other Internet users. This collection of applications enables
individuals to share information (including videos, photos, news items, and
audio footage) and create virtual communities on the web. The previous growth
in the amount of information in digital form has been replaced by growth in the
communication of that digital information.[2]

Whilst it is perhaps too early to tell how these emerging media developments will
fundamentally change corporate communication in the long run, their explosive use
in recent years suggests that these technologies are driving a shift in how people
engage with one another and with organizations. It is quickly changing how dia-
logues occur, how news about organizations is generated and disseminated, and how
stakeholder perceptions are shaped and relationships forged. Consider, for example,
the increasing internet access of individuals around the world. Two thirds of the
world's population have visited a blogging or networking site, and the time spent at
these sites is growing at more than three times the rate of overall internet growth.[3]
Every one of those individuals with access, as well as of course every connected
organization, can in principle become a global publisher of content. Additionally, the
widespread use of technologies such as camera phones and digital cameras means
that the individual citizen can instantly become a potential photojournalist or, with
the spread of video capabilities, a documentary film-maker. For example, at the G20
protests in London in 2009, a fund manager from New York who was in London
on business, used his digital camera to film the protests and captured the moment
when Ian Tomlinson, a newspaper vendor, was assaulted by the police and, as a
result, later on collapsed and died. The footage, whilst shot by an amateur, created
a huge news story. Besides this shift in news production towards 'citizen journalists',
a further notable development is the decline in the usage of traditional news media.
Newspapers have suffered a significant decline in interest and use, as readers and
users flock to the internet and to alternative news sources. Whatever the long-term
changes of these developments may be, approaches to corporate communication will
require at least some reinvention as these new media continue to evolve.

Whilst these new media play an important and growing role within corporate
communication, there is, at the same time, often confusion amongst corporate
communicators and academic researchers alike as to what term is most appropriate –
'social media' or 'Web 2.0' – to describe this emerging area. These terms are often
used interchangeably and what adds to the confusion is that these terms themselves
also evolve in their definition as new technologies and applications emerge. The term
social media became established particularly after the creation of social networking
sites such as Facebook (in 2004). Besides these specific sites, social media has been
more broadly defined as involving all kinds of online or digital technologies through
which people create, share and exchange information and ideas. The term Web 2.0,

on the other hand, describes a general ideological and technological shift in the use of online technologies. The basic idea is that the web has evolved from being a platform where content is created and published by individuals or organizations to one where content and applications are continuously generated and modified by all users in a participatory and collaborative fashion. The creation and 'publication' of websites, in other words, is indicative of Web 1.0, whereas blogs, wikis and collaborative projects are hallmarks of Web 2.0. For the purpose of this chapter, we use the term social media as inclusive of Web 2.0. In essence, Web 2.0 provides the platform for the evolution of social media and their use within corporate communication. Social media are accordingly defined as 'a group of Internet-based applications that build on the ideological and technological foundations of Web 2.0, and that allow for the creation and exchange of user-generated content'.[4]

One way of understanding the new media environment in which organizations nowadays operate is to distinguish it from more traditional media. Traditional media, for the most part, involve one-way messaging techniques through which organizations speak to an audience. An internal news magazine or a TV advert, for example, reaches in one instant a multitude of employees or prospective customers. The underlying model of these media is one of 'broadcasting' – a model of mass communication whereby an organization informs or tries to persuade many members of a particular stakeholder audience at once (see Table 3.1). With such a model, stakeholders are on the receiving end of a corporate message, as 'audiences', and can only actively decide to consume the message or not. The process of communication, in other words, is largely initiated and determined by the sending organization.

Social media, in comparison, are probably best characterized as a form of 'crowd-casting'; they enable stakeholders of an organization to self-organize as a 'crowd' in order to produce and disseminate content about an organization. Stakeholders are

TABLE 3.1 The difference between the traditional and new media environment

	Traditional media environment	New media environment
Communication approach	*Broadcasting*: stakeholders as audiences receive messages from the organization in a controlled and planned manner	*Crowd-casting*: stakeholders as participants produce or forward content about the organization
Communication model	One-to-many	Many-to-one, many-to-many
Underlying principle	*Corporate positioning*: planned and controlled transfer of corporate messages and campaigns	*Content generation*: impromptu and free generation and dissemination of corporate content
Key metaphors	Medium, channels	Platforms, arenas
Rules of communication	Fixed and controlled	Messy and emergent
Costs of content production/ publishing threshold	Expensive/high	Cheap/low

no longer passive 'audiences', but active 'participants' in the communication about an organization. Crowd-casting may actually involve organizations first disseminating details of a specific issue or seeding a conversation in a community, with the community on its own account generating discussion and forming perspectives and solutions on the issue. As such, from the organization's perspective it may include 'push' and 'pull' elements where an organization first engages a community of stakeholders and builds a network of participants ('push') and then harnesses the network for new insights ('pull'). However, in many other instances, the crowd or community may be fully self-initiated and have only limited ties to the organization. Such ties are not actually needed for stakeholders to collect, produce and disseminate content on an organization, as the costs, and thus the threshold, for producing content have become extremely low. Any individual can set up a blog or use the available social networking sites to start communicating about organizations and connect with like-minded others. The only needed resource is often simply having the time.

The shift from broadcasting to crowd-casting implies a fundamental change in thinking for corporate communicators about how they approach their stakeholders and communicate with them. The traditional guiding principle for many practitioners was the idea of releasing messages in a planned and controlled manner to build, manage and maintain a strong reputational 'position' in the minds of their stakeholders groups. This *positioning* model of communication is one where practitioners start with their own objectives, develop extensive communication plans and then assume that through creative and powerful adverts, PR campaigns and other media, the organization's reputation can be strengthened or maintained. This principle is one that no longer works, or at least not fully, in a social media environment (see Case Study 3.1 for an example). Instead, social media necessitate a shift in thinking about the underlying principles of corporate communication – from the controlled and planned release of corporate messages (*corporate positioning*) to the community-wide *generation of content* about organizations. Content generation defines corporate communication as a joint activity between an organization and its stakeholders, where, in principle, stakeholders can just as easily initiate a conversation as an organization can. As a result, the process of communication also shifts from one based on exchanging carefully crafted messages in a controlled and almost scripted manner to one that is much more messy and open-ended: with social media, stakeholders can produce and disseminate various forms of content (such as commentary, discussions, texts and visual materials) with often unpredictable consequences as to whether particular content on an organization will 'stick'. The unpredictability is largely associated with whether content, including rumours and positive or negative commentary on organizations, spreads within a given or self-generated community, or not.

The content that is generated about an organization can be initiated by stakeholders, but may just as well have been created by organizations. Communication practitioners are increasingly thinking in this respect about how they may themselves generate content on their organizations and spread positive word-of-mouth through their social media presence. This social media presence is, from an organizational perspective, then typically divided into owned, paid and earned media. The distinction is now commonly used and highlights how companies have become their own content generators in the form of media or channels that are directly owned, such as a company website or a blog with branded content (such as the makeup.com website owned by L'Oréal – see Case Example 2.1) or partially 'owned' channels or properties on Facebook, LinkedIn or YouTube (such as the Lego YouTube channel mentioned in Chapter 2). Paid and earned media then in turn refer to channels and media through which companies try to increase traffic to their owned properties, or simply try to spread the word on their company and its products and services. Paid media refers to paid-for adverts, links or promotional banners on other social media channels that are meant to drive traffic to owned properties. Such paid media may simply involve Google Ads, but may also involve paying influential bloggers or vloggers to refer to a website (as in the case of makeup.com in Case Example 2.1). Earned media, finally, refers to online-generated word-of-mouth about an organization, oftentimes manifesting itself in 'viral' tendencies, mentions, shares, reposts, reviews, recommendations or other content picked up by third-party sites. Whilst it is not directly owned by an organization, such content is valuable in and of itself (in terms of fostering goodwill and positive feelings towards the organization), and it may furthermore drive traffic to owned properties as individuals become interested in these company-owned media. Table 3.2 summarizes the differences between owned, paid and earned media, and their possible interconnections in an online setting.

3.3 CLASSIFYING SOCIAL MEDIA

Building on the distinction between broadcasting and crowd-casting, we now turn towards defining social media more specifically. One useful way of understanding social media, and its difference from traditional broadcasting media, is by looking at the degree to which the medium facilitates individual involvement and allows for rich forms of interaction when individuals and organizations use such media.[5]

On the media-related dimension, social presence theory states that media differ in the degree of 'social presence' – defined as the acoustic, visual and physical contact that individuals can have with one another as they communicate, such that they feel that they are both 'present'. Social presence is generally enabled by the intimacy and immediacy of a medium and can be expected to be somewhat lower for more digital and mediated forms of communication (e.g. telephone conversation, e-mail) than for direct interpersonal interactions (e.g. face-to-face discussion). However, a defining characteristic of many social media is that they mimick personal face-to-face interactions and have almost comparable levels of richness. Traditional broadcasting media were quite 'poor' in this respect, allowing for little interaction or feedback and offering, in most instances, a simple encoded message.

When social presence is high, it generally leads to a greater degree of involvement of individuals in the interaction and also potentially higher degrees of commitment. A closely related media theory is media richness, which states that media differ in their degree of richness – that is, the amount of information and cues that can be exchanged between individuals in real time, as they are communicating. Rich media,

TABLE 3.2 Differences between owned, paid and earned media in an online setting

Media type	Definition	Examples	Role in online setting	Benefits	Challenges
Owned media	Online media that an organization owns and thus controls	Website Branded content Blog Facebook page Twitter account YouTube channel	1. Generate interest in the organization and its products or services (directly or indirectly) 2. Engage stakeholders and build relationships with them	Control Cost efficiency Ways of engaging stakeholders (as opposed to direct persuasion)	No guarantees of engagement Potential scepticism towards organization
Paid media	Paid for content or exposure on other (non-owned) online media	Display ads Paid search Sponsored links	1. Direct advertisment of the organization and its products or services 2. Channel that feeds owned media and may on occasion create earned media	Immediacy Control	Clutter Declining reach and response rates Credibility (when seen as straightforward advertising)
Earned media	Stakeholder-generated online word-of-mouth about the organization that, in effect, becomes the 'medium'	Word-of-mouth Online chatter and buzz Viral spread of content	1. Earned media may generate traffic to owned media 2. Owned and paid media in turn may create (further) earned media and potentially trigger an ongoing 'viral' spiral of content to be generated about the organization	Most credible and authentic May live on (stakeholders become true 'advocates' of the organization)	No control Can be negative Hard to measure

such as face-to-face conversations or instant messaging (e.g. WhatsApp), allow for a frequent updating of information and give individuals the opportunity to provide feedback to one another so that they can gradually build up a common understanding. Poor media, such as written documents or a corporate advert, on the other hand, require that information is encoded and included as part of a medium, but such information can only be retrieved and cannot be actively discussed between the producer and any possible consumers of the medium.

Another dimension to consider concerns the intentions and objectives of individuals when they actually use social media. Here, the focus is on the actual *use* of the medium by individuals or organizations, rather than on any given characteristics of a medium. A defining characteristic of social media is that they bring individual stakeholders into the picture and they may, to a greater or lesser extent, use a medium for their own purposes. In particular, they may at least in part use the medium to create a certain impression of themselves, possibly to influence others but also to create a self-image that is in line with their desired personal identity. Such a self-presentation is typically achieved through a degree of self-disclosure – that is, the release of some personal information (thoughts, feelings, likes, etc.). Disclosing such information is a crucial aspect of social media as it allows individuals to exchange views and build relationships. Such disclosure and self-presentation of individual stakeholders, who are actively involved in the generation of content about issues or organizations, distinguish social media from broadcasting media such as advertising, editorials, newsletters and the like. In addition, social media themselves differ in their general capacity to allow individuals to socially interact with one another, and in such a way that their goals of impression formation and self-disclosure are achieved.

When we relate the two dimensions together, it creates a classification scheme of social media, as displayed in Figure 3.1. As highlighted, web-based collaborative projects (e.g. Wikipedia) and blogs score the lowest on media presence and richness, as these media often involve simple text-based exchanges. Content communities and networking sites are relatively higher in media presence and richness, as they include more interactive features that enable more direct communication between the individuals within the community. Virtual worlds, finally, are highest in presence and richness, as these media mimic human face-to-face interaction in a virtual environment.

On the other hand, blogs usually score higher than collaborative projects in terms of the degree of self-presentation and self-disclosure, whereas collaborative projects typically have a more specific purpose and content (e.g. specific work projects). Similarly, social networking sites such as Facebook allow for more self-disclosure than content communities such as YouTube. And, finally, virtual social worlds are premised on a higher degree of human-like natural interaction and self-disclosure, whereas virtual game worlds are more restricted in terms of the roles and behaviours afforded to the interacting individuals.

Based on this classification, we will briefly discuss each of these social media. As part of this discussion, we will also highlight the opportunities and risks offered by each medium for corporate communication.

Blogs are a controlled web-based medium that enable an individual or group of individuals (bloggers) to publish information in a diary or journal style. Bloggers control the information that they publish and moderate comments that viewers (non-authors) add to the blog. The statistics in blog usage point to an increasingly proactive and prolific population: approximately 175,000 new blogs are created every day. These developments suggest that corporate communication practitioners have to monitor and engage with influential bloggers, including opinion leaders, industry analysts and journalists. The other option is for an organization to maintain or sponsor a corporate blog that opens the organization up to conversations with all stakeholders, including the media. One of the first companies to start a corporate blog was Microsoft. Robert Scoble, when he was still employed at Microsoft, wrote a daily blog on technology which often promoted Microsoft products like Tablet PCs and Windows Vista, but he also frequently criticized his own employer and praised its competitors. His blog was read by many independent software developers and technology journalists around the world and made Microsoft's image more humane with this particular community. In February 2005, he became the first person to earn the newly coined term of 'spokesblogger', defined as an official spokesperson for an organization in that he or she develops, writes and edits an organization's blog.[6] The spokesblogger, whilst seemingly publishing an independent blog, often does not speak only for themselves, but also on behalf of their employer or the organization that they represent. Another example involves McDonald's use of a blog (entitled 'Open for Discussion') for a number of years to discuss ethical and social responsibility issues openly with its community of stakeholders. The company also reacted openly to comments that were posted, demonstrating a very open and involving attitude towards the issues that were raised and the individuals involved.

Generally speaking, the advantage of corporate blogging is that it allows stakeholders, including journalists, to engage in a direct and unfiltered conversation with the organization. Increasingly, journalists are also actively searching the blogosphere for information on organizations. According to a 2008 *PR Week* survey, nearly 73 per cent of responding journalists admitted using blogs when researching stories.[7] This provides a powerful argument for organizations to have a presence with their own sponsored blog. In addition, research has found that blogs can create a personal connection with users, facilitate positive attitudes towards the company and encourage supportive word-of-mouth.[8] One potential risk, on the other hand, for organizations who use or support blogs is that once they encourage employees to be active on blogs, they also have to deal with the consequences of employees writing negatively about the organization.

Collaborative projects involve the joint and simultaneous collaboration between individuals in an online setting. Within collaborative projects, a further distinction exists between wikis – websites where users add, remove and change mainly text-based content – and social bookmarking applications, that allow individuals to collectively rate internet links or media content. The best-known example of a wiki is the online encyclopaedia Wikipedia, which, amongst other things, features detailed reports on many corporations. Importantly, Wikipedia is also frequently used as a source of information by consumers, and this presents a real challenge to corporations. Specifically, Wikipedia reports corporate news almost instantaneously and, coupled with the fact that it is largely produced by 'citizen journalists' and members of the public, the information that is listed may not always be factually correct or thoroughly checked (although, over time, the collective wisdom often leads to a revision and updating of the contents). Whilst externally collaborative projects and wikis present some challenges to organizations, within the organization these kinds of application are often used to enable and support collaborative work (see, for example, the case study of IBM in Chapter 9). Cisco, for example, provides a digital platform for employees to interact and collaborate, including a video-based teleconferencing facility that allows employees around the globe to interact face-to-face with another. As in this example, whilst collaborative projects have typically been a medium of low richness, the addition of other applications such as video conferencing enhances their overall degree of richness.

Social networking sites allow users to present personal information and create profiles of themselves, and to share these in turn with others. This sharing typically leads to the formation of a small network or community of friends and/ or colleagues, who exchange e-mails and instant messages with each other. The medium is relatively rich in that users can upload images, videos, links to other sites, audio files and blogs (yet it is short of direct face-to-face interaction). Facebook and LinkedIn are well-known social networking sites and are particularly popular amongst younger internet users. Companies such as General Electric also have their own social networking sites, with many Facebook-like features (see Case Example 14.1). Facebook in particular is still growing in terms of its usage. In the light of the scale and prominence of Facebook, more than 700,000 businesses have also set up active pages on the site.[9] Whilst in most cases these Facebook pages are simply meant to provide a presence for an organization, these sites may, at the same time, be an important channel to reach certain consumers and to strengthen their ties with the organization and its brands. Some companies have gone even one step further and use Facebook as a direct marketing and distribution channel. However, the challenge for organizations increasingly is to have a 'discrete' presence on Facebook in the personal context of users which is not about 'selling' but about creating a personal image for the company and its brands, and in such a way that it presents interesting content for users that strengthens or reaffirms the company's image and reputation.

Content communities are applications through which users share media content. Such media content could include text, photos, videos or PowerPoint presentations. Obviously, from a corporate perspective, content communities present the risk that copyrighted materials or corporate documents are shared without the express permission of the organization. Whilst many content communities have rules in place against this, the distributed and social nature of the medium means that, frequently, illegally acquired or reproduced content is still being shared. On the other hand, the opportunity for organizations lies in the reach of content communities such as YouTube that provide them with significant possibilities to make contact with users and position their brands. Companies can also set up their own YouTube channel, where they present corporate videos such as recruiting promos, keynote speeches and press announcements, or make their corporate and brand adverts available to watch.

Recent examples from the energy sector include BP's 'Energy Lab'. The company invites participants to join BP in tackling the challenges of saving energy and making the environment cleaner through the adoption of eco-friendly behaviours. Under the heading of 'Tips to Living Greener', individual citizens are encouraged to contribute their 'real tips', to 'tweet your tip' and to 'share this site and get friends involved'. Further, BP has used its YouTube channel to convey information on such issues as its commitment to repair the damage done following the 2010 Deepwater Horizon oil disaster. Individual citizens have been free to post responses as part of the community, including negative commentary about the company, to which BP has responded in an attempt to keep the discussion alive. BP realized that starting an open community comes with potential challenges and risks, which the company has taken in its stride.

The reach of YouTube indeed comes with a real reputational risk, in that consumers or other stakeholders can share and produce videos that put a company in a bad light. A recent example of this is the protest song *United Breaks Guitars* by a Canadian musician which he posted on YouTube after failing to get any acknowledgement from the airline based on his earlier complaints and letter writing. The song went viral and became an embarrassment for United Airlines, which quickly promised to reimburse the musician and to learn from the case in terms of its customer service.

In *virtual social worlds*, users can adopt a certain persona and essentially live a virtual life similar to their own real life. They create an avatar (a virtual person) and then interact in a three-dimensional virtual environment. Given that there are hardly any restrictions to how individuals choose to manifest themselves within virtual social worlds such as Second Life, the application most closely approximates human natural interaction and richly supports various ways in which individuals (or, rather, their virtual alter egos) present themselves. Perhaps reflecting its richness, the medium has been adopted by organizations for marketing and communication purposes, but also to foster interaction internally between employees. On the marketing side, companies are able to advertise and promote their products. Firms such as Toyota have also set up flagship stores within Second Life, to present digital equivalents of their real-life products. Virtual social worlds have also found use in terms of recruitment strategies and communication with prospective employees. Companies such as T-Mobile, eBay and Verizon run recruitment fairs in Second Life, in the hope of promoting themselves to creative and technologically savvy candidates. Companies can also use virtual social worlds internally as a platform for organizing internal meetings and for knowledge exchange. Cisco and IBM offer their employees custom avatar creation tools and maintain corporate islands that foster exchanges between staff. Yet, besides the potential of the medium, it also comes with certain constraints. First of all, it may mimic real-life interaction, but it is still not the same thing. Second, not all of a company's stakeholders may be familiar with the medium or actively using it; this clearly presents limits to its use for communication purposes. In some senses, therefore, it may present a specific and complementary channel, but not a primary means of engaging with stakeholders.

Virtual game worlds are like virtual social worlds, with the difference being that, in this case, users are restricted in how they behave themselves and also in the roles, as avatars, that they adopt. Most of these games involve multiple players who engage in an online role-playing game. These games run over the web and are also supported by standard game consoles such as Microsoft's Xbox and Sony's PlayStation. An example of a virtual game world is *World of Warcraft* which involves millions of online users. Whilst these games are popular, they are more restricted in terms of their potential for corporate communication. It may be possible for organizations to advertise and promote themselves within a game, but, compared to virtual social worlds, the medium offers far less opportunity.

This classification highlights the broad categories of social media and their possible use as part of corporate communication. It is important to realize, however, that new applications constantly emerge and may attract a following. As such, the classification should not be seen as set in stone. Furthermore, new applications may emerge that, in a sense, fall in between the types categorized in Figure 3.1. For example, microblogging such as Twitter largely follows the description of blogging, yet it is also more interactive than the classic blog. Twitter allows for the quick and real-time exchange of messages, for example regarding corporate announcements or crisis episodes, and can quickly create an 'ambient awareness' and common sentiment about an organization amongst users. For example, in 2013, HMV employees sent real-time tweets on the music chain's official Twitter account as workers were being laid off and the chain was facing bankruptcy. Employees vented their anger at what they

		Social presence/Media richness		
		Low	Medium	High
Self-presentation/ Self-disclosure	High	Blogs	Social networking sites (e.g. Facebook)	Virtual social worlds (e.g. Second Life)
	Low	Collaborative projects (e.g. Wikipedia)	Content communities (e.g. YouTube)	Virtual game worlds (e.g. World of Warcraft)

FIGURE 3.1 Classification of social media

Source: Kaplan, A. and Haenlein, M. (2010) 'Users of the world, unite! The challenges and opportunities of social media', *Business Horizons*, 53 (1): 61.

considered the 'mass executions' at the company they 'loved'. When management regained control of the medium, the damage had already been done with individual customers, employees and other members of the public wading in and criticising the company for how it was handling the situation. In 2010, a similarly quick sentiment was established through tweets against H&M after a student found bags of its unsold clothes dumped in the garbage by store personnel. Shocked that the clothes had not been donated to charity, *The New York Times* featured the story and it quickly got amplified on Twitter as the 'trashgate' incident. H&M was taken off guard and was rather slow to react to the evolving social media crisis.

In other words, social media such as Twitter offer advantages and opportunities for corporate communication, as well as potential risks. Such risks are largely brought about by the immediacy of the medium, which means that the personal views or opinions of an individual (such as the student who spotted the unsold bags of H&M clothes) can quickly cascade into becoming the majority opinion of a large group of people, who press the organization for answers and for making a change. On the other hand, the advantages are also clear. Social media empower individuals and citizens to get involved in corporate issues or even, when given the chance, in the governance and management of organizations. BP's 'energy arena', for example, empowers individual citizens to get involved in energy-related discussions, and has as a virtual forum potentially a much broader reach and possibility of involvement than the traditional 'town hall meetings' that companies such as BP used to have for this purpose. Physical town hall meetings limited the number of people who could come because of the location and timing, essentially precluding large groups of citizens from taking part.

 CASE EXAMPLE 3.1

GENERAL ELECTRIC: CAMPAIGNING THROUGH SOCIAL MEDIA

In 2008, General Electric redeveloped its digital communication platforms, including its intranet and its external-facing website. The intranet came to include GE Connect, a Facebook-like internal network which allows staff to maintain personal sites and profiles, to write blogs and to develop knowledge-sharing and discussion sites. GE also has an interactive external website, where employees post videos about their work and thus act as brand ambassadors. A particularly popular feature is a correspondence site on the intranet (called InsideGE) where employees can debate stories and issues in an unfettered manner. In 2009, GE Aviation faced a threat to funding for the F-35 fighter-jet engine it was developing for the US military, an issue that sparked huge interest with employees inside the firm. Debating the issue on InsideGE, employees decided that they should collectively lobby politicians on the issue. Rather than a more traditional corporate communication approach of telling GE's story via the media or via a targeted public affairs strategy, employees initiated their own grassroots approach. About 12,000 employees from all parts of GE sent letters to the senators of their own states, asking the US government to keep funding the engine. Each employee wrote a personal letter and framed the appeal around their own interests, as individual citizens, and also argued for preserving jobs and local technology expertise. The initiative not only helped in getting the resolution passed, it also marked a new dawn for internal and external communication within GE. It led to the realization that employees can collectively voice issues and communicate with external stakeholders such as government and do not need traditional news media in the process. According to Sangita Malhotra, corporate communication manager at GE, companies like GE need to grow with these developments, rather than attempt to turn back the clock. New media are not only here to stay, but also offer new opportunities internally in terms of harnessing employees' creativity and identification and externally in terms of crafting conversations about the company and its activities.

Question for reflection

Reflect on the way in which employees mobilized themselves and communicated directly to the senators of their state. Do you think that a process like this should be supported or managed by a corporate communication practitioner; and if so, how and to what degree?

Source: This case study was informed by Palmer, M. (2010) 'Time to connect', *Financial Times*, 22 March.

3.4 CHALLENGES AND OPPORTUNITIES

The constant evolution of social media, with new applications emerging or bundled together, offers some clear challenges to corporate communication practitioners. Technological developments are moving so quickly that for many of them it is hard to keep up. Recent research amongst corporate communication practitioners indicates that many still need to become fully familiar and comfortable with the ins and outs of these new technologies and work out how they might be used most effectively for their organizations.[10] This is perhaps not that surprising as there are no clear rules, benchmarks or tried-and-tested principles yet on the use of social media. Most evidence to date is still anecdotal, and in some senses specific to each company. In addition, new developments take time to settle, and as such it is only natural that practitioners are struggling to keep up and make sense of the changes in front of them. Most practitioners are at present fully at ease with using tools like e-mail and the intranet, are comfortable with blogs and podcasts, but are more reserved towards other tools like social networks and virtual worlds.[11] This partly indicates where they see opportunities for corporate communication, but it also reflects a more general model of how new technologies are diffused – it takes time before new technologies and their uses are fully documented, understood and established as tools within corporate communication. Yet, those communication practitioners who, as early adopters, master the use of social media tools and are able to track their effects are generally held in greater esteem by their peers and by the CEO in the organization, which reflects the significance that is now attributed to the use of these tools within organizations.[12]

Besides the challenges that they present, social media also offer clear opportunities. One such opportunity is that, in some senses, the advent of social media presents a further step in the integration of marketing and public relations under the umbrella of corporate communication (Chapter 2). Social media such as Facebook and Twitter allow companies to engage more directly with customers, employees and other stake-holders. As such, these tools are more interactive and inclusive in nature compared to more traditional advertising and marketing channels that focus on strategic messaging and persuasion. The traditional one-way outreach of marketers is, in other words, being complemented by the opportunity of having two-way conversations with stakeholders that can build reputational capital and brand equity. In this sense, marketing and public relations are growing even further together, so much so that organizations now increasingly rely on the broader corporate communication function to engage stakeholders with viral, word-of-mouth and buzz marketing initiatives to drive action through engagement. In other words, the growing role of social media solidifies the strategic role of corporate communication within the organization, with communicators being called on to navigate the organization through the new media landscape (see Case Study 3.1).

For corporate communication practitioners themselves, one further opportunity in using social media is that it allows the company to present a more human image of itself and to have a conversational voice. Conversational voice is defined as an engaging and natural style of communicating as perceived by the organization's stakeholders and as based on their direct communication with the organization.[13] When there is a genuine experience of such a 'human' corporate voice through Twitter feeds, blogs and social networking sites, it translates into positive feelings, a favourable image and strong stakeholder relationships. It addresses the conundrum of companies being able to communicate directly with multiple individual stakeholders across the globe. In the words of Searls and Weinberger, 'by acknowledging that, inevitably, many people speak for a particular company in many different ways, the company can address one of the most important and difficult questions: How can a large company have conversations with hundreds of millions of real people?'[14]

A further opportunity is that social media may foster or create a whole new range of stakeholder behaviours in support of the organization. Whereas traditional communication channels and tools are often more focused on individual cognitive and behavioural effects, with social media stakeholders can now share experiences, opinions and ideas about organizations, and organize for action, at scale. In other words, they can use social media to network with others and disseminate corporate news, whether good or bad. The dynamics of such dissemination may often take on a viral form, with news spreading exponentially from one person to the next and which in turn may quickly create a general mood amongst a large collective of social media users.

Besides disseminating news (say through Twitter), individual stakeholders may also use social media to organize themselves for action and to take concerted steps in favour of, or in some instances against, the organization. This feat offers challenges but also real opportunities to organizations in terms of word-of-mouth and peer-to-peer influence when individuals self-organize and may become advocates for the organization. The case study of Nestlé (Case Study 3.1) provides a well-known example of stakeholders, including activists and consumers, organizing themselves and mobilizing themselves against a corporation, but the same viral dynamic can also work in the other direction – with customers or activists, for example, becoming genuine advocates for an organization and using social media to mobilize further goodwill and supportive action. A recent industry report suggests that the future corporate communicator needs to have a deep insight into data and analytics and into behavioural science, so that he or she can prime or nudge individual stakeholders into becoming advocates for the organization and mobilizing others.[15]

The idea of priming or nudging is that with a few carefully chosen expressions or speech acts (such as positive announcements, pledged contributions or commitments, and emotive expressions) on Twitter or other social media platforms, organizations can try to mobilize individuals to produce and share content in favour of the organization. The influence that they have with nudging and priming is more indirect and not forced; organizations offer content that is suggestive and emotive, and may as such trigger reactions, rather than clearly directed to persuade. The best social media initiatives often involve such indirect priming and nudging techniques that are both immersive and emotive, and that promote various forms of content sharing and community building. To some extent, the use of nudging or priming through social media as a way of triggering reactions and generating publicity may in time replace traditional 'off-line' public relations campaigns or events. Recent analyses of successful social media initiatives suggest that 'the role of campaign events to generate publicity in service to a PR campaign may, in the future, be displaced by social media campaign tactics which belong to an entirely different ecosystem where the act of sharing social media content generates publicity in lieu of a campaign event'.[16]

The challenges and opportunities that social media present stem, in part, as mentioned, from the characteristics of these media and the forms of instantaneous communication they enable and afford. But whether these media truly harbour challenges or indeed opportunities also reflects the different mindsets of corporate communicators. Some communicators frame social media as generally harbouring the potential for reputation risk, and denounce the fact that they are no longer 'in control'.[17] In such a framing, social media are seen as a vehicle for disclosing or exposing information that may be harmful to an organization. An alternative framing, and one that is more alive to the opportunities of social media, is to view them as conversation starters and as ways of co-creating corporate reputation with an organization's stakeholders.

In the co-creation view, reputation is not simply given, as a position to be taken up or protected by communicators, but is an intangible asset that is established in relationships and thus co-constructed with stakeholders. Communication practitioners who adopt this co-creation frame realize that in a social media environment a reputation is shaped by the organization as well as by the community it embraces. They see the opportunities that social media provide to foster goodwill for their organizations, and believe that a reputation is not theirs to claim, but is constantly being established and re-established in interactions with their stakeholders, both on- and off-line.[18]

These different mindsets, or ways of thinking about social media, are also reflected in the social media strategies and tactical guidelines that organizations are starting to set up. Most organizations, including many of the largest listed corporations, still do not have a clear social media strategy or guidelines in place.[19] Only a small percentage of organizations have a social media strategy document that outlines what the company aims to achieve with its social media use and who can speak on behalf of the organization on different social media platforms and under what circumstances. Many organizations are, however, starting to develop tactical guidelines that suggest to employees how they can use social media, in either an official or private capacity at work. These guidelines tend to be either more restrictive or open, depending on whether social media are framed as reputational 'risks' or 'opportunities'. Practitioners and organizations who work from the 'risk' frame have guidelines that limit the free expression of certain topics or issues, suggest a specific voice and editorial style, and promote a more 'defensive' attitude in responding to negative comments online (see Case Study 3.1). When practitioners and organizations instead operate from an 'opportunity' frame, they embrace the technology and move beyond the question of whether employees should or should not be allowed to comment online. Practitioners in these organizations proactively develop staff to become 'ambassadors' or 'evangelists' for their organizations. They argue that the spontaneously expressed views of staff in a social media environment are usually far more authentic and credible than central messages released or broadcast by the organization. Such an open and supportive approach towards social media use does, however, require thorough training, an active monitoring of social media content and, where needed, editorial services to support and assists employees.

A recent example of the 'risk' versus 'opportunity' framing of social media is the case of how Ikea responded in the summer of 2015 to a spontaneous social media movement inviting everyone online to come and play hide and seek within one of its stores. The movement was triggered when one customer listed playing hide and seek in Ikea as one of the 30 things she would like to do before her 30th birthday. She had created a Facebook event and had invited her friends and family, who themselves had invited many others. Soon, on- and off-line media got wind of the initiative and it became a trending topic on Twitter. In the end, 13,000 people signed up for the event. Instead of responding defensively or negatively, Ikea played ball, contacted the customer and offered a game of hide and seek in one of its Belgian stores for 500 people (a game with many more would have been dangerous). With its spontaneous response, Ikea got a lot of positive publicity.

Spotting such opportunities, however, requires that practitioners actively monitor the social media environment and know what people are saying about the organization and its products and services. Depending on the degree to which organizations are in the public eye and newsworthy, this may involve either a few or literally thousands of conversations happening at any one time. Whilst communication practitioners may find it hard to keep track of all these conversations, as they are taking place in real time, they can manage the flow of information by creating Google Alerts for all the relevant search terms for an organization (brands, leaders, products and services, competitors, etc.), by using social media sites such as Social Mention where they can search the web in real time, and by using a desktop or mobile application for Twitter and other social networks to manage existing social media accounts and sort and track content as it is being generated. Some organizations also pay for social media monitoring services, or, as in the case of Nestlé (see Case Study 3.1), have now brought such services in-house.

In summary, social media are changing the environment for corporate communication. Their success often hinges on the degree to which their use meets one (or more) of the so-called PARC principles for success: whether their use is participatory (stimulating interaction with the community), authentic (engaging in conversations without forced attitudes or a false demeanour), resourceful (providing an audience or community with helpful information) and credible. In this way, these media also offer strikingly different uses and opportunities for corporate communicators, compared to more traditional broadcasting media. At the same time, however, instead of drawing a clear dividing line between broadcasting and crowd-casting, organizations often think 'through the line' about the best possible media mix to communicate with their stakeholders. Many social media campaigns lead to online conversations and engagement, which in turn lead to off-line engagement, further online conversations and potentially massive media coverage. Similarly, off-line campaigns and events may carry over into an online setting as well as trigger media coverage, similarly affecting the reputation of the organization. In other words, communication practitioners need to work out what the best possible mix of on- and off-line media is for their organization and the brands they work for, which may still very much involve broadcasting channels along social media initiatives (see Chapter 6). Besides such tactical choices, social media do, as we have seen, signal the need for more transparency and authenticity. The implication for corporate communicators is that they have an important role to play to support their company in openly and honestly communicating about its decisions and affairs (beyond any private, confidential or proprietary information) through all of its social media. Because if there are any outright discrepancies, or concerns about the organization not being true to its values, trying to hide certain information or not acting in character, this is very quickly picked up in the social media environment by individual stakeholders who in turn may quickly organize themselves for action and point out the lack of 'authenticity'.

CASE STUDY 3.1

NESTLÉ'S RESPONSE TO GREENPEACE'S SOCIAL MEDIA CAMPAIGN

On 17 March 2010, Greenpeace posted a spoof video online which criticized Nestlé for acquiring palm oil, which is used in products such as Kit Kat and Rolo. The criticism related to the sourcing of palm oil from unsustainable producers in Indonesia who are levelling rainforests, and in doing so threaten the remaining habitat of orangutans. The video featured an office worker who opens a Kit Kat bar to take a break but then essentially consumes an orangutan finger rather than chocolate. Greenpeace posted the video on YouTube, after its direct discussions with the company had stalled. Greenpeace felt that Nestlé should have followed other companies such as Unilever, Kraft and Shell which had ended their contract with their unsustainable palm oil suppliers. One supplier in Indonesia, the Sinar Mas Group, in particular, was known to burn forests to clear land for palm oil plantations. Besides contributing directly to an increase in carbon emissions, the clearing of land also endangered already threatened species such as Sumatran tigers and elephants, and orangutans. According to Greenpeace, it had targeted Nestlé as it is 'the largest food and drinks company in the world, and already a major consumer of palm oil – the last three years have seen Nestlé's use of palm oil almost double. Considering its size and influence, it should be setting an example for the industry and ensuring its palm oil is destruction free. Instead, Nestlé continues to buy from companies like Sinar Mas, that are destroying Indonesia's rainforests and peatlands'.

(Continued)

(Continued)

When the video was posted, it took Nestlé by surprise. In a direct attempt to quell the storm, the company decided to ask YouTube to remove the video for copyright infringement. Yet, this had the opposite effect. Visitors who wanted to view the video saw the following statement: 'This video is no longer available due to a copyright claim by Société de Produits Nestlé S.A.' The video itself was quickly reposted on other sites such as Vimeo, as well as the Greenpeace site. Arguably, it also came across, even unwittingly, as an admission of guilt, and very quickly the protest went viral with the video being shared amongst protestors and consumers, and with many of them turning to the company's Facebook site. There, thousands joined to post negative comments. The initial censorship had thus mobilized social media activists, whose actions on the Facebook page were being re-tweeted and reached a global audience. Interestingly, these activists had not been part of the Greenpeace action, but had very quickly organized themselves around what they saw was an important campaign.

The moderator of the Nestlé Facebook page was woefully unprepared for this kind of onslaught and became more bitter and rude in his responses. Instead, a more diplomatic and humane tone would probably have been fitting, but it demonstrated how unprepared Nestlé was in terms of a social media strategy. The moderator threatened Facebook users with the removal of posts on its fan page that contained altered versions of the company's logos such as a Kit Kat logo that had been altered to read 'killer'. This led to a further discussion between one Facebook user and the Nestlé moderator, which ran as follows:

Nestlé: 'To repeat: we welcome your comments, but please don't post using an altered version of any of our logos as your profile pic – they will be deleted.'

Facebook user: 'Hmmm, this comment is a bit "Big Brotherish", isn't it? I'll have whatever I want as my logo pic thanks! And if it is altered, it's no longer your logo is it!'

Nestlé: 'That's a new understanding of intellectual property right. We'll muse on that. You can have what you like as your profile picture. But if it's an altered version of any of our logos, we'll remove it from this page.'

Facebook user: 'Not sure you're going to win friends in the social media space with this sort of dogmatic approach … Social media is about embracing your market, engaging and having a conversation rather than preaching.'

Nestlé: 'Thanks for the lesson in manners. Consider yourself embraced. But it's our page, we set the rules, it was ever thus.'

This and other similar exchanges only fuelled the fire further, and rather than being a single offhand comment, the sarcastic tone of the moderator continued. His comments were widely re-tweeted and further swelled the number of visitors to the Facebook site. By 18 March 2010, the Greenpeace video had been reposted on YouTube, Vimeo and other sites, and had been watched more than 300,000 times. The video, together with the Facebook comments, also gained major news coverage around the world. The issue, in other words, had gone mainstream with reports on Sky News and NBC and newspaper coverage in *The Guardian*, *The Wall Street Journal* and *The New York Times*. Nestlé's reputation was severely damaged and there was a slight dip in the share price the day after. As one Facebook fan wrote:

'Hey PR moron. Thank you for doing a far better job than we could ever achieve in destroying your brand.'

The campaign had built such a momentum that Nestlé found itself not only cornered by Greenpeace and social media activists but also by its own consumers who threatened to boycott the firm. On 19 March, the company apologized for its handling of the comments on its Facebook site: 'This [deleting logos] was one in a series of mistakes for which I would like to apologize. And for being rude. We've stopped deleting posts, and I have stopped being rude.' On the same day, Nestlé announced on its Facebook site its intention to use sustainable palm oil by 2015: 'Hi everyone – We do care and will continue to pressure our suppliers to eliminate any sources of palm oil which are related to rainforest destruction. We have replaced the Indonesian company Sinar Mas as a supplier of palm oil for further shipments.' Greenpeace, however, continued to challenge Nestlé for its sourcing of palm oil, claiming that some of its sourcing was still indirectly linked to Sinar Mas. The company then announced on 13 April that its chairman had written to Greenpeace to call for a 'moratorium on the destruction of rainforests' and to work together in achieving this goal. In May 2010, Nestlé joined the Roundtable for Sustainable Palm Oil, a partnership of companies and other parties aimed at eliminating unsustainable production. The company also moved ahead with its target of only sourcing certified palm oil by 2015 and had conducted an in-depth analysis of its supply chain to ensure transparency and report on its progress. The company chose The Forest Trust (TFT) as a credible external partner that would audit and certify the sustainability of its palm oil suppliers.

A year later, Nestlé also added the new post of Global Head of Digital and Social Media to its corporate communication team. The incumbent in the role, Peter Blackshaw, set up a 'digital acceleration team' as part of Nestlé's efforts to monitor social media sentiment 24 hours a day. When issues connected to Nestlé emerge in social media, the team coordinates internally with the relevant departments but also externally with suppliers, campaigners and consumers, to work out a response. In addition, Nestlé's executives from around the world are made aware of the team's efforts and achievements, and are able to visit the team at its base in Switzerland to learn about managing social media communications. In the end, Nestlé realized that engaging with its critics was more effective than trying to control and shut down discussion on social media.

Questions for reflection

Reflect on the role of content communities and social networking sites, as social media, in how the initial Greenpeace campaign escalated into a full-blown crisis for Nestlé.

How would you characterize the initial response from Nestlé to the emerging crisis and to its critics, and should the company have taken a different approach instead?

Source: Informed by www.ft.com/intl/cms/s/0/90dbff8a-3aea-11e2-b3f0-00144feabdc0.html; www.greenpeace.org.uk/nestle-palm-oil; and www.independent.co.uk/environment/green-living/online-protest-drives-nestl-to-environmentally-friendly-palm-oil-1976443.html

3.5 CHAPTER SUMMARY

In this chapter, we have provided an overview of the changing media environment of corporate communication. The chapter started by setting the scene for developments around social media. We then provided a classification of social media that puts the characteristics of each medium in perspective and highlights their potential use as part of corporate communication. The chapter ended by summarizing the practical benefits of using social media as part of corporate communication.

 ──── DISCUSSION QUESTIONS ────

Think of a number of high-profile cases where social media were used either effectively or ineffectively by organizations. What, in your opinion, were the key conditions that made it a success, or in fact less so?

The new media landscape is changing the production and dissemination of corporate content, including news coverage on corporate organizations. What are the main challenges in this respect for organizations and what can communication practitioners do in response?

KEY TERMS	
Media richness	Media presence
Social networking sites	Blogs
Microblogging	Content communities
Virtual social worlds	Virtual game worlds
Collaborative projects	Conversational voice
Technological diffusion	Metrics

 ──── FURTHER READING ────

Argenti, Paul A. and Barnes, Courtney M. (2009) *Digital Strategies for Powerful Corporate Communications*. New York: McGraw-Hill.

Scott, David Meerman (2013) *The New Rules of Marketing and PR: How to Use Social Media, Online Video, Mobile Applications, Blogs, News Releases and Viral Marketing to Reach Buyers Directly*. London: Wiley, 4th edition.

Want to know more about this chapter? Visit the companion website at: https://study.sagepub.com/cornelissen5e to access videos, web links, a glossary and selected journal articles to further enhance your study.

NOTES

1. Argenti, P.A. and Barnes, C.M. (2009) *Digital Strategies for Powerful Corporate Communications*. New York: McGraw-Hill; Groysberg, B. and Slind, M. (2012) *Talk, Inc.: How Trusted Leaders Use Conversation to Power Their Organizations*. Boston, MA: Harvard Business School Press.

2. Komito, L. (2008) 'Information society policy', in Hearn, G. and Rooney, D. (eds), *Knowledge Policy: Challenges for the 21st Century*. Cheltenham: Edward Elgar, 87–101, quote on pp. 87–8.

3. Nielsen (2009, March) 'Global faces and networked places' (www.nielsen.com/content/dam/corporate/us/en/newswire/uploads/2009/03/nielsen_globalfaces_mar09.pdf).

4. Kaplan, A.M. and Haenlein, M. (2010) 'Users of the world, unite! The challenges and opportunities of social media', *Business Horizons*, 59–68, quote on p. 61.

5. Kaplan and Haenlein (2010).

6. *The Economist* (2005) 'Robert Scoble, Microsoft's celebrity blogger', 10 February.

7. Washkuch, F. (2008) 'State of transition: Media survey 2008', *PR Week*, 30 March.

8. Yang, S.U. and Kang, M. (2009) 'Measuring blog engagement: Testing a four-dimension scale', *Public Relations Review*, 35: 323–24.

9. Hird, J. (2010) '20+ mind-blowing social media statistics' (http://econsultancy.com/blog/5324-20+-mind-blowing-social-mediastatistics-Revisited).

10. Eyrich, N., Padman, M.L. and Sweetser, K.D. (2008) 'PR practitioners' use of social media tools and communication technology', *Public Relations Review*, 34: 412–14; Porter, L.V., Sweetser, K.D. and Chung, D. (2009) 'The blogosphere and public relations: Investigating practitioners' roles and blog use', *Journal of Communication Management*, 13 (3): 250–67; Porter, L., Sweetser Trammell, K.D., Chung, D. and Kim, E. (2007) 'Blog power: Examining the effects of practitioner blog use on power in public relations', *Public Relations Review*, 33: 92–5.

11. Eyrich et al. (2008); Macnamara, J. and Zerfass, A. (2012) 'Social media communication in organizations: The challenges of balancing openness, strategy and management', *International Journal of Strategic Communication*, 6 (4): 287–308.

12. Diga, M. and Kelleher, T. (2009) 'Social media use, perceptions of decision-making power, and public relations roles', *Public Relations Review*, 35: 440–42.

13. Kelleher, T. (2009) 'Conversational voice, communicated commitment, and public relations outcomes in interactive online communication', *Journal of Communication*, 59: 172–88.

14. Searls, D. and Weinberger, D. (2000) 'Markets are conversations', in Levine, R., Locke, C., Searls, D. and Weinberger D. (eds), *The Cluetrain Manifesto: The End of Business as Usual*. New York: Perseus, 75–114, quote on p. 110.

15. Arthur W. Page Society (2012) 'Building Belief: A New Model for Activating Corporate Character and Authentic Advocacy [report]' (www.awpagesociety.com/insights/building-belief/).

16. Allagui, I. and Breslow, H. (2016) 'Social media for public relations: Lessons from four effective cases', *Public Relations Review*, 42: 20–30, quote on p. 20.

17. Macnamara and Zerfass (2012).

18. Stohl, C., Etter, M., Banghart, S. and Woo, D. (2015) 'Social media policies: Implications for contemporary notions of corporate social responsibility', *Journal of Business Ethics*, 1–24.

19. Barker, M., Barker, D., Bormann, N. and Neher, K. (2013) *Social Media Marketing: A Strategic Approach*. Boston, MA: Cengage Learning.

Conceptual Foundations

2

In Part 2, we explore the basic concepts that are used in corporate communication and provide the theoretical background to the management of corporate communication in practice. Subjects that are addressed include the concept of stakeholders, models for stakeholder communication and engagement, the importance of an organization's corporate identity, image and reputation, and the subject of corporate branding.

After reading Part 2, the reader should be familiar with the basic vocabulary and theoretical concepts in corporate communication and understand the importance of stakeholder communication for contemporary organizations.

Stakeholder Management and Communication

4

CHAPTER OVERVIEW

The management of relationships with stakeholders is, both in theory and practice, one of the main purposes of corporate communication. The chapter starts with an introduction to the concept of stakeholders, followed by an overview of different management and communication models that organizations use to communicate and engage with their stakeholders.

4.1 INTRODUCTION

Contemporary organizations increasingly realize that they need to communicate with their stakeholders to develop and protect their reputations. The significance of stakeholder management partly came about because of pressures from governments and the international community promoting the stakeholder perspective. A range of stakeholder initiatives and schemes have sprung up in recent years at the industry, national and transnational levels, including the UN Global Compact Initiative, the Global Reporting Initiative, the World Bank's Business Partners for Development and the OECD's Guidelines for Multinational Companies. These initiatives and schemes emphasize the wider responsibilities of organizations to *all* stakeholders and society at large. Stakeholder management, more than any other subject in business, has profound implications for corporate communication. It requires that managers think strategically about their business overall and about how they can effectively communicate with stakeholders, including customers, investors, employees and members of the communities in which the organization resides.

The chapter outlines how stakeholder management developed, as well as how that theory can be used to establish communication strategies for organizations. Managers of many corporate organizations realize that now more than ever they need to listen to and communicate with a whole range of stakeholder groups to build and maintain the reputation of their companies. We begin the chapter with an explanation of the basic theory behind stakeholder management and then make a link with corporate communication and the use of stakeholder theory in practice.

4.2 STAKEHOLDER MANAGEMENT

Theoretically, the now widespread adoption of the stakeholder perspective in business marks a move away from a neo-classical economic theory of organizations to a socio-economic theory. The neo-classical economic theory suggests that the purpose of organizations is to make profits in their accountability to themselves and to shareholders, and that only by doing so can business contribute to wealth for itself as well as society at large.[1] The socio-economic theory suggests, in contrast, that the question of 'who counts' extends to other groups besides shareholders who are considered to be important for the continuity of the organization and the welfare of society. This distinction between a conventional neo-classical perspective and a socio-economic or stakeholder perspective on the management of organizations is highlighted by the contrasting models displayed in Figures 4.1 and 4.2.[2]

In Figure 4.1, the organization is the centre of the economy, where investors, suppliers and employees are depicted as contributing inputs (such as investments, resources, labour), which the 'black box' of the organization transforms into outputs for the benefit of customers. Each contributor of inputs is rewarded with appropriate compensation, and, as a result of competition throughout the system, the bulk of the benefits will go to the customers. It is important to note that in this 'input–output' model, power lies with the organization, on which the other parties are dependent, and that the interest of these other parties and their relationship to the organization are only financial.

The stakeholder model (Figure 4.2) contrasts with the input–output model. Stakeholder management assumes that all persons or groups who hold legitimate interests in an organization do so to obtain benefits and there is, in principle, no priority for one set of interests and benefits over another. Hence, the arrows between the organization and its stakeholders run in both directions. All those groups which have a legitimate 'stake' in the organization, whether purely financial, market-based or otherwise, are recognized, and the relationship of the organization with these groups is not linear but one of interdependency. In other words, instead of considering organizations as immune to government or public opinion, the stakeholder management model recognizes the mutual dependencies between organizations and various stakeholder groups – groups that are affected by the operations of the organization, but can equally affect the organization, its operations and performance.

The picture that emerges from the stakeholder perspective is far more complex and dynamic than the input–output model of strategic management that preceded it. More individuals and groups with legitimate interests in the organization are recognized and accounted for, and these individuals and groups all need to be considered, communicated with and possibly accommodated by the organization to sustain its financial performance and to secure continued acceptance for its operations. One significant feature of the stakeholder model is that it suggests that an organization needs to be considered 'legitimate' by both 'market' and 'non-market' stakeholder groups. This notion of legitimacy stretches beyond financial accountability to include accountability for the firm's performance in social and environmental terms.

Framing accountability through this concept of legitimacy also means that organizations engage with stakeholders not just for *instrumental* reasons but also for *normative* reasons. Instrumental reasons point to a connection between stakeholder management and corporate performance. Stakeholder management may lead to increases in revenues and reductions in costs and risks as it increases transactions with stakeholders (e.g. more sales or more investments) or as a reputational buffer is created for crises or potentially damaging litigation. Normative reasons appeal to underlying concepts such as individual or group 'rights', 'social contracts', morality, and so on. From a normative perspective, stakeholders are persons or groups with legitimate interests in aspects of corporate activity; and they are identified by this interest, whether the corporation has any direct economic interest in them or not. The interests of all stakeholders are, in effect, seen as of some intrinsic value to the organization, in this view. That is, each group of stakeholders merits consideration for its own sake and not merely because of its ability to further the interests of some other group, such as the shareholders.

Instrumental or normative reasons for engaging with stakeholders, however, often converge in practice, as social and economic objectives are not mutually exclusive and as 'doing good' for one stakeholder group delivers reputational returns which are easily carried over and may impact the views of other stakeholder groups. So, whilst communication with a particular stakeholder group may have been started for normative, even altruistic reasons – to be a 'good corporate citizen' as an end in itself, so to speak – the gains that this delivers in terms of employee morale, reputation, and so on, are often considerable and clearly of instrumental value to the organization.

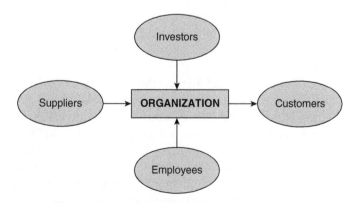

FIGURE 4.1 Input-output model of strategic management

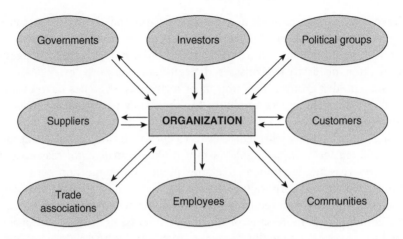

FIGURE 4.2 Stakeholder model of strategic management

4.3 THE NATURE OF STAKES AND STAKEHOLDERS

Having sketched out some of the theoretical background to stakeholder manage-ment, it is helpful to devote a bit more space to discussing the concepts of 'stake' and 'stakeholder'. The standard definition of a stakeholder is the one provided by Edward Freeman: 'A stakeholder is any group or individual who can affect or is affected by the achievement of the organization's purpose and objectives.'[3]

A stake, which is central to this definition and to the notion of stakeholder in general, can be described as 'an interest or a share in an undertaking, [that] can range from simply an interest in an undertaking at one extreme to a legal claim of owner-ship at the other extreme'.[4] The content of stakes that are held by different persons and groups is varied and based on the specific interests of these individuals or groups in the organization. Special interest groups and NGOs, for example, may demand ever higher levels of 'corporate social responsibility' from an organization. Investors, for their part, may apply relentless pressure on that same organization to maximize short-term profits. Stakes of different individuals and groups are thus varied and may be at odds with one another, putting pressure on the organization to balance stakeholder interests.

Edward Freeman was amongst the first to offer a classification of all those groups who hold a stake in the organization. In his classic book, *Strategic Management: A Stakeholder Approach*, Freeman considered three types of stakes: equity stakes, economic or market stakes, and influencer stakes. Equity stakes, in Freeman's termi-nology, are held by those who have some direct 'ownership' of the organization, such as shareholders, directors or minority interest owners. Economic or market stakes are held by those who have an economic interest, but not an ownership interest, in the organization, such as employees, customers, suppliers and competitors. Finally, influencer stakes are held by those who do not have either an ownership or economic interest in the actions of the organization, but who have interests as consumer advocates, environmental groups, trade organizations and government agencies. By considering these types of stakes, Freeman specified the nature of stakes in terms of the interest of various groups in the organization – whether this interest is primarily economic or moral in nature – and whether this interest is bound in some form through a contract or (moral) obligation.

One standard way of looking at stakes is indeed to assess whether the interest of a person or group in an organization is primarily economic or moral in nature. In this respect, Clarkson suggests thinking of primary and secondary groups of stakeholders, with primary groups being those groups that are important for financial transactions and necessary for an organization to survive.[5] In short, in Clarkson's view, a primary stakeholder group is one without whose continuing participation the organization cannot survive. Secondary stakeholder groups are defined as those who generally influence or affect, or are influenced or affected by, the organization, but they are not engaged in financial transactions with the organization and are not essential for its survival in strictly economic terms. Media and a wide range of special interest groups fall within this secondary group of stakeholders. These secondary stakeholders do, however, have a moral or normative interest in the organization and have the capacity to mobilize public opinion in favour of, or against, a corporation's performance, as demonstrated in the cases of the recall of the Tylenol product by Johnson & Johnson (favourable) and the *Exxon Valdez* oil spill (unfavourable).

A second way of viewing stakes is to consider whether stakeholder ties with an organization are established through some form of contract or formal agreement, or not. Charkham talked about two broad classes of stakeholders in this respect: contractual and community stakeholders.[6] Contractual stakeholders are those groups who have some form of legal relationship with the organization for the exchange of goods or services. Community stakeholders involve those groups whose relationship with the organization is non-contractual and more diffuse, although their relationship is nonetheless real in terms of its impact. Contractual groups, including customers, employees and suppliers, are formally tied to an organization because they have entered into some form of contract; the nature of their interest is often economic in providing services or extracting resources from the organization (Table 4.1). Community stakeholders, on the other hand, are not contractually bound to an organization. This includes groups such as the government, regulatory agencies, trade associations and the media, who are nonetheless important in providing the authority for an organization to function, setting the general rules and regulations by which activities are carried out, and monitoring and publicly evaluating the conduct of business operations.

In summary, the notion of having a legitimate stake in an organization is rather 'inclusive' and ranges from economic to moral interests, and from formal, binding relationships as the basis of a stake to more diffuse and loose ties with the organization. This 'inclusiveness' implies that organizations ideally communicate and engage with all of their stakeholders. A particular way in which this 'inclusive' nature of the stakeholder concept is shown is in corporate social responsibility (CSR) initiatives that have been adopted by many organizations in recent years. These initiatives are a direct outcome of the shift from an 'input–output' model to a stakeholder model of strategic management (Figures 4.1 and 4.2). CSR includes philanthropy, community

TABLE 4.1 Contractual and community stakeholders

Contractual stakeholders	Community stakeholders
Customers	Consumers
Employees	Regulators
Distributors	Government
Suppliers	Media
Shareholders	Local communities
Lenders	Pressure groups

involvement and ethical and environmentally friendly business practices. The drive for CSR came with the recognition of the need for business to deliver wider societal value beyond shareholder and market value alone (see Chapter 14).

4.4 STAKEHOLDER COMMUNICATION

The stakeholder model of the organization suggests that the various stakeholders of the organization need to be identified and that they must be addressed according to the stake that they hold. In practice, this comes down to providing stakeholders with the type of information about the company's operations that they have an interest in. Financial investors and shareholders, for instance, will need to be provided with financial information concerning the organization's strategy and operations (e.g. through annual reports and shareholder meetings), whilst customers and prospects need to be supplied with information about products and services (e.g. through advertising, sales promotions and in-store communication). Each of these stakeholder groups, on the basis of the stake(s) that an individual holds in an organization, looks for and is interested in certain aspects of the company's operations. Whilst the interests of stakeholders are intricately varied, and, at times, even at odds with one another (e.g. staff redundancies are a blow to the workforce, but may be favoured by shareholders and investors who have an interest in the financial strength and continuity of the firm), it is important that an organization provides each stakeholder group with specific information and builds a strong reputation across exchanges with all of these stakeholders.

In order to do so, managers and communication practitioners typically start by identifying and analysing the organization's stakeholders, their influence and interest in the organization. In this way, they have a clearer idea what the information needs of stakeholders are, what specific positions they have on an issue or in relation to a corporate activity, and what kind of communication strategy can to be used to maintain support or counter opposition. A basic form of stakeholder identification analysis involves answering the following questions that capture the essential information for effective stakeholder communication:

Who are the organization's stakeholders?

What are their stakes?

What opportunities and challenges are presented to the organization in relation to these stakeholders?

What responsibilities (economic, legal, ethical and philanthropic) does the organization have to all its stakeholders?

In what way can the organization best communicate with and respond to these stakeholders and address these stakeholder challenges and opportunities?

A similar approach is to use a map or model to identify and position stakeholders in terms of their influence on the organization's operations or in terms of their stance on a particular issue related to the organization. There are two general mapping devices or tools that managers and communication practitioners can use for this task: the stakeholder salience model and the power–interest matrix. Both mapping devices enhance practitioners' knowledge of stakeholders and their influence, and enable them to plan appropriate communication strategies. Such mapping exercises should be carried out on an ongoing basis, but can also be performed in relation to issues or corporate decisions at a particular point in time.

Stakeholder salience model

In this model, stakeholders are identified and classified based on their salience to the organization. Salience is defined as how visible or prominent a stakeholder is to an organization based on the stakeholder possessing one or more of three attributes: power, legitimacy and urgency. The central idea behind the model is that the more salient or prominent stakeholders have priority and therefore need to be actively communicated with. Lesser or hardly salient stakeholders have less priority and it is less important for an organization to communicate with them on an ongoing basis.

The first step of the model is to classify and prioritize stakeholders according to the presence or absence of the three key attributes: power (the power of the stakeholder group upon an organization); legitimacy (the legitimacy of the claim laid upon the organization by the stakeholder group); and urgency (the degree to which stakeholder claims call for immediate action).[7] Together, these three attributes form seven different types of stakeholders, as shown in Figure 4.3.

The three stakeholder groups on the edges of Figure 4.3 are classified as *latent* stakeholder groups which are groups possessing only one attribute:

1. *Dormant stakeholders*: those who have the power to impose their will on others but because they do not have a legitimate relationship or an urgent claim, their power remains dormant. Examples of dormant stakeholders include those who wield power by being able to spend a lot of money or by commanding the attention of the news media. Dormant stakeholders such as, for example, prospective customers, however, have little or no interaction with the organization. But because of their potential to acquire a second attribute (urgency or legitimacy), practitioners should be aware of such stakeholders and their potential impact on the organization.

2. *Discretionary stakeholders*: those who possess legitimate claims based on
    interactions with an organization but have no power to influence the
    organization, nor any urgent claims. Recipients of corporate charity, for
    instance, fall within this group.
3. *Demanding stakeholders*: those who have urgent claims, but neither the
    power nor legitimacy to enforce them. These groups can therefore be
    bothersome but do not warrant serious attention from communication
    practitioners. That is, where stakeholders are unable or unwilling to acquire
    either the power or the legitimacy necessary to move their claim to a more
    salient status, the 'noise' of urgency is insufficient to move a stakeholder
    claim beyond latency. For example, a lone demonstrator who camps near a
    company's site might be embarrassing to the company or a nuisance to
    employees and managers of an organization, but the claims of the
    demonstrator will typically remain unconsidered.

Three further groups are considered and classified as expectant stakeholders and are
groups with two attributes present:

Dominant stakeholders: those who have both powerful and legitimate claims,
giving them a strong influence on the organization. Examples include
stakeholder groups who regularly transact with or have strong binding
relationships with organizations such as employees, customers, owners and
significant (institutional) investors in the organization. They have power because
there is always the possibility that they may decide to withhold their investment
or labour, for example.

Dangerous stakeholders: those who have power and urgent claims, but lack
legitimacy. They are seen as dangerous as they may resort to coercion and even
violence. Examples of unlawful, yet common, attempts at using coercive means
to advance stakeholder claims (which may or may not be legitimate) include
wildcat strikes, employee sabotage and terrorism.

Dependent stakeholders: those who lack power, but who have urgent, legitimate
claims. They rely on others for the power to carry out their will, at times
through the advocacy of other stakeholders. Local residents of a community in
which a plant of a large corporation is based, for instance, often rely on lobby
groups, the media or another form of political representation to have their
concerns voiced and considered by a company.

The seventh and final type of stakeholder group that can be identified is:

Definitive stakeholders: those who have legitimacy, power and urgency. In other
words, definitive stakeholders are powerful and legitimate stakeholders who, by
definition, need to be communicated with. When the claim of a definitive
stakeholder is urgent, communication practitioners and other managers have a
responsibility to give it priority and attention. Shareholders, for example, who
are normally classified as dominant stakeholders, can become active when they
feel that their legitimate interests are not being served by the managers of the

company in which they hold stock, and then they effectively act as definitive stakeholders. When the actions of such powerful shareholders may, for example, imply the removal of senior executives, communication practitioners and managers of the organization urgently need to attend to their concerns.

Once all the organization's stakeholders have been classified according to their salience, communication practitioners will have an overview of which stakeholder groups require attention and need to be communicated with. Based on the classification, they can develop communication strategies to most appropriately deal with each stakeholder. For example, dominant and definitive stakeholders of the organization, such as employees, customers and shareholders, need to be communicated with on an ongoing basis. Most organizations have ongoing communication programmes for these stakeholders, including newsletters, corporate events and an intranet for employees, advertising and promotional campaigns for customers and financial reports, investor briefings and the annual general meeting for shareholders. In addition, many organizations will often communicate directly with members of the local communities in which they operate (dependent stakeholders) and will respond to dangerous stakeholders if the actions of those stakeholders affect others, including the company's employees. Organizations typically do not communicate on an ongoing basis with latent stakeholder groups including dormant, demanding and discretionary stakeholders.

The stakeholder salience model is a useful diagnostic tool for communication practitioners. They often use the tool on an ongoing basis, in recognition of the fact that the classification of stakeholder groups is not given once and for all.

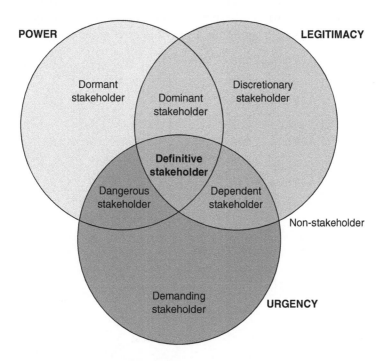

FIGURE 4.3 Stakeholder salience model

Because of changes in public opinion, market environments, or because of a particular crisis for the organization, stakeholder groups may 'move' in the classification and may accordingly become more or less salient, and thus more or less important for communication.

The power–interest matrix

A second mapping device is based on the same principles as the stakeholder salience model. The general objective is to categorize stakeholders on the basis of the power that they possess and the extent to which they are likely to have or show an interest in the organization's activities. Practitioners would estimate stakeholders on these two variables and plot the location of the stakeholders in the matrix. Figure 4.4 displays these variables and the four cells in which stakeholders can be located.[8]

Similar to the stakeholder salience model, the idea again is that communication practitioners can formulate appropriate communication strategies on the basis of identifying and categorizing stakeholders. In particular, the reaction or position of 'key players' (quadrant D) towards the organization's decisions and operations must be given key consideration. They need to be constantly communicated with. Similarly, those with a high level of interest in the organization but with a low level of power or influence (quadrant B) need to be kept informed of the organization, so that they remain committed to the organization and may spread positive word-of-mouth to others. Stakeholders in quadrant C are the most challenging to maintain relationships with as, despite their lack of interest in general, these stakeholders might exercise their power in reaction to a particular decision or corporate activity. Practitioners should also remain sensitive to the possible movement of stakeholders from one quadrant to another when, for example, levels of interest in the organization change.

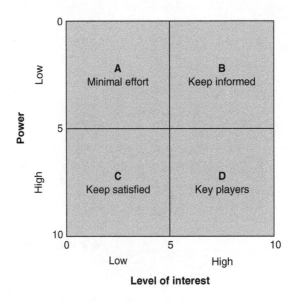

FIGURE 4.4   The power–interest matrix

Both mapping devices provide an overview and ordering of the importance and influence of particular stakeholders to an organization in general terms. Based on this ordering, organizations know how intensely they need to communicate with particular groups and also often already have a sense of what the key messages should be. In other words, these mappings give an insight into whether stakeholders should only be kept informed of decisions of the organization or its stance on a particular issue, or instead whether stakeholders should be actively listened to and communicated with on an ongoing basis. In broad terms, those stakeholders who are salient or have a powerful interest in the organization need to be communicated with so that they continue to support the organization. Important stakeholders such as customers, employees, suppliers and shareholders in any case need to be listened to and may also need to be actively considered in the choices and decisions that the organization makes. Figure 4.5 displays these differences between a strategy of simply providing information or disseminating information with stakeholders in order to raise their awareness, on the one hand, versus a strategy of actively communicating with stakeholders and incorporating them in the organization's decision-making, on the other.

An *informational strategy* is simply a strategy of informing someone about something. Press releases, newsletters and reports on a company website are often simply meant to make information available about the organization to its stakeholders. Such a strategy may create awareness of organizational decisions and may also contribute to a degree of understanding of the reasons for these decisions. A second strategy that organizations can use is a *persuasive strategy* whereby an organization, through campaigns, meetings and discussions with stakeholders, tries to change and tune the knowledge, attitude and behaviour of stakeholders in a way that is favourable to the organization. Corporate advertising and educational campaigns, for example, are often used to create a favourable image for the organization and to 'sell' a particular kind of understanding of the organization's decisions, its corporate values and its products and services. A third strategy that organizations may use is a *dialogue strategy* in which both parties (organizations and stakeholders) mutually engage in an exchange of ideas and opinions. A dialogue strategy involves the active consultation of stakeholders and, at times, even the incorporation of important stakeholders into the organization's decision-making. It involves working towards a process of mutual understanding and mutual decisions rather than strategic self-interest on the part of the organization. As Figure 4.5 highlights, there is a difference, however, within this strategy between an approach of *involving* stakeholders, soliciting their input

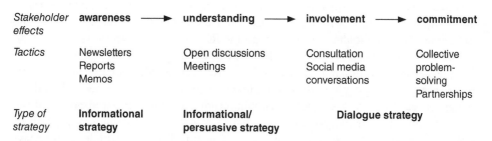

Stakeholder effects	awareness ➝	understanding ➝	involvement ➝	commitment
Tactics	Newsletters Reports Memos	Open discussions Meetings	Consultation Social media conversations	Collective problem-solving Partnerships
Type of strategy	**Informational strategy**	**Informational/ persuasive strategy**	**Dialogue strategy**	

FIGURE 4.5 Stakeholder communication: from awareness to commitment

and feedback through, for example, social media conversations, and one of *engaging* stakeholders to get their ongoing commitment through, for example, joint partnerships (see also Chapter 13). The strategy of joint partnerships of an organization with key stakeholders such as customers or suppliers is the most intensive form of communication and reflects situations where the two sides share mutual interests and are strongly committed to one another.

The use of each of these strategies will depend on the salience and power interest of a stakeholder group and the need for active engagement with stakeholders to build long-term relationships with them and to provide them with opportunities to connect with the organization. To give an example, when powerful institutional shareholders challenge a company's executive payment and reward scheme, they become definitive stakeholders who not only need to be actively communicated with, but ideally would also at the very least be consulted in future decisions about such matters (a dialogue strategy).

This is exactly the scenario that BP faced in April 2016, when 59 per cent of its shareholders revolted against a £14 million pay package for its CEO in a year in which the company recorded significant financial losses and cut thousands of jobs. BP had tabled the pay package at its annual general meeting and had informed shareholders about it beforehand in its annual report. The shareholder revolt, however, indicated that BP would have been wise to seek active consultation earlier. In the wake of the criticism, the company's chairman said that BP would now solicit advice from its shareholders: 'Let me be clear. We hear you. We will sit down with our largest shareholders to make sure we understand their concerns and return to seek your support for a renewed policy', he said.

Schematically, these three strategies have been described as a one-way symmetrical model of communication (informational strategy), a two-way asymmetrical model of communication (persuasive strategy) and a two-way symmetrical model of communication (a dialogue strategy), as shown in Figure 4.6.

In the first model, communication is always one-way, from the organization to its stakeholders. There is no listening to stakeholders or an attempt to gather feedback in this model. The aim is simply to make information available to stakeholders. However, the relationship between the organization and stakeholders is still 'symmetrical'. This means that communication practitioners aim to report, objectively, information about the organization to relevant stakeholders and do not try to persuade them regarding particular understandings, attitudes or behaviour. In other words, there is no explicit persuasive intent on the part of the practitioners which is labelled an 'asymmetrical' relationship between an organization and its stakeholders, as that would involve a situation where the interests of the organization are emphasized at the expense of the interests of its stakeholders. In the second model, communication flows between an organization and its stakeholders and is thus labelled two-way communication. For example, an organization may gather feedback from stakeholders on how the organization is being perceived and understood. However, the two-way asymmetrical model is 'asymmetrical' because the effects of communication are unbalanced in favour of the organization. The organization does not change as a result of communicating with its stakeholders; instead, it only attempts to change stakeholders' attitudes and behaviours. The third model, the two-way symmetrical model, consists of a dialogue rather

Informational strategy: one-way symmetrical model of communication

Persuasive strategy: two-way asymmetrical model of communication

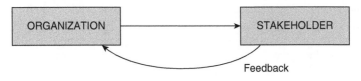

Feedback

Dialogue strategy: two-way symmetrical model of communication

FIGURE 4.6 Models of organization–stakeholder communication

than a monologue. Communication again flows both ways between an organization and its stakeholders, but unlike the previous model, the goal is to exchange views and to reach mutual understanding between the parties. Both parties recognize the 'other' in the communication process and try to provide each other with equal opportunities for expression and for a free exchange of information.[9] British American Tobacco (Case Example 4.1) is an example of a company that has engaged with stakeholders on a whole range of social and environmental issues within its supply chain and in the marketing of its products.

—▢—— CASE EXAMPLE 4.1 ————————————————

BRITISH AMERICAN TOBACCO (BAT) AND STAKEHOLDER DIALOGUE

British American Tobacco (BAT) is the world's most international tobacco group, with brands sold in more than 180 markets. The company is amongst the most profitable corporations in the world, delivering exceptional value to shareholders. Over the past ten years, for example, shareholders received a total return of 486 per cent on their investments, compared to 3 per cent for the 100 top listed corporations in London (the FTSE 100) as a whole. BAT's strategy is firmly focused on growing the business towards a strategic vision of regaining overall leadership in the global tobacco industry. The company recognizes that realizing its vision is, at least in part, dependent on effectively managing stakeholder relationships. BAT's products pose significant health risks for individual consumers, which in turn affects the provision and costs of healthcare in countries around the world. The company has been criticized for this, with many advocacy groups calling for an outright prohibition of smoking.

(Continued)

(Continued)

BAT itself takes a different ethical stance; the company recognizes that its products pose risks to health, but it constantly emphasizes that these products are legal, that calls for prohibition are exceptionally rare and that about a billion adults globally choose to smoke. In other words, their social responsibility does not extend to the responsible choices made by adults, or indeed the public costs associated with these choices. Instead, the company's corporate social responsibility efforts are aimed at improving its overall standards of business conduct and it has adopted 'a responsible approach to doing business from crop to consumer'. As part of this approach, the company is working on the elimination of child labour in the industry, provides support for leaf-growing communities, is tackling illicit trade and is curbing carbon emissions. Whilst BAT does not actively campaign on the risks of smoking, its websites contain information on these risks. Corporate communication staff have also set up a dialogue forum with key stakeholders on social and environmental issues connected to the business. The feedback gained from stakeholders is used to set progressive targets on its social and environmental reporting. It also gives the company an insight into what stakeholders believe are the most contentious topics. In response, BAT has acted on a number of these topics, resulting in the development of youth smoking prevention programmes and investment in the development of cigarettes with reduced toxicants that are less harmful to consumers.

Since 2013, the company has been changing its approach to social and environmental reporting. Instead of an annual comprehensive sustainability report, corporate communication staff will now produce shorter, more focused sustainability communications throughout the year. One part of this approach involves producing and disseminating periodic issue-specific reports to provide stakeholders with more in-depth information on the topics that are of most interest to them, and in this way foster a dialogue with them about these issues and the company's progress on them.

Question for reflection

Consider the stakeholder communication strategy (Figure 4.5) of BAT in relation to social and environmental issues. Is this the right strategy, or do you think an alternative strategy would have been better or more sufficient?

Each of these different strategies also requires different media or channels to communicate with stakeholders. Communication media or channels such as reports, adverts and face-to-face communication vary based on their capacity to process and channel 'rich' exchanges. A 'rich' exchange involves the ability to provide immediate feedback between the two parties, the ability to personalize and adapt messages based on responses, and the ability to express and articulate the message in different ways.[10] Media that facilitate such 'rich' exchanges are central to a dialogue strategy and, to some extent, also feature in a persuasive strategy. These include face-to-face consultations and meetings, social media such as Facebook and Twitter and personalized documents such as letters or memos. Media that are less able to facilitate 'rich' exchanges, such as impersonal written documents (e.g. a financial report) or print or TV adverts, are associated with an informational strategy where there is no direct need for the stakeholder to directly respond to the message. Face-to-face communication (or its simulated virtual equivalent, such as Facebook or Twitter) is the richest medium because it allows immediate feedback so that interpretations can be checked and subsequent communication can be adjusted. 'Rich' media are also useful for discussing ambiguous, sensitive, controversial or complex issues with stakeholders of the organization in order to overcome different frames of reference. Media of low 'richness' restrict immediate feedback and are therefore less appropriate for resolving ambiguous, sensitive, controversial or complex issues. However, an important point is that media of low richness are effective for reporting well-understood messages and standard data (such as, for example, reporting on financial performance).

4.5 STAKEHOLDER ENGAGEMENT

In recent years, communication practitioners have increasingly realized the importance of engaging with stakeholders directly to further understanding around specific issues, to strengthen the goodwill and reputation of the organization, and to generally build more long-term and lasting relationships. Rather than focusing on a single instance of communication or of exchanging goods, they see the opportunities in changing the very nature of the relationship between the organization and its stakeholders from 'management' to 'collaboration' and from 'exchange' to 'engagement'. This development brings with it a shift in thinking about stakeholders as being managed by and for the benefit of corporate organizations (managing 'of' stakeholders) to the idea of developing mutually supportive and lasting relationships (managing 'for' stakeholders). 'Engagement' implies a two-way symmetrical model of dialogue and consultation through which communication practitioners build stakeholder relationships that are reciprocal, evolving and mutually defined, and that are a source of opportunity and competitive advantage.[11]

A summary of this change in focus is given in Table 4.2. The 'old' approach of stakeholder management consists of different practitioners and departments in the organization 'managing' interactions with stakeholders, often from the perspective of their own function or department. Another characteristic of the 'old' approach is the attempt to 'buffer' the claims and interests of stakeholders to prevent them from interfering with internal operations and instead trying to influence their attitudes and opinions. In this approach, in line with a persuasion strategy, an organization is trying either to insulate itself from external interference or to actively influence stakeholders in its environment through such means as contributions to political action committees, lobbying and corporate advertising. The 'new' approach of stakeholder engagement, in contrast, involves an emphasis on stakeholder relationships across the organization. The aim here is to build long-term relationships, or 'partnerships', and to seek out those stakeholders who are interested in more direct engagement and possibly collaboration. The 'new' approach is more in line with a dialogue strategy with its emphasis on 'bridging' stakeholder claims and interests. Bridging occurs when organizations seek to adapt their activities so that they conform with the external interests and expectations of important stakeholder groups. It suggests that an organization actively tries to meet and exceed regulatory requirements in its industry and goes out of its way to meet its stakeholders' expectations.

TABLE 4.2   Characteristics of the 'old' and 'new' approaches to organization–stakeholder relationships

Stakeholder management	Stakeholder engagement
Fragmented amongst various departments	Integrated management approach
Focus on managing relationships	Focus on building relationships
Emphasis on 'buffering' the organization from stakeholders interfering with internal operations	Emphasis on 'bridging' and creating opportunities and mutual benefits
Linked to short-term business goals	Linked to long-term business goals
Idiosyncratic implementation dependent on department's interests and personal style of manager	Coherent approach driven by mission, values and corporate strategies

There are many examples of this change in approach to organization–stakeholder relationships. For example, many leading brands such as Saab, LEGO and Harley Davidson now involve their customers in long-term relationships by incorporating them in their internal research and development (R&D) processes and through participation in branded online communities. Another good example is the way in which Starbucks has moved form an arm's-length relationship with key stakeholders to a direct dialogue through social networking sites that allows key stakeholders to influence the direction of the company (Case Study 4.1). Yet another example is the way in which Novo Nordisk, a pharmaceutical manufacturer of insulin, uses Twitter to provide a discussion forum for diabetes care and to openly discuss its sustainability initiatives. These channels provide Novo Nordisk with a personal and direct way of communicating with interested stakeholders, and the company also uses these channels as a platform for actively listening to suggestions and responses from stakeholders. An important rule within Novo Nordisk is that these Twitter feeds cannot mention products directly or indirectly, and are thus sheltered from marketing influence so as to ensure an open dialogue with diabetes sufferers, healthcare professionals and others interested in the broader cause.

The degree to which companies generally engage with all of their stakeholders, and particularly non-market groups such as local communities, interest groups and social movements, varies, however, between sectors and industries. One important driver of such differences is the dominant logic of senior managers in an organization. Recent research[12] demonstrates that managers may collectively conceptualize the firm's relationship with the broader society in three distinct ways and this in turn determines how the company engages with stakeholders. A dominant logic is a collective cognitive construct that reflects how top managers conceptualize their business, and which they enact and reinforce through decisions, strategies and actions taken towards stakeholders.

First of all, their default logic may be one of a strict commercial logic, where economic considerations, such as profit, growth and efficiency are paramount, and where social value and actively collaborating with stakeholders are seen to come at the expense of economic returns. Second, the logic of senior managers may be one of collaboration for competitive gain, where companies collaborate with stakeholders to create value and, in doing so, gain competitive advantage, reputation and a capacity for innovation. Compared to the strict firm-centric commercial logic, this logic recognizes, to a much greater extent, the interconnections with various stakeholder groups in society, and it tends to involve interactions and relationship building beyond single transactions. The third and most 'extended' conceptualization is one of social value creation, not only for the corporate organization but also for other actors and groups in society. This final logic is – compared to the other two – the most complex for managers to work out, as it requires that they actively think through the bidirectional and positive links between social and economic value and recognize the interdependence between the wellbeing of the organization and that of society. The emphasis, in other words, is on 'joint value creation'.[13] This logic of joint or social value creation is, however, generally more taxing for managers than thinking in terms of a more straightforward commercial logic.

The dominant logic is thus an important driver as it directs attention to particular stakeholders and how companies choose to engage (or not) with them. In some senses, the enactment of the logic through decisions, actions and communication makes it a self-fulfilling prophecy in that those actions, once they are taken, reinforce the overall logic. Managers in turn then become further convinced of their business model. For managers, at the outset there is also no way of determining whether the strict commercial logic is more likely to lead to competitive gain than the more stakeholder-oriented logics. Whilst collaborating with stakeholders means that companies devote time and resources to them, and possibly away from economic production, it may unlock additional potential for value creation. The key here is that when companies develop trusting relationships with stakeholders, these stakeholders are more likely to share nuanced information that can spur innovation and allow the company to better deal with changes in the environment. In such circumstances, stakeholders are also more likely to reciprocate and continue to transact with organizations. They may even become advocates for the organization who, through word-of-mouth and peer-to-peer influence, communicate favourably about the company to others. This information sharing, reciprocity and advocacy lead to direct competitive gains, which are gains that are sustainable because of the strong ties that companies have established with stakeholders.[14] One clear caution associated with this analysis, however, is that for competitive advantage to be achieved, the benefits of engaging with stakeholders must generally exceed the costs. The costs of stakeholder engagement include the time that managers spend on communicating and managing relationships with stakeholders, as well as the direct allocation of other resources to them. It is possible that a company allocates too much time and resources to stakeholder engagement. Also, those managers and companies who desire to create social value may end up allocating too many resources to stakeholders directly, and may as such be 'giving away the store' to stakeholders. In other words, the crux for managers is to conceptualize a sufficiently detailed logic on how the company engages stakeholders, and to ensure that the appropriate amount of time, resources and dedication goes into managing those stakeholder relationships.

CASE STUDY 4.1

STARBUCKS COFFEE COMPANY AND STAKEHOLDER ENGAGEMENT

Starbucks, generally considered to be the most famous specialty coffee shop chain in the world, today has over 23,000 stores worldwide. Many analysts have credited Starbucks with having turned coffee from a commodity into an experience to savour. Starbucks has always felt that the key to its growth and its business success would lie in a rounded corporate brand identity, a better understanding of its customers and a store experience that would generate a pull effect through word-of-mouth. Howard Schultz, Starbucks' founder and chairman and CEO, had early on in the company's history envisioned a retail experience that revolved around high-quality coffee, personalized, knowledgeable services and sociability. So Starbucks put in place various measures to make this experience appealing to millions of people and to create a unique identity for Starbucks' products and stores.

Schultz felt that the equity of the Starbucks brand depended less on advertising and promotion and more on personal communications, on strong ties with customers and with members of the local community and on word-of-mouth. As Schultz put it:

> If we want to exceed the trust of our customers, then we first have to build trust with our people. A brand has to start with the [internal] culture and naturally extend to our customers … Our brand is based on the experience that we control in our stores. When a company can create a relevant, emotional and intimate experience, it builds trust with the customer … we have benefited by the fact that our stores are reliable, safe and consistent where people can take a break.

Stakeholders as partners

Schultz regarded the baristas, the coffee makers in the stores, as his brand ambassadors and considered the company's employees as long-term 'partners' in making the company's strategic vision a reality. This commitment to employees is also anchored in Starbucks' mission statement which, amongst other things, states that the company aims to 'provide a great work environment and to treat each other with respect and dignity'.

From its founding onwards, Starbucks has looked on each of its stores as a billboard for the company and as directly contributing to building the company's brand and reputation. Each detail has been scrutinized to enhance the mood and ambience of the store, to make sure everything signals 'best of class' and reflects the personality of the community and the neighbourhood. The company has gone to great lengths to make sure that the store fixtures, the merchandise displays, the colours, the artwork, the banners, the music and the aromas all blend to create a consistent, inviting, stimulating environment that evokes the romance of coffee and signals the company's passion for coffee.

Just as treating employees as 'partners' is one of the pillars of Starbucks' culture and mission, so is contributing positively to the communities it serves and to the environment. Each Starbucks store supports a range of community initiatives and causes and aims to be a long-term 'partner' to the communities in which it trades.

At the community level, Starbucks store managers have discretion to make money donations to local causes and to provide coffee for local fund-raisers.

Because of these initiatives, consumers and members of the community in which Starbucks operate associate the Starbucks brand with coffee, accessible elegance, community, individual expression and 'a place away from home'. Besides engaging in long-term relationships with customers, employees and communities, Starbucks is also known for its social progressive ethos and collaborates with non-governmental organizations (NGOs) in promoting the production and consumption of 'fair trade' coffee. Back in 2000, Global Exchange, an NGO dedicated to promoting environmental, political and social justice around the world, criticized the company for profiting at the expense of coffee farmers by paying low prices and not buying fair trade coffee beans. Whilst the company is, at times, still being criticized for its aggressive tactics in the coffee market, it has tried to collaborate with various organizations to promote the consumption of fair trade coffee. Starbucks has been an ongoing contributor to CARE, a worldwide relief and development foundation, specifying that its support should go to coffee-producing nations. The company also began a partnership in 1998 with Conservation International, a non-profit organization that promotes biodiversity in coffee-growing regions, to support producers of shade-grown coffee, which protects the environment.

Managing stakeholder issues

Despite its best efforts, however, Starbucks was recently criticized for its poor handling of two issues, which demonstrate the broader challenges for big corporations such as Starbucks to manage their stakeholder relationships in a balanced and ethical way. The first issue emerged in March 2007 when Starbucks was accused of attempting to block Ethiopia's desire to trademark some of its most famous coffees. Premium coffee is a growing market, and to benefit from the rising demand the Ethiopian government set out to trademark three coffee-growing regions of the country associated with its finest beans: Sidamo, Yirgacheffe and Harar. With trademarks, the country could charge distributors a licensing fee for their use and claim intellectual property rights over its coffees. The European Union, Japan and Canada all approved the trademark scheme. Starbucks, however, initially objected to the trademarks and was working with its industry lobbyists to pressure the US Patent and Trademark Office to turn down Ethiopia's trademark applications. Unbeknown to the Ethiopian government, Starbucks had also itself a year earlier tried to trademark Shirkina Sun-Dried Sidamo. Attaining trademark certification would have conferred Starbucks with a number of benefits, including recognition of the ownership of the trademark and exclusive use of the brand name, both in the USA as well as potentially (upon registration) abroad.

As a result of Starbucks' efforts, the Office approved the trademarking of Yirgacheffe but has continued to refuse the registration of Sidamo and Harar as they refer to generic names for a type of coffee. The outcome of this decision is directly felt by Ethiopian farmers. Whereas US retailers generally earn up to $28 per kilogram, farmers were receiving as little as $1 per kilogram (of the retail price). In the case of Yirgacheffe, the price has, however, increased substantially for Ethiopian farmers, who now collect up to $4 per kilogram, with estimates that they could secure up to $8 per kilogram over the coming years.

(Continued)

(Continued)

Oxfam took up Ethiopia's cause in a media campaign, generating some 70,000 complaints against Starbucks from consumers and the general public. In response, Starbucks launched a media counter-offensive, publicly rebuking Ethiopia's efforts. The company claimed that licensing would be more appropriate than trademarking the three coffee regions, and argued that 'the trademark application is not based on sound economic advice and that the proposal as it stands would hurt Ethiopian coffee farmers economically'. The active blocking of the Ethiopian government led to a public relations crisis for Starbucks, with the normally ethically minded company accused of acting tough with one of the world's poorest countries.

To defuse the situation, Starbucks agreed a wide-ranging accord with Ethiopia to support and promote its coffee, ending the dispute over the issue. Starbucks also offered to promote Ethiopia's coffees in its stores, regardless of any decision by the US Patent and Trademark Office. The company furthermore pledged that it was going to build sustainable long-term partnerships with Ethiopian farmers, but this never materialized and it has focused its efforts since on offering support and capacity-building services through Farmer Support centres in Africa and the Caribbean. In addition, the company sponsors Conservation International through cause-related marketing efforts to replant coffee trees for every bag of coffee sold in one of its stores.

In December 2012, Starbucks found itself in another difficult situation, when it emerged that over the course of 14 years of trading in the UK the company had paid only £8.6 million in tax and nothing in the last three years. The reason for this is that despite having revenues of over £3 billion over this period, the company's accounting scheme meant that profits were channelled to Ireland and the Netherlands where these were more favourably taxed. Customers were outraged over the issue. They, in effect, felt let down by the company and its pledge to care about the communities and societies in which it operates. David Cameron, the then Prime Minister, also openly criticized Starbucks: 'Companies need to wake up and smell the coffee, because the customers who buy from them have had enough.' In response to the media backlash and the effect it was having on customers, Starbucks promised a further £20 million as a 'gift' for 2013 and 2014 on top of the tax that it legally owed the British taxman. UK Uncut, a group that protests against corporate tax avoidance in the UK, said that Starbucks' announcement was not enough and that they would continue to stage actions at Starbucks stores up and down the country. Politicians also branded the move by Starbucks as 'odd' and as a PR gimmick in that paying tax is not 'voluntary' but a legal requirement. Starbucks admitted in turn that the degree of hostility and emotion of customers, politicians and the media over the issue had 'taken us a bit by surprise' and that the move was an attempt to rebuild trust with its customers.

Engaging stakeholders through social media

Alongside managing these specific issues, Starbucks uses social media to reach out directly to stakeholders and to strengthen the brand and community ties around the company. The company has active strategies for Facebook and Twitter, posting unique feel-good and eye-catching content, including helpful tips for coffee aficionados, subtle sales messages to its customers and stories of its community outreach and volunteering events. The company's social media team also responds directly on Facebook and Twitter to information requests or comments online and actively seeks out social media users who mention Starbucks in their own timeline, in either a positive or negative way, to get in touch with the company for follow-up. In addition, for some time, Starbucks ran the Starbucks V2V site, which was a social networking site that the company ran up until 2008 where people were able to connect on global relief causes and community issues. The networking site was closely connected to the company; many people on the site either worked for Starbucks or were loyal customers or members of the community. The company directly facilitated the discussion and supported the identified causes and issues. On another site that is still live (www.mystarbucksidea.com), people can suggest ideas for products, store experiences and community involvement. Most of the people on the site are loyal customers and in this way Starbucks is able to give them a direct voice in the company. Dedicated communication staff 'listen' to the ideas being discussed, provide customers with information on what the company is doing and may help develop these ideas into action.

Questions for reflection

1   Consider the importance for Starbucks of developing long-term relationships and partnerships with different stakeholders. Should the company develop relationships with all of its stakeholders or only a select few?
2   What strategies and models of communication should the company use for communicating with its different stakeholder groups? What opportunities are provided by social media for stakeholder communication?

4.6 CHAPTER SUMMARY

This chapter has described the importance of stakeholder management within contemporary organizations. It has provided the theoretical background to the concept of stakeholders and discussed different strategies and models which communication practitioners can use to identify and analyse the key stakeholders of the organization and communicate and engage with them.

 DISCUSSION QUESTIONS

1.   What is the difference between a stakeholder and a shareholder?

2.   What are the main advantages for organizations when they adopt a stakeholder approach to their strategy and communication? Can you give examples of companies that you believe do this well?

3.   In your view, should an organization engage in a dialogue with all of its stakeholders all of the time, or rather only with some of them or simply only on particular occasions such as when there are specific issues or crises?

KEY TERMS

Corporate social responsibility
Dialogue strategy
Economic/market stake
Equity stakes
Influencer stake
Informational strategy
Legitimacy

Neo-classical economic theory
Persuasive strategy
Socio-economic theory
Stakeholder
Stakeholder engagement
Stakeholder salience
Power–interest matrix

 FURTHER READING

Browne, J. (2015) *Connect: How Companies Succeed by Engaging Radically with Society*. London: Wiley.
Husted, Bryan W. and Allen, David B. (2011) *Corporate Social Strategy: Stakeholder Engagement and Competitive Advantage*. Cambridge: Cambridge University Press.

Want to know more about this chapter? Visit the companion website at: https://study.sagepub.com/cornelissen5e to access videos, web links, a glossary and selected journal articles to further enhance your study.

NOTES

1. Friedman, M. (1970) 'The social responsibility of business is to increase its profits', The *New York Times* Magazine, 13 September.
2. Donaldson, T. and Preston, L.E. (1995) 'The stakeholder theory of the corporation: Concepts, evidence, and implications', *Academy of Management Review*, 20 (1): 65–91.
3. Freeman, R.E. (1984) *Strategic Management: A Stakeholder Approach*. Boston: Pitman, p. 6.
4. Carroll, A.B. (1996) *Business and Society: Ethics and Stakeholder Management*. Cincinnati, OH: South-Western College Publishing, p. 473.
5. Clarkson, B.E. (1995) 'A stakeholder framework for analyzing and evaluating corporate social performance', *Academy of Management Review*, 20 (1): 92–117.
6. Charkham, J.P. (1992) *Keeping Good Company: A Study of Corporate Governance in Five Countries*. Oxford: Oxford University Press.
7. Mitchell, R.K., Agle, B.R. and Wood, D.J. (1997) 'Toward a theory of stakeholder identification and salience: Defining the principle of who and what really counts', *Academy of Management Review*, 22 (4): 853–86.
8. Based on Mendelow, A., *Proceedings of 2nd International Conference on Information Systems*, Cambridge, MA; also cited in Johnson, G. and Scholes, K. (1993) *Exploring Corporate Strategy: Text and Cases*. London: Prentice Hall International, 3rd edition, 176–77.
9. Based on Grunig, J.E. and Hunt, T. (1984) *Managing Public Relations*. New York: Holt, Rinehart and Winston; Deetz, S. (2006) 'Dialogue, communication theory, and the hope of making quality decisions together: A commentary', *Management Communication Quarterly*, 19: 368–75; Morsing, M. and Schultz, M. (2006) 'Corporate social responsibility communication: Stakeholder information, response and involvement strategies', *Business Ethics: A European Review*, 15: 323–38.

10. Based on Daft, R.L. and Lengel, R.H. (1986) 'Organizational information require-ments, media richness and structural design', *Management Science*, 32 (5): 554–71; and Kaplan, R.S. and Norton, D.P. (2001) *The Strategy-focused Organization: How Balanced Scorecard Companies Thrive in the New Business Environment*. Boston, MA: Harvard Business School Press.
11. Based on Svendsen, A. (1998) *The Stakeholder Strategy: Profiting from Collaborative Business Relationships*. San Francisco: Berrett-Koehler; Andriof, J., Waddock, S., Husted, B. and Rahman, S.S. (2002) *Unfolding Stakeholder Thinking: Theory, Responsibility and Engagement*. Sheffield: Greenleaf.
12. Crilly, Donal and Sloan, Pamela (2012) 'Enterprise logic: Explaining corporate attention to stakeholders from the "inside-out"', *Strategic Management Journal*, 33: 1174–93; Harrison, Jeffrey S., Bosse, Douglas A. and Phillips, Robert A. (2010) 'Managing for stakeholders, stakeholder utility functions, and competitive advantage', *Strategic Management Journal*, 31: 58–74; see also Porter, M.E. and Kramer, M.R. (2011) 'Creating shared value', *Harvard Business Review*, 89 (1/2): 62–77.
13. Porter, M.E. and Kramer, M.R. (2006) 'Strategy and society: The link between competitive advantage and corporate social responsibility', *Harvard Business Review*, December, 1–15.
14. Harrison, Jeffrey S., Bosse, Douglas A. and Phillips, Robert A. (2010) 'Managing for stake-holders, stakeholder utility functions, and competitive advantage', *Strategic Management Journal*, 31: 58–74; Husted, Bryan W. and Allen, David B. (2011) *Corporate Social Strategy: Stakeholder Engagement and Competitive Advantage*. Cambridge: Cambridge University Press.

Corporate Identity, Branding and Corporate Reputation

5

CHAPTER OVERVIEW

One of the primary ways in which organizations manage relationships with stakeholders is by building and maintaining their corporate reputations. Reputations are established when organizations consistently communicate an authentic, unique and distinctive corporate identity towards stakeholders. Drawing on frameworks from theory and practice, the chapter discusses how organizations manage their corporate identity in order to establish, maintain and protect their corporate reputations with different stakeholder groups.

5.1 INTRODUCTION

In the previous chapter, we discussed the importance for organizations of communicating with different stakeholders for both moral (legitimacy) and instrumental (profit) reasons. We also highlighted the challenges that organizations face in dealing with the different expectations and demands of stakeholders. One way in which organizations have addressed these challenges is by strategically projecting a particular positive image of the organization, defined as a corporate identity, to build, maintain and protect strong reputations with stakeholders. Such strong reputations lead to stakeholders accepting and supporting the organization. Strong reputations also give organizations 'first-choice' status with investors, customers, employees and other stakeholders. For customers, for instance, a company's reputation serves as a signal of the underlying quality of an organization's products and services, and they therefore value associations and transactions with firms enjoying a good reputation. Equally, employees prefer to work for organizations with a good reputation. They tend to commit themselves to highly reputable firms, where they may work harder and may even engage in innovative and spontaneous activity above and beyond the 'call of duty'.

The chapter focuses on how organizations manage the process by which they project a particular corporate image of themselves and come to be seen and evaluated in a particular way by their stakeholders. The chapter starts by outlining traditional frameworks and principles of managing corporate identity and reputation, followed by more recent models on corporate branding. After a discussion of the basic theory, we turn to practice and demonstrate how these frameworks and principles can be used within corporate communication.

5.2 CORPORATE IDENTITY, IMAGE AND REPUTATION

The emphasis that organizations, both in theory and practice, place on managing their corporate image suggests a preoccupation with how they *symbolically* construct an image (as a 'caring citizen', for example) for themselves through their communication and how in turn that image leads them to be seen in particular symbolic terms by important stakeholders. In other words, corporate image management adds an important symbolic dimension to corporate communication and the process by which organizations communicate with their stakeholders. Corporate communication is not only seen as a matter of exchanging *information* with stakeholders (an informational or dialogue strategy; see Chapter 3) so that they can make informed decisions about the organization, but also as a case of *symbolically* crafting and projecting a particular image for the organization. In many actual instances of corporate communication, these two dimensions may blend together and may be hard to separate. For example, when Tesco, a UK retailer, announced its sponsorship of Cancer Research UK, it provided people with information regarding the decision about its sponsorship (to fund research into the prevention, treatment and cure of cancer) and tied the sponsorship into the promotion of its Healthy Living range of products to support a healthy lifestyle. At the same time, through the sponsorship, the company aimed to project an image of itself as a caring and responsible corporate citizen contributing to the fight against one of the deadliest diseases around.

Investing in the development of a corporate image for the organization has further strategic advantages for organizations. These can be summarized under the following headings:

Distinctiveness: a corporate image may help stakeholders find or recognize an organization. When consistently communicated, a corporate image creates awareness, triggers recognition and may also instil confidence in stakeholder groups because these groups will have a clearer picture of the organization.[1] Inside the organization, a clear and strong image of the organization can help raise motivation and morale amongst employees by establishing and perpetuating a 'we' feeling and by allowing people to identify with their organizations.

Impact: a corporate image provides a basis for being favoured by stakeholders. This, in turn, may have a direct impact on the organization's performance when it leads to stakeholders supporting the organization in the form of, for example, buying its products and services, investing in the company or not opposing its decisions.

Stakeholders: any individual may have more than one stakeholder role in relation to an organization. When organizations project a consistent image of themselves, they avoid potential pitfalls that may occur when conflicting images and messages are sent out. Employees, for example, are often also consumers in the marketplace for the products of the company that they themselves work for. When companies fail to send out a consistent image (often by failing to match all their internal and external communications), it threatens employees' perceptions of the company's integrity: they are told one thing by management, but perceive something different in the marketplace.

For these reasons, corporate image management is seen as an important part of corporate communication. In theory and practice, the original set of concepts that was introduced to describe this particular aspect of corporate communication involves corporate identity, corporate image and corporate reputation. More recently, the term corporate branding has gained traction in describing the way in which companies aim to develop and build strong symbolic reputations with their stakeholders.

The original concept of corporate identity grew out of a preoccupation in the design and communication communities with the ways in which organizations present themselves to external audiences. Initially, the term was restricted to logos and other elements of visual design, but it gradually came to encompass all forms of communication (corporate advertising, sponsorship, etc.) and all forms of outward-facing behaviour in the marketplace. The German corporate design specialists Birkigt and Stadler proposed one of the first models of corporate image management (Figure 5.1).[2] Birkigt and Stadler's model put particular emphasis on the concept of corporate identity which they defined as consisting of the following attributes:

symbolism: corporate logos and the company house style (stationery, etc.) of an organization

communication: all planned forms of communication including corporate advertising, events, sponsorship, publicity and promotions

behaviour: all behaviour of employees (ranging from managers and receptionists to front-line staff such as salespeople and shop assistants) that leaves an impression on stakeholders.

Through these three attributes, organizations communicate and project an image of themselves to their stakeholders. Birkigt and Stadler also argued that the image that organizations project through symbolism, communication and behaviour is often also the way in which they are perceived by their stakeholders. The latter concept they called corporate image which involves the image of an organization in the eyes of stakeholders.

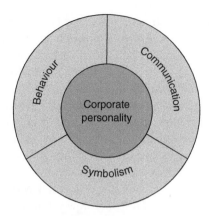

FIGURE 5.1 The Birkigt and Stadler model of corporate identity (Birkigt, K. and Stadler, M. (1986) *Corporate Identity: Grundlagen, Funktionen und Fallbeispiele.* © 1998 mi-Wirtschaftsbuch, MünchnerVerlagsgruppe GmbH, München. www.m-vg.de/mi/. All rights reserved.)

One important implication of the Birkigt and Stadler model is that corporate identity is seen as quite a broad concept which encompasses more than corporate logos or corporate advertising campaigns. Because of its breadth, the concept also has a bearing on different functional areas within the organization. Communication practitioners often hold only direct responsibility for corporate symbolism and communication, whilst product and brand managers are responsible for the positioning of products and services, and human resource staff and middle managers for incentivising and supporting employee behaviour.

A second important implication of the original Birkigt and Stadler model is that it suggests that corporate identity, as the outward presentation of an organization through symbolism, communication and behaviour, should emerge from an understanding of the organization's core mission, strategic vision and the more general corporate culture of an organization. The mission and vision represent the basic who and what of an organization; what business the organization is in and what it wants to be known and appreciated for. An organization's mission often already includes a statement on the beliefs that constitute the organization's culture and underpin its strategy and suggests how the organization wants to be known by stakeholder groups outside the organization. Birkigt and Stadler labelled the notion of core values in the organization's culture, mission and vision as the organization's corporate personality. Design guru Wally Olins articulates the difference between corporate personality and corporate identity as follows:

> Corporate personality embraces the subject at its most profound level. It is the soul, the persona, the spirit, the culture of the organization manifested in some way. A corporate personality is not necessarily something tangible that you can see, feel or touch – although it may be. The tangible manifestation of a corporate personality is a corporate identity. It is the identity that projects and reflects the reality of the corporate personality.[3]

In other words, corporate identity involves the construction of an image of the organization to differentiate a company's position in the eyes of important stakeholder groups. Corporate personality, on the other hand, is based on deeper patterns of meaning and sense-making of people within that same organization and includes the core values that define the organization.

The French sociologists Larçon and Reitter added a further dimension to the concept of corporate identity when they argued that it not only involves the visible outward presentation of a company, but also the set of intrinsic characteristics or 'traits' that give the company its specificity, stability and coherence.[4] In their view, a corporate identity is not merely a projected image in the form of visual design and communication, but is also fundamentally concerned with 'what the organization is' – the core of the organization as it is laid down in its strategies and culture. This notion of corporate identity 'traits' has also been referred to as an 'organizational' identity as opposed to a 'corporate' identity, again to make the distinction between core values that people share within the organization ('organizational identity') and the outward presentation and communication of those values through symbolism, communication and behaviour ('corporate identity').

The management experts Albert and Whetten, who were amongst the first to define this notion of 'organizational' identity, similarly talked about specific characteristics or 'traits' of an organization in all its strategies, values and practices that give the company its specificity, stability and coherence. They argued that just as individuals express a sense of personal distinctiveness, a sense of personal continuity and a sense of personal autonomy, equally organizations have their own individuality and uniqueness. And just as the identity of individuals may come to be anchored in some combination of gender, nationality, profession, social group, lifestyle, educational achievements or skills, so an organization's identity may be anchored in some combination of geographical place, nationality, strategy, founding, core business, technology, knowledge base, operating philosophy or organization design.

For each organization, according to Albert and Whetten, its particular combination of identity anchors imbues it with a set of distinctive values that are core, distinctive and enduring to it.[5] For example, many would argue that Sony's differentiation in the marketplace is quality consumer products, and they certainly do have ability in that area. But what makes Sony truly distinctive is the company's core value of 'miniaturization', of producing ever smaller technology. This feature of miniaturization, which goes hand in hand with a drive for technological innovation, is at the heart of Sony's organizational identity or corporate personality. At the same time, this organizational identity has been carried through in all products, services and communications; that is, in Sony's corporate identity. Similarly, Virgin, a company that is active in very different markets (e.g. airlines, music stores, cola and mobile phones) has meticulously cultivated the value of 'challenge' with all of its employees. Headed by its flamboyant CEO Richard Branson, Virgin has carried through its core organizational identity of 'challenge' in its distinctive market positioning of David versus Goliath: 'we are on your side against the fat cats'. This projected corporate identity has led to the widespread perception that Virgin is a company with a distinctive personality: innovative and challenging, but fun.

Figure 5.2 summarizes the process of corporate identity management as originally articulated by Birkigt and Stadler. The aim of corporate identity management is to establish a favourable image, or reputation, with the organization's stakeholders which it is hoped will be translated by such stakeholders into a propensity to buy that organization's products and services, to work for that organization or to invest in it (organizational performance). In other words, a good corporate reputation has a strategic value for the organization that possesses it. It ensures acceptance and legitimacy from stakeholder groups, generates returns and may offer a competitive advantage as it forms an asset that is difficult to imitate. A good corporate reputation, or rather the corporate identity on which it is based, is an intangible asset of the organization because of its potential for value creation, but also because its intangible character makes replication by competing firms more difficult.[6] Figure 5.2 shows the corporate identity mix (symbolism, communication and behaviour of members of the organization) as based on the organization's core values in its history and culture and which inform every part of its strategy.

Theoretically, the concept of identity thus refers both to strategic communication with external stakeholders as well as to internal patterns of meaning-making and identification within the organization. To make this distinction more clearly, it is useful to briefly discuss the three main theoretical traditions of identity in management research: social identity, organizational identity and corporate identity.[7] Whilst these concepts overlap, they are, at the same time, distinct in terms of their primary definition and focus. Social identity, first of all, refers to how individuals define themselves in terms of membership of certain groups, such as a profession or department. Organizational identity refers to the overall self-definition of the organization, often described as an answer to the question of 'who we are' as an organization. Corporate identity, finally, refers to the distinct image that is projected by an organization and its members to external stakeholders (Table 5.1).

The concept of social identity emerged from social psychological research that examined the causes and consequences of individuals seeing themselves, and being seen by others, as part of a social group. A core idea here is that such group memberships contribute to a person's sense of self. The theory of social identity suggests that once

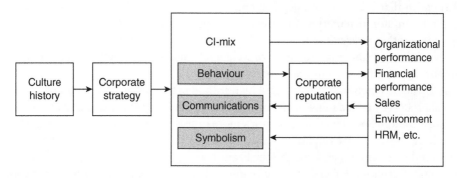

FIGURE 5.2 Corporate identity in relation to corporate reputation

Source: Based on Van Riel, C.B.M. and Balmer, J. (1997) 'Corporate identity: The concept, its measurement and management', *European Journal of Marketing*, 31: 342.

TABLE 5.1 Definitions of the social, organizational and corporate identity constructs

Construct	Definition	Illustrations
Social identity	Individuals' knowledge that they belong to certain groups, together with the emotional and value significance of that group membership	I am an engineer and am proud to be in this department
Organizational identity	The shared meaning that an organization is understood to have that arises from its members' awareness that they belong to it	As an organization, we know that we are good at A but bad at B
Corporate identity	The distinctive public image that an organization communicates that influences stakeholders' image and reputation of that organization	Company X excels in A, which brings real benefits to customers

individuals define themselves in terms of such group membership, they seek to achieve or maintain positive self-esteem by positively differentiating their own in-group from a comparison out-group on some valued dimension. This quest for positive distinctiveness means that when people's sense of self is defined in terms of 'we' (i.e. social identity) rather than 'I' (personal identity), they strive to see 'us' as different from, and preferably better than, 'them' in order to feel good about who they are and what they do.

Different group memberships within organizations in turn may lead to distinct social identities around professions or departments, or based on other groupings such as gender, ethnicity or seniority. A challenge for organizations is to ensure that groups do not differentiate themselves within the organization from one another and in an unhealthy way that unsettles the common orientation and goals of the organization. For example, when people strongly identify with their profession, with a department or with a particular business unit, they may value other parts of the organization more negatively compared to themselves.

The concept of organizational identity is one level up from a focus on specific groups to that of the entire organization. The primary interest at this level is whether besides any group memberships, individuals have a common sense of what values and traits they share as an organization. Organizational identity has a specific strategic purpose in that it cuts across departmental and other group boundaries and aims to foster a common orientation for everyone in the organization. As such, it may also provide another source for identification and a sense of belonging for members of the organization and may furthermore channel their energies into behaviours that support the organization in realizing its goals.

A further distinction between social identity and organizational identity involves the actual process by which individuals form a sense of who they are, either as a group or as an organization. Social identity assumes a more or less automatic categorization, where people define themselves and others as belonging to certain groups. This categorization rests on the principle that through socialization and prior experiences, people's under-standing of group memberships is fully internalized as a set of categories that people have in their heads. In many cases, such categories may have become taken for granted, so much so that individuals simply define and see themselves as engineers, technicians, administrators or managers, to name but a few examples.

Organizational identity, on the other hand, is described as an active process of collective sense-making within the organization, in contrast to accessing and retrieving an internalized set of categories (Figure 5.3). Sense-making highlights the active production and negotiation of shared meaning at the organizational level. Individuals from various functional backgrounds, levels of seniority and departments come, in effect, together to produce a joint understanding of 'who they are as an organization'. The crux here is that unless a particular social identity dominates an organization – say, an organization being an engineering-driven firm – individuals need to develop common ground about who they are at this organizational level. Organizational identity, in other words, involves a sense-making process in which individuals collectively come to define those features and values of the organization that are 'central, enduring, and distinctive in character [and] that contribute to how they define the organization and their identification with it'.[8] When in turn they themselves strongly identify with those features and values, this leads to a sense of 'oneness with the organization',[9] meaning that they feel that they belong to the organization and embody its values.

Organizational identity is thus more malleable than social identity and corporate communication practitioners have an important role in facilitating dialogue about the definition of the organization's identity. They also have this role in ensuring that the company has a clearly articulated definition of its identity, which can then in turn

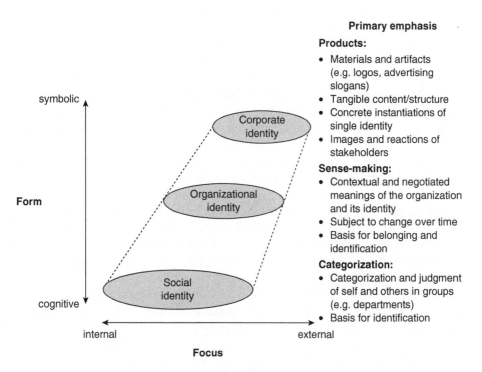

FIGURE 5.3 The relationship between social, organizational and corporate identity

Source: Adapted from Cornelissen, J.P., Haslam, S.A. and Balmer, J.M.T. (2007) 'Social identity, organizational identity and corporate identity: towards an integrated understanding of processes, patternings and products', *British Journal of Management*, 18: S1–S16.

feature in corporate identity campaigns. The general principle that corporate communication practitioners work from is that the corporate identity – the picture of the organization that is presented to external stakeholders – is grounded in the core values and traits that members of the organization themselves associate with the organization and that define the organization's mission and vision (organizational identity).

Making sure that the corporate identity that is presented is rooted in the organizational identity not only offers a distinctive edge in the marketplace, but also ensures that the image that is projected is authentic, rather than cosmetic, and also carried and shared by members of the organization. In this context, corporate identity and organizational identity can best be seen as two sides of the same coin within corporate communication. Developing a corporate identity must start with a thorough analysis and understanding of the organization's core values in its mission, vision and culture, rather than rushing into communicating what might be thought to be the company's core values in a superficial manner. Equally, it is the case that whatever picture is projected to external stakeholders has an effect on the beliefs and values of employees, and thus on the organizational identity, as employees mirror themselves in whatever messages are being sent out to external stakeholder groups.[10]

Figure 5.3 presents a summary of these definitional differences between social, organizational and corporate identity. The figure basically highlights these differences on the basis of whether the focus is primarily internal (e.g. employees) or external (e.g. customers) to the organization, and whether the form, or the way in which identity is manifested, is cognitive or symbolic. At the cognitive or psychological end of the dimension, identity is defined as involving a mental framework, categorization or agreed-on set of beliefs and attributions in the minds of individuals. The symbolic end of the same dimension defines identity as the symbolic manifestation or projection (through language, artefacts and behaviour) of an identity.

Figure 5.3 also again emphasizes that organizational identity and corporate identity are naturally connected, in that organizations want to present a coherent, distinctive and authentic image of themselves to external stakeholders. This point is reinforced by studies into 'excellent' companies carried out over the past few decades. Writers such as Hamel and Prahalad, Peters and Waterman, and Collins and Porras, have found that what truly sets an 'excellent' company apart from its competitors in the marketplace, in terms of the power of its image and products, can be traced back to a set of values and related competencies that are authentic and unique to that organization and therefore difficult to imitate. Collins and Porras, in their analysis of companies that are industry leaders in the USA, argue that 'a visionary company almost religiously preserves its core ideology – changing it seldom, if ever'.[11] From this adherence to a fundamental set of beliefs or a deeply held sense of self-identity, as Collins and Porras point out, come the discipline and drive that enable a company to succeed in the rapidly changing, volatile environments that characterize many contemporary markets.

5.3 CORPORATE BRANDING

Reputation scholars Fombrun and Van Riel carried out comparative analyses of the corporate reputations of the most visible and reputable organizations across the world.

Based on stakeholder evaluations of companies within different countries, they found that organizations with the strongest reputations are, on average, characterized by high levels of *visibility* (the degree to which corporate themes are visible in all internal and external communication), *distinctiveness* (the degree to which the corporate identity or positioning of the organization is distinctive), *authenticity* (the degree to which an organization communicates values that are embedded in its culture), *transparency* (the degree to which an organization is open and transparent about its behaviour) and *consistency* (the degree to which organizations communicate consistent messages through all internal and external communication channels) in corporate communication.[12] In other words, a key driver for the strength of an organization's reputation is the degree to which the values that it communicates are not only authentic but also distinctive.

Many communication practitioners indeed draw heavily on the idea of uniqueness or distinctiveness in corporate identity because it encapsulates the idea that the organization needs to express its uniqueness in the market and with other stakeholders. The principle behind this idea is that it enables an organization to

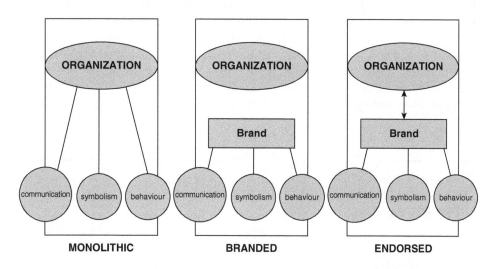

Identity structure	Definition	Example
Monolithic	Single all-embracing identity (products all carry the same corporate name)	Sony, BMW, Virgin, Philips
Endorsed	Businesses and product brands are endorsed or badged with the parent company name	General Motors, Kellogg, Nestlé, Cadbury
Branded	Individual businesses or product brands each carry their own name (and are seemingly unrelated to each other)	Procter & Gamble (Ariel, Ola), Electrolux (Zanussi), Unilever (Dove)

FIGURE 5.4 Monolithic, endorsed and branded identities

differentiate itself from its competitors and to attain a preferred 'position' in the minds of consumers and other stakeholders (see Chapter 3). Recently, the term 'corporate branding' has become fashionable alongside corporate identity to highlight the importance of distinctiveness. The idea of an organization as a brand is a logical extension of the product branding approach, with its original focus on products and brand benefits and on individual consumers. The notion of a 'corporate brand' was also inspired by Wally Olins' framework on monolithic corporate, endorsed and branded identities. Figure 5.4 displays these three types of identities.

The monolithic corporate identity refers to a corporate brand: a structure where all products and services, buildings, official communication and employee behaviour are labelled or branded with the same company name. Examples include Disney, Coca-Cola, Nike, McDonald's, Wal-Mart and BMW. The fully branded identity refers to a structure whereby products and services are brought to the market, each with their own brand name and brand values. Companies such as Unilever and Procter & Gamble have traditionally followed this branded identity structure where neither the company's name nor its core values figured in the positioning and communication of its products. This branded strategy traditionally made sense for Unilever and Proctor & Gamble as they were addressing very different market segments through the different products in their product portfolio. An increasing number of organizations that were previously branded giants are, however, changing their organizations into monolithic corporate brands. Unilever is an example of an organization that has moved in the direction of a monolithic identity, with the purpose of having its product brands more strongly associated with the company name (Case Example 5.1).

 CASE EXAMPLE 5.1

UNILEVER: FROM A BRANDED GIANT TO A MONOLITHIC CORPORATE BRAND

Back in 2005, Unilever announced that the corporate name would appear more prominently on all of its products. The announcement formed part of the company's long-term strategy and was driven by the company's belief that many consumers were demanding more and more from the companies behind the brands, increasingly bringing their views as citizens into their buying decisions. The logo of the company was redesigned, bringing together 25 different icons representing Unilever and its brands. The redesigned logo and its more prominent place on products and in advertising were meant to highlight the company behind the products to consumers, employees, investors and other stakeholders.

The initial redesign of the logo also went hand in hand with a strategic repositioning of the brand portfolio. The brand portfolio had involved 1,600 disparate products that did not coherently relate to each other or to a singular business objective. Unilever, in other words, had become too diffuse, lacking a coherent brand identity and a unifying driver of growth. The design agency Wolff Olins redesigned the logo and helped conceptualize the strategic identity-defining idea for the company at the time, which was that all its brands should bring 'vitality to life'. The brand portfolio was reduced to around 400 brands with each brand meeting customers' 'needs for nutrition, hygiene, and personal care with brands that help people feel good, look good and get more out of life'.

This initial repositioning and redesign of the Unilever logo already brought it up front, as a monolithic brand, rather than being in the background for consumers and other stakeholders alike. In recent years, CEO Paul Polman has further redefined the strategy for the corporation around its Sustainable Living Plan. Established in 2010, the Plan sets the company on an ambitious course of transformational change through which it aims to alter the world in environmental and social terms for the better. The Plan also underscores the notion that individual product brands need to add a social purpose to their brand positioning, with the company finding that those brands that do this well are growing much faster. With this new chapter in the company's history, the Unilever brand and logo are further evolving into a 'trust mark of sustainability', in the words of its chief marketing officer.

Question for reflection

What do you think about the strategic repositioning of Unilever and its move towards becoming a corporate brand? Apart from any other strategic reconsiderations, do you think this will help the company strengthen the reputation of its products?

One important reason for organizations to move from branded to endorsed and monolithic identities is that monolithic identities have become enormously valuable assets – companies with strong monolithic identities, and the reputations associated with them, can have market values that are more than twice their book values – and can save money as marketing and communication campaigns can be leveraged across the company. Many brand rankings such as the ones published by Interbrand and *Business Week* confirm the impact of monolithic identities on companies' financial performance. The 2015 Interbrand ranking of the most valuable brands, for example, features corporate giants such as Disney, Apple, General Electric, IBM, Microsoft, Google, McDonald's, BMW and Amazon at the very top of the list. Not surprisingly, therefore, many academic writers and communication professionals have emphasized the importance of branding the entire organization and of focusing communication and marketing on the organization rather than on individual products and services. Where previously the brand portfolio strategy of an organization may have been geared towards the branded end, with different consumer brands targeted at separate market segments, increasingly companies consolidate their portfolio around a more limited monolithic or endorsed range. This reflects not only that customers and consumers are increasingly interested in the corporation behind the brand, but also the recognition that the point of difference from competitor brands often rests on corporate values, company-wide technology and IP, or specific organizational capabilities. This is easily spotted in technology and automotive brands, but also, for example, in clothing brands. Burberry, for instance, has different consumer brands, such as Burberry Prosum (high-end couture and runway fashion), Burberry London (easy to wear styles) and Burberry Brit (casual wear), for different market segments, but the crucial point of difference for consumers lies in the quintessentially British heritage and classic design capability of the company around, for example, the iconic tartan pattern.

The branding terminology that puts this insight further in perspective is the notion of points-of-parity and points-of-difference between brands.[13] Points-of-parity are features and associations that are not necessarily unique to the brand but may be shared by other competing brands. They may nonetheless still be important to consumers and other stakeholders as 'hygiene factors'. In other words, these features may not be the prime reason for liking or choosing a brand, but their absence can certainly be a reason to exclude or discount a brand. A point-of-difference, on the other hand, is a feature or association that consumers and other stakeholders find relevant and believe they cannot find with competing brands. It forms the basis for superiority over competing brands. This terminology highlights two things: first, and as mentioned, points of difference for customers and consumers buying specific products and services are increasingly based on organizational capabilities, values or technology, or more generally associations with the company or corporate brand. Second, it suggests that besides a claim for distinctiveness, a degree of similarity to other companies and their products and services may also be important. HSBC, for example, has claimed a distinctive value of being 'the world's local bank', whereby the company claims to tune its global scale to the local demands of individual customers. At the same time, HSBC has claimed very similar values as its competitors (Barclays, Citigroup, BNP and ING) regarding being a global or international institution that is focused on 'customer service', 'value creation', 'professionalism' and 'technological and financial innovation'.

The distinctive identity of the organization is the core foundation of corporate branding and forms a key differentiator in the marketplace. In this sense, the idea of corporate branding is in principle not that different from the more traditional idea of corporate image management. As Majken Schultz, one of the leading writers on corporate branding puts it, the focus in corporate branding is on how an organization can formulate an enduring corporate identity that is relevant to all its stakeholders.[14] Similar to corporate image management, corporate branding is aimed at all stakeholders of the organization, which contrasts the concept with product branding which is exclusively focused on (prospective and current) customers and consumers. Schultz further emphasizes that the core of corporate branding is the alignment between the company's vision, culture and image. Culture and image relate to how the organization and its identity are seen by employees (culture) and the company's external stakeholders (i.e. the external image). The vision of senior managers adds a strategic dimension in that by setting directions for possible ways of changing or transforming who we are as an organization, it may change how the company is seen internally and externally. For example, the vision of senior managers in Unilever of strengthening and highlighting the corporate brand behind its products is one that sets a strategic direction for the company. It fundamentally changes the identity of the organization and how it is seen by customers and other stakeholders (image). Importantly, it also presents a break from the company's past strategy and internal culture where brand and product managers had executive responsibility for planning communication and marketing strategies (culture). The new identity thus goes hand in hand with a new culture that fosters collaboration between managers and employees and a commitment to a monolithic Unilever identity.

As in this example, the role of all employees (not just communication and marketing staff) becomes much more important in corporate branding as employees are the brand ambassadors of the organization. Ideally, the identity behind the corporate brand would thus pervade the entire organization, from top to bottom. Organizations often therefore provide support to employees in the form of brand manuals, intranet resources and brand briefings or workshops to ensure that employees do not just know about the corporate brand but also live and enact it as part of their day-to-day jobs, regardless of whether those jobs involve direct contact with stakeholders or not.[15]

5.4 ALIGNING IDENTITY, IMAGE AND REPUTATION

Generally speaking, in order to manage the company's reputation it is strategically important for organizations to achieve 'alignment' or 'transparency' between its internal identity and its external image. According to reputation experts Fombrun and Rindova, transparency is 'a state in which the internal identity of the firm reflects positively the expectations of key stakeholders and the beliefs of these stakeholders about the firm reflect accurately the internally held identity'.[16] Along these lines, many practitioners, consultants and researchers stress the importance of alignment between (a) the organizational culture as experienced by employees, (b) the corporate vision as articulated by senior managers, and (c) the corporate image or reputation in the minds of external stakeholders. Importantly too, where these elements are non-aligned (so that, for example, corporate rhetoric does not match the experienced reality), a range of sub-optimal outcomes are anticipated, including employee disengagement and customer dissatisfaction.

A useful way of analysing the alignment between an organization's vision, culture and image or reputation is the toolkit developed by Hatch and Schultz.[17] The toolkit (Figure 5.5) consists of a number of diagnostic questions based on three elements:

- *vision*: senior management's aspirations for the organization
- *culture*: the organization's values as felt and shared by all employees of the organization
- *image*: the image or impression that outside stakeholders have of the organization.

The questions each relate to a particular interface between the three elements and are meant to identify the alignment between them. The first set of questions involves the interface between vision and culture – that is, how managers and employees are aligned. They are:

- Does the organization practise the values it promotes?
- Does the organization's vision inspire all its subcultures?
- Are the organization's vision and culture sufficiently differentiated from those of its competitors?

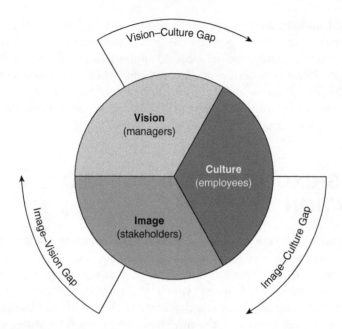

FIGURE 5.5   Toolkit to assess the alignment between vision, culture and image

Source: Schultz and Hatch (2003) 'The Vision-Culture-Image (VCI) Model', *California Management Review*, 46(1): 10. Reprinted with permission.

There is a potential for misalignment (*vision–culture gap*) here when senior management moves the organization in a strategic direction that employees do not understand or support. For example, senior managers may establish a vision that is too ambitious for the organization to implement and that is not supported by its employees.

The second set of questions involves the interface between culture and image and is meant to identify potential gaps between the values of employees and the perceptions of stakeholders outside of the organization. The questions are:

- What images do stakeholders associate with the organization?
- In what ways do its employees and stakeholders interact?
- Do employees care what stakeholders think of the organization?

Misalignment between an organization's image and organizational culture (*image–culture gap*) leads to confusion amongst stakeholders about what a company stands for. For example, employees of the organization may not practise what the company preaches in its advertising, leaving a tarnished image with its stakeholders.

The final set of questions addresses the interface between vision and image. The key objective here is to find out whether management is taking the organization in a direction that its stakeholders support. The questions are:

- Who are the organization's stakeholders?
- What do the stakeholders want from the organization?
- Is the organization effectively communicating its vision to its stakeholders?

There is potential for misalignment (*image–vision gap*) here when organizations do not sufficiently listen to their stakeholders and create strategic visions that are not aligned with what stakeholders want or expect from the organization.

Based on these three sets of diagnostic questions, organizations can monitor the alignment between their vision, culture and image so that they can make adjustments accordingly. All three interfaces are equally important to an organization in order to make sure that the identity or image that is projected to stakeholders is carried by both senior managers (vision) and employees (culture) and furthermore understood and appreciated by stakeholders (image). A classic example of an organization that failed to sufficiently align its vision, culture and image is British Airways in its design of a new identity in the late 1990s that was not picked up nor appreciated by its staff and customers.

Robert Ayling, the CEO of British Airways at the time, articulated together with his senior managers a vision for the company of becoming 'the undisputed leader in world travel'. This vision was coupled with a repositioning of the company in 1997 which involved blending the traditional British values of the company with new values of cosmopolitanism and global appeal. To give this repositioning shape, BA unveiled a striking new visual identity scheme. The 50 ethnic designs commissioned from artists around the world were meant to adorn the tailfins of BA's entire fleet, as well as ticket jackets, cabin crew scarves and business cards. Over the next three years, the idea was that the new look would gradually replace the sober blue and red livery and crest along with the traditional motto 'to fly, to serve' which dated back to 1984. The decision to change was based on the CEO's foresight about the consolidation of the airline industry around a few international players and on a piece of market research in the early 1990s which had suggested that passengers viewed the airline as staid and stuffy. The vision of senior managers within BA was that the repositioning presented the airline with an opportunity not just to tone down its national origins and project a more modern image, but also to reposition itself as a 'citizen of the world' in recognition of the fact that 60 per cent of BA's passengers came from outside the UK.

The colourful designs did attract tremendous free publicity at the time, with the front pages of most British newspapers featuring large colour photos. But they also generated more controversy than anticipated, with many seeing the revamp as extravagant, confusing or, in the case of the then Prime Minister Margaret Thatcher, a national betrayal. At the launch of the new designs, Margaret Thatcher famously draped her handkerchief over one of the new designs. The backlash was disappointing, but Ayling hoped, at the time, that these emotionally charged reactions from the more conservative-minded sections of the British public would soon blow over. However, the negative news coverage of the new designs endured and carried over to BA customers and the general public in the UK who then voted with their feet (i.e. a vision–image gap). BA customers appreciated the company's traditional values and British heritage which they felt were being lost with the new designs and repositioning. In addition to repainting the planes' tailfins, the company had also decided to remove the British flag from all its aircraft. This triggered a strike by cabin crew who apparently did not agree with the new corporate values and also felt that they had not been included in consultations on the new vision (i.e. a vision–culture gap). Employees not only disagreed with the new vision, they also did not share and live the new values of a multicultural ethos as communicated in the new designs. Because they did not embody these values, there was thus real potential for a gap between what the company communicated (cosmopolitanism) and employee behaviour which was still firmly rooted in a sense of Britishness and stakeholder images (i.e. an image–culture gap). Before it came to that, Ayling and his senior management team acknowledged that they had made a wrong decision and abandoned the design programme. When Rodd Eddington took over from Ayling as CEO in 2000, one of his first actions was to announce a return to British livery and he reintroduced the Union Flag on each tailfin of the BA fleet.

The vision–culture–image toolkit provides communication practitioners with crucial insights into the alignment between the different parts of the company's identity and allows them to spot gaps that need to be repaired or redressed. The vision–culture interface, for example, captures the extent to which the aspired identity for the company, as laid out in the vision of senior managers, connects with the experienced identity on the ground and in the hearts and minds of employees. If managers are not preparing employees for a shift in identity, as in the British Airways case, a crucial gap in perception between managers and employees may result. The vision–image and culture–image interfaces capture the degree to which the promoted and expressed identity by the company is also how the company is being seen and what it is appreciated for by stakeholders. The importance of these two interfaces is that if corporate organizations are, in communications and behaviour, out of step with stakeholder expectations for too long, then the performance and continuity of the organization will be at risk.

However, when the image or reputation of stakeholders is broadly consistent with the projected images in communication, symbolism and behaviour, it ensures that the organization is respected and understood in the way in which it wants and aims to be understood.[18] Yet, when there is a gap between the projected identity of an organization and the way in which it is regarded, an organization is not standing out on its own turf and may not have a strong enough individual reputation as a result. Its reputation is then based on more general associations with the industry in which the organization is based or is informed by reports from the media. Shell, for instance, in the wake of the Niger Delta crisis, realized that its poor reputation since the 1990s had, more often than not, been based on media reports and the tainted image of the oil industry than on its own identity and the values that were at the heart of its business and operations. Shell has since put considerable effort into a rethinking of its identity and values, redesigning systems for stakeholder management and running global corporate identity campaigns to close the gap between its identity and reputation.

Corporate organizations, in other words, benefit from continuously analysing the alignment between their vision, culture and image, and in the context of changing and shifting stakeholder expectations over time. This also means that an identity that was once fit for purpose – such as Polaroid and Eastman Kodak's innovative edge in instant film – may no longer have traction. As stakeholder expectations are shifting, this may be the downfall for some companies, but, at the same time, it also creates opportunities for others to change their identities and make the most of the changing scene in their industry. This is essentially what British Airways aimed to do in the context of a consolidating and deregulated airline industry, and companies such as BP and Shell tried to do, in the wake of growing criticism in the late 1990s, in restyling themselves as sustainable and environmentally responsible corporations.

A key question, however, is when organizations should decide to go for a full-scale overhaul of their identity in a changing environment. This requires not only a great deal of foresight, but also a considered judgment. The guidance that Hatch and Schultz provide is that they generally warn companies against hyper-adaptation, where instead of their own inner strengths they are quickly fashioning images to meet with fleeting stakeholder expectations. Instead, it seems that the key point is to wait for the onset of a defining moment when a new set of conventions across stakeholders or a new cultural story is emerging. In that way, a truly new foundation emerges that can be used for identity and brand-building. This, in effect, has been a formula for iconic identity changes, such as Sam Palmisano changing IBM's identity from a hardware to an integrated solutions and service provider in the context of changing customer expectations (see Case Study 9.1).

As in the case of IBM, the CEO and the senior management team are the most obvious patrons of organization-wide identity questions, as well as of the way in which these are translated into mission and vision documents and spread throughout the organization. When in a similar way Carlos Ghosn took the helm at Nissan in 1999, he personally led the restoration and strengthening of Nissan's identity, which had become sloppy, weak and insufficiently exploited. Alongside a restructuring and cost-cutting programme to boost productivity and profitability (for which he took a lot of flak), Ghosn revamped Nissan's identity of quality engineering and the uniquely Japanese combination of keen competitiveness and a sense of community. He ensured that through his own performance and commitment, as well as through internal communication, these values trickled down through the ranks to embrace all employees.

As the example of Nissan shows, it is important that a sense of organizational identity is internalized by members of the organization, so that they can live and enact the company's values in their day-to-day work. Particularly those members of the organization who represent it in the eyes of stakeholders such as the CEO, front-office personnel and front-line staff (salespeople, retail staff), and of course those who are responsible for marketing and communication, need to have a fine grasp of the organization's core ideology and values. Senior managers, with the help of senior communication practitioners – as the experts on stakeholder management – can facilitate this understanding by articulating and actively communicating the company's values to all staff within the organization through policy documents, briefings, identity workshops and internal communication (see Chapter 10 for more details).

CASE STUDY 5.1

BMW: AN EXERCISE IN ALIGNING IDENTITY, BRAND AND REPUTATION

BMW, the German car manufacturer, has been strategically focused on premium segments in the international car market. With its BMW, Mini and Rolls-Royce brands, the company has become one of the leading premium car companies in the world. BMW's strong identity and marketing campaigns are often credited as a crucial part

(Continued)

(Continued)

of the company's continuing success. For the last couple of years, BMW has been rated as the most valuable automotive brand in the world.

At the heart of the BMW identity are four values: dynamism, aesthetics, exclusivity and innovation. These values have been central to the company's leadership in design and are consistently communicated across all its corporate communication, corporate design and consumer advertising as well as through the behaviour of managers, designers and retail staff. The brand consultancy Interbrand argues that these four brand values align customers' images and associations with the vision and culture of BMW.

BMW has long focused on innovation but made it the driving force for its product development process and its philosophy at the end of the 1990s. Since then, the company has put a lot of emphasis on its research and development (R&D), making it a core element of its corporate strategy. The innovation process within BMW is aimed at systematically channelling potential innovations to the actual product development stage, and to ensure that the company can maintain its positioning around producing technologically advanced cars. Besides its focus on innovation, the company has also been a powerhouse of creative and aesthetic designs of cars. According to Christopher Bangle, global chief of design for BMW until 2009, 'our fanaticism about design excellence is matched only by the company's driving desire to remain profitable'. Bangle sees the company's core value as being 'an engineering-driven company whose cars and motorcycles are born from passion'. In his words: 'We don't make "automobiles", which are utilitarian machines you use to get from point A to point B. We make "cars", moving works of art that express the driver's love of quality.'

Besides innovation and aesthetics, the company's other values of dynamism (or driving dynamics) and exclusivity are carried through in all of the company's communication to consumers and other stakeholders. They feature as brand promises in dealer and customer materials, including showroom interior designs, tradeshow materials, advertising and customer promotion packages. Particularly through its advertising, the BMW brand has come to be associated with the words 'driving' and 'performance'. The company's taglines in many adverts have, for a long time, been 'The Ultimate Driving Machine' and 'Sheer Driving Pleasure'. According to marketing guru Al Ries, this association with 'driving' was a very powerful component of BMW's brand as it led consumers to associate BMW with high-performing cars. This association also reinforced the design excellence of BMW and nurtured for customers the importance of feelings and pleasure derived from driving an advanced car.

Branding the entire corporation

Besides a strict focus on cars, as products, BMW has also tried to bolster a strong image or reputation for the entire company. Corporate and consumer adverts have, for example, over the years highlighted the innovation culture of the company. These ads communicate BMW's independence and freedom to pursue innovative ideas, as it is neither owned by nor part of a division of another company. These advertisements still feature the tagline 'The Ultimate Driving Machine', but place little emphasis on its high-performance features. The focus instead is on the theme of BMW as a 'company of ideas', where radical design and ideas are encouraged as a way of supporting the tagline around performance. With this series of ads, the company reinforces the alignment between its internal culture and external image. The series has also made employees and existing and loyal customers proud of the company's success story.

BMW has also embarked on a series of ambitious sustainability initiatives, something which it highlights in recent corporate print adverts. The adverts stress BMW's achievements in developing fuel-saving engines, clean production facilities and state-of-the-art recycling techniques. BMW also suggests in these adverts that it is 'intent on playing our part in actively shaping the future – for the long term. We do so both for the common good and for the sake of the environment: in the interests of our customers – and, naturally, in the interests of our company, its employees and its shareholders. Because sustainability secures all our futures.'

The company in fact aims to integrate sustainability throughout the entire value chain, as it believes that sustainability will become a must in the premium segment of carmakers. As such, embracing sustainability issues, and being at the forefront of development, will give BMW a competitive edge. According to the Dow Jones Sustainability Index, BMW is the world's most sustainable carmaker, having being ranked at the top since 2005. The company has been driven to develop increasingly better solutions to sustainability issues on the basis of its strong innovation culture, but also to meet the growing expectations of its stakeholders. BMW in fact believes that sustainability is core to innovation nowadays and that it can as such be incorporated into the company's identity and brand. A good example of this way of thinking is the BMW i series of electric vehicles. The i3 has the same sleek design that customers expect of BMW and was in 2014 ranked as third amongst all electric cars sold worldwide.

Stakeholder engagement

From 2011 onwards, BMW has also initiated a number of stakeholder dialogue sessions in major cities across the world to get direct input from stakeholders on sustainability issues and goals. These face-to-face sessions are, in the company's words, a

> new format for on-going exchange with our stakeholders around the world. The goal is to create a comprehensive learning process for the constant development of ideas – which will allow us to align our company's goals with the needs and expectations of a global society. This dialogue helps us identify trends early, strengthen our commitment to society and reach our sustainability goals.

In recent years, these dialogue sessions have become split between separate sessions with experts and with students. BMW has even set up a specific stakeholder engagement policy to foster and coordinate stakeholder dialogue sessions across global and local operations. The company believes that such sessions will be immensely helpful; the policy states that 'gaining stakeholders' input on and responding to their needs regarding social and environmental issues can improve decision-making and accountability and positively influence our license to operate, our competitive advantage, and our long-term success'. In this way, then, BMW aims

(Continued)

(Continued)

to listen to its stakeholders on important issues as well as have another means in place to ensure an effective alignment between its vision and strategy, its internal culture and the company's external image or reputation.

Questions for reflection

1 Describe the alignment between vision, culture and image for BMW and discuss how BMW manages this alignment, and whether there is the potential for gaps between them.
2 Does the emphasis on sustainability change the identity and brand of BMW, and can it, in your view, be easily incorporated alongside, or as part of, the traditional four values of the company?
3 Consider the four traditional values of the identity and brand positioning of BMW. Are these values authentic, distinctive and unique from the perspective of consumers and other stakeholders in the premium car market?

Source: This case study is based on Bangle, C. (2001) 'The ultimate creativity machine: How BMW turns art into profit', *Harvard Business Review*, January, 5–11; and documents drawn from bmw.com.

5.5 CHAPTER SUMMARY

The chapter has outlined the theoretical background to the frameworks and concepts that organizations use to build strong and distinctive images or reputations with their stakeholders. One important observation that was made is that communication practitioners need to look inside their organizations for the core values that define the organization and that can give them a competitive edge in communications with internal and external stakeholders. Indeed, many organizations which have not thought seriously about their corporate identity and whether their profile is appreciated by stakeholder groups, often appear to hire and fire outside agencies with regularity, trying to find the one with the ability to 'sell' a message that people do not seem to be 'buying'. In other words, such organizations have not given enough care to crafting an identity that is authentic and distinctive, and also meaningful to stakeholders.

 ──── DISCUSSION QUESTIONS ────

Pick a company with which you are familiar or that you have worked for in the past. Describe the alignment between the company's vision, culture and image. Are there any gaps between these elements?

Identify a company with a world-class reputation in its industry. What, in your opinion, has been the main driver of its reputation?

KEY TERMS

Brand(ed) identity
Corporate brand
Corporate identity
Corporate personality
Culture
Design
Brand portfolio

Symbolism
Organizational identity
Corporate image
Corporate reputation
Vision
Alignment
Social identity

 FURTHER READING

Hatch, Mary Jo and Schultz, Majken (2008) *Taking Brand Initiative: How Companies Can Align Their Strategy, Culture and Identity through Corporate Branding*. San Francisco: Jossey Bass.
Morley, Michael (2009) *The Global Corporate Brand Book*. Basingstoke: Palgrave Macmillan.

Want to know more about this chapter? Visit the companion website at: https://study.sagepub.com/cornelissen5e to access videos, web links, a glossary and selected journal articles to further enhance your study.

NOTES

1. Dowling, G.R. (2001) *Creating Corporate Reputations*. Oxford: Oxford University Press.
2. Birkigt, K. and Stadler, M. (1986) *Corporate Identity: Grundlagen, Funktionen und Fallbeispiele*. Landsberg am Lech: Verlag Moderne Industrie.
3. Olins, W. (1978) *The Corporate Personality: An Inquiry into the Nature of Corporate Identity*. London: Design Council, p. 212.
4. Larçon, J.P. and Reitter, R. (1979) *Structures de pouvoir et identité de l'entreprise*. Paris: Nathan.
5. Albert, S. and Whetten, D.A. (1985) 'Organizational identity', in Cummings, L.L. and Staw, B.M. (eds), *Research in Organizational Behavior*. Greenwich, CT: JAI Press, pp. 263–95.
6. Weigelt, K. and Camerer, C. (1988) 'Reputation and corporate strategy: A review of recent theory and applications', *Strategic Management Journal*, 9: 443–54.
7. Cornelissen, J.P., Haslam, S.A. and Balmer, J.M.T. (2007) 'Social identity, organizational identity and corporate identity: Towards an integrated understanding of processes, patternings and products', *British Journal of Management*, 18: S1–S16.
8. Gioia, D.A. and Thomas, J.B. (1996) 'Identity, image and issue interpretation: Sensemaking during strategic change in academia', *Administrative Science Quarterly*, 41: 370–403, quote on p. 372.
9. Ashforth, B.E. and Mael, F. (1989) 'Social identity theory and the organization', *Academy of Management Review*, 14: 20–39.
10. Dutton, J.E. and Dukerich, J.M. (1991) 'Keeping an eye on the mirror: Image and identity in organizational adaptation', *Academy of Management Journal*, 34: 517–54.
11. Hamel, G. and Prahalad, C.K. (1994) *Competing for the Future*. Boston, MA: Harvard Business School Press; Peters, T.J. and Waterman, R.H. (1982) *In Search of Excellence:*

Lessons from America's Best Run Companies. New York: Harper & Row; Collins, J.C. and Porras, J.I. (1997) *Built to Last: Successful Habits of Visionary Companies.* New York: Harper Business.

12. Fombrun, C. and Van Riel, C.B.M. (2004) *Fame and Fortune: How Successful Companies Build Winning Reputations.* London: FT Prentice Hall.

13. Keller, K.L. (2008) *Strategic Brand Management.* Upper Saddle River, NJ: Prentice-Hall, 3rd edition.

14. Schultz, M. (2005) 'A cross-disciplinary perspective on corporate branding', in Schultz, M., Antorini, Y.M. and Csaba, F.F. (eds), *Corporate Branding: Purpose/People/Process.* Copenhagen: Copenhagen Business School Press, 23–55.

15. Mitchell, C. (2002) 'Selling the brand inside', *Harvard Business Review*, January: 99–105.

16. Fombrun, C. and Rindova, V. (2007) 'The road to transparency: Reputation management at the Royal Dutch/Shell', in Schultz, M., Hatch, M.J. and Larsen, M.H. (eds), *The Expressive Organization.* Oxford: Oxford University Press, 76–96.

17. Hatch, M.J. and Schultz, M. (2001) 'Are the strategic stars aligned for your corporate brand?', *Harvard Business Review*, February: 128–35; Schultz, M. and Hatch, M.J. (2003) 'Cycles of corporate branding: The case of the LEGO Company', *California Management Review*, 46: 6–26; Hatch, M.J. and Schultz, M. (2008) *Taking Brand Initiative: How Companies Can Align Their Strategy, Culture and Identity through Corporate Branding.* San Francisco: Jossey Bass.

18. Bouchikhi, H. and Kimberly, J. (2007) *The Soul of the Corporation: How to Manage the Identity of Your Company.* Upper Saddle River, NJ: Pearson Education/Wharton School Publishing.

Corporate Communication in Practice

3

Part 3 explores practical issues in corporate communication: it deals with the questions of how communication strategies are developed and put into practice, and how professionals can monitor and research the effects of their activity. These issues are discussed in two separate chapters, but are part of an integrated process of moving from strategy and planning to actions and outcomes.

After reading Part 3, the reader will be familiar with crucial steps in developing an overall communication strategy, in planning and producing creative and effective communication programmes and campaigns, and in researching the effects of those programmes and campaigns on the organization's stakeholders.

Communication Strategy and Strategic Planning

6

┌─── CHAPTER OVERVIEW ───┐

The chapter describes the process and content of developing and planning a communication strategy for an organization. The process refers to the practical steps in developing a communication strategy across stakeholders and in line with the overall corporate strategy of an organization. The content refers to formulating specific messages to change stakeholder views and behaviours and the use of specific message styles that creatively articulate those themes in an organization's communication to stakeholders. Combining the process and content dimensions of strategy, the chapter offers a strategic planning model for developing and executing a communication strategy.

6.1 INTRODUCTION

Managing corporate communication requires a communication strategy that lays out a direction for the organization and describes the activities that are undertaken by communication practitioners to strengthen or maintain the reputation that an organization has amongst its stakeholders. A communication strategy, in other words, starts with formulating a desired reputational position for the organization in terms of how it wants itself to be seen by its different stakeholder groups. When such a broad-based objective is set, communication practitioners translate that aspiration into specific communication programmes and campaigns aimed at both internal and external stakeholder audiences.

The first part of the chapter discusses the process of strategy making in corporate communication. This section describes how a communication strategy is developed in interactions between practitioners from different communication disciplines and with support from the top of the organization, including its chief executive officer (CEO).

The second part of the chapter elaborates on the content of a communication strategy in terms of what, at their core, such strategies normally consist of and how they guide the design and planning of particular communication programmes and campaigns of an organization. The third and final part of the chapter presents a strategic planning model that combines the process and content dimensions of communication strategy. The model provides practitioners with a goal-directed but flexible method to plan and implement communication strategies for their organization.

6.2 DEVELOPING A COMMUNICATION STRATEGY

A communication strategy involves the formulation of a desired position for the organization in terms of how it wants to be seen by its different stakeholder groups. Based on an assessment of the gap between how the company is currently seen (*corporate reputation*) and how it wants to be seen (*vision*) (Chapter 5), a communication strategy specifies a strategic intent, on which possible courses of action are formulated, evaluated and eventually chosen. Communication strategies typically involve a process of bringing stakeholder reputations in line with the vision of the organization, in order to obtain the necessary support for the organization's strategy. In other cases, a communication strategy may be about reinforcing the existing reputations of stakeholders if those are broadly in line with how the organization wants itself to be seen.

A range of paradigms or different ways of thinking exist on the *process of strategy making*.[1] How strategies are formed within organizations has become variously depicted in these different paradigms as following a rational planning mode, in which objectives are set out and methodically worked out into comprehensive action plans, as a more flexible intuitive or visionary process, or as rather more incremental or emergent in nature, with the process of strategy formation being rather continuous and iterative. Each of these paradigms varies in whether the process of strategy formation is characterized and described as 'top-down' or 'bottom-up' in the organization, as deliberate and planned or as ad hoc and spontaneous and as analytical or visionary.

Besides the diversity and the distinct views presented by each of these different paradigms, there is also consensus on the following three points:

> *Strategy formation consists of a combination of planned and emergent processes.* In practice, strategy formation involves a combination of a logical rational process in which visions and objectives are articulated and systematically worked out into programmes and actions, as well as more emergent processes in which behaviours and actions simply arise ('emerge') yet fall within the strategic scope of the organization. The same combination of planned and emergent processes of strategy formation can also be observed at the level of communication strategy. In practice, communication strategy typically consists of pre-structured and annually planned programmes and campaigns, as well as more ad hoc, reactive responses that 'emerge' in response to issues and events that emerge in an on- or off-line setting.

Strategy involves a general direction and not simply plans or tactics. The term strategy is itself derived from the Greek 'strategos', meaning a general set of manoeuvres carried out to overcome an enemy. What is notable here is the emphasis on *general*, not *specific*, sets of manoeuvres. Specific sets of manoeuvres are seen as within the remit of translating the strategy into programmes or tactics. In other words, strategy embodies more than plans and tactics, which often have a more immediate and short-term focus. Instead, strategy concerns the organization's direction and positioning in relation to stakeholders in its environment for a longer period of time.

Strategy is about the organization and its environment. Related to the previous point, the emphasis for managers is to make long-term, strategic choices that are feasible in the organization's environments. Managers who manage strategically do so by balancing the mission and vision of the organization – what it is, what it wants to be and what it wants to do – with what the environment will allow or encourage it to do. Strategy is therefore often adaptive in that it needs to be responsive to external opportunities and threats that may confront an organization. A broad consensus exists in the strategy literature that strategy is essentially concerned with a process of managing the interaction between an organization and its external environment so as to ensure the best 'fit' between the two.

From a strategic perspective, corporate communication is in fact an important 'boundary-spanning' function between the organization and the environment.[3] As a boundary-spanning function, corporate communication operates at the interface between the organization and its environment. It helps to gather, relay and interpret information from the environment as well as represent the organization to stakeholders in the outside world. Seeing corporate communication as a strategic boundary-spanning function requires in turn that communication professionals are involved in decision-making on the corporate strategy itself. Such a view of communication means that communication strategy is not just seen as a set of goals and tactics at the functional or operational level – at the level of the corporate communication function – but that its scope and involvement in fact stretch to the central and most senior level of the organization as well.

At this corporate level, where strategy is concerned with the corporate mission and vision, communication practitioners can aid senior managers in developing strategies for interaction with the environment. They can, for example, support strategic decision-making through their 'environmental scanning' activities. Environmental scanning may assist corporate strategy-makers in analysing the organization's position and identifying emerging issues which may have significant implications for the organization and for future strategy development. At this corporate level, communication practitioners can also bring identity questions and a stakeholder perspective into the strategic management process, representing the likely reaction of stakeholders to alternative strategy options, and thereby giving senior management a more balanced consideration of the attractiveness and feasibility of the strategic options open to them. Finally, communication practitioners of course also facilitate the implementation of the corporate strategy by helping to communicate the organization's strategic intentions to both internal and external stakeholders, which can help avoid misunderstandings that might otherwise get in the way of the smooth implementation of the organization's strategy. With such involvement in the corporate strategy of an organization, the communication strategy itself will also be more substantial as opposed to just a set of tactics. And in an era of stakeholder management, successful companies are the ones where a corporate communication strategy is not divorced from the organization's overall corporate strategy, to which it must contribute if it is to have a genuine strategic role.[4]

In summary, a corporate strategy is concerned with the overall purpose and scope of the organization to meet its various stakeholders' expectations and needs. A corporate strategy provides a strategic vision for the entire organization in terms of product, market or geographical scope or matters as fundamental as ownership of the organization. A vision often also articulates how the company wants to be seen by its various stakeholder groups. A communication strategy in turn is a functional or operational strategy concerned with how corporate communication can develop communication programmes towards different stakeholders to achieve that vision and to support the corporate objectives in the corporate strategy.

Figure 6.1 illustrates this dynamic between the corporate strategy and the corporate communication strategy. On the one hand, the decisions that are made at the level of the corporate strategy need to be translated into specific communication programmes for different stakeholders. In the words of Kevin Rollins, former CEO of Dell: 'The job of a senior manager is to determine which elements of the overall strategy you want to communicate to each constituency.' Rollins, together with Dell's senior communication managers, decides how they 'break messages up into pieces and try to give the right piece to the right audience'.[5] At the same time, corporate communication and communication strategies need to be linked to the corporate strategy. This link consists of advising and informing the CEO and senior executives on stakeholder and reputation issues so that these can be factored into the overall corporate strategy and the company's strategic vision. Michael Dell, the founder of Dell, articulates this link by saying that 'communications are an essential part of what you have to offer to customers and shareholders'. In his view, 'communications has to be in the centre to be optimally effective' and for it to support the corporate strategy.[6]

This nested model of strategy formation, in which a corporate strategy and communication strategy are seen as interrelated layers in the total strategy-making structure of the organization, depends on a number of conditions. First of all, it goes against strict 'top-down' views of strategy formation where strategy is seen to cascade down from the

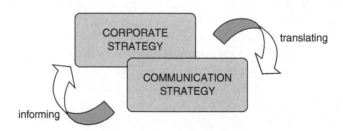

FIGURE 6.1   The link between corporate strategy and communication strategy

corporate to the business unit and ultimately to the functional level of corporate communication, with each level of strategy providing the immediate context for the next, 'lower' level of strategy making. Strategy making generally fares better when it does not strictly follow such a rigid, hierarchical top-down process. Instead, it should be more flexible and at least in part decentralized so that business units and functions such as corporate communication are encouraged to initiate ideas that are then passed upward for approval at the appropriate senior management level. From this perspective, business units and functions may be responsible not only for developing strategic responses to the problems or opportunities encountered at their own level ('translating' in Figure 6.1), but may sometimes initiate ideas that then become the catalyst for changes in strategy throughout the organization ('informing' in Figure 6.1). Communication practitioners, for instance, may pass their ideas in relation to stakeholders at the functional level to the CEO and senior management level and may as such initiate a revision of corporate strategy in terms of how the organization needs to build and maintain relationships with those organizational stakeholders who have the power to influence the successful realization of its corporate goals.

The input of corporate communication practitioners into corporate strategy and other operational areas of activity in the organization requires that these professionals have relevant managerial expertise and skills. Specifically, it requires that professionals are able to formulate the importance and use of communication in the context of general organizational issues and objectives. Surveys of the PR and corporate communication profession repeatedly stress that effective communicators are those who speak the same language as senior executives and have a deep understanding of the business and its strategy.[7] Practitioners need to have knowledge of the industry or sector in which the organization operates and of the nature of the strategy-making process, and need to have a strategic view of how communication can contribute to corporate and market strategies and to different functional areas within the company. Instead of a purely 'technical' approach to communication that is only focused on the production of communications materials, a managerial role requires that a professional is able:

> to bring thoughtfully conceived agendas to the senior management table that address the strategic issues of business planning, resource allocation, priorities and direction of the firm. Instead of asking what events to sponsor and at what cost, [professionals] should be asking which customer segments to invest in and at what projected returns ... instead of asking how to improve the number of hits to the website, [professionals] should be asking who their key stakeholders are and how to get more interactive with them.[8]

Having practitioners in an organization who can enact a managerial role is crucial for corporate communication to be involved in decision-making that concerns the overall strategic direction of the organization. And when communication professionals are involved at the decision-making table, information about relations with priority stakeholders gets factored into the process of corporate decision-making and into corporate strategies and actions. This would mean, amongst other things, that senior communication professionals are actively consulted concerning the effects of certain business actions (e.g. staff lay-offs, divestiture) on a company's reputation with stake-holders, and even have a say in the decision-making on it, instead of being called in afterwards, after the decision has been made, to draft a press release and to deal with any communication issues emerging from it.

Communication practitioners who are expected to adopt a managerial role, how-ever, do not always meet the requirements for competencies and skills associated with the manager role. This may be partly the result of a lack of career development opportunities and professional support within their organizations. Many commu-nication professionals lack knowledge and skills in financial management, in the strategy-making process, and in the use of communication in organizational develop-ment and change. As a result, these professionals and the communication disciplines that they represent may be sidelined by companies and treated as a peripheral man-agement discipline – one viewed as unimportant to the overall functioning of the corporation. In such instances, senior managers may believe that communication adds little to corporate performance as it is a 'fluffy' discipline that is insufficiently focused on the practicalities and demands of the business.

6.3 STRATEGIC MESSAGING AND CONTENT PLATFORMS

The content of a communication strategy is influenced by the process by which it is formed and by the different individuals and layers in the organization who have had a stake in it. Ideally, the content of the strategy starts from an organization-wide assessment of how the organization is seen by different stakeholders (reputation) in the light of the organization's vision (vision) at a particular point in time. The gap between the reputation and the vision, as mentioned, forms the basis for the formu-lation of a strategic intent: the change or consolidation in the company's reputation that is intended. The strategic intent in turn is translated into strategic messages – or content platforms – that are designed to change or reinforce perceptions in line with the vision of how the organization wants itself to be known.

To illustrate this process, consider the example of Wal-Mart. The company is the biggest in the USA, but has for years been ranked at the bottom of the US retail sector, mostly due to reports of underpaying its workers, of relying on imported goods from China and of aggressively driving local stores out of business. Wal-Mart has realized that it has to improve its image on each of these fronts, and particularly the reputa-tion it has for unfairly treating its employees. This image is out of step with its vision of being a fair and transparent employer, with competitive pay and opportunities for those who want to work hard and better themselves. The company also realizes that higher levels of employee satisfaction translate directly into customer satisfaction, and thus into a stronger economic performance.

Based on this gap, the strategic intent of Wal-Mart's communication strategy is defined for 2016 as changing stakeholder views – from a company that treats its work-ers rather harshly and unfairly to an aspired image of a company that offers a fair workplace with competitive pay and opportunities for advancement. To achieve its strategic intent and to claim this aspired reputational position in the minds of stake-holders, Wal-Mart has identified a number of strategic messages or content areas that the company consistently communicates to different stakeholders. These content areas include stories around competitive pay, including the above-average hourly wage that the company offers, around the collegial but hard-working culture at the company and around the opportunities for advancement that Wal-Mart offers to its employees. Wal-Mart has, for example, increased the size of its digital communications team which has turned the company's blog and website into an active news site that publishes its own content on each of these areas. The team has run stories on individual employees, giving a glimpse of their working lives, as well as their hobbies and life outside of work – humanizing its workers and in turn humanizing the company. The site publishes two or three new stories a week and posts video features and profiles of its employees every two weeks. Since becoming more proactive in its communication, Wal-Mart believes that there has been a 15 per cent lift in reputation for the company – mostly in terms of a change in how people view Wal-Mart as treating its employees.

As in this example, themed messages relate to specific capabilities, strengths or values (as 'themes') of an organization. These messages are continuously and consist-ently communicated to stakeholders to achieve the strategic intent of changing or consolidating the company's reputation. Such a themed message may involve a com-pany's specific capability, such as the ability of an organization to develop innovative products, its general strengths or achievements such as the care that it has demon-strated in support of its employees and the general community in which it operates (which is what Wal-Mart claims), or particular values associated with the company's identity such as its claimed integrity or transparency. Themed messages are direct translations of the strategic intent: they emphasize an aspect (achievement, capabil-ity or value) that the organization wants to become associated with in the mind of important stakeholder groups. These messages are in turn marked as relevant content areas that the organization wishes to publish and communicate; content that it hopes will then translate into real changes to its reputation. Themed messages are at the level of a news story, advert, blog post or any other form of communication trans-lated into different message styles that communicate the claim about the company's capabilities, strengths or values in a convincing way (Figure 6.2).

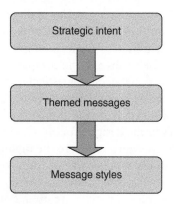

FIGURE 6.2   Stages in formulating the content of a communication strategy

TABLE 6.1 Alternative message styles

Functional orientation	Symbolic orientation	Industry orientation
Rational message style	Symbolic association message style	Generic message style
	Emotional message style	Pre-emptive message style

There are in fact various ways to communicate themed messages. Several relatively distinct message styles have developed over the years and represent various ways in which corporate messages are communicated to different stakeholder groups.[9] Table 6.1 summarizes five message styles and groups them into three categories: functional orientation, symbolic orientation and industry orientation. Functionally oriented messages refer to tangible, physical or concrete capabilities or resources of an organization. Symbolically oriented messages appeal to the psychosocial needs, preferences and experiences of stakeholders. An industry orientation message style does not necessarily use any particular type of functional or psychosocial appeal, but is designed to achieve an advantage over competitors in the same industry. Finally, it is important to note that, as is the case with most categorization schemes, the message styles covered in the following section sometimes overlap in specific examples of corporate communication practice. In other words, distinctions are sometimes very fine rather than perfectly obvious, and a particular corporate communication strategy may simultaneously use multiple message styles in relation to themed messages.

Rational message style: in this approach, an organization makes a superiority claim about its products or achievements based on a distinctive advantage in its capabilities, size or resources (including technology). The main feature of this message style is identifying an important difference that can be highlighted and then developing a claim that competitors either cannot make or have not chosen to make. The claim is seen as 'functional' because it addresses a basic need or expectation of stakeholders. The message style is labelled rational because it follows a basic argumentation structure where the grounds for the claim for superiority are supplied through supporting information. For example, when Alcatel-Lucent Technologies claims a superior ability to develop and deliver network solutions to clients, it is based on its distinctive and proven track record in research and development in network technology (the company is associated with the world-renowned Bell Labs and the company's engineers have won many prizes for their ground-breaking technologies including Nobel Prizes). Similarly, BMW claims a superior ability in engineering aesthetically pleasing, high-performance cars that is backed up by the company's long-standing emphasis on innovation and aesthetics in the design process (Case Study 5.1). The rational message style can be effective in cases where the organization can claim a distinctive advantage in its capabilities, size or resources. In cases where the organization cannot claim such an advantage or where such an advantage is easily matched, alternative message styles are used. For example, organizations typically do not use a rational message style when they communicate about their corporate social responsibility (CSR) because standards for performance in such areas are not typically obvious or transparent (Chapter 13) and, as such, performance can often be easily matched by competitors. In addition, a hard-hitting rational message style may also be seen as socially unacceptable for communicating about CSR.

▌ RATIONAL MESSAGE STYLE ▐

1 *Definition*: a superiority claim based on actual accomplishments or delivered benefits by the organization

2 *Conditions*: most useful when the point of difference cannot be readily matched by competitors

3 *Content*: informational in the form of a claim that is supported with information as the grounds for the claim.

Symbolic association message style: whereas the rational message style is based on promoting physical and functional differences between an organization and its competitors, a symbolic association message style involves psychosocial rather than physical differentiation. The aim with this message style is to develop an image for the organization and to differentiate the organization psychologically from its competitors through symbolic association. In imbuing the organization with a symbolic image, communicators draw meaning from the culturally constituted world (that is, the world of symbols and values) and, through communication, transfer that meaning to the organization. The core of this message style consists of identifying a set of symbols and values that, through repeated linkage with the organization, may come to be associated with that organization. One example of this message style is the way in which organizations link themselves through sponsoring to values associated with a sport or certain cause. Another example of this message style involves corporate value statements whereby an organization explicitly states values or moral attributes that guide its conduct. AstraZeneca, for instance, lists the values of integrity, honesty and trust as central to how the company engages with its different stakeholders. These values express the moral sentiments and social capital that make organizations legitimate in the eyes of stakeholders. AstraZeneca also gives examples of how the company tries to live up to its values in specific practices. Similar to sponsorship, these value statements are meant to link the company with general (culturally shared and recognized) moral values and sentiments which may then become associated with the organization.

A symbolic association message style may also be described as 'transformational' because it associates the organization with a set of culturally shared experiences and meanings which, without corporate communication, would not typically be associated with the organization to the same degree. Such communication is transforming (versus informing) by virtue of endowing the organization with a particular symbolic image that is different from any of its competitors.

SYMBOLIC ASSOCIATION MESSAGE STYLE

1 *Definition*: a claim based on psychological differentiation through symbolic association

2 *Conditions*: best for homogeneous organizations where differences are difficult to develop or easily duplicated, or for messages around areas such as CSR or social capital that are difficult to communicate in concrete and rational terms

3 *Content*: transformational in the form of endowing the organization with a particular image through association with culturally shared and recognized values or symbols.

Emotional message style: an emotional message style is another form of symbolically oriented communication. By using this message style, organizations aim to reach stakeholders at a visceral level. One approach may be to use emotional appeals in corporate communication to regulate the emotional responses of stakeholders. The display of emotions may, for example, lead to greater levels of involvement and affiliation with an organization. Starbucks, for example, incorporates emotional appeals around love, joy and belonging into its in-store communication which has led to consumers associating the Starbucks brand with community, individual expression and 'a place away from home' (Case Study 4.1). Displays of positive emotions may also stimulate supportive, sharing and expansive behaviours of stakeholders, whilst the display of negative emotions may lead to distancing and avoidance. A good example of this message style involves the launch of Orange back in 1994. At the time, the mobile phone market in the UK was a confusing place for customers. Digital networks had just been introduced, but few people yet understood the benefits and most members of the general public were worried about the safety of mobile technology. On top of this, Orange also faced an uphill task in differentiating itself as the last entrant in a market which already included BT, Cellnet and Vodafone. In response, Orange launched an advertising campaign which communicated the positive emotions afforded by using mobile phones (friendship, love, freedom) and assured people that the negative emotions (fear, safety) that they may have had concerning the introduction of this new technology were unfounded. In considering an emotional message style, it is important for organizations to make sure that the display of emotions is seen as authentic. If stakeholders perceive references to emotions to be inauthentic, an emotional message style may backfire. In the case of Starbucks, for example, the company's emotional message style has been verified as authentic by stakeholders because of the genuine enthusiasm, friendliness and professionalism conveyed by employees.

EMOTIONAL MESSAGE STYLE

1 *Definition*: attempts to provoke involvement and positive reactions through a reference to positive (or negative) emotions

2 *Conditions*: effective use depends on the perceived authenticity of the professed emotion and on the relevance of the emotion to stakeholders

3 *Content*: appeals to specific positive or negative emotions (e.g. romance, nostalgia, excitement, joy, fear, guilt, disgust, regret).

Generic message style: an organization employs a generic strategy when making a claim that could be made by any organization that operates in the same industry. With this message style, the organization makes no attempt to differentiate itself from competitors or to claim superiority. This message style is most appropriate for an organization that dominates a particular industry. For example, Campbell's soup dominates the prepared-soup market in the USA, selling nearly two-thirds of all soup. Based on its market dominance, the company has run advertising campaigns that stimulate demand for soup in general, rather than Campbell's soup in particular. The rationale behind this message style was that any advertising that increased overall soup sales would also naturally benefit Campbell's sales. Along similar lines, Novo Nordisk's 'changing diabetes' message emphasizes the company's long-standing leadership in developing products for the diagnosis and treatment of diabetes. Given Novo Nordisk's grasp on the worldwide diabetes market, the campaign communicated, in the company's words, 'a clearly differentiated corporate position in the global diabetes market'.

GENERIC MESSAGE STYLE

1 *Definition*: a straight claim about industry or cause with no assertion of superiority

2 *Conditions*: a monopoly or an extreme dominance of industry

3 *Content*: a general claim (to stimulate demand for product category or raise awareness of cause).

Pre-emptive message style: a second message style that involves an industry-wide orientation is employed when an organization makes a generic-type claim but does so with a suggestion of superiority. Pre-emptive communication is a clever strategy when a meaningful superiority claim is made because it precludes competitors from saying the same thing. For example, many electronics firms can potentially claim to be about developing technological products that are advanced but easy to operate and designed around the needs of the customer, but no other firm could possibly make such a claim after Philips made it part of its generic 'sense and simplicity' campaign. This claim could have been made by many other electronics firms such as Sony and Samsung, but in appropriating this claim with its implicit assertion of superiority Philips pre-empted competitors from using the simplicity tact in promoting their own organizations. Another example of the pre-emptive message style involves Exxon Mobil's claim of 'taking on the world's toughest energy challenges', which invokes its superior operational efficiencies and capabilities in drilling for oil in hard-to-reach places. In doing so, the company differentiates itself from its nearest competitors on a relevant industry-wide capability and suggests that it is leading the initiative to meet the increasing demand for energy.

⌐ PRE-EMPTIVE MESSAGE STYLE ¬

1 *Definition*: a generic claim with a suggestion of superiority

2 *Conditions*: changing industry, allowing a company to take a position on an issue connected to that industry

3 *Content*: a claim of industry-wide leadership on a relevant issue or capability.

 ——— CASE EXAMPLE 6.1 ————————————————

TOYOTA: A ROCKY ROAD AHEAD

Toyota Motor Corporation (TMC) became the world's largest vehicle manufacturer in 2008, offering a full range of models from mini-vehicles to large trucks. Toyota and its luxury line, Lexus, have been amongst the top automotive brands in terms of reliability, quality and long-term durability. Until recently, Toyota had also been one of the most profitable carmakers. But in 2010 the company's fortune changed. In January 2010, the company announced that it would temporarily shut down production at six assembly plants in North America and suspend sales of its most popular models, including the Camry, the best-selling car in the USA. The week before, the company had already recalled 2.3 million vehicles with faults in the accelerator pedals.

Challenges ahead

These announcements and recalls seriously damaged the carmaker's reputation for producing good quality, reliable cars at reasonable prices. Recent customer polls and market surveys put Toyota clearly behind its competitors. For example, Ford vehicles, long considered as also-rans, are now showing 'world-class reliability', beating the Toyota Camry in the segment of mid-size cars. If Toyota can no longer rely on its superior quality and reliability to appeal to customers, its vehicles will inevitably be judged increasingly on more emotional criteria, such as their design and styling, and the experience of driving a Toyota car. But this is not an area that has traditionally been Toyota's strength, nor has the company been consistently communicating such experiential or emotional benefits to its consumers. The company therefore finds itself in a bit of a dilemma. Mr Toyoda, the current president, believes that the company needs to return to its strengths (reliability) as well as add new spice to its cars. In October 2009, Toyoda addressed an audience of Japanese journalists and said that the company was in a spiral of decline, unless it could reinvent itself. Mr Toyoda had been reading *How the Mighty Fall*, a book on how previously mighty companies may step into a cycle of decline. The decline leads to a downward spiral triggered by an undisciplined pursuit of growth and by being out of touch with the changing values and expectations of customers and other stakeholders. When Mr Toyoda took over in 2009, he immediately ordered a back-to-basics overhaul of product development across the firm's global operations. He has also been challenging his company's engineers to make less dull cars. At the Tokyo motor show in October 2009, he stated publicly: 'I want to see Toyota build cars that are fun and exciting to drive.' As Morizo, the alter ego under which he blogs, he even went a step further. In his blog, he commented on the cars at the show: 'It was all green. But I wonder how many inspired people get excited. Eco-friendly cars are a prerequisite for the future, but there must be more than that.'

Mr Toyoda's challenge lies in rebuilding and extending Toyota's reputation from the initial focus on the safety, sustainability and reliability of its cars, to a reputation that stresses the emotional fun and enjoyment of driving Toyota cars. He may have to keep the company's traditional strengths – the dependability and affordability of its cars – whilst adding the emotional benefits that he feels customers appear to demand.

Question for Reflection

Consider the overall communication strategy of Toyota, including its strategic intent, the themed messages and message styles in Toyota's communications. Given the challenges ahead for Toyota, how would you change the communication strategy in terms of strategic intent, themed messages and message styles?

Source: This case example is based on *The Economist* (2009) 'Struggling giants: Toyota slips up', 9 December; *The Economist* (2010) 'The machine that ran too hot', 25 February; *The Economist* (2010) 'Getting the cow out of the ditch', 11 February; *The Economist* (2010) 'No quick fix', 4 February (other quotes throughout the text); Collins, J. (2009) *How the Mighty Fall: And Why Some Companies Never Give In*. New York: Random House.

Five general message styles have been discussed and categorized as functional, symbolic or industry-oriented. These strategic alternatives to communicating corporate messages provide a useful aid to understanding the different approaches available to communicators and the factors influencing the choice for a particular message style. The message styles should, however, not be seen as mutually exclusive. In fact, organizations may use different message styles to communicate different messages to different stakeholders, as illustrated by the case example of Toyota (Case Example 6.1).

In the following section, we will discuss in more detail how organizations develop and plan particular communication programmes and campaigns as part of a communication strategy. These programmes and campaigns include different themed messages that may be communicated through multiple message styles.

6.4 PLANNING AND EXECUTING COMMUNICATION PROGRAMMES AND CAMPAIGNS

The planning of communication programmes and campaigns starts from the basic model presented in Figure 6.2, but with added detail on communication objectives, the segmentation of target audiences, the media strategy and the budgeting of the programme or campaign. Figure 6.3 presents this strategic planning framework. The framework consists of seven steps, starting with the strategic intent, and is illustrated by the case study of Lenovo (Case Study 6.1). Before we outline these steps in detail, it is worth clarifying the distinction between communication programmes and campaigns.

A communication programme involves a coherent set of activities targeted at internal and external audiences, which may include outreach activities, community initiatives and other ways in which organizations communicate with stakeholder audiences. A communication programme is a broader concept than the idea of a communication campaign which is typically more short-lived and focused on a single event or activity, such as a product launch. In other words, campaigns are restricted to a single point in time and build to a decision point for stakeholders. A programme

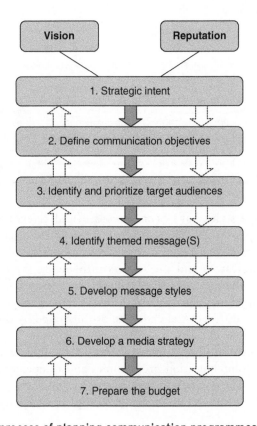

FIGURE 6.3 The process of planning communication programmes and campaigns

is like a campaign in that it may consist of similar types of events or activities, but it differs in the sense that it does not have a pre-set endpoint. A programme is generally put in place to address the ongoing needs for reputation building as laid down in the overall communication strategy, and is reviewed periodically to determine whether its objectives have been met. All or parts of a programme will be continued as long as there is a need for communication with stakeholders, and in order to strengthen or maintain a company's corporate reputation.

The framework that is presented can be used for the planning of both programme- and campaign-level activities. In other words, it can be used to drill down to the specifics of a campaign or may stay quite general and broad in focus, in detailing the overall programme of the communication strategy. The fact that communication practitioners can cycle back and forth between programme and campaign elements and their interconnections, highlights that the framework should be used in a flexible and pragmatic manner, reflecting the fact that a strategy is not fixed or set at a certain point in time but is an ongoing and evolving process.

Step 1: Strategic intent

At the onset of a communication programme or campaign, it is important to refer back to the organization's overall communication strategy and the identified strategic intent. Roughly speaking, the strategic intent formulates a change or consolidation of stakeholder reputations of the organization. It is based on the gap between how the organization wants itself to be seen by important stakeholder groups and how it is currently seen by each of those groups. The strategic intent articulates a set of general goals at the level of the reputation of the organization.

Step 2: Define communication objectives

Based on the strategic intent, communication practitioners then need to set specific communication objectives for a communication programme or a specific campaign. Here, practitioners may decide to develop specific programmes or campaigns for particular stakeholder groups (e.g. employees, shareholders and investors, customers) or instead to develop a general corporate programme or campaign that addresses all of them. In both cases, however, practitioners need to define objectives in terms of whether they are seeking to change or consolidate a particular stakeholder's awareness, attitude, more general reputation with them, or behaviour. In line with the strategic intent, successful communication consists of appealing to stakeholders with a particular message, so that they react favourably to it and change or consolidate a specific supportive behaviour as regards the organization such as investing in an organization or buying its products. Communication objectives should be as tightly defined as possible: specific, measurable, actionable, realistic and timely (SMART):

> *Specific*: objectives should specify what it is that the practitioner wants to achieve (e.g. change in awareness of, change of reputation) with a particular stakeholder group.

> *Measurable*: practitioners should be able to measure whether they are meeting the objectives or not. This often consists of identifying clear indicators (e.g. a

percentage change in behaviours supportive of the organization) that can be measured and afterwards used to evaluate the success of the programme or campaign.

Achievable: objectives should be achievable and attainable in the light of current stakeholder reputations of the organization and the competitive landscape.

Realistic: objectives need to be realistic in light of the resources and budget that are provided for a particular programme or campaign.

Timely: objectives should also specify the time frame in which they need to be achieved. Communication objectives often include a 'window' of 1–2 years after the programme or campaign to measure the direct impact of a programme or campaign.

Well-articulated objectives are measurable in that they specify a time frame and the number of people that the programme or campaign sets out to reach and affect. It is then possible for communication practitioners to evaluate and determine whether objectives have been met.

Step 3: Identify and prioritize target audiences

Organizations have many stakeholder groups. Obviously, organizations cannot communicate with all of them, and practitioners therefore use the stakeholder salience model and the power–interest matrix (Chapter 4) to identify the most important stakeholder groups. Once important stakeholder groups have been identified, practitioners need to segment those groups into more specific target audiences that are prioritized for a particular programme or campaign. For example, the stakeholder group of 'employees' includes many segments of different groups (e.g. top management, middle management, front-line staff, back-office personnel, administrative staff) which may not all need to be addressed within a particular programme or campaign. A target audience is defined as the segment of individuals (from a particular stakeholder group) that is the focus ('target') of a particular programme or campaign.

Step 4: Identify themed messages

Based on the identified communication objectives and selected target audiences, practitioners need to decide what the core message should be. The core message aimed at a particular target audience often evolves directly from how the organization wants to be seen. For example, Wal-Mart's intent to be seen as a fair and responsible employer provides a core message that can be translated into a specific campaign format and message style (Step 5 below). Themed messages may relate to the organization as a whole or to more specific areas such as products and services, CSR or financial performance, in which case they may be primarily relevant to particular stakeholder groups.

Step 5: Develop message styles

A message can be told in different ways using one of the five message styles laid out in section 6.3. The message styles involve the creative concept that articulates the appeal of the message and brings it to life through the use of catchy slogans, an appropriate framing in words and visual stimuli (pictures, images, logos and the typographic setting of a message). As discussed, the use of a particular message style depends on certain conditions and expectations of stakeholders: for example, an organization may adopt a rational message style when it communicates its financial growth and potential to investors at the annual general meeting by referring to its recent financial results and the growth of the market in which it operates. Simultaneously, an organization may adopt a symbolic association style by sponsoring a sports event or cause in an attempt to build a general corporate image that may lead to recognition and favourability with all of its stakeholder groups. In short, an organization can use multiple message styles simultaneously to communicate with different target audiences. At the same time, an organization often uses the same message style to communicate about certain specific areas, such as its products and services, its general corporate position, CSR or its financial performance. Wal-Mart, for example, has reinstated the phrase 'Our People Make the Difference' on employees' name badges – a symbolic message that communicates to customers the customer focus and abilities of Wal-Mart employees.

Step 6: Develop a media strategy

The sixth step in the process involves identifying the media that can carry the message and its creative execution and can reach the target audience. In developing the media strategy, the overriding aim is to identify the most effective and efficient means of reaching the target audiences within the given budgetary constraints. Practitioners need to consider criteria such as the reach and coverage of the target audience (to what extent does a particular medium reach subjects within the target audience so that they are exposed to the message at least once?), the creative match of the medium with the message (to what extent does the medium support a particular message style and creative format?), competitors' use of the media (to what extent do competitors use the same medium?) and the ability of media to enable dialogue and interaction with the audience (does the medium simply supply information or does it also allow interaction with the organization?). Media selection is ideally 'zero-based',[10] meaning that rather than repeating a pre-fixed and standard choice for a medium that may have worked in the past, the most appropriate medium is chosen in the light of these criteria. In other words, practitioners need to stay open to the wide range of media options available to them (e.g. free publicity, video conferencing, promotions, meetings with stakeholders, sponsoring), rather than heading straight for tried-and-tested media or ones they have simply used in the past. Practitioners also need to decide on the right mix of media for a particular communication programme or campaign. For example, when an organization launches a new product, it will need to use a range of media, including mass media advertising to generate awareness, marketing public relations and branded content to generate excitement and interest in the product, and sales promotions to stimulate people to try the product. Within the constraints of the budget, practitioners will aim to select multiple media and need to specify how these media complement each other in the achievement of communication objectives, and at which point each medium is put to use within the time frame of the programme or campaign. With such choices, practitioners are also increasingly trying to establish a seamless integration of on- and off-line media – sometimes called an 'omnichannel' approach – so that messages reinforce each other and drive stakeholders towards the desired effect in cognitive, emotional or behavioural terms.

Step 7: Prepare the budget

Finally, it is important to budget for the communication programme or campaign. Most of the budget is often spent on media buying, with the remaining amount going towards the production of the programme or campaign (including the hiring of communication consultants, advertising professionals and copy editors) and the evaluation of results. Based on the budget that is available for a particular programme or campaign, practitioners may have to revise the previous steps, select a different mix of media and/or adjust their communication objectives.

In fact, the process model is indeed often dynamically used, rather than what the model might suggest is a linear progression of steps. The current environment for corporate communication (Chapter 3) requires that practitioners cycle back and forth between the different steps (as indicated by the dotted arrows in Figure 6.3), feed forward and plan their own programmes or campaigns, but also make the most of opportunities that suddenly present themselves. Communication strategies should remain agile, such that they can be adapted to changing circumstances and so that intermediate insights can be fed into the planning cycle.[11] Furthermore, the move from one step in the model to the next is also not a simple cascading down, but involves interpretations, negotiations and best guesses, and is as such always open to revision.

Therefore, instead of developing and writing lengthy communication plans, communication practitioners are probably best served by a flexible and to-the-point planning model, such as the one highlighted in Figure 6.3. This model allows them to plan ahead whilst remaining flexible enough in adapting to changing circumstances and feedback. Such adaptation requires, however, that they keep an open mind and a reflective attitude, and do not simply assume that their job is done once they have put the details of a strategy on paper.

Finally, when the entire programme or campaign is planned and has been executed, it will be evaluated for its results – which is the subject of Chapter 7. Effectiveness of the programme or campaign can be evaluated on the basis of process and communications effects. Process effects concern the quality of the communication programme or campaign (in terms of intelligence gathered, the detail that has gone into the planning, the appropriateness of message content and overall organizational support) and whether the programme has been executed in a cost-effective manner. Communication effects include the range of cognitive and behavioural effects of targeted stakeholder audiences that the programme or campaign aimed to achieve. Here, it is important to identify suitable impact measures (i.e. changes in awareness, attitude and reputation, or behaviour) rather than relying on interim measures of communication effects such as media coverage or simple exposure,[3] and to evaluate the effects achieved against the targets or benchmark set with the objectives of the communication programme or campaign.

CASE STUDY 6.1

LENOVO: DEVELOPING A GLOBAL BRAND

In 2004, Lenovo – China's largest personal computer (PC) maker – acquired IBM's PC division for $1.75 billion. With the deal, the company set out to become a global technology giant and became a multinational corporation overnight with 20,000 employees operating in 138 countries. The acquisition was judged by Lenovo as a strategic move as it would help internationalize the company and as IBM's customer base and skills would complement the strong presence of Lenovo in China. Where Lenovo's focus had been on small businesses and consumers, IBM had long targeted corporate and enterprise customers. As part of the deal, Lenovo also gained the right to use the IBM brand name on its products for up to five years, along with two major products: the established IBM ThinkPad laptop and ThinkCentre desktop brands. Whilst the acquisition made a lot of sense from a strategic and marketing standpoint, and provided Lenovo with the opportunity to expand, it also meant that the company had to refashion its branding and communication to match its new international status and market reach.

Becoming an international company

The culture of the acquired IBM division consisted of the same values of customer focus, innovation and trustworthiness as Lenovo. The two companies also shared the same performance-driven culture and a focus on meritocracy, based in part on the fact that Lenovo had originally modelled itself on HP and IBM. When the deal was announced, however, there was uncertainty about how IBM's existing customers would react to the new organization, and similarly there was a concern amongst IBM staff that the Chinese side would come to dominate the combined organization. The CEO of the new Lenovo, however, announced a management restructuring that successfully integrated both organizations. Half of the most senior positions in the organization went to American, Australian, European and Indian colleagues, reflecting the company's new international composition and scope. English also became the official working language in Lenovo. The post-acquisition integration succeeded in part because of the complementary skills and assets shared between the two companies, but also because of a realization amongst employees that the company was in fact a truly international organization that combined the best of the East and the West. As one executive explained: 'From the original Lenovo we have the understanding of emerging markets, excellent efficiency and a focus on long-term strategy. From IBM we have deep insights into worldwide markets and best practices from Western companies. So we view Lenovo as a new world type of company.' The company uses the corporate tagline of 'New world. New thinking', which communicates its global outlook and the innovation-driven focus of the company.

(Continued)

(Continued)

Building a global brand

The Lenovo brand name was derived from 'le-' which came from the original Chinese company's name of Legend, and 'novo', signifying new or innovative. However, back in 2004, the awareness and perception of the Lenovo brand around the world was far from ideal (step 1 – strategic intent). At the time, Lenovo carried out some market research to get a handle on the transition from a local to a globally respected brand. Lenovo staff talked to over 4,000 customers and the concerns that surfaced were that with the new company structure innovation would slow down, quality would suffer and service and support would be outsourced overseas. To quickly neutralize the third point, Lenovo structured the original deal with IBM in such a way that it included ongoing worldwide service and support from IBM via its existing global service infrastructure. As for the first two concerns, Lenovo realized that it had to reassure customers that innovation and quality would not only be maintained and protected, but that this would actually increase because of the determination and strict focus of Lenovo on the PC market. As Deepak Advani, Chief Marketing Officer, explained at the time: 'we knew we had to show that innovation and quality would not decrease. Customers would have to experience all this for themselves. The proof had to be in the pudding.' The company looked at various branding alternatives and decided to focus on a dual strategy that would consist of raising awareness and building up a favourable image of Lenovo as a corporate brand, and continuing to strengthen the Thinkpad product brand so as to drive intention to purchase and customer loyalty (step 2 – define communication objectives). The reason for this strategy was to lift the brand equity of the Thinkpad series and to extend its existing customer base, whilst, at the same time, building up and reinforcing the strength of the overall Lenovo brand. As one of the marketing executives explained: 'What we wanted was to maintain the Thinkpad brand and use that brand's strength to build the Lenovo brand. We realized that it would be naive to choose one over the other and we needed to take a flexible view of the transition.' The target audience consisted primarily of existing Lenovo and IBM customers and new prospects, but the aim was also to build a strong corporate image of Lenovo with the general public across the world (step 3 – target audiences).

Up to 2003, the corporate brand had furthermore been defined in emotional terms (step 4 – themed messages). The theme of dreaming, as a close association with imagination, had been the key brand proposition, with the overall tagline 'only if you dream'. With the acquisition of IBM, the Lenovo brand itself was redefined in more rational and straightforward terms around 'efficiency' and 'innovation', which it was felt, at the time, would differentiate the company from major low-cost players such as Dell and Acer who focus on supply chain efficiencies and inventory turnovers. Lenovo also believed that this combination set them apart from innovation-driven companies such as Sony and Apple. The Chief Marketing Officer reasoned that this corporate brand promise was in line with the culture and identity of the firm and as laid down in its mission statement: 'We put more innovation in the hands of more people so they can do more amazing things.' This understanding and definition of the corporate brand formed the basis for their corporate advertising and the tagline of 'Lenovo: for those who do'. The tagline is meant to communicate the innovation- and service-driven focus of the company to develop 'tools' which come to life and find a purpose in the hands of customers. The text of their more recent 2011 adverts, for example, reads 'We make the tools. You make them do. Lenovo, for those who do' (step 5 – develop message styles).

Telling the story

To implement this overall brand strategy, Lenovo planned a significant new Thinkpad product launch, but with a specific media strategy (step 6 – develop a media strategy). First, the company ran a worldwide advertising campaign in 2005 where every ad signed off with 'Thinkpad' instead of Lenovo. The objective was to focus on the product, to maintain Thinkpad sales momentum and to reassure existing and prospective customers that little had changed since the acquisition. The second campaign, 'Thinkpad unleashed', went one step further and ran during the Turin Winter Olympics opening ceremony in 2006. This gave it a huge global reach and broadcast the overall message that Lenovo was not just maintaining the status quo but making the Thinkpad even better than the original IBM product. It also empha- sized a focus on corporate and enterprise clients with the slogan 'carried by those who carry companies'. The advertising campaign sat alongside Lenovo's sponsor- ship deal for the Turin Winter Olympics, which strengthened its visibility and brand awareness. Lenovo's market research demonstrated afterwards that the sponsorship had given a major boost to the brand's reputation, primarily in China and Brazil. The third phase of the campaign built on this link to the corporate brand and stressed that the Lenovo brand stood for innovation. In 2005, Lenovo spent $250 million on worldwide marketing, with over 80 per cent spent on television and print advertising and the remainder allocated to the internet, outdoor and other media. However, rival companies such as Dell had a much greater share of voice, outspending Lenovo on marketing and communications in all the major markets around the world. In response, Lenovo has not increased its advertising and marketing budget to match its rivals (step 7 – prepare the budget), but has looked at sponsorship and public relations options to work primarily on awareness and brand image. Together with Ogilvy and Mather, the company created a $100 million campaign with online ads, television and print advertising around the 2008 Beijing Olympics. Lenovo has also provided PCs to microfinance organizations and to students with limited financial means. Yet, unaided awareness of the Lenovo brand is still low outside China, par- ticularly in major markets such as Germany, India and the USA. Whilst the company is now the largest PC maker worldwide, the recognition and knowledge of its brand by customers still lags. In addition, its increasing visibility as one of the world's lead- ing brands has led to increased expectations amongst its loyal customers. This was most recently demonstrated by the crisis that the company found itself in when its existing customers got angry about the adware software that had been installed on newly sold laptops. Such adware puts the privacy and security of customers at risk, as it allows hackers to easily steal encrypted data and passwords.

Questions for reflection

1   Reflect on the brand-building and communication efforts made to establish Lenovo as a global brand. What decisions made sense as part of the planning framework?
2   What do you think the company needs to do now to strengthen awareness of the brand and its reputation across the world? Can you describe a new cycle of activity for Lenovo to achieve this?

Source: Informed by Quelch, John A. and Knoop, Carin-Isabel (2006) 'Lenovo: Building a global brand', Harvard Business School Case 507-014, July; and lenovo.com

6.5 CHAPTER SUMMARY

The chapter has described the process and content of corporate communication strategy. The process refers to the different individuals and groups that are involved in strategy formation and the way in which they work together to shape and formulate a communication strategy. The content refers to the themed messages within corporate communication and the message styles that are adopted to communicate those messages to different stakeholders. The chapter combined these process and content dimensions as part of a planning model that can be used to specify and implement a communication strategy for an organization.

 ——— DISCUSSION QUESTIONS ———

1. What is the difference between a themed message and a message style?

2. Select an industry or sector with which you are familiar or that you have worked for in the past. Identify the themed messages and message styles used in messages released by organizations in this industry or sector. Are their communication strategies comparable or different? What might explain this similarity or difference?

3. Reflect on the stages of the planning model; in the current media environment (see Chapter 3), how flexible or agile do you think communication planning has to be?

KEY TERMS

Environmental scanning
Communication strategy
Corporate strategy
Emotional message style
Boundary spanning
Generic message style
Communication programme
Strategic planning
Omnichannel approach

Pre-emptive message style
Rational message style
Strategic intent
Symbolic association message style
Themed message
Vision
Campaign
'Zero-based' selection
Communication effects

 ——— FURTHER READING ———

Moss, Danny and DeSanto, Barbara (2012) *Public Relations: A Managerial Perspective*. London: Sage.
Smith, Ronald D. (2012) *Strategic Planning for Public Relations*. New York: Routledge, 4th edition.

Want to know more about this chapter? Visit the companion website at: https://study.sagepub.com/cornelissen5e to access videos, web links, a glossary and selected journal articles to further enhance your study.

NOTES

1. See, for instance, Mintzberg, H., Ahlstrand, B. and Lampel, J. (1998) *Strategy Safari: The Complete Guide through the Wilds of Strategic Management*. London: Prentice-Hall/ Financial Times.
2. Grunig, J.E. and Repper, F.C. (1992) 'Strategic management, publics and issues', in Grunig, J.E. (ed.), *Excellence in Public Relations and Communication Management*. Hillsdale, NJ: Lawrence Erlbaum, 122–23.
3. Argenti, P., Howell, R.A. and Beck, K.A. (2005) 'The strategic communication imperative', *MIT Sloan Management Review*, Spring, 83–9, quote on pp. 86–87.
4. Argenti et al. (2005).
5. Argenti et al. (2005).
6. USC Strategic Communication and Public Relations Centre (2010) survey on Communications and Public Relations General Accepted Practices (GAP).
7. Gronstedt, A. (2000) *The Customer Century: Lessons from World-class Companies in Integrated Marketing and Communications*. London: Routledge, quote on p. 203.
8. Based on Shimp, T.A. (2003) *Advertising, Promotion and Supplemental Aspects of Integrated Marketing Communications*. Fort Worth, TX: Dryden Press; Thompson, K.E. and Rindova, V. (2007) 'Starbucks: Constructing a multiplex identity in the specialty coffee industry', in Lerpold, L., Ravasi, D., Van Rekom, J. and Soenen, G. (eds), *Organizational Identity in Practice*. London: Routledge, 157–73.
9. Jones, J.P. (1992) *How Much is Enough?* New York: Lexington Books; Rossiter, J.R. and Danaher, P.J. (1998) *Advanced Media Planning*. Boston: Kluwer.
10. Van Ruler, B. (2015) 'Agile public relations planning: The Reflective Communication Scrum', *Public Relations Review*, 41, 187–94.

Research and Measurement

7

CHAPTER OVERVIEW

Research and evaluation is a cornerstone of a professional approach to corporate communication. Research helps in establishing the effects of corporate communication on the organization's reputation in the eyes of its stakeholders. It has an evaluative role in tracking changes in corporate reputation as well as an important formative role in suggesting the extent to which communication strategies are working and whether they may need to be revised. The chapter outlines principles and methods for research and evaluation within corporate communication, including methods for evaluating the effects of communication programmes and campaigns as well as standardized methods and metrics for measuring corporate reputations.

7.1 INTRODUCTION

Previous chapters have discussed the strategic role of corporate communication in developing and maintaining strong and favourable reputations with stakeholders upon whom the organization depends for its performance and survival. At the heart of this role lies an understanding of the fundamentals of reputation and of measuring any changes in such reputations to drive business strategy and communications. In strategically focused communication departments, senior communication managers use research as the bedrock for the formulation of communications objectives for the organization and to help formulate and design specific communication programmes and campaigns. Over the years, many communication experts and scholars have recognized the importance of research for corporate communication, both in a direct and an indirect sense. Research is of course, first of all, important to gather feedback on communication strategies and more generally to get a sense of the overall profile and reputation that is attributed to an organization. In this way, research gives a direct assessment, which will indicate whether objectives have been achieved and may also, in a more formative manner, guide communication practitioners to either reinforce or revamp their communications to stakeholders. Indirectly, research is important as it may improve the perception of the value of corporate communication in the eyes of chief executive officers (CEOs) and other senior managers in an organization. When corporate communication objectives and campaigns are directly informed by research, it suggests that the function is, like other functions in an organization, similarly focused on results and on the practicalities and demands of the business. Such perceptions, as an indirect effect of doing research – rather than relying on intuition or informal feedback alone – are important for corporate communication to secure a seat at the decision-making table and to make sure that research evidence and information about relations with priority stakeholders get factored into the process of decision-making and into any corporate strategies and actions.[1]

The purpose of this chapter is to discuss the practical issues around research, including applied methods for researching and evaluating the impact of particular communication strategies and standardized metrics for measuring corporate reputations. The first section of the chapter deals with research methods for researching the impact of communication programmes and campaigns and is focused on the direct outcomes of a specific planned set of messages. The subsequent section focuses on more general ways of measuring the reputation of an organization in the minds of stakeholders that are not specifically tied to any specific communication activity. Compared to specific programmes or campaigns at a specific point in time, this involves a more generalized evaluation which has been built up gradually. In other words, this section focuses on the general profile and reputation of an organization, and suggests issues to consider when planning and carrying out such research. These issues consist of what kinds of questions to ask during a research project, and the advantages and disadvantages of qualitative versus quantitative research methods.

Whilst most of the chapter is practical in orientation, the final section includes a discussion of the theory behind measuring communication effects. This particular section is more academic in focus, but provides helpful additional reading to understand the basic assumptions behind principles of research and evaluation in practice.

7.2 RESEARCH AND EVALUATION

Communication practitioners use research throughout the planning, execution and evaluation stages of a particular communication programme or campaign, as demonstrated in Figure 7.1. The way they use research changes as the programme or campaign evolves; practitioners may use pre-campaign, or formative, surveys, for example, to better understand the problems or issues they are aiming to address and to help in segmenting stakeholder audiences. They may also use focus groups to explore the feasibility of a campaign in terms of changing people's opinions regarding key issues or to help them pre-test or refine message strategies. Increasingly, communication practitioners are also making use of social media as a way of experimenting

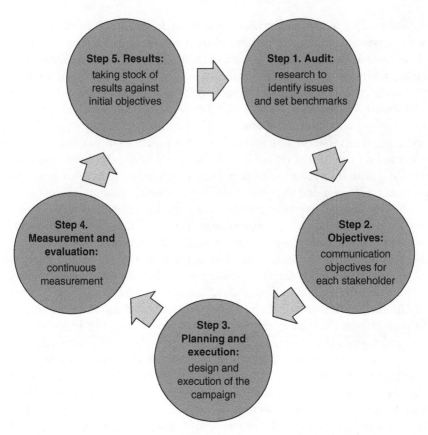

FIGURE 7.1   Research and evaluation as part of communication campaigns

with and testing the reception of key messages (in terms of wording, visuals and format) before rolling them out to broader audiences. In addition, afterwards and once a programme or campaign has run, research provides important benchmarks against which results achieved by the programme or campaign can be measured. Using research throughout the planning process thus helps in delivering results and in improving on past performance, but, as mentioned, it also gives much needed credibility with other senior managers in the organization. Organizations of course are looking for a concrete return on investment and research gives them an indication of what communication is contributing to the organization and its objectives in light of the budget and resources invested in corporate communication.

At its most basic level, research simply is about collecting information, and practitioners can use a number of methods to gather information, each with their own strengths and weaknesses. One basic form of research that is often used, even unwittingly, is informal research which consists of casual interactions with key stakeholders or experts to define issues and to get a better understanding of any problems informing a communication programme or activity. The main disadvantage of informal research is that it may not be a systematic effort across stakeholder groups and is likely to be unrepresentative. Any information therefore may be subject to biases, in terms of who was asked (and who was not), which may seriously undermine the ability to draw strong conclusions from the information gathered. Formal research methods include more systematic data-gathering methods that are set up for the purpose at hand (e.g. finding out about a problem or issue) and are sensitive to issues of representativeness in sampling stakeholders. These methods include, for example, focus groups, surveys and content analyses. A focus group is a semi-structured group discussion facilitated by a researcher whereby the researcher tries to dig deep into the underlying motivations around an issue or a problem. Focus group sessions are taped or recorded and the recorded data (i.e. verbal transcripts or audio-visual recordings) are analysed using qualitative methods, which basically means that researchers interpret responses instead of trying to count them. Surveys are structured questionnaires which are sent to a representatively sampled part of a population, such as customers or employees. Survey methods are quantitative in nature; the attempt is to record in numbers the level of awareness, attitudes or behaviours of the population in relation to certain issues or circumstances. Such methods may also be analytical in nature when there is an attempt to explain why certain circumstances, attitudes and behaviours exist amongst members of a specific population. Advanced forms of statistical analyses (e.g. statistical regressions) are then used to test hypotheses concerning relationships amongst a group of variables under study. In many cases, surveys serve both descriptive and analytical purposes, for example to profile and describe the characteristics of customers (descriptive) and to explain their consumption behaviour (analytical). Content analysis, as another formal research method, is a scientific method used for describing communication content in a quantitative, or numerical, form. Many practitioners use content analysis to monitor and track media coverage of issues and of organizations. Such analyses are often carried out with the use of statistical software packages for the coding and tabulation of news coverage in terms of frequency of coverage and the overall tone or sentiment (favourable versus unfavourable) of the reporting.

As already mentioned, a key suggestion is that research and evaluation should be an integral part of the planning process for communication programmes or campaigns. The entire sequence, with research and evaluation at the heart of it, is broken down into five stages. Figure 7.1 displays the planning cycle.

The stages of the cycle are as follows:

Audit: this stage consists of taking stock of and analysing existing data, with research being used to identify issues as well as to create benchmarks. This stage is often also called formative research, which is the data on which practitioners will build their communication programme or campaign.

Objectives: this stage involves setting objectives that follow from the audit, and in line with the organization's general business objectives. Objectives are broken down by stakeholder audience and timescale, and are specified in measurable terms. Objectives are often specified in terms of any changes in awareness, attitude and behaviour of stakeholders that an organization aims for.

Planning and execution: this stage involves deciding on the design and execution of the programme or campaign, which may involve a pre-testing of messages and of the choice of media channels and tactics.

Measurement and evaluation: this stage is the first of several possible types of programme or campaign measurement, or continuous measurement. During the programme or campaign, communication practitioners can ask themselves whether they are getting the desired results, or whether the campaign needs to be adjusted. This may involve monitoring the execution and any costs associated with it as well as taking stock of the initial results achieved.

Results: the final stage involves an assessment of the overall post-programme or post-campaign results, and identifying any potential issues or learning points that may inform the audit stage and a new cycle of activity.

A good example of this cycle, with research and measurement providing a valuable input into communication campaigns, is that of FedEx (Case Example 7.1). The company extensively surveyed stakeholder opinion on a re-alignment of its operations and a new branded structure, with the survey results informing communications aimed at specific stakeholder groups.

 CASE EXAMPLE 7.1

FEDEX: FROM A PORTFOLIO OF BRANDS TO A SINGLE COMPANY

FedEx was founded in 1973 as an overnight delivery company. It has since established itself as a leading company in global air transportation, securing a strong reputation for service and reliability. The company faced some stiff competition from rival UPS and several novel ventures in the express carrier market during the 1990s. In addition, FedEx acquired Caliber Systems – which included a suite of logistics and express companies – in the late 1990s. Both these developments triggered the need within the FedEx corporation to rethink its corporate brand and communication. In particular, there was the belief that rather than slowly assimilating these companies whilst keeping marketing activities separate, customers increasingly requested a 'one-stop' transportation interface – a single point of contact with the same company. In January 2000, FedEx responded and rolled out a single corporate brand across all its operating companies. The company name was badged on all its services and operations, with sub-brands such as FedEx Express for express services and FedEx Freight for less-than-truckload services. Whilst the structural alignment within FedEx and the choice for a monolithic brand made a lot of sense, strategically stakeholders were initially not convinced. Media journalists were sceptical of the new structure and questioned its viability, employees continued to identify with their own operational units and financial analysts felt that the new structure did not provide additional synergies over the model of having a portfolio of separate brands and companies.

Bill Margaritis, the Vice President for Corporate Communication at the time, aimed to address these stakeholder opinions through a campaign that set out to gain recognition for the new business model and that would also help in creating acceptance and support across stakeholder groups. Before the campaign was developed, Margaritis and his team carried out extensive research on the current awareness of, and attitude towards, the new FedEx structure (step 1: audit). They surveyed employees, journalists and financial analysts, who each expressed a lack of understanding and even scepticism about the new model. Margaritis used these research findings to develop change communication programmes internally that would create understanding of the new structure (steps 2 and 3: objectives, planning and execution). The research also led them to intensify their efforts to convince journalists and financial analysts of the advantages of the new structure and to demonstrate to them some early successes.

The themes for the change campaign, which was labelled as 'The Change Ahead', and for the exchanges with journalists and analysts came directly out of the initial research study. For the media, for example, Margaritis felt that it would be key to demonstrate the positives of the new structure and to nip any negative rumours in the bud - a point that had been drawn out by the initial survey. He therefore set up a system for educating the media. Margaritis and his team identified an inner circle of media contacts and conducted personal briefings with these journalists to forge and strengthen relationships with them and to reinforce messaging and reduce any gaps in understanding. They also set up a 'FedEx Truth Squad', analogous to political campaign tactics. This squad monitored the media coverage of FedEx in real time and kicked into action when inaccuracies or negative news were reported, which were then immediately corrected or challenged. Continuous measurement during and after the initial communication efforts (step 4: measurement and evaluation) demonstrates that media coverage turned increasingly supportive of the new business model. The Truth Squad had done its job effectively; few inaccuracies about the new structure had been reported. Employees demonstrated an improved understanding of how the new structure worked. Customer successes proved the merits of the business model and the power of having an integrated brand. The FedEx brand has since gone from strength to strength; since 2001 FedEx has been ranked amongst the top 100 global brands (in the Brand Finance and Interbrand rankings) and is also recognized for its strong corporate reputation (as measured by the Reputation Institute) (step 5: results). In turn, when the company had such positive news to tell, this informed a new cycle of activity; FedEx, for example, released a series of global ads in 2002 that celebrated the company's achievements and reputational accolades and which recognized the importance of FedEx employees.

Question for reflection

Reflect on the research and planning cycle (Figure 7.1) and how it was used within FedEx. Could the same results have been achieved without research informing their messaging along the way?

Source: This case study draws on a presentation delivered by Bill Margaritis at the Institute for Public Relations' 2010 Annual Distinguished Lecture and Awards Dinner, New York City, November.

The advantage of seeing research and evaluation as part of a cycle of interrelated activities is of course that each cycle of activity can be more effective than the preceding cycle if the results of evaluation are used to make adjustments to a programme or campaign, or even to future communication efforts. In addition, it also draws attention to research and evaluation at different stages of the cycle: before the planning and execution of a programme or campaign, during its implementation, and of course in terms of assessing its overall results after the programme or campaign. Evaluation is here broadly defined as the use of research for informing and assessing the conceptualization, design, execution and effects of communication programmes or campaigns. In the audit stage, research consists of gathering data on an issue in order to inform the development of a programme or campaign. Such research may involve gathering data through informal contacts with stakeholders, colleagues or experts and examining any available secondary data (e.g. past surveys) to get a sense of the issues. If necessary, practitioners may decide to conduct primary research, as in the example of FedEx (see above), to get to a more detailed understanding of the issues with each stakeholder group. During the planning and preparation of the programme or campaign, practitioners may pre-test the appropriateness of messages and the way in which such messages are presented. Reputation expert Charles Fombrun proposes that companies systematically map and audit their 'messaging profile'; that is, how their corporate image is projected and communicated through print, visual, video and web-based communications.[2] The execution or implementation of the programme or campaign in turn is associated with continuous measurement and evaluation of the outputs in terms of, for example, the amount of on- and off-line media coverage received or the number of stakeholders who have received or attended to the messages and activities. In this stage, the monitoring of such output effects may lead to real-time adjustments in the course of the programme or campaign. Finally, in the results stage, research and evaluation attempt to establish the actual outcomes in terms of awareness, attitude and behavioural changes achieved by a programme or an activity. Here, research and evaluation go one step further in moving from outputs (e.g. the amount of media coverage as established through newspaper clippings) to outcomes (e.g. the number of people who have changed their opinions and who behave towards the organization as desired). The entire sequence of effects is displayed in Figure 7.2.

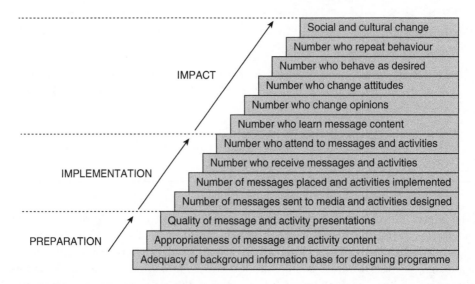

FIGURE 7.2   Stages and levels of evaluation

Increasingly, communication practitioners recognize the value of measuring outcomes over outputs. The so-called Barcelona Principles 2015 for communication measurement highlight measuring outcomes (rather than outputs) as a key principle, or best practice, for the industry and profession.[3] The reasoning behind this principle is that outputs do not capture closely enough what really has changed in stakeholders' behaviour as a result of a programme or campaign. Outputs are, in other words, only a 'proxy' and may help practitioners guess the impact of their programme or campaign, but are simply just that: good guesses. The Barcelona Principles therefore advise against relying only on proxy measures, such as using the 'advertising value equivalent' or AVE (i.e. the amount of on- and off-line coverage received in relation to a campaign or an event, measured in terms of equivalent advertising spend). Whilst the AVE or any other output proxy (e.g. followers on Twitter, likes on Facebook) may provide a rough way of guessing the effects of communication, truly researching outcomes instead requires primary research through focus groups, content analysis and surveys, in order to determine, with a higher degree of accuracy, the strengths of the effects that have been achieved with a programme or campaign.

7.3 METHODS AND MEASURES

At the 'impact' level (Figure 7.2), research focuses on the number of people in the target audience who have seen the message, digested its contents, and have in turn changed their views of and behaviours towards the organization in a favourable way. Routinely carrying out research on impact, or overall effects, is crucially important for communication practitioners in order to evaluate whether their communication programmes and campaigns are effective.

Table 7.1 describes a number of research methods that communication practitioners can use for such effects research. These methods vary in terms of whether they involve qualitative or quantitative methods. Qualitative methods are 'open' in their design, in that with such methods practitioners invite respondents to describe an organization in their own words, which generally leads to rich descriptions and insights. Quantitative methods, on the other hand, are more closed techniques of data collection and analysis and ask respondents to rate the organization and its campaigns on a set of pre-defined questions and scales. The advantage of such structured or closed techniques is that it facilitates comparison across respondents and allows practitioners to more easily generalize an overall picture of the effects of a programme or campaign.

1. *Interviews*: this method involves open interviews with individuals from the targeted audience for a programme or campaign where they are asked to reflect on their perceptions of the organization and their views of the recent programme or campaign. These kinds of interviews are typically semi-structured, in that the researcher aims to ask a number of general questions about campaign elements, but also leave ample space for the respondent to articulate their views in detail and without interruption. The responses can then be further content-analysed to document general interpretations and the associations arising from the campaign as a way of determining its

TABLE 7.1 Corporate reputation research methods

Methodology	Techniques	Data collection	Number of respondents	Ease of analysis	Costs
Qualitative	Unstructured interview	Oral interview: each respondent is asked to reflect on their views of an organization and explain why (with or without use of visual aids)	10-40	Moderate/Low	Moderate
	Focus group	Group discussion: in a group, respondents discuss their views of the organization and explain why (with or without use of visual aids)	5-10 (each group)	High	Moderate
	Repertory grid	Oral interview: each respondent is asked to pick two out of three statements which match the organization best or worst and explain why. These are subsequently grouped in sets that compare the organization on certain attributes to other firms	10-40	Moderate	Low
	Laddering	Oral interview: each respondent is asked to reflect on beliefs about the organization aimed at discovering means-ends relations (e.g. why an individual assigns a certain reputation to a firm)	10-25	Low	High
Quantitative	Survey	Questionnaire: respondent ratings of attributes of the firm and its overall reputation based on Likert scales	50 or more	Moderate/ High	Moderate

overall effect. The advantage of the interview method is that it is tuned to individual respondents and allows them to answer freely. The downside is that the method is quite time-consuming and it may accordingly be difficult to get a big enough sample of respondents.

2. *Focus group*: this method consists of bringing together an entire group of people from the target audience who are asked to share their views on an organization and in relation to a recent communication programme or campaign. At the beginning of the session, individuals are asked to articulate their general views of the organization. This part of the session is a brainstorming exercise, so there are no true or false answers regarding the associations and attributes that are mentioned. After this brainstorming session, they are shown examples from the communication programme or campaign and asked whether this changed or reinforced their views. The change in perceptions can then be visually captured in a diagram or figure. The method is very easily carried out and has the advantage that the practitioner gets a great deal of in-depth insights into the way in which individuals perceived the campaign or programme, and compared to their prior views of the organization. The obvious limitations of a focus group are that it only captures the views of a limited group of people and may, at times, lead to biased effects where the research setting cues more positive responses in the group.

3. *Survey*: this is a more structured and quantitative research design. With a survey, respondents are asked to record their views of the organization and its recent campaigns based on a set of pre-specified questions. Respondents are asked to respond to various statements describing the campaign. The respondent then indicates to what extent they agree or disagree with each statement. The advantage of surveys is a larger sample of respondents and surveys also allows practitioners to measure responses explicitly and in a quantitative manner, which enables statistical analysis and comparison across respondents. Surveys are also easy to administer, but may in comparison not be able to capture the richness and detail of more open methods.

4. *Panel study*: panel studies are a type of longitudinal study that permits practitioners to collect data over time. Panel studies typically involve the same method of data collection as surveys, but are different in terms of the research design. Panel studies record changes in each sample member over time, and as a result of exposure to programmes or campaigns, typically by having the same participants complete questionnaires. Surveys, on the other hand, are cross-sectional in nature, meaning that they provide an immediate picture of participants' views as they currently exist, but provide little information on how those views were formed or change over time. A strength of panel studies, in other words, is that they allow practitioners to track changes over time and to document the effectiveness of particular programmes or campaigns in changing or reinforcing the views of the target audience. The downside is that a panel study is quite labour-intensive, and is therefore typically outsourced to market research agencies who conduct such research on a company's behalf.

Besides choosing a particular method, communication practitioners also need to determine what general effects form the basis of their research and evaluation. This obviously follows from the initial objectives of the campaign and whether the anticipated effects were cognitive, such as awareness and knowledge of the organization; affective, including liking the campaign and the way in which it invokes certain emotions; or behavioural, in stimulating certain behavioural actions in the target audience. A key issue here is to define these effects in precise terms in order to tease out how they may be connected and may have led to a net result in the minds and behaviours of the target audience. For example, practitioners may want to identify whether a campaign raised awareness of the positioning of the company in the minds of the target audience. Awareness could then be measured in an aided or unaided way (i.e. priming the respondent about the company, or not), and in relation to other companies. A practitioner may then in turn analyse whether any changes in awareness had a knock-on effect in terms of greater knowledge about the company or even a more favourable position towards the company. In other instances, practitioners may be focused on specific behavioural effects, such as whether a programme or campaign has increased customer loyalty and the so-called net promoter score (NPS). An NPS is the degree to which a customer is likely to recommend a company or its products and services to a friend, colleague or anyone else in their social environment. The score can be calculated based on responses to an administered survey that directly asks the question on a Likert scale or by identifying the recommendations that were made in social media networks such as Twitter and Facebook.

Generally speaking, being precise about the effect or effects that are of interest, and about how such effects can be measured, is crucial. Some effects are based on directly identifiable or observable variables, such as the net promoter score, which is one single question that can be asked in a survey. Similarly, effects such as online sentiments are discrete variables and can therefore often be automatically tracked with a sentiment analysis. Other effects, however, relate to broader concepts or constructs, such as a company's trust, legitimacy or reputation. These effects are typically a composite of more specific cognitive, emotional and behavioural variables. Trust, for example, depends on knowledge and a strong emotional affect, such that a member of the target audience is willing to commit him- or herself to an organization. The public relations scholar Jim Grunig, for example, identifies trust as both cognitive – with individuals having the knowledge and belief that an organization has the ability to do what it says it will do – and affective – with individuals perceiving the organization as fair and just and as reliable in doing what it promises to do. Similarly, legitimacy is a multi-dimensional construct that involves the degree to which individuals know about an organization, are familiar with its position and activities, and accept its position as in line with taken-for-granted values, norms and expectations about its industry. Legitimacy, in other words, involves cognitive effects around awareness and knowledge, as well as social judgments of the appropriateness of a company's actions when evaluated against its nearest rivals. The next section focuses in more detail on the construct and measurement of corporate reputation, which is similarly a broader concept rather than a single variable.

7.4 MEASURING CORPORATE REPUTATION

Research and evaluation can be used to inform specific communication programmes or campaigns. Although it may be used throughout the cycle of planning a programme or campaign, as we have seen, the scope of such research is often confined to a particular programme of activity or campaign. As such, it is often defined as a one-time study, focused on and limited to a particular communication activity at a particular point in time.

At the same time, many communication practitioners continuously measure reputations with stakeholders to understand what stakeholders think of an organization, whether this is in line with the projected corporate identity of the organization, and whether the organization is generally accepted and valued. This kind of research is not limited to a particular campaign or activity, but is carried out on a continuous basis to gauge stakeholder support for the organization. As such, it is more general in scope; it is focused on the general profile, or reputation, that the organization enjoys in the minds of stakeholders, rather than being tied to a particular activity such as a programme or communication campaign.

Communication practitioners also carry out this kind of reputational research to find out what values the company is known and respected for and indeed whether the projected values in communication, symbolism and behaviour are actually salient in the minds of stakeholders. This will provide them with an important strategic indication as to whether the company's identity is at all valued and whether it has been successfully communicated. In the first scenario, when a company's identity in itself is not valued enough, managers may want to redefine their organization, strategies and operations with values that do matter to stakeholders and make a difference in the marketplace (Chapter 5). In the second scenario, when an identity is not effectively communicated or understood, management needs to rethink the company's stakeholder engagement programmes and the visibility and effectiveness of the communication campaigns that it has previously used (Chapter 6). Getting feedback from reputation research is, in other words, an important step in the process of developing and refining corporate communication strategies, including stakeholder engagement and communication programmes.

Such feedback can be gathered through two broad types of reputation research: (a) publicly syndicated rankings and (b) company-specific reputation research. Table 7.2 provides a summary of two publicly syndicated international reputation rankings. Besides these two well-known international rankings, companies are also frequently ranked in the countries in which they operate in national rankings of the 'best employers' or the 'strongest brands' or corporate reputations in a particular country.[4] Such publicly syndicated rankings are performed annually by various research firms or media organizations and involve a standardized comparison between firms. These rankings are also typically set up as panel studies (see above) so as to gauge changes in the reputations of firms over time. These kinds of syndicated rankings enjoy popularity with managers but have obvious limitations in that they often fail to account for the views of multiple stakeholder groups, and appear to be primarily tapping a firm's visibility in a particular setting and its financial performance and assets.

The Fortune reputation ranking, for instance, is known for its financial bias and the high correlation between all of the measure's nine (previously eight) attributes. This means that these nine attributes produce, when factor analysed, one factor, so that a company tends to rate high, average or low on all nine attributes.[5] These publicly syndicated rankings converge on a number of areas, including financial performance, product quality, employee treatment, community involvement, environmental performance and a range of other organizational issues (such as supporting equality of opportunity and diversity, good environmental performance, improved ethical behaviour, and so on) (Table 7.2). But these rankings do not take into account that stakeholder opinions vary and that stakeholder groups attend to very different cues when forming an opinion of an organization. Some stakeholder groups would not be at all interested in some of these areas or would in any case not rate them in their evaluation of the company. Furthermore, the distinctive values that a company may project, and that are extracted from its organizational identity or corporate personality, are not necessarily captured by these publicly syndicated measures.

When communication practitioners plan to set up their own company-specific reputation research, they need to be conscious of the fact that a corporate reputation is not just a general impression but an evaluation of the firm by stakeholders. According to reputation expert Charles Fombrun, a corporate reputation is 'a perceptual representation of a company's past actions and future prospects that describe the firm's overall appeal to all of its key constituents when compared to

TABLE 7.2 Corporate reputation rankings

	Fortune's 'most admired corporations'	Reputation Institute's RepTrak Pulse
Method and sample	Annual survey of over 10,000 senior executives, outside directors and financial analysts	Annual survey of a large sample of consumers (approx. 60,000) who are asked to evaluate the 600 largest companies in the world
Measure	Ranking is based on the compilation of assessments given by respondents of the ten largest companies in their own industry on nine criteria of 'excellence'	Ranking is based on averaging perceptions of trust, esteem, admiration and good feeling obtained from a representative sample of 100 local respondents who are familiar with the company
Attributes included	Quality of management, quality of products and services, innovativeness, long-term investment value, financial soundness, ability to attract, develop and keep talented people, responsibility to the community and the environment, wise use of corporate assets, global acumen	Four attributes: trust, esteem, admiration and good feeling about a company (as reflections of the company's performance, quality of products and services, innovative ability, care for employees, governance, corporate social responsibility and professional leadership)

other leading rivals'.[6] Whereas corporate images concern the immediate impressions of individual stakeholders when they are faced with a message that comes from an organization, reputations are more endurable evaluations that are established over time. Theoretically, a corporate image may be defined as the immediate set of associations of an individual in response to one or more messages from or about a particular organization. In other words, it is the net result of the interaction of a subject's beliefs, ideas, feelings and impressions about an organization at a single point in time. Corporate reputation can be defined as a subject's collective representation of past images of an organization (induced through either communication or past experiences) that is established over time. Images might vary in time due to differing perceptions, but reputations are more likely to be relatively inert or constant, as individuals and stakeholders retain their assessment of an organization built in over time. Gray and Balmer, two academics, illustrate this distinction between the image and reputation constructs:

> Corporate image is the immediate mental picture that audiences have of an organization. Corporate reputations, on the other hand, typically evolve over time as a result of consistent performance, reinforced by effective communication, whereas corporate images can be fashioned more quickly through well-conceived communication programmes.[7]

These properties of the reputation construct provide the basis for developing operational measures and for surveying opinions of important stakeholder groups. First of all, the time dimension (as reputation is an established perception over time) needs to be factored into the measurement process by having respondents evaluate a company (*vis-à-vis* its nearest rivals) *generally* instead of having them reflect on a single instant (e.g. a crisis) or image (e.g. a campaign) in relation to that company. Second, reputation is a perceptual construct, so simple proxy measures of the assets, performance or output of a particular organization will not be enough. And third, measurement and also the sampling of respondents need to account for the various attributes upon which an organization is rated by different stakeholder groups.

Different types of research techniques may be used to gather reputational data. These techniques can be used when a company does not buy into a panel study such as the RepTrak Pulse but aims to set up and conduct reputation research of its own with its own stakeholder groups. In doing so, the aim of a company will be to account for the diversity of opinions of its stakeholder groups and to gain a clearer view of the attributes that these different groups actually find important and rate the organization on. Table 7.3 displays the two broad classes of research techniques, qualitative and quantitative, that may be used either separately or in combination for such reputation research.

Qualitative research, such as in-depth interviews with individual stakeholders or focus group sessions with selected groups of stakeholders, is one option. These qualitative techniques are more open in nature; they allow selected stakeholders to delve into their associations with the organization as they see them. This usually provides very rich and anecdotal data of stakeholder views of the company. Quantitative research, where stakeholders are asked to rate the organization (and its nearest rivals)

TABLE 7.3   Research methods for campaign evaluation

Method	Research design	Data collection	Ease of collection and analysis	Costs
Interviews	Qualitative	Open interviews	High	Low-moderate
Focus group	Qualitative	Brainstorm session	Moderate	Low-moderate
Survey	Quantitative	Questionnaire	High	Low-moderate
Panel study	Quantitative	Questionnaire	Moderate	Moderate

on a number of pre-selected attributes, is another option. Quantitative research leads to more discrete data that can be statistically manipulated, but is less rich and may also be less insightful (i.e. it reflects to a lesser extent the particular lens of the individual stakeholder). The choice of either qualitative or quantitative research techniques is based on content issues as well as pragmatic and political considerations. Qualitative techniques are chosen when the attributes upon which an organization is rated are simply not yet known, or when there is a need for a comprehensive, detailed and rich account of stakeholders' perceptions of and associations with the organization. Quantitative surveys are preferred when the attributes upon which an organization is rated are to a large extent known, allowing for a structured measurement across large sections of stakeholder groups. Many organizations also opt for quantitative surveys as these are relatively easy to administer and process and as they provide them with a 'tangible' indication (that is, a number). Figure 7.3 illustrates the reputations of two organizations through an attribute rating that produces such numerical values. A 'tangible' indication is also one of the motives for organizations to buy into panel studies such as the RepTrak Pulse, which provides practitioners with a score that they can work with and sets a benchmark for future years.

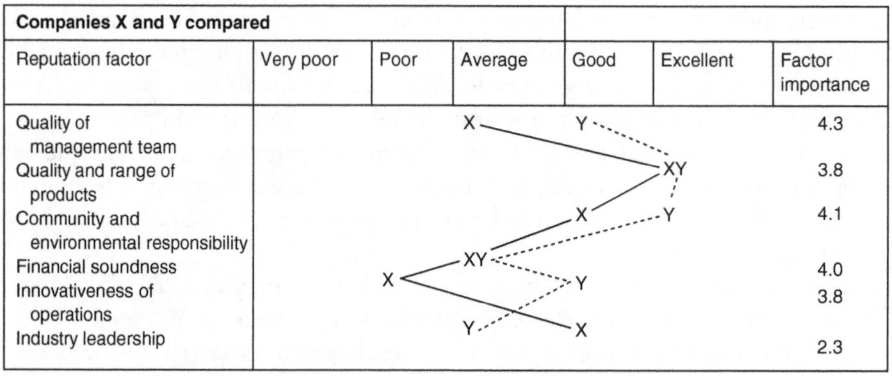

Companies X and Y compared						
Reputation factor	Very poor	Poor	Average	Good	Excellent	Factor importance
Quality of management team			X	Y		4.3
Quality and range of products					XY	3.8
Community and environmental responsibility				X	Y	4.1
Financial soundness		X	XY	Y		4.0
Innovativeness of operations						3.8
Industry leadership			Y	X		2.3

FIGURE 7.3   The corporate reputation of two companies compared

7.5 THEORIES ON MEASURING THE EFFECTS OF COMMUNICATION

Historically, communication scholars have thought in different ways about the effects of communication. At the start of the twentieth century, the mass media were assumed to be omnipotent in their effect – messages, once communicated, were directly consumed and acted on by willing audiences. In the 1950s and 1960s, mass communication experts changed quite radically in their assessment as they noticed that, on closer examination, mass media campaigns were having little effect. One belief at that time was that campaigns often simply reinforced existing beliefs or attitudes, rather than changing an audience's attitudes or behaviours. In the early 1970s, Mendelsohn stepped into the fray with a more realistic diagnosis of effects and a more optimistic prognosis for communication practitioners.[8] He simply believed that both sides had some truth to them; campaigns often failed because communicators overpromised, assumed audiences would automatically receive and accept messages, and blanketed audiences with messages that were not properly targeted and therefore likely to be ignored or misinterpreted. Mendelsohn's claims still appear to hold today; most campaigns fail these days because they overpromise or because they are insufficiently tuned to a particular target audience. Mendelsohn also offered a very helpful prescription for communicators: target your messages and set reasonable goals and objectives that are not only achievable but demonstrate a sound knowledge of the current levels of awareness, beliefs and behaviours of your target audience.

Essentially, at the heart of Mendelsohn's recommendations is a critique of traditional linear models of communication and communication effects. McGuire, another communication scholar, suggested a receiver-oriented view as an alternative, commonly known as the hierarchy of effects theory of persuasion.[9] The model is based on the assumption that campaign messages have to achieve several intermediate steps before a member of a target audience moves from exposure to a message to actual desired behavioural changes (see back to Figure 6.2). Exposure is of course a necessary step for any effect on a target audience, but exposure may not automatically assume attention to the message. A message must attract at least a basic level of attention to succeed, and this implies that communicators need to be clear about the messages and the message style, and need to design messages in such a way that they attract attention. This may involve particular visuals such as colours and positive images, which may draw in the audience, as well as simple, catchy or counter-intuitive phrases. At the same time, although people will orient themselves to messages with appealing sounds and visual effects, research has shown that they may stop paying attention if a message seems irrelevant or uninteresting to them. Messages that come across as relevant will sustain attention and will trigger the interest or involvement of the target audience. Any change in attitude or behaviour towards a company, in turn, then requires a sustained number of reinforcing messages. In particular, being motivated to take certain supportive behaviours towards an organization, say of buying products or shares, often requires a series of messages or a specific set of convincing reasons to follow through. The benefits offered in a message, whether functional or emotional, essentially need to outweigh the cost, and must seem realistic and easy to obtain. McGuire's greatest insight was to suggest that the effectiveness of messages depends on audience factors and on different stages leading up to any change in behaviour, as the ultimate effect. With this hierarchy of effects, he also suggested a way for communicators to calculate the attrition rate, moving from exposure effects to attention, interest and attitude to behavioural effects. This brings a certain sense of realism to the process of understanding and measuring effects. Communication practitioners and public relations agencies often want to assume that exposure will produce success in terms of reputation, and often focus on exposure or output measures such as the mentioned advertising value equivalent. However, the likelihood of continued success along each step is probably far less than they assume. McGuire estimated a drop of 50 per cent with each step from sending a message out to exposure to, in turn, the desired behavioural effects, making the final outcome only a fraction of the original number of the target audience that was originally exposed to the campaign (see Figure 7.4). The theory has found its uses as a campaign planning tool amongst communication professionals and agencies. The public relations agency Ketchum, for example, uses a communication effectiveness yardstick, fashioned in the image of the hierarchy of effects model.

The hierarchy of effects model has, however, a basic limitation: it incorporates the assumption that recipients of a campaign will process messages in a logical way, carefully considering the message in a rational manner to decide whether they wish to perform the proposed behaviour. Of course, people do not always act rationally, and indeed some messages and message styles appeal to emotions or symbolic values and associations. Two alternative theoretical models have therefore since gained ground as another way of looking at communication effects. Both models

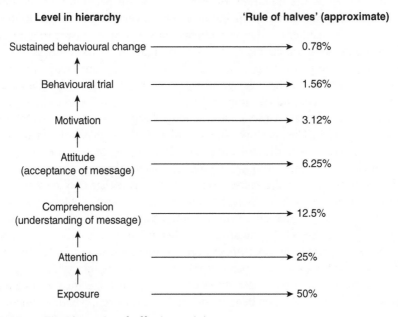

FIGURE 7.4   The hierarchy of effects model

allow for other kinds of appeals beyond logical or rational appeals, and both also recognize the importance of prior beliefs and involvement with an issue or a topic as a critical factor that determines success.

The first alternative to the hierarchy of effects theory is the elaboration likelihood model (ELM).[10] According to ELM, people process messages differently depending on their involvement with an issue. Those people who are interested will be more involved and will elaborate on a message in detail, whereas those with less interest will not process messages deeply. The result is that persuasion may be designed as following one of two possible routes:

1. The first central route emphasizes logical and careful consideration, or systematic processing. This route is desirable if a target audience can be reached easily and when the audience has a moderate to high degree of involvement with an issue or with the organization in question. The effect may also be more sustained, providing that audience members agree with the conclusions once they have systematically processed the message.

2. The second, peripheral, route, on the other hand, forgoes logical arguments in favour of more emotionally or heuristically based strategies of processing. With this route, an audience simply short-circuits the processing of the message to their own beliefs or interests, which may range from logical elements of the content of the message to the presentation and other factors associated with a message, such as the attractiveness or likeability of the message or the credibility of the media source. The effect of the peripheral route may be less pronounced long-term, although it may achieve changes more quickly because it requires less thoughtful consideration.

The second alternative effects model, that of framing, comes from research in anthropology and linguistics, which found their way into communication science.[11] The earliest work on framing traces back six decades to Gregory Bateson, an anthropologist, and also to the sociologist Erving Goffman, who both described words and nonverbal interactions as intimating larger culturally rooted frames which help individuals interpret messages through the lens of existing cultural beliefs and worldviews. In the 1970s, cognitive psychologists Daniel Kahneman and Amos Tversky continued this line of thinking and studied framing in experimental designs to understand risk judgments and consumer choices.[12] They found that the different ways in which a message is presented or framed – apart from the content itself – can result in very different responses, depending on the terminology used to describe the problem or the visual context provided in the message. In a nutshell, models of framing assume that messages consist of three parts: the activation of an overall frame in terms of certain keywords of formulations, the manifest or latent reasoning or arguments as part of that frame, and the connection with deeper and culturally shared categories of understanding that supports and legitimizes the framing as a whole. A good example of the way in which framing works is how climate change has been framed within public and policy debates. Some politicians and corporate executives, for example, have referred to climate change as scientifically uncertain and hence as not warranting any drastic or immediate policy actions. Others have framed the topic as essentially conflicting with the goal of economic growth and progress; any actions to curtail current levels of consumption, for example, would hurt economic activity including jobs. Scientists and environmental advocates, on the other hand, have framed climate change as a real immediate crisis and about doing the right thing (morality); in other words, even if the science cannot fully predict how the effects of global warming will work out, we need to do something collectively, and sooner rather than later, to avoid leaving the world in a poorer state for future generations. Essentially, the same issue is framed in different ways, and in doing so these messages attempt to appeal to underlying cultural associations and beliefs. For communicators who wish to break through the communication barriers of partisan identity and cultural beliefs, messages need to be tailored to a specific medium and audience, using carefully researched metaphors, allusions and examples that trigger a new way of thinking about the personal relevance of issues such as climate change. Framing, in other words, is about selecting and highlighting certain dimensions of an issue, and as such giving it higher salience and relevance than alternative readings. To make sense of issues, audiences use frames provided by organizations and the media as interpretive shortcuts, but integrate these framed presentations with pre-existing interpretations forged through personal experience, ideology and beliefs, as well as their social identity. Framing, in other words, is about convincing an audience through a particular highlighted interpretation and arguments, as well as by appealing to underlying cultural values or beliefs.

7.6 CHAPTER SUMMARY

The chapter has outlined practical issues and principles around research and measurement, including methods associated with programme- and campaign-based research and evaluation as well as methods for measuring corporate reputations. One important distinction that was made is between one-time studies of effects after a programme or campaign and standardized benchmarking studies of the reputation of an organization, which essentially measures stakeholder evaluations that have been built up over time. Research on both programmes and campaigns and general corporate reputations is useful for practitioners to guide and inform the formulation of communication strategies and their choice of messages (Chapter 6) and, more generally, to demonstrate the effectiveness of communication in changing stakeholder opinions and their support of the organization.

—— —— DISCUSSION QUESTIONS ——

1. Describe the advantages of using quantitative versus qualitative methods for evaluating the outcomes of a particular communication programme or campaign. On what basis would you choose the one over the other type of method?

2. What are the main weaknesses of Fortune's well-known ranking of corporate reputations?

3. What is the difference between the concepts of corporate image and corporate reputation?

4. Pick a number of corporate brands with strong reputations. Which one of the presented communication effects models (hierarchy of effects, elaboration likelihood model, framing) best describes your responses to the campaigns and messages around each of these brands?

KEY TERMS

One-time studies	Focus group
Benchmark studies	Laddering
Qualitative methods	Informal techniques
Corporate identity	Publicly syndicated rankings
Corporate image	Repertory grid
Quantitative methods	Formative evaluation
Corporate reputation	Formal techniques
Elaboration likelihood model	Hierarchy of effects
Framing	Communication effects

 FURTHER READING

Cutlip, S.M., Center, A.H. and Broom, G.H. (2012) *Effective Public Relations*. London: Prentice-Hall, 11th edition.

Stacks, Don and Michaelson, David (2010) *A Practitioner's Guide to Public Relations Research, Measurement and Evaluation*. New York: Business Expert Press.

Want to know more about this chapter? Visit the companion website at: https://study.sagepub.com/cornelissen5e to access videos, web links, a glossary and selected journal articles to further enhance your study.

NOTES

1. See, for example, Lauzen, M.M. (1995) 'Public relations manager involvement in strategic issue diagnosis', *Public Relations Review*, 21: 287–304; Fombrun, Charles J. and Cees, B.M. Van Riel (2004) *Fame and Fortune: How Successful Companies Build Winning Reputations*. London: FT/Prentice Hall.

2. Fombrun, C. (1996) *Reputation: Realizing Value from the Corporate Image*. Cambridge, MA: Harvard University Press, 72.

3. For more details on the Barcelona Principles 2015, see http://amecorg.com/barcelona-principles-2-0/

4. Fombrun, C.J. (2007) 'List of lists: A compilation of international corporate reputation ratings', *Corporate Reputation Review*, 10: 144–53.

5. Fryxell, G.E. and Wang, J. (1994) 'The Fortune Corporate Reputation Index: Reputation for what?', *Journal of Management*, 20: 1–14.

6. Fombrun, C.J. (1996) *Reputation: Realizing Value from the Corporate Image*. Cambridge, MA: Harvard Business School Press.

7. Gray, E.R. and Balmer, J.M.T. (1998) 'Managing image and corporate reputation', *Long Range Planning*, 31 (5): 685–92, quote on p. 687.
8. Mendelsohn, H. (1973) 'Some reasons why information campaigns can succeed', *Public Opinion Quarterly*, 37: 50–61.
9. McGuire, W. (1981) 'Theoretical foundations of campaigns', in Rice, R. and Paisley, W. (eds), *Public Communication Campaigns*. Beverly Hills, CA: Sage, 41–70.
10. Petty, R.E. and Cacioppo, J.T. (1986) *Communication and Persuasion: Central and Peripheral Routes to Attitude Change*. New York: Springer-Verlag.
11. See, for example, Hallahan, K. (1999) 'Seven models of framing: Implications for public relations', *Journal of Public Relations Research*, 11: 205–42; Entman, R.M. (1993) 'Framing: Toward clarification of a fractured paradigm', *Journal of Communication*, 43 (4): 51–58.
12. Kahneman, D. (2011) *Thinking, Fast and Slow*. New York: Farrar, Straus and Giroux.

Specialist Areas in Corporate Communication

4

Part 4 explores four of the most important specialist areas in corporate communication: media relations, employee communication, issues management and crisis communication. These four areas involve stakeholder groups whose goodwill is important to an organization and its corporate reputation. Each of these areas also involves specialist knowledge, tools and techniques around communicating to each of these stakeholder groups, including journalists and media organizations, investors and shareholders, activist groups and NGOs and an organization's employees.

After reading Part 4 of the book, the reader should be familiar with effective approaches to media relations, employee communication, issue management and crisis communication.

Media Relations

8

┌─────────────── CHAPTER OVERVIEW ───────────────┐

Communicating with the media is a central area of activity in corporate communication. Drawing on theories from mass communication and practical examples, the chapter outlines how journalists and media organizations work and how news coverage and content may have an impact on corporate reputation. The chapter also explores the use and effectiveness of specific media relations techniques (media-monitoring services, press releases and press briefings) as well as strategies around new media and digital communication platforms.

└───┘

8.1 INTRODUCTION

Working with the media is what most people associate with corporate communication. Media relations involves managing communication and relationships with the media – all the writers, editors and producers who contribute to and control what appears in the print, broadcast and online news media. From a corporate communication standpoint, these news media are important as channels for generating publicity and because their coverage of business news may influence many important stakeholders including investors, customers and employees. Many corporate communication practitioners therefore see the news media as an important 'conduit' for reaching their stakeholders, rather than as a stakeholder or audience themselves.

This chapter explores how journalists and news organizations operate and how corporate communication practitioners can best liaise with them and can develop effective communication strategies to influence their news coverage in broadcast, print and online media. The aims of the chapter are, first of all, to provide an introduction to the roles and values of news journalists and news media organizations and to discuss their importance in terms of the impact of news coverage on corporate reputation. Based on this overview, the chapter continues by exploring the relationship between corporate communication practitioners and journalists and discusses various traditional tools and techniques such as media research and press releases used by communication practitioners to manage this relationship. The final section of the chapter considers the changing media landscape with the explosion of new Web 2.0 media such as blogs, social networking sites and other powerful digital communication platforms. These new media present clear challenges to organizations in terms of presenting the company image and telling the company's story, and require organizations to develop digital corporate communication strategies.

8.2 JOURNALISM AND NEWS ORGANIZATIONS

The news media involve a variety of organizations with the core operational process of production and dissemination of news content through various media (newspapers, radio, TV and the internet). The production of news content typically involves two levels: (1) journalists who, on an individual basis, consult sources and write news stories, and (2) other parties within the news organization (e.g. copy editors) who, based on their news routines, edit stories before they make it into print.[1] This distinction between journalists and news routines is important for corporate communication practitioners because it illustrates the variety of influences on the production of news content and points to the limited degree of control that journalists producing stories about organizations actually have on the whole process, including the final printed words that make up the news story.

Journalists may talk to sources, cover a beat and write a story, but, at the same time, not even recognize their own story when the story goes to print. This is because, at the level of *news routines*, there are many other people involved in the writing process who affect the story, such as the fact checker who verifies that the names of people, organizations and places mentioned are all spelled correctly. Copy editors may check that quotes are appropriately attributed to sources in a way that minimizes conflict and controversy. Layout and design specialists may be involved and check that news stories do not go over a certain word limit and that the story is designed within the format of the outlet and probably with an idea of how to attract readers. Moreover, the newspaper editor may decide that what was once a business news story should be a front page article for a much broader audience. In such a case, the lead paragraphs would need to be re-written to change from a business or strict financial perspective into a public interest perspective, attracting a much wider reading audience typical of the front page. When there is a strong set of news routines within a news organization, it means that the journalist is, to an extent, writing for the needs of the editorial desk to which they are assigned: a national news desk, a local news desk, the financial/business news desk or perhaps even an international news desk or the arts. On the other hand, when news routines are absent or less strong, there may be more flexibility for a journalist to write the story from a preferred angle and in a way in which they would like to write it. For example, an internet blog written by an individual journalist is subject to less rigorous scrutiny and further editing than an article published in a daily newspaper.

For journalists, writing for the needs of the desk is their way of ensuring that their story makes it into print. Whilst no journalist ever writes a story without the intent of it getting picked up, whether the story is published or not is not their call. Moreover, journalists do not have a say on the final printed story, what the headline of the story is or which photographs will be included (if any) with their story. Those decisions lie with their editors, including the front page editor, national editors, business/financial editors and arts/community editors, amongst others. Editors decide based on multiple potential stories what is, in terms of timing and readership, the relevance of a particular story for the medium's audience. For journalists themselves, the pressure of writing for a news desk is sometimes experienced as a hindrance in their work and produces conflict with their professional ideals of objectivity, fairness and impartiality. Many journalists share a set of values based on seeking information and maintaining a measure of independence from all organizations including their own.[2]

News routines within a media organization may also reflect a certain ideology (a set of normative principles and values) or political orientation that is shared by journalists and editors of that organization. This has sometimes been described as a 'media logic', which refers to the ideological frame of reference of a news organization which influences how editors and journalists see, interpret and cover political, corporate and social affairs. A logic, in other words, underpins media coverage, including how material is organized, the style in which it is presented, the focus or emphasis, and the grammar and wording of an article.[3] For example, *The New York Times* has been characterized as 'the editor's paper' and *The Washington Post* as the 'reporter's paper', referring to the levels of bureaucracy that exist between them. Similarly, articles in *The Guardian* newspaper are generally in sympathy with the middle-ground liberal to left-wing end of the political spectrum. This logic, or ideology, may have a direct bearing on the way in which news about organizations is reported. A recent study commissioned by the BBC Trust found that programmes on the BBC (e.g. *The Money Programme*, *Radio Five Live* and the *10 O'Clock News*) failed to represent shareholders' and employees' perspectives on corporate stories in favour of a consumer perspective. The study criticized the BBC business editors' often rather negative and narrow views of business and made three recommendations: the BBC should (1) address the lack of knowledge of business issues amongst editorial staff, (2) widen 'the range of editorial ideas and programming about business', and (3) 'ensure compliance in business coverage with standards of impartiality'.[4] Hence, ideology matters in terms of how organizations are covered in the news media and whether this will largely consist of 'good' or 'bad' news coverage.

8.3 THE EFFECTS OF NEWS COVERAGE ON CORPORATE REPUTATION

In general, media coverage of an organization can have a significant influence on the corporate reputation of that organization. Ranging from reports on annual results to investigations of corporate issues, media coverage may often have an 'amplifying' effect on a company's reputation when 'good' or 'bad' news is reported. Whilst media coverage does not strictly determine a company's reputation or the way in which stakeholders think about an organization, it does have an impact in terms of highlighting an issue or increasing the already held positive or negative view of an organization.[5]

This amplifying effect has often been studied through the lens of agenda-setting theory. This theory was traditionally developed in mass communication and public opinion research but has recently been extended to the domain of corporate reputation. The agenda-setting hypothesis underlying the theory is that the frequency with which the media report on a public or political issue determines that issue's salience in the minds of the general public.[6] In other words, 'The press may not be successful much of the time in telling people what to think, but it is stunningly successful in telling its readers what to think about'.[7]

The basic idea behind agenda-setting theory is that news media communicate a wealth of information when they report on organizations, politics, the economy or issues of social and human concern. In doing so, they also signal to their viewers, readers or audience which issues are salient for these topics. Over time, and through repeated mention of the same issues, such issues may become lodged in the public's mind. The public, in other words, will use the input from the media to decide which issues are important. The news media thus 'set' the public agenda.

Agenda-setting theory distinguishes two levels of agenda setting. The first level relates to the objects of news coverage, such as political candidates, nation states or organizations. The focus here is on the salience of a particular organization and the degree to which it readily comes to mind when a particular topic, such as an issue or industry, is being discussed. Whereas the first level of agenda setting deals with the salience of objects, the second level goes one step further and is linked to the concept of framing by suggesting that the news media can also influence *how* people think about a topic by selecting and placing emphasis on certain attributes or associations, and ignoring others. The focus here is not only on whether people think about a topic, but also on how they do so in terms of certain associations or affective judgments.

First-level agenda setting occurs when Shell, for example, comes first to mind for members of the general public when it receives more media attention than other petroleum companies. By covering certain organizations, the media may prime awareness of an organization and certain content about that organization. Second-level agenda setting is apparent when the public associates Shell primarily with a particular issue (e.g. renewable energy or the environmental damage in the Niger Delta) that has received much attention in the news during a particular period.

Studies have tested both levels of agenda setting. In one study, the coverage of US corporations in *The New York Times* was correlated with data on the public's awareness of those corporations and their associations with those corporations.[8] Positive results were found for both levels of agenda setting: results revealed that news coverage influences which corporations are salient in the public's mind, and the amount of media coverage devoted to certain corporate issues or attributes of an organization (e.g. workplace environment) are roughly in line with public associations regarding those corporations. A further study in the Netherlands confirmed the same agenda-setting effects of media coverage. This study also extended the basic agenda-setting hypotheses by testing the further hypothesis that the greater the salience of an issue associated with a company in media coverage, the better the reputation of the company that is seen to 'own' that issue. For example, news coverage on environmental issues in the petroleum sector may have benefited the reputation of BP for a number of years, as this organization was seen to take a leadership role in recognizing the ecological impact of business and the importance of reducing carbon emissions.[9] The company's recent retreat from investments in alternative energy and the 2010 oil spill in the Gulf of Mexico have since dampened its environmental image. As a result, BP is now more likely seen as a 'bad guy' in relation to environmental issues in the sector. Yet, other studies have been less conclusive: a 2007 study of the 28 most reputable corporations in the USA found little support for the agenda-setting hypothesis and for its influence on corporate reputation.[10] To some extent, these mixed findings may not be that surprising as it would otherwise suggest a rather linear model with news media reporting directly priming the salience of organizations and how people think about or modify their opinions about these organizations.

Yet, corporate reputation is formed through multiple interactions of individuals with an organization, and not only or even primarily through media coverage. Corporate reputations are also relatively inert over time; once established, they may act as a buffer against negative news and may as such neutralize or minimize the effect of negative news coverage on stakeholder opinions. The status and visibility associated with a strong corporate reputation may also mean that organizations get away scot-free when negative news is reported, although this is generally less so if the entire industry is implicated and tainted. Consider, for example, the banking or petroleum industries where negative news coverage has, by association, tarnished the image of most corporations in those sectors.

The second level of agenda-setting suggests that news coverage not only reports facts and neutral observations, but also conveys feelings through its stance and tone on the issue. This affective dimension has been talked about in terms of media favourability – 'the overall evaluation of a firm presented in the media … resulting from the stream of stories about the firm'.[11] Reputation expert David Deephouse used this term to suggest that the media not only convey information, they actually make and represent reputational assessments to their audiences. Deephouse referred to 'favourable' news coverage when an organization was praised for its actions or was associated with activities that should raise its reputation, whilst 'unfavourable' coverage referred to reporting in which an organization was criticized for its actions or associated with actions that should decrease its reputation. A 'neutral' rating identified a story that was the 'declarative reporting of role performance without evaluative modifiers'.[12] Deephouse found evidence suggesting that the higher the level of media favourability, the higher the level of an organization's performance. Whilst the media does not directly impact on an organization's performance (the media are an intermediary between organizations and stakeholder opinions and actions), this finding has one central implication for corporate communication practitioners: they should seek to cultivate positive evaluations by the media through releasing well-placed stories that report on organizational actions (e.g. charitable giving, CSR initiatives) or significant newsworthy events.

Although the majority of agenda-setting studies examine the relationship between media coverage and public opinion, this leaves open the question of how the agenda is formed in the first place. There is significant evidence that corporate communication practitioners are crucial to the formation of the media agenda. This process is often described as agenda building, which involves discussions and debates amongst multiple groups, including journalists and communication practitioners, but also policymakers and interest groups.[13] Yet, particularly through information subsidies, such as news conferences, press releases and campaigns, corporate communication can have a profound impact on shaping news content. However, as we will explain in the following section, the relationship between corporate communicators and journalists is not uni-directional. News coverage is often the result of interactions between them, with each side impacting one another throughout the process.

Finally, agenda-setting theory may also explain why certain companies are generally more well known and listed more highly on reputation rankings (e.g. the *Fortune* or *Financial Times* rankings) than others. Companies included in these rankings are prominent on the media agenda and are more likely to be prominent on the public agenda, whilst those companies that are outside of these rankings are far less likely to be prominent in the public's mind.[14] The news media often rely on large and well-known corporations for information subsidies, and there is evidence to support the claim that only companies with significant corporate reputations – whether good or bad – are used as information sources.[15] Organizations that are not well known or are less visible (e.g. large corporations in business-to-business industries) are often ignored because of their low levels of newsworthiness, or simply because the media are not familiar with them. This has of course significant implications for the media's role as a watchdog when only certain organizations are monitored and covered in the news, and other organizations are given little attention or even simply ignored and stay outside of the public eye.

8.4 FRAMING NEWS STORIES

The relationship between communication practitioners and journalists has often been described as adversarial. Journalists often have a negative opinion about communication practitioners, in part because they feel that there is a clear divide between their interests: according to journalists, communicators think about the needs of their companies first and less about what journalists need. Past research has also found that journalists felt that practitioners withheld information, were not always objective and certainly not focused on issues of public interest.[16] On the other hand, communication practitioners are less negative about journalists and are often eager to work with them. However, communication practitioners also realize that journalists have their own agenda and may frame news about the company in line with their news routines and the ideology of the news organization that they work for (see section 8.2). Whilst communication practitioners and journalists have different agendas and thus different angles on news related to a company, they do realize that they are interdependent: journalists need and often use information provided by communication practitioners and, equally, practitioners and the companies that they work for often need the media as a conduit to generate coverage on the company and to reach important stakeholders such as the financial community, customers, prospective employees, government and the general public. According to some reports, as much as 80 per cent of news reports about companies is prompted and delivered by communication practitioners.[17] The realization of this interdependence has led to a further specialization of media or press relations within corporate communication: many large companies have a dedicated press office or media team dealing with the general media, which subsumes or is separate from investor relations professionals who deal with financial media such as *The Wall Street Journal* and *The Financial Times*.

When corporate communication practitioners propose a particular story (in the form of, for example, a press release) to a journalist, they engage in two separate but related processes. The first is to solicit interest in the story topic itself. The second is to make sure that the story is framed in a way that is consistent with the organization's preferred framing (i.e. how the organization would like to have its story told). In many instances, news coverage may directly feature parts of a press release or corporate report; yet, in other cases, communication practitioners and journalists may discuss and exchange alternative viewpoints.[18] Such exchanges are essentially *negotiations* about how news is *framed*.[19] Framing theory is a theoretically rich approach that has been used to understand and investigate communication and related behaviours in a wide range of disciplines, including psychology, speech communication, organizational decision-making, economics, health communication, mass communication and political communication. Framing theory focuses on how messages are created in such a way that they connect with the underlying psychological processes of how people digest information and make judgments. Because people cannot possibly attend to every little detail about the world around them, framing in communication is important because it helps shape the perspectives through which people see the world. The notion of framing is best understood metaphorically as a window or portrait frame drawn around information that delimits the subject matter and, thus, focuses attention on key elements within it. Hence, framing involves processes of *inclusion* and *exclusion* of information in a message as well as *emphasis*. The communication scholar Entman summarized the essence of framing as follows:

> Framing essentially involves selection and salience. To frame is to select some aspects of perceived reality and make them more salient in the communicating text, in such a way as to promote a particular problem definition, causal interpretation, moral evaluation and/or treatment recommendation for the item described.[20]

In the context of corporate communication, framing theory suggests that communication practitioners *frame* a particular corporate decision, issue or event in such a way that it furthers and promotes the interests of the organization. This frame which features in a press release, in corporate reports on the company's website, in speeches of spokespersons and the CEO is labelled the *corporate frame* that is provided to the media and to the general public. Journalists and editors, on the other hand, may interpret and represent the same decision, issue or event in a different way. *News framing* refers to the way in which news is selectively portrayed by the media in an effort to explain news or ideas about organizations in familiar terms for a broader audience. How a news item is framed also largely depends on the political views and ideology of journalists and their news organizations. Much research in mass communication has documented how journalists use dominant frames on politics, society and corporations to construct an understanding for their audience. Journalists often use such frames unconsciously as they relate to deeply ingrained assumptions about the social world.[21]

Because of their different interests, communication practitioners and journalists may frame the same decision, issue or event in completely different ways. Skilful communication practitioners therefore play on journalists' knowledge and views to propose stories that follow dominant news frames, fit certain categories of content and resonate with a journalist's notion of expectations of their audience. In doing so, they are able to align a story proposal (corporate frame) with a story expectation (news frame) which leads to a greater probability of the story being placed and reported. The skill in media relations, in other words, is often in spotting the stories or the angles that can turn corporate news into media news or bring a corporate story into a global news story. This process is referred to as the *alignment* of frames between practitioners and journalists.

Because not all journalists are necessarily going to frame a story in the same way, communication practitioners often find themselves engaged in *frame contests* with journalists. Market models of journalism suggest that journalists will deliberately strive to frame stories in ways that resonate with what journalists perceive to be the largest segment of their audience. For example, in July 2006, a trader with Citigroup committed suicide by climbing over a barrier and jumping from the 16th floor of the bank's Canary Wharf offices. Despite evidence that the trader had committed suicide because of mental depression, many newspapers (including *The Telegraph*) framed the suicide in inverted commas (i.e. as 'suicide') and openly suggested a link to work pressures in the investment banking industry. Journalists from these newspapers chose to frame the news in what turned out to be a biased and inaccurate way because of a link with reader expectations and despite any evidence of trading irregularities or substantial losses.

How, then, can communication practitioners avoid such frame conflicts? The alignment of frames is more likely when the substance of the corporate frame relates to common norms and expectations about business and society. For example, The Body Shop's (see Case Example 8.1) long-standing focus on social equality and fair trade aligns with some journalists' expectations of the role of business in society. Frame alignment is also more likely when practitioners and journalists openly discuss an issue, decision or event so that a journalist is more likely to understand the other side. The opportunity for such an open discussion presupposes of course that communication practitioners have developed a relationship with journalists in which both parties respect each other.

—⬭—— CASE EXAMPLE 8.1 ————————————

L'ORÉAL'S TAKEOVER OF THE BODY SHOP

On 17 March 2006, The Body Shop International Plc (The Body Shop), a retailer of natural-based and ethically sourced beauty products, announced that it had agreed to be acquired by beauty giant L'Oréal in a cash deal worth £652 million. The Body Shop, a cosmetics retailer which promotes itself based on ethics, fair trade and environmental campaigning, was founded in 1976 by Dame Anita Roddick. Roddick started her first Body Shop in 1976 in Brighton in the UK. The store sold around 15 lines of homemade cosmetics made with natural ingredients such as jojoba oil and rhassoul mud. From its early days, The Body Shop was associated with Roddick's social activism. The windows of the early Body Shop outlets, for example, featured posters of local charity and community events. From the start, Roddick was very critical of the environmental insensitivity of big business and called for a change in corporate values.

Profits-with-a-principle

The Body Shop's core brand identity is its 'profits-with-a-principle' philosophy and the brand was closely marketed in combination with a social justice agenda. This was a revolutionary idea at the time and The Body Shop developed a loyal customer base. By the late 1970s, the company had grown into a number of franchise stores around the UK. Growing at a rate of 50 per cent annually, The Body Shop was getting a lot of media attention for its social activism, including its 'save the whales' campaign with Greenpeace in 1986. Following some disagreements with Greenpeace, Roddick discontinued the relationship and instead formed an alliance with Friends of the Earth in 1990. The Body Shop also teamed up with Amnesty International and from the 1990s onwards became very vocal in its support for international human rights.

At the time of the takeover, L'Oréal was and still is one of the largest and most successful cosmetics companies in the world with 17 global brands in its portfolio. The company had successfully strengthened its market dominance by promoting its major brands such as L'Oréal Paris and Lancôme, and by acquiring and internationalizing popular local brands such as Ralph Lauren, Redken, Maybelline and Garnier. L'Oréal became interested in the acquisition of The Body Shop as the takeover would provide the company with a new perspective on retailing (specialty stores, direct-sales business), a brand capable of generating publicity in developing markets (China, Russia, India), an entry into the 'masstige' market (premium mass cosmetics), a foothold in the fair trade movement, as well as additional revenues. At the same time, L'Oréal realized that it had not been previously associated with ethics or fair trade and had been criticized in the past for its use of animal testing in the production of cosmetics. Therefore, a takeover of The Body Shop would present L'Oréal with some communication challenges.

Announcing the takeover

When the deal was finalized between the two companies, both L'Oréal and The Body Shop came out with press releases and video clips to announce and rationalize the deal and to communicate the advantages to both parties. These press releases and video clips were made available on an online newsroom. L'Oréal's chairman and CEO Lindsay Owen-Jones issued a written statement. Adrian Bellamy (chairman of The Body Shop), Peter Saunders (CEO of The Body Shop) and Anita Roddick (non-executive director) all issued pre-recorded video clips with answers to questions about the takeover. The transcripts of these video releases were also made available as press releases. Adrian Bellamy said: 'I'm extremely positive about the deal. We'll be stronger as part of the L'Oréal group than by sailing our own boat. We'll be able to share its global platform and experience.' Similarly, L'Oréal's chairman and CEO Owen-Jones said: 'We have always had great respect for The Body Shop's success and for the strong identity and values created by its outstanding founder, Anita Roddick.' He also added:

(Continued)

(Continued)

> A partnership between our two companies makes perfect sense. Combining L'Oréal's expertise and knowledge of international markets with The Body Shop's distinct culture and values will benefit both companies. We are delighted that The Body Shop has agreed to unanimously recommend our offer to the company's shareholders. We look forward to working together with The Body Shop management, employees and franchisees to fulfil The Body Shop's independent potential as part of the L'Oréal family.

L'Oréal also said that the management team at The Body Shop would be retained and that the company would continue to operate as a separate company to preserve its own identity.

In her own press release, Roddick justified the deal by saying that L'Oréal wanted to learn from The Body Shop's value-based management. She denied that she had sold out and maintained that The Body Shop's values and focus on social development would not change. As she stated in the press release:

> I do not believe that L'Oréal will compromise the ethics of The Body Shop. That is after all what they are paying for and they are too intelligent to mess with our DNA ... I want to make things happen, to spread human values wide in business if I possibly can. And this sale gives us the chance to do so.

She added:

> The campaigning, the being maverick, changing the rules of business – it's all there, protected. And it's not going to change. That's part of our DNA. But having L'Oréal come in and say we like you, we like your ethics, we want to be a part of you, we want you to teach us things, it's a gift. I'm ecstatic about it. I don't see it as selling out.

Roddick also mentioned that she hoped that The Body Shop values would rub off on the way in which L'Oréal does business:

> But with L'Oréal now, the biggest cosmetics company in the world, for them to partner with us on our projects in 35 countries in the world, I think it's amazing, amazing. They could work with our Nicaraguan farmers who sell us 70 tons of sesame oil. How many tons could they use? A thousand? I mean it's mind-blowing in terms of poverty eradication.

Media reporting

The media reported the takeover on the same day (17 March 2006) that the deal was finalized and announced. Initially, news coverage consisted of reports on the details of the takeover with quotes from the press releases of L'Oréal's Owen-Jones and of Anita Roddick. The BBC, for example, quoted from Roddick's press release in which she said that 'this [the takeover] is the best 30th anniversary gift The Body Shop could have received'. *The Guardian* published the same quote from Roddick, along with another demonstrating the complementary link that Roddick mentioned in her press release: 'L'Oréal has displayed visionary leadership in wanting to be an authentic advocate and supporter of our values.' However, later that afternoon, *The Guardian* online edition published an article on a call by animal welfare activists to boycott The Body Shop. A coalition of activist groups including Naturewatch opposed L'Oréal's policy on the testing of cosmetics ingredients on animals. None of the other newspapers reported the same or a similar story on the same day.

Editorial pieces in subsequent weeks only incidentally picked up on the nature of the relationship between the two companies. For example, an article in *The Economist* on 25 March 2006 questioned the complementary but independent link between the two companies. The article suggested that it would be difficult for L'Oréal not to adopt any cross-selling practices across Body Shop outlets. Rhetorically, the article asked: 'Will L'Oréal really be able to resist slipping its ethically challenged wrinkle cream onto the shelves next to the bracing and naturally inspired body scrubs offered by The Body Shop?' However, by and large, the news media and the general public accepted the claim from Roddick and Owen-Jones that The Body Shop would remain an independent entity, with the upshot that its value-based practices and social change campaigns could have a wider impact with the support of L'Oréal. Part of this news framing may be attributed to the strong media presence of Roddick, who, with her frank style of communicating, convinced many journalists of the rationale of the deal.

Questions for reflection

Discuss the framing of the takeover of The Body Shop by L'Oréal in terms of the concepts of frame alignment and frame contests. Why do you think that some media reported frames and quotes from corporate press releases whilst others published alternative frames about the takeover?

When the takeover was announced, The Body Shop issued pre-recorded interviews to journalists. In your view, should The Body Shop have done anything else (e.g. face-to-face interviews, press conference) to influence the news coverage and framing of the takeover?

Communication practitioners use a wide range of tools and techniques to obtain news coverage and to monitor reporting on their organization over time. These include press releases, press conferences, interviews, online newsrooms and media monitoring and media research. We will briefly discuss each in turn.

Press release: the aim of press releases is to transfer news to journalists so that it can be made public. Press releases are more likely to be used and placed in a news medium when they refer to newsworthy events or items that are current and have a human interest or appeal, when the release is written in a factual (as opposed to judgmental) manner and with a clear heading and lead (first paragraph) into the topic.

- When writing a press release, communication practitioners should keep the expectations, preferred frames and deadlines of the different media in mind. Different media organizations and media forms (TV, print, internet) involve different reporting styles, timetables and deadlines. The print journalist, for example, will employ a pyramid scheme where the most important information is shared first in the article, and as the article increases in length, the information appearing further down will be deemed less important. In contrast, the radio journalist will try to share all of the information early on. Moreover, a reporter who is assigned to a business or financial desk will be concerned about angles from the perspective of business audiences and the implications for financial performance and financial markets. The public affairs reporter will be more concerned about the public angle. A feature writer will be more concerned about the human interest angle.

- As mentioned, it is important that practitioners are sensitive to the dominant frames and interests of journalists and their news organizations so that there is a greater likelihood of frame alignment. Another point is the time frame of different news media. Television and the internet are 'fast' media in the sense that a topic or article, once it is finished, is published directly, whereas newspapers are slower in that they wait for publication until the next deadline. Magazines have even longer deadlines. This time frame, which is short for internet and television, is of importance to corporate communication practitioners, because the chance of incorrect reporting is greater for these fast media.

- For a number of years, the automated distribution of press releases, as a PR activity, was quite popular online. However, in recent years, many of the automated press release distribution services have become less successful in generating interest amongst journalists and other stakeholders, creating less subsequent traffic to a company's site. There is instead an emphasis again on a more targeted approach, with press releases being written for, and channelled to, relevant media outlets. On the other hand, there is an increasing trend in automated software packages being used to help write press releases, particularly for basic news items such as corporate earnings and stock market performance that can be easily arranged into text-based structures for reporting. Press agency AP, for example, has been using Wordsmith software that produces 4,300 such press releases per quarter – which is effectively 14 times more than what, in the same time, would be manually achieved by AP's reporters and editors.

Press conference: another tool of disseminating information to the news media involves inviting journalists to a press conference. Press conferences are normally organized around fixed periods in the calendar when organizations release financial results or share corporate information at the annual general meeting with shareholders. Incidentally, there may also be ad hoc press conferences around an issue or crisis (e.g. product defects, accidents) (see Chapters 10 and 11) in order to provide journalists with up-to-date information. An important element of the press conference is that it allows journalists to address questions to the company executives gathered at the event. This 'interactive' feature distinguishes a press conference from a press release. A press conference is therefore more applicable when information cannot be conveyed in a standardized, written form or when the information involves a controversial or sensitive issue (see Chapter 10). In preparation for a press conference, communication practitioners need to draw up a list of journalists and editors whom they would like to invite to the conference and brief them about the conference in time.

Interviews: journalists often request an interview with official spokespersons or with the CEO or other senior executives of the organization. For this purpose, communication practitioners need to offer executives advice and training on news angles in relation to corporate themes and on specific guidelines regarding the interview format. Such guidelines may consist of advising staff to keep 'control' of the interview by asking the journalist to call or come at a prearranged time, to brief them about the interview topics in advance and to supply them with a copy of the interview transcript and final article so that facts, opinions and attributions can be checked.

- In addition, CEOs and other executives who are likely to be interviewed by journalists over the telephone, face-to-face or in front of a camera need to be trained to be skilled communicators. Many organizations therefore instruct their CEO and senior executives in media training so that they stay on message, synchronize their body language with their verbal messages and can anticipate questions from journalists. When a CEO becomes an effective communicator, that can translate into admiration, respect and trust and a stronger overall corporate reputation.[22]
- *Media monitoring and research*: the most common type of media research consists of monitoring media relations efforts. Two of the most commonly used monitoring techniques are gate-keeping research and output analysis. In addition, many corporations also use syndicated media-monitoring services such as Carma International and Media Tenor:
- *Gate-keeping research*: a gate-keeping study analyses the characteristics of a press release or video news release that allow them to 'pass through the gate' and appear in a news medium. Both content and style variables are typically examined. For example, previous research has found that press releases dealing with financial matters (e.g. annual results) are more likely to be used than those dealing with other topics. Press releases that are aimed at the specific interests of the newspaper to which they are sent are also more likely to be published than general releases. Editors furthermore typically shorten news releases and rewrite them to make them easier to read before publication.[23]
- *Output analysis*: the objective of output analysis is to measure the amount of exposure or attention that the organization receives as a result of media relations. Several techniques can be used in output analysis. One way is to simply measure the total amount of news coverage (i.e. the total number of stories or articles) that appears in selected mass media. In addition, it is also possible to examine the tone (positive or negative) of stories or articles. Many communication practitioners systematically collect press clippings (copies of stories or articles in the press) and record the degree of exposure in terms of column inches in print media, the number of minutes of air time in the electronic media or the number of cites on the web.

- An often used measure for exposure is the 'advertising value equivalent' (AVE), which consists of counting the column inches of press publicity and seconds of air time gained and then multiplying the total by the advertising rate of the media in which the coverage appeared. It is not uncommon, using this measure, for communication campaigns and well-placed press releases to bring in the equivalent of many hundreds of thousands of, say, pounds, euros or dollars of advertising. However, AVE does not incorporate an evaluation of the tone of the stories or articles or the exposure of the organization compared to competitors. Another form of output analysis is to calculate the reach and frequency of media reporting on an organization. Reach is usually based on the total audited circulation of a newspaper or the estimated viewing or listening audience of TV or radio, whilst frequency refers to the number of times a story or an article about an organization is carried in the same medium.

- *Syndicated media-monitoring services*: countering the shortcomings of output analysis, a number of media research agencies (e.g. Carma, Media Tenor) have developed media-monitoring packages. These packages focus on measuring the total circulation or audience reached; the tone of the news stories or articles on the organization; the extent to which key messages (for example, in a press release) are picked up and communicated; and the share-of-voice compared to competitors or other comparable organizations. Philips, for example, uses the Carma media-monitoring tool to monitor news coverage on the firm compared to competing consumer electronics firms (e.g. Samsung, Sony) and other relevant firms (e.g. Shell which is also a Dutch corporation). The advantages of these tools involve the focus on outcome (share of voice and tone) as opposed to mere exposure or output, the automated analysis of mass media around the world and easy-to-use web portals which allow a communication practitioner to view real-time developments in media coverage.

Online newsrooms: in order to connect different platforms and media content, corporate communication practitioners have also increasingly developed online newsrooms, as a dedicated part of the company's website. These newsrooms are a one-stop shop for media relations; they typically include standard reports, speeches and press releases, but also tend to host dynamic content including videos, news feeds, widgets, podcasts and searchable archives of content. The general advantage of these newsrooms is that they provide journalists with information when they need it; they also help drive traffic to the company's website. In addition, they allow a company to get its content out in a way that responds to the way in which journalists nowadays search for company information on the internet. To stimulate usage by journalists, the design of these newsroom sites needs to be user-friendly and easy to navigate. In addition, dynamic content including image libraries and videos significantly enhances the experience of using the site. A good example of a company that quite early on developed an online newsroom with dynamic content is The Body Shop (see Case Example 8.1).

CASE STUDY 8.1

AMAZON'S SILENT RISE TO THE TOP

Amazon, the Seattle-based internet retailer, was started in 1994 as the 'Earth's biggest bookstore'. Besides selling books, the company has diversified into selling music and entertainment, as well as apparel, furniture, food, toys and jewellery. In recent years, the company has also added cloud infrastructure services to its remit and has become a producer of digital content, including Amazon Kindle, e-book readers, Fire tablets and Fire TV. Over the years, Amazon has slowly but steadily built its brand and reputation. Far from being just an online retailer, Amazon has become a true digital innovator, rivalling the likes of Google and Apple in its innovative prowess. The company is constantly innovating new digital products and offers a breadth of digital services, ranging from marketplaces bringing buyers and sellers of local services together to e-book lending services. This constant innovation of products that are, upon launch, almost immediately in high demand stems from founder Bezos' vision for creating what he calls the 'world's most consumer-centric company'.

Corporate silence

When he started Amazon in 1994, Jeff Bezos' personal traits – a competitive spirit, a loathing of taxes and government intrusion, a lack of sentimentality and a mistrust of the media – proved to be the perfect foundation for a young start-up that quickly gained ground. Those values appear to be, however, still very much alive in the company today, despite the fact that the company has become far bigger in size. In fact, Amazon is these days somewhat notorious for its lack of communication with the media. Some say that most of its communication efforts are not out in the open, but take place behind closed doors in the form of its communication staff lobbying legislators to pass, for example, favourable legislation on transporting Amazon packages through drones in the air and through longer delivery trucks on the ground. This may well be the case, as its media relations demonstrate a largely stony, silent effort. The company does not appear to be pushing its stories into the media, nor does it often seem compelled, even in the face of ongoing media criticism, to respond. This way of handling the press is perhaps not unique to Amazon; Apple, Google and other high-tech giants often say very little in the press. This may work when trying to keep new products under wraps, but it is perhaps less effective when the company is being criticized or attacked in the media, with its reputation hanging in the balance.

An ongoing dispute in book publishing

A recent issue that flared in the media was the struggle between Amazon and the Hachette book group. Hachette was very vocal on the negotiation and its fight, with Amazon saying very little. The issue involved the difference of opinion on the royalty payment for Amazon and the pricing of e-books, which were no longer set but open for discussion. Amazon did not want to abide by the price that was set by Hachette, so that it, in effect, can decide itself on the appropriate pricing of books. This, however, would affect authors who would

(Continued)

(Continued)

see their profits dwindle, and could in some cases not even make a profit at all. When the dispute continued, Amazon eliminated discounts and delayed the delivery time for books provided by Hachette, badly affecting the sales of Hachette books and pushing customers away for those titles. Throughout the dispute, Amazon remained largely silent, even when many well-known authors, readers and loyal customers waded in. In a post on its website, the company did, however, release a brief formal statement in which it declared that 'we are not optimistic that this will be resolved soon', seeing the issue as at the heart of its business model and the future of the publishing industry. In the same post, Amazon also oddly enough criticized the media for its 'narrow' coverage of the dispute with Hachette, but had undertaken no media efforts of its own to balance out such coverage.

A great place to work?

A second issue that emerged in the media in 2015 was a critique of the company's corporate culture. *The New York Times* published a scathing critique of a competitive and intense workplace environment faced by Amazon's white-collar employees. Whilst earlier coverage had detailed the conditions for workers in its warehouses, the *New York Times* feature documented what it saw as cruelty towards employees in the company's corporate headquarters, including gruelling working conditions and the rather harsh, even bullying, treatment of staff suffering personal crises, such as cancer and miscarriage. Confronted by the article, communication staff did not immediately respond to *The New York Times* or to the general media who, following the feature, had also started to write about the work conditions at Amazon. Jeff Bezos did, however, issue an internal e-mail to employees, saying that the article 'claims that our intentional approach is to create a soulless, dystopian workplace where no fun is had and no laughter heard'. Bezos writes: 'I don't recognize this Amazon and I very much hope you don't, either … I strongly believe that anyone working in a company that really is like the one described in the NYT would be crazy to stay. I know I would leave such a company'. In the e-mail, he also encourages staff to report the kind of negative experiences and management practices reported in the *New York Times* feature: 'Even if it's rare or isolated, our tolerance for any such lack of empathy needs to be zero.' Whilst the company has remained largely silent on the external front, the vice president of corporate affairs for Amazon, Jay Carney, interestingly did post a message on Medium a few months after the *New York Times* piece was first published. In it, he criticizes the lead journalist for not checking her sources and for offering a rather one-sided account of Amazon's corporate culture. Carney also writes that through all their conversations with the lead journalist on the article, they 'were repeatedly assured that this would be a nuanced story that dove into what makes Amazon an exciting and fun place to be, not just a demanding place to work'.

Apart from the question of what conditions at its headquarters may really be like, these two recent cases do reveal an interesting fact about Amazon. In contrast to what its steady rise in terms of the value of its brand and reputation would suggest, the company has been operating a very minimal approach to its media relations. Its record in terms of pushing stories in the press shows that Amazon has done very little of the kind, and equally when issues emerge in the media – such as the two issues described in this case – the company often remains silent, and for a prolonged period of time. It seems that communication practitioners in the company believe – and they may, at times, be right – that too strong a response to such issues may escalate them even further, turning them into real talking points in the public domain and affecting the company's reputation in turn. At the same time, with such a tacit response there is a real risk of such issues lingering and turning into a real crisis for the company, which may be one reason why, after a few months of silence, the company's vice-present of corporate affairs tried to set the record straight on the *New York Times* article.

Questions for reflection

1 Discuss the general approach of Amazon to the media; is this an approach that you think can be used by other companies and, if so, by which companies and in what industries?
2 What in your view are the potential risks and rewards for Amazon in staying out of the limelight and in being less vocal, or even silent, in response to media coverage on its business conduct?

8.5 CHAPTER SUMMARY

This chapter started with an overview of journalists and news organizations and of the production of news content. Given the importance of the news media for a company's reputation, the chapter continued by discussing ways in which professionals can frame news items in such a way that they are picked up by the press. The chapter also outlined various practical tools and techniques that communication practitioners use to obtain media coverage, build relationships with journalists and monitor reporting on their organization over time. Finally, the chapter concluded with a discussion of the new media landscape and of how organizations can develop digital communication platforms to support media relations.

 ———— DISCUSSION QUESTIONS ————

1. Describe the main tenets of the agenda-setting role of the news media.
2. What can communication practitioners do to increase the chances of a story being covered in the news media?

KEY TERMS	
Agenda setting	Journalist
Corporate frame	Media favourability
Frame alignment	Media monitoring
Frame conflict	News desk
Frame contest	News frame
Frame negotiation	News routine
Gate-keeping research	Output analysis
Media logic	Press conference
Interview	Press release
Online newsroom	Agenda building

─── 📖 ─── FURTHER READING ──────────────────────

Henderson, D. (2006) *Making News: A Straight-Shooting Guide to Media Relations*. New York: Harlem
   Writers Guild Press.
Lehane, C., Fabiani, M. and Guttentag, B. (2012) *Masters of Disaster: The Ten Commandments of Damage
   Control*. New York: Palgrave Macmillan.

Want to know more about this chapter? Visit the companion website at:
https://study.sagepub.com/cornelissen5e to access videos, web links, a
glossary and selected journal articles to further enhance your study.

NOTES

1. Deephouse, D.L. and Carroll, C.E. (2007) 'What makes news fit to print? A five-level framework predicting media visibility and favourability of organizations', Working Paper, Alberta
   School of Business.
2. See, for example, Lorimer, R. (1994) *Mass Communications*. Manchester: Manchester
   University Press.
3. See Altheide, D. and Snow, R.P. (1979) *Media Logic*. Beverly Hills, CA: Sage; Altheide, D.
   and Snow, R.P. (1991) *Media Worlds in the Postjournalism Era*. Hawthorne, NY: Aldine de
   Gruyter.
4. Conlan, T. (2007) 'BBC business news failing impartiality test, says report', *The Guardian*,
   26 May: 18; see also Berry, M. (2013) 'Hard evidence: How biased is the BBC?', *New
   Statesman*, 23 August.
5. Fombrun, C.J. and Shanley, M. (1990) 'What's in a name? Reputation building and
   corporate strategy', *Academy of Management Journal*, 33: 233–58.
6. McCombs, M. and Shaw, D. (1972) 'The agenda-setting function of mass media', *Public
   Opinion Quarterly*, 36: 176–87.
7. Cohen, B.C. (1963) *The Press and Foreign Policy*. Princeton, NJ: Princeton University
   Press, p. 120.
8. Carroll, C. (2004) 'How the mass media influence perceptions of corporate reputation:
   Agenda-setting effects within business news coverage', unpublished doctoral dissertation,
   The University of Texas at Austin.
9. Meijer, M. and Kleinnijenhuis, J. (2006) 'Issue news and corporate reputation: Applying the
   theories of agenda setting and issue ownership in the field of business communication',
   Journal of Communication, 56: 543–59.
10. Kiousis, S., Popescu, C. and Mitrook, M. (2007) 'Understanding influence on corporate
    reputation: An examination of public relations efforts, media coverage, public opinion, and
    financial performance from an agenda-building and agenda-setting perspective', *Journal of
    Public Relations Research*, 19 (2): 147–65.
11. Deephouse, D.L. (2000) 'Media reputation as a strategic resource: An integration of mass
    communication and resource-based theories', *Journal of Management*, 26: 1091–112, quote
    on p. 1097.
12. Deephouse (2000), p. 1101.
13. See, for example, Kiousis, Popescu and Mitrook (2007).
14. Carroll, C.E. and McCombs, M. (2003) 'Agenda-setting effects of business news on the
    public's images and opinions about major corporations', *Corporate Reputation Review*, 6:
    36–46.

15. Carroll (2004), p. 2.
16. See, for example, Belz, A., Talbott, A.D. and Starck, K. (1989) 'Using role theory to study cross perceptions of journalists and public relations practitioners', *Public Relations Research Annual*, 1: 125–39; Neijens, P.C. and Smit, E.G. (2006) 'Dutch public relations practitioners and journalists: Antagonists no more', *Public Relations Review*, 32 (3): 232–40.
17. Merten, K. (2004) 'A constructivist approach to public relations', in Van Ruler, B. and Vercic, D. (eds) *Public Relations and Communication Management in Europe*. Berlin: Mouton de Gruyter, 45–54; Elving, W.J.L. and Van Ruler, B. (2006) *Trendonderzoekcommunicatiemanagement* [Trend research communication management]. Amsterdam: University of Amsterdam.
18. Schultz, F., Kleinnijenhuis, J., Oegema, D., Utz, S. and Atteveldt, W.V. (2011) 'Strategic framing in the BP crisis: A semantic network analysis of associative frames', *Public Relations Review*, 38: 97–107.
19. See, for example, Hallahan, K. (1999) 'Seven models of framing: Implications for public relations', *Journal of Public Relations Research*, 11: 205–42.
20. Entman, R.M. (1993) 'Framing: Toward clarification of a fractured paradigm', *Journal of Communication*, 43 (4): 51–58, quote on p. 55.
21. See, for example, Hallahan (1999); Entman (1993); and Scheufele, B.T. (2006) 'Frames, schemata, and news reporting', *Communications*, 31: 65–83.
22. See, for example, Gaines-Ross, L. (2003) *CEO Capital: A Guide to Building CEO Reputation and Company Success*. Hoboken, NJ: Wiley; Hayward, M.L., Rindova, V.P. and Pollock, T.G. (2004) 'Believing one's own press: The antecedents and consequences of CEO celebrity', *Strategic Management Journal*, 25: 637–53.
23. Morton, L. and Ramsey, S. (1994) 'A benchmark study of the PR news wire', *Public Relations Review*, 20: 155–70; Morton, L. and Warren, J. (1992) 'Proximity: localization versus distance in PR news releases', *Journalism Quarterly*, 69: 1023–28; Walters, T., Walters, L. and Starr, D. (1994) 'After the highwayman: Syntax and successful placement of press releases in newspapers', *Public Relations Review*, 20: 345–56.

Employee Communication

9

| CHAPTER OVERVIEW |

Employees are a crucial stakeholder group for any organization. Organizations need to communicate with their employees to strengthen employee morale and their identification with the organization and to ensure that employees know how to accomplish their own, specialized tasks. The chapter discusses general strategies for communicating to employees. These strategies range from communication that makes employees feel comfortable speaking up and providing feedback to managers to using communication to stimulate innovation and creativity within networks and communities of practice.

9.1 INTRODUCTION

Organizations require employees to cooperate with one another to achieve the company's goals. Most organizations have divided complex activities up into more specialized tasks for individual employees. Whilst efficient, the pay-off of such specialization depends almost wholly on coordinating tasks and activities across employees. If an organization controls its members through top-down command and delegation, the individual needs of employees for autonomy, creativity and sociability may be frustrated. But, at the same time, if the organization fails to control its employees, it loses the ability to coordinate its employees' activities and will ultimately fail. Hence, organizations must find ways to meet their employees' individual needs and stimulate their creativity, whilst persuading them to act in ways that meet the organization's overall objectives. Organizations do so by adopting various strategies for communicating with employees. In the next section, we first define the general scope of employee communication. The chapter then goes on to discuss how employee communication may strengthen employees' identification with their organization.

The degree to which managers communicate with employees and involve them in decision-making has a direct impact on employee morale and their commitment to the organization. The final section of the chapter outlines how social media can be used within organizations to encourage employees to network and to form communities of practice that stimulate knowledge sharing, learning and innovation.

9.2 DEFINING EMPLOYEE COMMUNICATION

Contemporary organizations realize that their performance rests on effective communication with their employees. Many of the most reputable firms and 'most admired' organizations spend in fact more than three times as much on employee communication than their less admired counterparts.[1] Communicating routinely and effectively with employees is linked to employee commitment, productivity, job performance and satisfaction, as well as to a significantly lesser likelihood of employees leaving the organization. Given these direct benefits, it is perhaps not surprising that employee communication is a core area of corporate communication.

The terms that have often been used to label this area of corporate communication are 'employee communication', 'staff communication' and 'internal communication'. Traditionally, employee communication, which is the term used in this chapter, was defined as communication with employees internal to the organization. Such internal communication was distinguished from forms of external communication with stakeholders such as customers and investors. However, the advent of new technologies (e.g. blogs, e-mail) has meant that messages to employees do not always remain 'inside' the organization. These new technologies have blurred the boundaries between 'internal' and 'external' communication. Employees can nowadays distribute their own information about an organization electronically to outside stakeholders, sometimes without any gate-keeping or control from corporate communication professionals. On a blog, for example, employees can share their views and publish their grievances as well as organize and demand action from the organization. Indeed, with access to e-mail, blogs and social networking sites for sharing corporate information, many employees become somewhat like corporate communication professionals themselves.

Clearly, communication technologies have led to many changes in the workplace. Computer technologies have made it easier to produce, multiply, distribute and store written documents; to exchange messages over long distances and to work together and to execute meetings relatively independent of time and space. Employees are now often connected to each other by electronic means rather than through close physical proximity. E-mails, the intranet, video conferencing and podcasting are used by managers to communicate with employees and by employees themselves to stay informed of company news. IBM, for example, offers more than 5,000 audio and video podcast 'episodes' to employees, who can download these files and watch or listen to them at a convenient time. IBM feels that these podcasts are a useful way to disseminate corporate information in an efficient and engaging way.

If we look at the use of communication technologies within organizations, we can first of all distinguish two central areas of employee communication: (a) management communication, and (b) corporate information and communication systems. Management communication refers to communication between a manager and their subordinate employees. Communication in this setting is often directly related to the specific tasks and activities of individual employees as well as to their morale and wellbeing. Research on what managers do has demonstrated that managers spend most of their time communicating, and much of that time is spent in verbal, face-to-face communication.[2] Besides face-to-face communication, managers also increasingly use e-mail, video conferencing and enterprise software to communicate to their employees. Whilst the responsibility for management communication lies with managers themselves and not with the corporate communication department, communication practitioners often advise and support managers in their communication to staff. Communication practitioners in AstraZeneca, for example, have developed training materials for senior and middle managers to help them become better communicators.

Corporate information and communication systems (CICS) have a broader focus than the manager–employee dyad. CICS involve technologies and communication systems that broadcast corporate decisions and developments to all employees across the organization. The emphasis is on disseminating information about the organization to employees in all ranks and functions within the organization, in order to keep them informed about corporate matters. CICS is often the preserve of the communication department, charged with releasing information to employees through the intranet, e-mails and so-called 'town hall' meetings (i.e. large employee meetings where senior managers announce and explain key corporate decisions or developments). Corporate TV such as the digital FedEx Television Network or Nokia's digital broadcasting systems are also used as communication channels for reaching employees around the world.

Whereas management communication is often restricted to the specific interpersonal work setting of a manager and an employee, CICS may not differentiate content between groups of employees and typically relates to more general organizational developments rather than specific areas of work. As such, its more general contents are not tuned to the interests and circumstances of specific employees across the organization. Management communication, however, can more easily address various groups of employees, yet it misses the broader organizational picture. In other words, whilst distinct in scope, both areas of employee communication complement each other in ensuring that information flows vertically and horizontally across the organization. Without both forms of employee communication, a company's overall communication effort may be ineffective and its employees demotivated. One key implication for corporate communicators is to assess whether CICS and management communication work effectively in that together they cover and reach the entire base of employees – from, for example, managers and workers to consultants and trainees, and from full-time staff to employees on part-time contracts. The two together should also be used strategically to reach the twin objectives that organizations often have for employee communication: to provide relevant and specific information to employees to support them in their tasks and work objectives; and to build an organizational community with strong relationships between employees, and with employees strongly identifying with the organization.

The complementary nature of both forms of employee communication can also be understood through the concepts of downward and upward communication. Downward communication consists of electronic and verbal methods of informing employees about their organization, its performance and their own contribution and performance in terms they can comprehend. In other words, downward communication involves 'information flowing from the top of the organizational management hierarchy and telling people in the organization what is important (mission) and what is valued (policies)'.[3] Both management communication and CICS are central to downward communication; together, they provide employees with general information from the top of the organization (CICS) as well as with more specific information from their managers (management communication).

A good example of this kind of downward communication is the corporate calendar system within Siemens. The corporate calendar (Figure 9.1) lists events throughout the year at which the corporate strategy and corporate objectives are communicated to employees from different parts of the company. The calendar was developed by corporate communication practitioners who realized that employees were not always informed about the company's strategy in a timely and consistent manner. Communication practitioners raised the issue with the CEO and senior executives who agreed that the calendar system could be usefully incorporated into the corporate strategy as a way of implementing the strategy. The CEO and senior executives felt that the calendar would make an important contribution to the achievement of the corporate objectives as it provides a medium to report on the past

				AM		PM							
				8.00	10.00	12.00	2.00	4.00	6.00	8.00	10.00	12.00	
Events and corporate calender	Oct	Nov	Dec	Jan	Feb	Mar	Apr	May	Jun	Jul	Aug	Sep	Oct
Siemens Business Conference (incl. top+ award)													
Communication of key topics for the new fiscal year			▬ Groups, Regions, Corporate Units										
Target achievement, target agreements, staff dialogs, management dialogs	▬▬▬												
Structuring and integration of initiatives in the Group/Region planning process		▬▬▬▬▬▬▬▬▬▬▬▬▬▬▬▬▬▬▬											
Approval of Regional business plans										▬▬			
Review of Group plans by the Corporate Executive Committee											▬▬		
Quarterly reviews (Q2 with expanded circle of attendees)		(Q4)		(Q1)			(Q1)			(Q3)			
Regular reviews of initiatives in the Corporate Executive Committee	▬	▬	▬	▬	▬	▬	▬	▬	▬	▬	▬	▬	▬
Best practice sharing/ Best Practice Day			▬▬▬▬▬▬▬▬▬▬▬▬▬▬▬▬▬▬										
Training to support initiatives	▬▬▬▬▬▬▬▬▬▬▬▬▬▬▬▬▬▬▬▬▬												

FIGURE 9.1 The corporate calendar system at Siemens (calendar dating from 2003); reprinted with permission

year's targets and for setting binding priorities and objectives for the new fiscal year. As displayed in Figure 9.1, the Siemens Business Conference (SBS) marks the start of each fiscal year. This central communication event provides a platform for senior managers to report on the past year's targets and to set priorities and objectives for the new fiscal year. The SBS event is followed by management conferences in the business divisions, regions and corporate units. By streamlining management events, the corporate calendar ensures that all managers and employees hear about the past year's results and are given objectives for the coming period.

Upward communication, on the other hand, involves information from employees that is sent up to managers within the organization. It often involves information about the employee themselves, information about co-workers, information about organizational practices and policies, and information about what needs to be done and how it can be done. Allowing employees to communicate upwards is important because employees' ideas, responses to their working environment or critiques of the plans and ideas announced by managers may be used to find ways to improve an organization's overall performance and profitability. Upward communication is typically facilitated within the interpersonal setting of management communication. Managers can stimulate employees to voice concerns and to provide them with feed-back on practices, procedures and new organizational changes. At the same time, CICS may include communication systems such as message boards on an intranet and 'town hall' meetings, allowing employees to ask questions of senior managers and to ask for further information on corporate decisions or organizational developments.

9.3 EMPLOYEE COMMUNICATION AND ORGANIZATIONAL IDENTIFICATION

Generally speaking, when employees strongly identify with the organization that they work for, they are more satisfied in their work, they will be more coopera-tive and they will also demonstrate behaviour that is helpful to the organization.[4] Organizational identification, in other words, plays a significant role in many organi-zations. Organizational identification can be defined as: 'the perception of oneness with or belongingness to an organization, where the individual defines him or herself in terms of the organization(s) of which he or she is a member'.[5] Academic research has shown that organizational identification increases as a result of the perceived external prestige of the organization[6] and as a result of the degree of overlap between the personal identity of the employees and the identity of the organization. When employees perceive their organization to be associated with a strong reputation and prestige in the eyes of outsiders, they often feel proud to belong to that organiza-tion and may feel inclined to bask in its reflected glory. Employees identify with an organization partly to enhance their own self-esteem: the more prestigious an indi-vidual employee perceives their organization to be, the greater the potential boost to self-esteem through identification. Employees also identify more strongly with their organization to the degree that the corporate values and attributes of the organization (organizational identity) correspond with their own personal values. In other words, the higher the perceived fit between the values of an individual employee and the corresponding organization, the stronger the degree to which that employee identifies with their organization.

Employee communication in particular has a significant impact on organizational identification. Recent studies demonstrate that downward communication enhances organizational identification when the information transmitted is perceived as adequate and reliable.[7] Adequate information involves receiving useful and sufficient information about what is expected of employees in their work and regarding their contributions. The more adequate or specific the information to the employee involved, the higher the level of identification with that organization. Reliable information involves the perception that managers release information that is trustworthy and instrumental to the accomplishment of tasks. When information coming from management is perceived as reliable, employees are more likely to identify with their organization.[8] A further factor that has a significant impact on organizational identification involves the degree to which employees feel that they are listened to and are involved by managers when decisions are made. When employees feel that they participate in decision-making and are able to exert some control over their working life, they identify more strongly with their organization and are also generally more committed. Good employee communication, therefore, combines upward and downward communication in such a way that employees are well informed about the future directions of the organization (in particular the organization's strategies and policies) and are allowed to interact with management about their policies, and where this interaction has an impact on managerial decisions. In other words, employee communication is most productive, in the sense of eliciting employee commitment and organizational identification, if it is a two-way process of communication, rather than a one-way flow of feedback and instructions. The role of corporate communication practitioners and managers is therefore to use management communication and CICS in such a way that employee communication provides each employee with adequate information and opportunities to speak out, be listened to and get actively involved in the organization.

Again, the balance between downward and upward communication is key to fostering strong levels of employee identification. If employee communication in an organization is largely top-down, it may be experienced by employees as limiting and indeed as somewhat oppressive. The one-directional flow of information in the form of directives and commands may then in turn negatively shape employees' feelings and emotions as they try to perform the roles that are expected of them. Yet, without any opportunities to provide feedback or to speak up, they would feel that their professional roles and emotional wellbeing are suppressed or even controlled, with a direct effect on their commitment, morale and identification with the organization. On the other hand, if employees are provided with the means to express their opinions through upward communication and are able to exercise some influence over their workplace, their level of involvement, as well as the degree to which they identify with the organization, is bound to go up. The following case example (9.1) from India gives a good illustration of these communication principles.

 —— CASE EXAMPLE 9.1 ——

USING EMPLOYEE COMMUNICATION TO EMPOWER EMPLOYEES

Hindustan Petroleum Company Limited (HPCL) is the third largest oil company in India, with more than 11,000 employees. In 2003, the company initiated a series of workshops called Vision 2006, which allowed employees to discuss in small groups the strategic vision and direction of the company. Employees were able to talk freely, explored the various levels and parts of the organization, and tested each other's ideas and assumptions. Almost all of the company's employees participated in these workshops which lasted up to three days and involved professional coaches who facilitated the discussions. Whilst the leaders of the company realized that with these workshops they could open themselves up to all sorts of feedback, they quickly observed a remarkable convergence across the ideas that emerged from these workshops. As Arun Balakrishnan, the chairman and managing director from 2007 to 2010, remarked: 'It was amazing to see that irrespective of the level in the hierarchy, the vision statements that were coming out were almost the same, from the senior management down to unionized staff – especially the unionized staff.'[9] Each employee, whether a senior executive or union member, had to prepare a five-point vision statement for the company. When these statements were combined, they did not simply reinforce a particular vision, but also led to new ideas regarding the company's strategic direction. The most telling of these ideas was that unionized members pushed the company to go global. As one of the coaches during the workshops mentioned afterwards, the workshops not only redefined what business the company was in but also gave a sense of ownership of the vision to all those who had participated: 'People at large wanted the vision to be broad-based: "Instead of being a petroleum company, we should think of ourselves as an energy company." That kind of attitude was so powerful. People started feeling, "This is my vision." And changes in the vision did come about, because people wanted these things.'[10] The final and official version of the company's vision statement reflects these suggestions. In short, the organization still known as HPCL now aims to move beyond its original locale and business to become a global player in the energy market, a far-reaching vision that was identified and defined through input from employees.

Question for reflection

Reflect on the value of employee input into the formulation of a corporate vision and strategy. When do you think this is most valuable and when would you consider it as potentially less instrumental?

Source: Drawn from Groysberg, Boris and Slind, Michael (2012) *Talk, Inc.: How Trusted Leaders Use Conversation to Power their Organizations*. Boston, MA: Harvard Business School Press.

9.4 VOICE, SILENCE AND STIMULATING EMPLOYEE PARTICIPATION

Voice, silence and employee participation are terms used to refer to the degree to which employees speak up, are listened to and participate in organizational decision-making. Employee participation involves organizational structures and processes designed to empower and enable employees to identify with organizational goals and to exert power over decision-making. Unionization of the workforce, for example, is one way in which the interests of workers are represented and communicated to senior managers. In some organizations, participation is anchored in the very identity and corporate governance of the organization. Cooperative organizations, for example, are jointly owned and democratically controlled by all those who work for the organization. John Lewis, a successful cooperative chain of department stores in the UK, attributes much of its success to employee co-ownership, which the company feels has led to 'sky-high' levels of employee engagement.[11]

Whilst most organizations are not based on a form of employee co-ownership like John Lewis, employee participation has been an issue of concern as long as organizations have existed. Employees want a say in shaping their work lives, and organizations equally often feel that participation is desirable for a number of reasons, from genuine concern for the welfare of employees to a desire for the productivity benefits that can follow from employees engaging with their organization. However, even though participation is desirable, enabling employee participation is by no means straightforward.

The management scholars Morrison and Milliken have argued that there are often powerful forces in many organizations that prevent employees from participation and that force them to withhold information about potential problems or issues.[12] They refer to such withholding of information as organizational silence. When employees share a perception that speaking up is unwise or without any consequence, they remain silent. Such silence in turn may mean that vital upward information is not passed on to managers. Morrison and Milliken pointed to two factors that often systematically cause employees to feel that their opinions are not valued and that thereby discourage them from speaking up. The first factor relates to managers' fear of receiving negative feedback from employees. There is evidence to suggest that senior and middle managers often feel threatened by negative feedback, whether this information is about them personally or about a decision or course of action with which they identify. Managers often feel a strong need to avoid embarrassment, threat and feelings of vulnerability or incompetence. Therefore, they are likely to avoid any negative information and negative feedback coming from subordinates. The second factor that may influence organizational silence involves a set of managerial beliefs which suggest that managers know best about organizational matters. The basic assumption underlying such beliefs of managers is that, because of information asymmetries, employees will not have a broad enough understanding of the organization. The information that employees therefore provide about organizational matters is seen as not relevant or up-to-date compared to the knowledge that managers already have. This particular belief is quite strong in managers who view their role as one of directing and controlling, with employees assuming the role of unquestioning followers (see Figure 9.2).

If the dominant belief of managers in an organization is that employees are not sufficiently knowledgeable about what is best for the organization, then it is reasonable

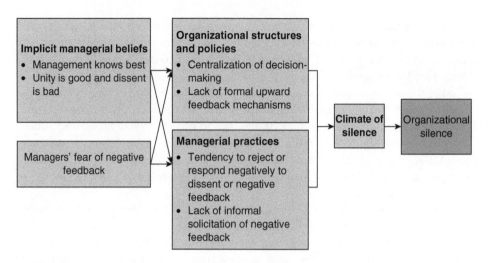

FIGURE 9.2 The conditions and processes leading to organizational silence

Source: Adapted from Morrison, E.W. and Milliken, F.J. (2000) 'Organizational silence: A barrier to change and development in a pluralistic world', *Academy of Management Review*, 25: 706-25, figure on p. 709.

for managers not to involve them in decision-making processes. In turn, participative forms of decision-making that involve employees will be seen by managers as not worth the time and effort they require. Excluding employees from decision-making is also a way to avoid dissent and negative feedback and, thus, will also stem from fear of negative feedback. In many organizations, although there may be the appearance of some forms of participative decision-making (e.g. task forces, committees), managers still often attempt to hold on to their decision-making authority. And when managers fear negative feedback from employees, they are unlikely to engage in seeking much informal feedback from subordinates. Instead, managers may be more inclined to seek feedback from those who are likely to share their perspective and who are, thus, unlikely to provide negative feedback.

The fear of negative feedback and the belief that upward information is often of little value will also be associated with a lack of mechanisms for soliciting employee feedback after decisions are made. Using procedures such as employee surveys or 360-degree feedback will be unlikely, because there will be a tendency to believe that little of value will be learned from them and because negative upward feedback will be seen as a challenge to management's control. It is important to realize that these various managerial beliefs and practices contributing to silence may operate at multiple levels of an organization. For example, middle managers and work supervisors may hold these beliefs and exhibit day-to-day practices that impede upward communication, whilst corporate communication practitioners and senior executives feel that employee feedback and involvement is a key performance indicator.

Organizational silence can damage the organization in that it blocks negative feedback and, hence, an organization's ability to detect and correct errors. Without negative feedback, errors within an organization may persist and may even intensify, because corrective actions are not taken when needed. The quality of decision-making may also be affected by organizational silence. Potentially useful viewpoints and alternatives from the perspective of employees are not considered. The effectiveness of organizational decision-making will be compromised because of the restricted information available to managers. The tendency of managers to discourage employee opinions and feedback is also likely to elicit negative reactions from employees. Employees may come to feel that they are not valued and that they lack control over their work. When employees feel that they are not valued, they will also be less likely to identify with the organization.

The concept of organizational silence is closely related to the concept of communication climate. Communication climate is defined as the internal environment of information exchange between managers and employees through an organization's formal and informal networks.[13] A communication climate is characterized as 'open' when information flows freely between individuals, groups and departments, and it is characterized as 'closed' when information is blocked. Organizational silence corresponds to a 'closed' communication climate because it involves a shared and widespread feeling amongst employees that speaking up is of little use, leading them to withhold potentially valuable information. In an 'open' communication climate, in contrast, employees feel free to express opinions, voice complaints and offer suggestions to their superiors. In such a climate, information also passes without distortion upward, downward and horizontally throughout the organization. Employees feel that they have enough support from their managers so that they can give information to them without hesitation, confident that superiors will readily accept it, whether good or bad, favourable or unfavourable. In an 'open' communication climate, employees also know that their information will be seen as valuable, and hence sending communication upward may have an effect.

9.5 SOCIAL MEDIA, NETWORKS AND COMMUNITIES OF PRACTICE

Downward and upward communication largely reflect the hierarchy of the organization, with managers communicating to employees on an individual basis or in work teams, and with employees speaking up and potentially participating in decision-making at higher levels in the organization. Hierarchy often stems from the vertical structure as depicted in the organizational chart of an organization (see Chapter 2). The vertical structure refers to the way in which tasks and activities are allocated to employees and located in the hierarchy of authority within an organization. The solid vertical lines that connect the boxes on an organization chart depict this vertical structure and the authority relationships involved, with senior and middle managers being located higher up in the hierarchy than employees. Communication that strictly follows such hierarchical lines, either downwards or upwards, is often by its very nature about control and command, and about supporting the coordination of specialized tasks across employees and departments. Besides such vertical communication, many organizations have started to use other media and means of communication to harness the creative potential and energy of their employees. Companies such as Cisco,

Dell and General Motors have initiated digital platforms and networking tools for dialogue and conversation between managers and employees. These platforms replace a one-way communication structure with systems that enable interactive dialogue between employees. Common features on such platforms include online databases, where users can create and edit content in a dynamic, collaborative fashion; online message boards and blogs; and file- and video-sharing sites.

These digital platforms foster networking between employees that, in a sense, breaks with the formal lines of communication across hierarchical lines. The networks that employees subsequently form through communication can be quite varied, ranging from communication within a group of young professionals who are at the same stage in their career, to a community of people with an interest in a particular technology, to networks based on social interests. Academic research into communication networks makes a distinction between production networks, which are primarily formed around the accomplishment of work tasks; innovation networks, which emerge around the creation, development and diffusion of new ideas; and maintenance networks, which serve to develop and maintain social relationships at work.[14] Obviously, these types may overlap, such as when a group of co-workers start to develop strong social bonds between them and form a maintenance network. For corporate communicators, it is often useful to have a good sense of the communication patterns and networks in an organization, so that they know what networked groups exist and can figure out how best to communicate with such groups.

An interesting aspect of network dynamics in the context of innovation is the notion of the 'strength of weak ties'.[15] The sociologist Mark Granovetter, who developed the idea, suggests that we often value so-called strong ties in social and organizational settings that are based on strong durable relationships with others and on frequent communication. However, such strong ties may also lead to an in-group mentality where you mirror each other's ideas and points of view, making it harder to generate new ideas. Instead, weak ties between individuals – such as between occasional acquaintances, relative outsiders or different subject experts – are more likely to lead to a challenging of taken-for-granted assumptions and to combining different ideas that may potentially lead to significant innovations.

One interesting form of network in the workplace today is what has been labelled as a 'community of practice'. These are networks of communication that bind employees together with a common focus on a particular project or because of shared professional interests. Communities of practice are based on the idea of self-organization through coordinated activity. Jean Lave and Etienne Wenger, who popularized the idea, defined a community of practice as a group of people informally bound together by common interests.[16] Such communities are not only self-managing, similar to self-managing work teams, but also self-designing in pursuit of social connections and a common social identity as well as mutual learning and knowledge development. An organization can consist of many different communities of practice that, once formed, can cross departmental and divisional boundaries, or any other dimension of formal hierarchical structure. Structure exists in emerging networks of social connections between individuals and groups. The community model suggests that although the group itself may not literally be in one and the same place, members are connected as a group and bound together through their common interests.

In this respect, Wenger suggests that 'members of a community are informally *bound* by what they do together – from engaging in lunchtime discussions to solving difficult problems – and by what they have learned through their mutual engagement in these activities'. He also argues that 'communities of practice are not a new kind of organizational unit', but that they are 'a different cut on the organization's structure – one that emphasizes the learning that people have done together rather than the unit they report to, the project they are working on, or the people they know'.[17] In other words, communities of practice 'set their own boundaries' around themselves and largely through collaborating together. Examples of communities of practice are found in many organizations and have been called by different names at various times, including 'learning communities' at Hewlett-Packard Company, 'family groups' at the Xerox Corporation, 'thematic groups' at the World Bank, 'peer groups' at British Petroleum (BP) and 'knowledge networks' at IBM Global Services (see Case Study 9.1). According to Wenger, it is important that boundaries of communities of practice remain fairly flexible so that the expertise within them is not sheltered from other communities and so that a community avoids becoming insular. With *flexible boundaries*, communities of practice learn through the knowledge that they develop within them as well as through any further knowledge from other communities that they may bring in and assimilate. In recent years, a growing list of interactive digital platforms, often labelled as 'Web 2.0', give employees the ability to freely communicate with one another and to build communities around shared interests. Much like Facebook and LinkedIn, internal social networks allow users to create personal profiles, post messages and correspond with other community users. These networks can be password-protected and can grow organically, based on the interests that are shared between employees. The IBM case study provides a good example of how digital platforms can be used to support the development of communities of practice.

CASE STUDY 9.1

TRANSFORMING IBM

International Business Machines (IBM) is one of the largest information technology and services companies in the world with almost 400,000 employees and operations in more than 170 countries. Through the development of the personal computer in the 1980s, the company had become an industry leader. In the 1990s, however, IBM moved from being the most profitable company in the world and an industry leader to one with negative earnings and sliding revenues. This had a major impact on the workforce of more than 400,000 at the time, who had grown accustomed to a tradition of life-long employment at the best place to work in the world. However, the total workforce had to be cut over the course of several years. After these crisis years, culminating with an $8.1 billion net loss in 1993, IBM began a steady climb towards

(Continued)

(Continued)

profitability with a net income of $7.7 billion in 2001. In 2002, IBM found itself in a solid position again, given its wide range of products and its unparalleled research excellence (IBM had received more patents than any other company for each year in the previous decade). Sam Palmisano, who became CEO in 2002, recognized, however, that these capabilities would not be enough. He felt that he also needed to unite IBM's vast resources to create customized solutions on behalf of its customers, and to do that he needed to develop a deep level of social integration within IBM. In 2002, this was a huge challenge given the changes and turmoil that the company had gone through in the previous decade. As he assumed control in 2002, Palmisano recognized that the task would be one of uniting IBM's global workforce behind a common set of values and through stimulating collaborative work. When employees could share strong connections with one another, and be united in purpose, horizontal interaction and innovation at the behest of customers would be a lot easier.

Changing the internal culture

However, because of the turmoil of the 1990s, whatever values the employees had previously shared between them had been lost. By 2002, many of IBM's more than 325,000 employees had no idea that there were any common IBM values other than driving up profits. Longer-term employees had also become disenfranchised with the company, their trust in the company shaken by lost job security and reduced benefits. Palmisano and his top executives recognized that something had to be done. From the start, they reasoned that a top-down approach would not work with a highly educated and cynical workforce. IBM employees generally have strong feelings about their work and would probably not appreciate a prescriptive approach that circumscribes the company's values for them. Palmisano's team therefore decided to set up an online discussion forum, using a technology that was pioneered by IBM in 2001. The forum was open to all IBM employees and facilitated the free and open expression of ideas. The team felt that this forum would be the right venue for focusing IBM's global workforce on a recommitment to corporate values. It fitted with the mobility of IBM's workforce and its flexible work arrangements. The team initially produced a set of three proposed value phrases (commitment to the customer, excellence through innovation, integrity that earns trust) that were put online in 2003 to start the online discussion. On 21 July 2003, Palmisano announced the exercise on the IBM intranet, inviting IBMers across geographies, divisions, levels and functions to participate in the discussion. Over the next three days, an estimated 50,000 IBMers monitored the discussion and 10,000 comments were posted. Many of these comments revolved around how to realize and live particular values, not around the wording or the substance of the values themselves. Besides many cynical comments, employees also pointed to the formulation of common values that could bring the company together. As Palmisano recalls:

> IBMers by the tens of thousands weighed in. They were thoughtful and passionate about the company they want to be a part of. They were also brutally honest. Some of what they wrote was painful to read, because they pointed out all the bureaucratic and dysfunctional things that get in the way of serving clients, working as a team or implementing new ideas. But we

were resolute in keeping the dialog free-flowing and candid. And I don't think what resulted – broad, enthusiastic, grass-roots consensus – could have been obtained in any other way.

At the end of the online session, the executives collated and analysed the comments, which led to an announcement in November 2003 of the new company values. These were 'dedication to every client's success', 'innovation that matters – for our company and the world' and 'trust and personal responsibility in all our relationships'. When these values were posted on the intranet as 'our values at work', more than 200,000 IBMers viewed them within a few weeks and employee responses indicated that there was strong support for the three chosen values. In October 2004, IBM held a second values-related online discussion, this time on the practical issues involved in the implementation of the values. Many ideas for how this could be done were posted by employees. After this session, Palmisano announced with his trademark clarity a range of initiatives, both internal and external, that would help in realizing the hard work of living these values. These initiatives included efforts to overhaul corporate programmes, align performance management and compensation with the values, invigorate training and support individuals in forming innovation-driven communities of practice. Once the key values had been identified, Palmisano and his communication executives also re-crafted the IBM story in the image of these values. The IBM story details how IBM and its predecessor companies have always been infused by human values, focused on developing innovations that matter to the world and that support progress, and defined by the best customer service. Whilst these values may have been more or less prominent at various stages in the company's history, the IBM story suggests that they have always been there at a deeper level. As such, they can also act as a guide to the future direction of the company.

Communities of practice

Besides this value-driven initiative, Palmisano also recognized the importance of communities of practice within IBM. These communities consist of informally connected groups of employees who discuss, often in an online setting, different areas of expertise. Although they are formed informally, the company supports them through software tools that facilitate the interaction between employees across the globe. Communities of practice within the organization were initially started in 1995 with informal networks of professionals managing domains of knowledge around IBM's technological competencies (such as enterprise systems management, application development, testing methods and practices, product platform), marketing competencies (such as e-business, package integration, mergers and acquisitions) and industry sector competencies (such as automotive, chemicals and petroleum, distribution, finance and insurance, and healthcare). In 2000, there were over 60 unique communities of practice and about 76,000 professionals who participated through web-based software (ICM asset web) which connects individuals to different communities. These professionals were also supported through an information portal that allowed them direct access to different IBM data sources. Within these communities, professionals handle knowledge in the above domains as well as intellectual capital; they gather, evaluate, structure and disseminate knowledge that is shared amongst

(Continued)

(Continued)

community peers and across customer projects and they also manage related intellectual capital consisting of methods, processes, tools, assets, reported experiences and any other documentation associated with delivering services and considered of value by the business or community. All of these communities evolve with some assistance from the corporate organization. Whilst they are self-managing, they tend to seek support from the organization, usually to obtain some level of organizational recognition, support and access to the common technology infrastructure. Many of these communities, particularly ones that are fully formed, are characterized by a lot of development and learning within their boundaries, with professionals working together to build and sustain the community as well as to solve business problems and exploit business opportunities. Indeed, professionals in such fully formed communities often see it as their joint responsibility to pool knowledge and work together to address the business issues presented to them and to create new products (new solutions, new offerings, new methods) in the process.

Recognizing the importance of these communities of practice, the company introduced the On Demand Workplace in 2003, an online technology which centralized the support for communities of practice and allowed employees across the globe to share and transfer knowledge. This online workplace helps employees to search for the profile of other IBMers, and also provides products and technologies that connect people and business processes.

These communities of practice, together with the value-based initiative, help bring IBMers together, creating stronger social connections between them and providing a platform for collaboration and innovation. They are thus a central part of the company's market-driven strategy. Palmisano explains: 'If three fifths of your business is manufacturing, management is basically supervisory ... but that no longer works when your business is primarily based on knowledge'. Instead, he argues, 'if you are going to build a business based on continual innovation and new intellectual capital, you are signing up for total dependence on the creativity and adaptive skills of your workforce'. Hence, common values and communities of practice that cut across divisions, departments and levels are key to developing innovative solutions for clients. Again, in the words of Palmisano: 'how else can we get our people in far-flung business units with different financial targets and incentives working together in teams that can offer at a single price a comprehensive and customized solution – one that doesn't show the organizational seams?'

Questions for reflection

1   Reflect on employee communication within IBM from the perspective of employees. How can communication with staff be characterized in terms of upward and downward communication and in terms of employee participation and voice?

2   IBM has supported the development of communities of practice within its organization. Would you expect such communities to be equally useful in other organizations and industry sectors that are, to a lesser extent, focused on constant innovation?

Source: This case study is based on Weeks, J. and Barsoux, J. (2010) IBM: The value of values. IMD case study; and on Kanter, R. and Bird, M. (2009) IBM in the 21st century: The coming of the globally integrated enterprise. Harvard Business School case study.

9.6 CHAPTER SUMMARY

The chapter started by defining the role of employee communication in terms of its impact on employee commitment, morale and organizational identification. One significant message in the chapter has been the importance of combining downward and upward communication between management and employees in such a way that employees feel valued, feel that they are listened to and feel that they can speak up about organizational decisions, practices and relationships with their colleagues. Besides upward and downward communication, organizations may also support employees with digital communication platforms for setting up communities of practice to encourage learning and innovation.

 ——— DISCUSSION QUESTIONS ———

1. Describe in your own words how, in an ideal scenario, communication flows between managers and employees in an organization. Can you give examples from your own experience in organizations to support your account?

2. Social media and new work-based technologies are changing employee communication. How, in your view, can these media and technologies be used to improve learning and innovation, as well as cohesion amongst employees? Which organizations, in your view, are doing this particularly well?

KEY TERMS

Communication climate

Organizational identification
Organizational silence
Emotions
Upward communication
Communities of practice
Networks

Corporate information and communication systems
Employee participation
Employee voice
Management communication
Downward communication
Social media
Weak ties

——— FURTHER READING ———

Birkinshaw, Julian (2012) *Reinventing Management: Smarter Choices for Getting Work Done*. London: Wiley, revised and updated edition.

Spender, J.-C. and Strong, Bruce (2014) *Strategic Conversations: Creating and Directing the Entrepreneurial Workforce*. Cambridge: Cambridge University Press.

Want to know more about this chapter? Visit the companion website at: https://study.sagepub.com/cornelissen5e to access videos, web links, a glossary and selected journal articles to further enhance your study.

NOTES

1. Seitel, F.P. (2006) *The Practice of Public Relations*. Prentice Hall, 10th edition.
2. See, for example, Hales, C.P. (1986) 'What do managers do? A critical examination of the evidence', *Journal of Management Studies*, 23: 88–115; Tengblad, S. (2006) 'Is there a "new managerial work"? A comparison with Henry Mintzberg's classic study 30 years later', *Journal of Management Studies*, 43: 1437–61; Birkinshaw, Julian (2012) *Reinventing Management: Smarter Choices for Getting Work Done*. London: Wiley.
3. Andrews, P.H. and Herschel, R.T. (1996) *Organizational Communication: Empowerment in a Technological Society*. Boston, MA: Houghton Mifflin.
4. See, for example, Dutton, J.E., Dukerich, J.M. and Harquail, C.V. (1994) 'Organizational images and member identification', *Administrative Science Quarterly*, 39: 239–63.
5. Mael, F.A. and Ashforth, B.E. (1992) 'Alumni and their alma mater: A partial test of the reformulated model of organizational identification', *Journal of Organizational Behavior*, 13: 103–23, quote on p. 104.
6. Dutton et al. (1994); Smidts, A., Pruyn, A.T.H. and Van Riel, C.B.M. (2001) 'The impact of employee communication and perceived external prestige on organizational identification', *Academy of Management Journal*, 44: 1051–62.
7. Smidts et al. (2001); Bartels, J., Pruyn, A.T.H, De Jong, M.D.T. and Joustra, I. (2007) 'Multiple organizational identification levels and the impact of perceived external prestige and communication climate', *Journal of Organizational Behavior*, 28: 173–90; Bartels, J., Peters, O., de Jong, M. D. T., Pruyn, A.Th.H. and Van der Molen, M. (2010) 'Horizontal and vertical communication as determinants of professional and organizational identification', *Personnel Review*, 39 (2): 210–26.
8. Christensen, L.T., Cornelissen, J.P. and Morsing, M. (2007) 'Corporate communications and its reception: A comment on Llewellyn and Harrison', *Human Relations*, 60: 653–61.
9. Groysberg, Boris and Slind, Michael (2012) *Talk, Inc.: How Trusted Leaders Use Conversation to Power their Organizations*. Boston, MA: Harvard Business School Press, p. 38.
10. Groysberg and Slind (2012), p. 39.
11. De Vita, E. (2007) 'John Lewis: Partners on board', *Management Team*, August: 44–47.
12. Morrison, E.W. and Milliken, F.J. (2000) 'Organizational silence: A barrier to change and development in a pluralistic world', *Academy of Management Review*, 25: 706–25.
13. See, for example, Conrad, C. and Scott Poole, M. (2012) *Strategic Organizational Communication in a Global Economy*. Fort Worth, TX: Harcourt, 7th edition.
14. Monge, P.R. and Contractor, N.S. (2003) *Theories of Communication Networks*. New York: Oxford University Press.
15. Granovetter, M.S. (1973) 'The strength of weak ties', *American Journal of Sociology*, 81: 1287–303.
16. Lave, Jean and Wenger, Etienne (1991) *Situated Learning: Legitimate Peripheral Participation*. Cambridge: Cambridge University Press.
17. Wenger, Etienne (1998) 'Communities of practice: Learning as a social system' (www.co-i-l.com/coil/knowledge-garden/cop/lss.shtml) [first published in *Systems Thinker*].

Issues Management

10

| CHAPTER OVERVIEW |

Organizations are increasingly challenged by activist groups, communities and governments on issues of public concern. A key role for communication practitioners is not only to analyse and understand how such issues evolve and may affect their organizations, but also to work out the appropriate communication strategies for dealing with such issues. The chapter discusses effective principles of issues management, ranging from reactive communication strategies to proactive advocacy to influence public policy and government regulation.

10.1 INTRODUCTION

Issues management is a rapidly growing area of activity within corporate communication. It has grown partly as a result of many high-profile public issues that have emerged in recent years. Whilst such issues have always existed within the public domain, the past decade has been particularly taxing on business leaders. The turn towards a so-called 'risk society' has created an emphasis on health and safety, environmental concerns, security and terrorism, and financial risk and regulation.[1] All of these issues are, to a greater or lesser extent, alive in the public mind. Indeed, the general public often expects a corporate response on these issues. Corporate organizations therefore increasingly realize that instead of fighting public opinion, a more effective approach would be to advocate their own positions to the public and to key political decision makers. Organizations have therefore begun investing in issues management programmes, including corporate advertising campaigns, advocacy and lobbying efforts and stakeholder engagement. The general principle behind such programmes is that by being knowledgeable about issues and government regulation and by getting involved in the development of public policy and stakeholder solutions, corporate organizations are better able to protect themselves from potentially damaging criticism whilst taking advantage of any positive opportunities that arise from engaging with stakeholders. In this chapter, we describe the general principles of issues management and discuss different issue-based communication strategies. We start the chapter with a brief introduction to the topic. We then discuss several principles and strategies of issues management in greater detail, and we end the chapter with a closer look at anti-corporate activism and influencing public policy.

10.2 DEFINING ISSUES

An issue can negatively affect the reputation of an organization. A fraud allegation, for example, may damage a company's reputation as a financially solid and reliable investment target. Similarly, a product recall may lead to public concern about the safety and reliability of a company's products. Strictly speaking, an issue can be defined as: (a) a public concern about the organization's decisions and operations that may or may not also involve (b) a point of conflict in opinions and judgments regarding those decisions and operations. For example, when Mattel recalled millions of toys in 2007 because of dangerously high levels of chemicals and toxins, the recall became an issue of public concern about the safety of the company's supply chain and manufacturing in China. Mattel, however, acknowledged the problem and hence there was no difference of opinion with customers and members of the general public about the severity of the issue and about the necessity of a product recall.

In many instances, before issues become connected to an organization and before activists, the public or stakeholders campaign for a specific organization to change, such issues often already exist as a matter of concern in public debates within society. For example, in many contemporary societies, healthy eating and obesity were already issues of public concern before they became connected to organizations such as Coca-Cola and McDonald's. Similarly, there has been an ongoing concern about executive pay and remuneration in many Western societies which has often led to direct action against large corporations. When in April 2016 shareholders of BP voted against a pay rise for the CEO in the face of record losses and whilst the company was cutting thousands of jobs, they acted on a 'mood' against 'fat cat pay' and 'excessive remuneration' that was already present in investment circles and the wider public domain.

Howard Chase, a well-known expert on issues management, defines an issue as 'an unsettled matter which is ready for a decision'.[2] Chase emphasizes that an issue often involves a matter that is in contention between an organization and another party and requires decisive action of the organization in order to protect its reputation. He also suggests that issues and crises are closely related as an issue may develop into a crisis.

A *crisis* is defined as an issue that requires not just decisive but also immediate action from the organization. The necessity of immediate action may be triggered by, for example, mounting public pressures, intense media attention or because of the direct danger (in case of an accident, product tampering or faulty products) to employees, customers or members of the general public. The organization theorist

Karl Weick defines a crisis as a critical and intense issue that threatens the very existence of an organization in terms of its basic assumptions, values and ways of operating.[3] For example, when Shell attempted to dispose of the Brent Spar oil rig in the North Sea, its actions led to a public boycott and to legislation that not only damaged its reputation but also challenged the company to change its basic assumptions and values regarding the environmental impact of its business.

A useful way of thinking about the distinction between issues and crises is to consider the process of how issues develop over time. Figure 10.1 displays how issues emerge and how over time they may become more salient and potent as a result of media attention and greater public concern. As indicated on the left of the figure, there are many 'latent' issues that may become 'active' because of media attention or because of a coalition of stakeholders mobilizing themselves in relation to the issue. At this stage, it is important for organizations to monitor and scan the environment for shifts in public opinion on latent issues that stakeholders may connect with the organization and its industry. AstraZeneca, for example, continuously monitors opinions around the world on animal testing for medical purposes. This issue of animal testing is seen as 'latent' or dormant because of the generally positive attitude to responsible animal testing in the developed world. In addition, many governments often side with pharmaceutical companies against extreme acts of aggression by some animal rights activist groups. However, there is always the potential for the 'latent' issue to evolve into an 'active' issue when opinions on animal testing change. When that happens, the issue becomes salient in the public domain. The media often play a crucial role in this process of making issues 'active'. The media may magnify interest in the issue through news coverage or may be the party that brought the issue up in the first place.[4] After an issue has become 'active', it may develop into an 'intense' issue that increases the pressure on an organization to do something about the issue and avert it from evolving into a significant 'crisis'.

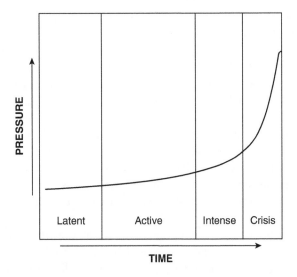

FIGURE 10.1 The development of an issue into a crisis

10.3 MANAGING ISSUES

The aim of this section is to present guidelines for the management of issues so that 'latent' and 'active' issues do not morph into 'intense' issues or a crisis. Although it may not always be possible to completely 'manage' issues, as communication practitioners cannot always foresee or control how an issue evolves, it is important that professionals are prepared and have communication strategies in place. The starting point for issues management involves scanning and monitoring the environment and detecting potential and actual issues. Environmental scanning and an analysis of the issue form the basis for deciding on an appropriate issue response strategy. The entire process of managing issues consists of the following stages: (1) environmental scanning, (2) issue identification and analysis, (3) issue-specific response strategies, and (4) evaluation.

Environmental scanning

All organizations exist in the context of a complex commercial, economic, political, technological, social and cultural world. This environment changes and is more complex for some organizations than for others: how this might affect the organization includes understanding historical and environmental circumstances, as well as expected or potential changes in environmental variables. This is a major task for communication practitioners because the range of variables is so great. Many of those variables will give rise to *opportunities* and others will exert *threats* on the organization. Whether environmental forces have such an impact on the organization, depends furthermore on how the organization itself, in terms of the *strengths* and *weaknesses* in its values, resources and competences, can respond to them. A problem that has to be faced is that the range of variables is likely to be so great that it may not be possible or realistic to identify and analyse each one. Thus, there is a need to distil a view of the main or overarching environmental impacts on the organization. Two analytical tools can be used for this: DESTEP analysis and SWOT analysis.

A DESTEP analysis is a broad analysis of the various *D*emographic, *E*conomic, *S*ocial, *T*echnological, *E*cological and *P*olitical developments and factors that are expected to have an impact on the organization and its operations. This includes a summation of factors such as government regulations (political) that affect the industry in which the organization operates, changing societal attitudes to certain industries and increasing demand for 'corporate citizenship' (social), and the effects of an economic slump and recession for the organization's supply and pricing strategies (economic). The DESTEP analysis provides a framework for summarizing and prioritizing all these factors. Through such a guided analysis of the environment, practitioners are able to describe the most important current environmental changes and to predict future ones.

A SWOT analysis stands for an investigation of the *S*trengths, *W*eaknesses, *O*pportunities and *T*hreats. The first half of this analysis – strengths and weaknesses – examines the company's position, its capabilities, operations and products *vis-à-vis* stakeholders, competitor activities, environmental trends and company resources. The second half of the SWOT takes this review further to examine the opportunities and threats identified within the environment, including, for instance, market opportunities, political regulation and shareholder activism. The result of the SWOT analysis should be a thorough understanding of the organization's status, of its standing with important groups in its environment and of the factors in the environment that may impinge on it. A SWOT analysis should be carried out in an objective and detailed manner, with evidence provided to support the points cited.

Together, these two analytical tools can help practitioners identify trends and detect potential issues in relation to the organization's operations and in relation to important stakeholder groups.

Issue identification and analysis

Through environmental scanning, communication practitioners will identify potential and emerging issues that they need to keep an eye on. A number of these emerging issues may become active in the public domain. Other issues may be identified as 'active' because the organization has marked them as important given their objectives and annual reporting. For example, as part of a company's integrated reporting (see Chapter 14) many managers now identify that the 'material issues' that arise from their company's operations are of consequence to their stakeholders and society at large, such as privacy and security issues for technology and service companies, access to medicine for pharmaceutical companies, responsible drinking for drinks manufacturers and climate and energy issues for resource-intensive manufacturers.

Regardless of how issues emerge and become active, once they have been identified as significant, such issues will have to be further analysed. The aim of issue analysis is to determine the present intensity of the issue in the public domain; how likely it is to trigger government action or impact on public opinion; the likelihood of the issue continuing; the ability of the organization to influence its resolution; and the key stakeholder groups and publics that are involved with the issue. 'Active' issues may concern stakeholders of the organization but also publics (e.g. activist groups) that the organization would not count as legitimate stakeholders but who nonetheless have mobilized themselves in relation to the issue and against the organization.

A useful device to analyse stakeholder and public opinion on a particular issue is the position–importance matrix. The position–importance matrix is very similar to the power–interest matrix (Figure 4.4), but is less concerned with the general salience or interests of stakeholders and is specifically concerned with the position of a stakeholder or public in relation to a particular issue. Stakeholders and publics are categorized in the matrix according to their position on a particular issue and according to their importance to the organization. Relevant stakeholders and publics are identified and assessed in terms of whether they oppose the organization on the issue or support it on the vertical axis. A numerical value of 0 to −5 is assigned to those stakeholders and publics opposing the issue and a value of 0 to +5 to those supporting it. The importance of stakeholders and publics to the organization and to an effective resolution of the issue is measured on a horizontal axis and varies from a value of zero (least important) to a value of 10 (most important). After stakeholders and publics are positioned on the two values, the location of the stakeholders and publics in the matrix is plotted. As displayed in Figure 10.2, four categories of stakeholders and publics result from this analysis:[5]

- *Problematic stakeholders/publics*: those stakeholders or publics who are likely to oppose or be hostile to the organization's course of action, but are relatively unimportant to the organization because they are not normally recognized as important stakeholders or publics and have little power to exert strong pressure on the organization.
- *Antagonistic stakeholders/publics*: those stakeholders or publics who are likely to oppose or be hostile to the organization's course of action and hold power or influence over the organization.
- *Low priority stakeholders/publics*: those stakeholders or publics who are likely to support the organization's course of action but are relatively unimportant in terms of their power or influence on the organization.
- *Supporter stakeholders/publics*: those stakeholders or publics who are likely to support the organization's course of action and are important to the organization in terms of their power or influence.

After the analysis and categorization are completed, the idea is that communication practitioners can work out communication strategies to most appropriately deal with each stakeholder or public. For example, practitioners may use educational programmes with 'problematic' stakeholders and publics to change their opinions on an issue and may prepare defensive statements or crisis plans in case such problematic stakeholders and publics form a coalition and together voice their discontent about the organization. Strategies for 'antagonistic' stakeholders or publics typically

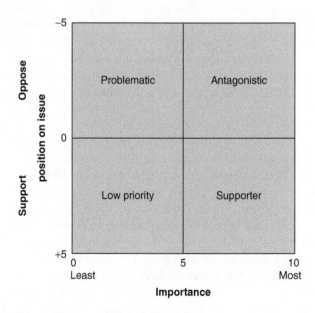

FIGURE 10.2   The position–importance matrix

involve anticipating the nature of their objections and developing and communicat-ing counter-arguments as well as bargaining with selected stakeholders or publics to win their support. Finally, strategies for 'low priority' stakeholders or publics often consist of educational programmes and promoting the company's involvement with these supporting stakeholders, whilst strategies for 'supporter' stakeholders or pub-lics often only involve a case of providing information to reinforce their position and possibly asking them to influence indifferent stakeholders.[6]

Besides analysing the opinions of stakeholders and publics on a particular issue, it is also important for communication practitioners to identify the current 'stage' of an issue. For example, it will be useful to know whether an issue can be classified as 'active' or 'intense', based on the amount of public debate about the issue and the pressure on an organization to do something about it. A useful framework in this respect is to think of the 'life cycle' of an issue (Figure 10.3) which consists of four stages: (1) emergence, (2) debate, (3) codification, and (4) enforcement. The basic idea behind the framework is that it is important for organizations to detect issues when they first 'emerge' and to engage publicly in the 'debate' on the issue. In doing so, organizations may be able to influence opinion in a favourable direction before the issue becomes 'codified' or defined within the public domain and 'enforced' through government legislation, industrial action or consumer boycotts. For exam-ple, when Greenpeace first raised the issue of Shell's disposal of the Brent Spar oil rig in the North Sea, Shell ignored the *emerging* issue and defended the disposal decision as 'business as usual' and as the 'best option with the least environmental damage'. The scientific evidence behind the decision convinced Shell that the company did not need to engage in any *debate* about the issue and explain its decision to the gen-eral public. The result was that Greenpeace's framing of the issue as an 'ecological disaster' and 'toxic dump' came to define how the general public viewed the issue (*codification*) – a view that was subsequently enforced through consumer boycotts and political action by many European governments (*enforcement*). The general principle that arises from the framework is that organizations need to detect issues early on

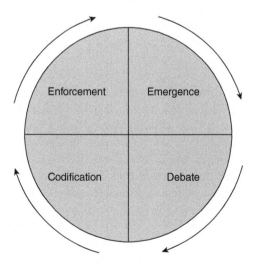

FIGURE 10.3 The 'life cycle' of an issue

because only in the early stages of 'emergence' and 'debate' can stakeholder or public opinion on an issue be influenced.

Issue-specific response strategies

The analysis of an issue provides the basis for identifying an appropriate response. The repertoire of issue-response strategies involves the following four options: (1) a buffering strategy, (2) a bridging strategy, (3) an advocacy strategy, and (4) a thought leadership strategy. The choice of any one of these four options is based on the 'intensity' of the issue, the importance of the issue to the organization's stakeholder groups, the values and beliefs of managers in an organization, as well as costs.

A buffering strategy is essentially an attempt to 'stonewall the issue' and delay its development. This strategy is one in which organizations attempt to continue with their existing behaviour by postponing decisions or by remaining silent. Buffering involves trying to keep claims from stakeholders or publics in the environment from interfering with internal operations. A good example of buffering involves Exxon Mobil's initial attempt to remain silent on the issue of climate change and avoid organizational ownership of the issue.

A bridging strategy, on the other hand, involves organizations being open to change and recognizing the issue and its inevitability. Bridging occurs when organizations reactively seek to adapt organizational activities so that they conform to external expectations of important stakeholders and publics. In response to those expectations, organizations attempt to find a way to accommodate them within the organization's plans and operations. For example, following criticism from their stakeholders, organizations may aim to be more transparent in reporting progress on their environmental performance and may actively engage in a dialogue with their stakeholders about environmental issues and expectations.

An advocacy strategy is an attempt to try to change stakeholder expectations and public opinions on an issue through issue campaigns and lobbying. With this strategy, organizations do not directly 'stonewall' an issue (buffering) or adapt to external expectations (bridging) but use campaigning and lobbying to alter the opinions and stakeholder expectations on an issue and often in such a way that these conform to the organization's present practices, output and values.[7] Such campaigning and lobbying may be either reactive, in response to continued criticism from stakeholders, or proactive, as a way of anticipating future expectations. The aim of advocacy is to persuade external stakeholders and publics that the organization's position on an issue is both rationally acceptable and morally legitimate. For example, a few years back Exxon Mobil lobbied governments on climate change and sponsored think-thank and campaigning organizations that have directly or indirectly taken money from the company. These organizations took a consistent line on climate change: that the science is contradictory, that scientists are split and that if governments took action to prevent global warming they would be endangering the global economy for no good reason. In other words, Exxon Mobil lobbied and campaigned to sow doubt about whether serious action needs to be taken on climate change.[8] In doing so, the company attempted to change public opinion on climate change and on the necessity of the company having to take direct action to curb carbon emissions.

A fourth, and final, strategy is thought leadership. With this strategy, a company identifies salient, emergent issues before these issues become active or intense and it then proactively stakes out a leadership position on the issue. Such a proactive strategy may be given by personal convictions of the CEO, market conditions or a generally changing industry or sector. Under the leadership of John Browne, BP, for example, restyled itself for some years as a leader in alternative energy besides fossil fuels, motivated by the winds of change that the company felt were sweeping through the industry and through society and that it thought would in time make sustainability norms the standard for the industry, rather than the exception. The company thus wanted to strategically position itself as at the vanguard of this broader change, so that, in effect, it would be seen as leading on it, rather than lagging behind and being stigmatized as an 'old oil' company. Similarly, Interface, the world's largest carpet manufacturer has been a thought leader on sustainability in an otherwise petrol and chemical-intensive industry. Driven by the epiphany of its former CEO, Ray Anderson, who wanted to leave a better world behind, Interface has developed sustainable innovations and progressed on a number of sustainability-related goals (such as the like-for-like recycling of carpet tiles) that save costs and increase customer loyalty, and are now also spilling over to other organizations in their supply chain and their industry.

Broadly speaking, organizations can choose between these four strategy options. Organizations can deny the existence of an issue and remain silent (buffering); they can recognize the issue, adapt their operations and actively communicate and engage with stakeholders (bridging); they can try to change stakeholder expectations and public opinions on an issue so that these expectations and opinions conform to current practices and values (advocacy); or they can proactively move on the issue, stake out a position and commit the company to progressive change on the issue (thought leadership). The choice of one of these strategies often depends on the 'intensity' of the issue and its importance to the organization's stakeholder groups, as well as on the values and beliefs of managers in an organization. As mentioned, BP took up a thought leadership position on the issue of climate change and their own environmental impact at the end of the 1990s because of mounting public pressure and their own stakeholders calling for change (although BP has since reverted its strategy and business model back to the extraction and refinement of fossil fuels). Exxon Mobil, on the other hand, did not even bridge on this particular issue, because the company's dominant coalition of senior managers and shareholders disputed the evidence on climate change and felt that an environmental stance would be in conflict with the company's economic principles.

Choosing any of these strategies determines how the organization communicates about the issue. For example, with a buffering strategy, organizations often communicate very little publicly on the issue but may issue defensive statements to the media that defend the company's policy or stance on a particular issue. A bridging strategy involves extensive reporting in the form of progress reports, briefings to journalists and issue-led campaigns. An advocacy strategy will typically consist of lobbying and campaigning on the issue. This may involve sponsorship of campaigning organizations or NGOs, a mass media corporate issue campaign and face-to-face presentations to key opinion leaders on the issue. And, finally, a thought leadership strategy involves intensive communication on the position of the organization in its sector or industry, trying to spread the word through various channels internally and externally and demonstrating how the company is trying to make a difference through its leadership on the issue. Often, thought leadership is initiated and carried by the top of the organization, including a CEO and senior managers who can credibly and authoritatively speak on the issue to the media, employees, politicians and other stakeholders of the organization.

The way in which organizations communicate about issues, whether from a bridging, buffering, advocacy or thought leadership angle, involves specific acts of framing. Issue framing refers to the purposeful efforts that communication practitioners take, whilst communicating, to shape the frames of interpretation of stakeholders or publics. Shell, as already mentioned, framed the Brent Spar issue as a sensible and legitimate 'business decision', supported by the UK government and scientific studies. Communication professionals within Shell defended the decision to the media and the general public and were told by senior executives to treat the situation as 'business as usual'. Greenpeace, on the other hand, framed the same event as a 'toxic time bomb' and as an 'environmental disaster'. Frames typically employ selection and salience to hold together or organize certain ideas in a communicating text, diagnose a situation and prescribe a course of action. This organizing function is often seen to be based on an 'underlying logic' that manifests itself at the level of a text, particularly in terms of stock phrases, keywords or metaphors that signify the larger frame and 'that [together] provide thematically reinforcing clusters of facts or judgments'.[9]

Frames also presuppose culturally familiar categories of understanding. Indeed, prototypical cultural phenomena may function as the central organizing theme or underlying logic of a frame, including cultural archetypes (e.g. heroes or victims), myths or mythical figures (e.g. David versus Goliath in Brent Spar) and ideologies or values (e.g. freedom of speech, environmental care). The invoked cultural frame may also, to a greater or less extent, be understood by stakeholders and considered as salient or taken-for-granted in relation to a specific issue. Case example 10.1 further illustrates the debates in framing that are often involved in publicly important corporate issues.

 —————— CASE EXAMPLE 10.1 ————————————————

THE FRAMING OF BONUS PAYMENTS AFTER THE CREDIT CRISIS

An interesting example of the debating and framing of an issue involves the case of bonus payments in banks after the global financial crisis of 2007–10. Billions of taxpayers' money was used to bail out many banks, supplying them with credit in the wake of the collapse of a global housing bubble which brought about a shortage of credit and a decline in trade. Governments around the world have since been developing schemes and legislation that would create better oversight and more stringent regulation of the banking sector. In an open letter in *The Wall Street Journal* on 9 December 2009, Gordon Brown, the then Prime Minister of the UK, and the former French president Nicolas Sarkozy argued that 'a huge and opaque global trading network involving complex products, short-termism and too-often excessive rewards created risks that few people understood. We have also learned that when crises happen, taxpayers have to cover the costs. It is simply not acceptable for them to foot the bill for losses in a deep downturn, while institutions' shareholders and employees enjoy all the gains as the economy recovers.'

Both men argued for stricter regulation that would ensure that compensation systems, and bonus payments in particular, limit the kind of excessive risk taking that was partly to blame for the financial crisis. In line with this view, the UK government announced a plan in December 2009 to tax bankers' bonus payments. The rationale for this was framed as in the public interest; besides recouping some of the investments made by taxpayers, it would also de-motivate or curb excessive risk taking associated with the bonus culture. Executives of banks in the UK, including ones that benefited from the government bail-out, however condemned the plans. On behalf of the British Bankers Association (BBA), Angela Knight pointed out that the banking industry generated significant jobs and taxes for the UK. She also mentioned a worry that London's reputation as a financial capital could be damaged and that it may risk an exodus of companies: 'We need to think about the message this will send outside the UK about Britain being a place to do business in.' Her main point was that banking is a viable industry that already does its fair share for the UK economy. She also questioned the practical consequences of such a measure, something that was echoed by other bank executives. The board of the Royal Bank of Scotland, which is almost wholly owned by the British taxpayer, for example, threatened to resign en masse if the Treasury of the UK government blocked bonus payments. Other executives have suggested that governments, even when they are a shareholder, should not interfere in remuneration decisions that are market driven. Lloyd Blankfein, the CEO of Goldman Sachs, feels strongly that his people must be rewarded for their efforts and skills. John Varley, former CEO of Barclays, drew an analogy with premiership football – superstar salaries have to be paid to the best staff, because otherwise they may go and work for the competition. The debate about bonus payments, as commercially crucial and legitimate rewards or as incentives to excessive risk taking, still rages on. Whilst no one would deny that exceptional effort, crea- tivity or hard work deserves an exceptional payment, the difficulty with bank bonuses may be that they are not necessarily associated with exceptional effort or ingenuity, nor do such payments always translate into long-term social and economic benefits. A recent paper by two economists, Thomas Philippon and Ariell Reshef, in the *Quarterly Journal of Economics* demonstrates that since the 1980s bankers' pay has risen by 80 per cent compared with the average wage. Only half of that rise, they argue, can remotely be justified by the increasing complexity and skills needed for modern-day banking, which in turn makes the average job in banking 40 per cent overpaid. A key issue in this respect is that the very system or market for talent and effort which bankers claim to be a part of, is at least in part one of their own making: bankers transact with themselves for huge fees and commissions and, on the back of that, attribute bonus payments to themselves.

Questions for reflection

1   How would you yourself frame the issue of bankers' pay? What kind of conceptualization or ideology does this presuppose?
2   Generally speaking, is it possible to combine frames around market competition and fair- ness and equality?

Source: This case study is informed by Brown, G. and Sarkozy, N. (2009) 'For global finance, global regulation', *The Wall Street Journal*, 9 December; Judge, E. (2009) 'Bankers hit back at "populist" bonus supertax', *The Times*, 7 December (quote from Angela Knight); and Philippon, T. and Reshef, A. (2009) 'Wages and human capital in the US financial industry: 1909-2006', NBER Working Paper No. 14644, January.

Evaluation

The final stage of the issues management process involves an evaluation of how the issue has developed and how stakeholder expectations and public opinions have changed. First of all, it is important for organizations to know what the 'stage' of the issue is and whether there is still an opportunity to influence public debate on the issue in question. In addition, depending on the strategy chosen by an organization, communication practitioners need to evaluate the success of their buffering, bridging, advocacy or thought leadership strategy. They need to find out whether and how stakeholder expectations and public opinions have changed, whether their activities contributed to a change in public opinion on the issue and whether the organization's response strategy has been appreciated by stakeholders and the general public.

10.4 INFLUENCING PUBLIC POLICY

One important part of issues management involves influencing public policy for-mation. Such influence may be indirect, through advocating a certain framing of an issue that may in turn influence government, or direct, through lobbying political action committees and industry coalitions. In 2003, for example, Fannie Mae, a mortgage provider in the USA, spent $87 million on an advertising cam-paign to help curtail the US Congress's efforts to create a more stringent regulator to oversee its operations and to have the authority to alter its capital standards. Together with direct lobbying, its efforts paid off and the legislation was never passed. Whilst the company had successfully campaigned and lobbied, the lack of stringent oversight led to accounting problems that had a big role in the 2007 crisis. Eventually, Fannie Mae was bailed out by the US government, in order to secure loans to home owners.

Investments in commercial lobbying and representation through political action committees and coalitions have grown significantly in recent years. Shaping or influ-encing government and public policy in this way is commonplace. The relevance of such activities stems of course from the fact that there is hardly an item of legislation which does not in some way encroach on business interests or impinge on organi-zational goals. A former Secretary to the Treasury in the UK government, Michael Portillo, observed that political lobbyists are 'as necessary to the political process as a thoroughly efficient sewage system is to any city'.[10] Despite its connotation, the analogy suggests that lobbying is not necessarily about 'spin doctoring', or indeed unethical or against the public interest. Instead, lobbying is a crucial part of the public policy process. Generally speaking, there are two competing views on the legitimacy of the corporate lobbying of government. There is the view that lobbyists, and the corporate organizations they work for, abuse the democratic system for their own selfish interests and that the growth in the industry, particularly in the use of political consultants, requires the imposition of greater controls over lobbying activities.

The alternative position is that lobbying is genuinely an intrinsic part of the democratic process because it can create a counter balance to potentially ill-informed or badly thought out policy decisions. Furthermore, it can be argued that government, including civil servants, actually depend on lobbyists for information and advice.

Besides direct lobbying, organizations also use political action committees and industry coalitions, and grassroots campaigning to influence government legislation. Together, these tools are considered as the main techniques for influencing government and public policy. Lobbying involves an individual (a lobbyist) designated by an organization or interest group to facilitate influencing public policy in that organization's or interest group's favour. Lobbying is typically done through directly contacting government officials. In the USA, *political action committees* (PACs) represent a fund for political donations made up of money from an organization's members or employees. The donations go to candidates and legislators who demonstrate favourable perspectives or behaviours around an organization's public policy goals. In principle, PACs are a means for organizations to support public policy in a way that agrees with their own political and legislative beliefs. In practice, many organizations use PACs to obtain access to government officials and to pursue their own direct interests.

Industry coalitions are an alliance of organizations in the same industry who, through direct lobbying or donations, attempt to have a voice in the policy-formation process. Many coalitions are permanent, with representatives located in political centres such as Washington, Beijing and Brussels. Whilst coalitions often adopt names and frame their mission in terms of the public interest, they may often be led and financed by narrow interests. For example, The National Wetlands Coalition in the USA involves – contrary to what its name may suggest – oil drillers, land developers and major gas corporations. Other coalitions may be more straightforward representations of an industry, such as the British Bankers Association (BBA) mentioned in Case Example 10.1. An example of a more narrowly financed political group is the financing by Coca-Cola of the Global Energy Network, a non-profit foundation that promotes exercise rather than diet as the way to combat obesity. When the media covered the network as a 'front group' for Coca-Cola in 2015, it led to a PR crisis for the firm. The company in turn changed the arrangement and the CEO wrote a letter to *The Wall Street Journal* vouching that they would, in the future, be more transparent about their funding arrangement and about their position on obesity.

Finally, *grassroots campaigning* involves an organization engaging with members of its own group and/or others with a stake in an issue to persuade legislators to support its public policy goals. Because legislators depend on voters in elections, constituent grassroots input is a powerful tool to influence legislators. There are several varieties of grassroots campaigning. Organizations, particularly public sector or not-for-profit organizations, may mobilize their own employees and/or association members. 'Third-party' grassroots campaigning is a term used for engaging public groups that may be impacted by an issue. Organizations may, for example, mobilize community groups affected by pending legislation.

10.5 ANTI-CORPORATE ACTIVISM

Issues management often also involves dealing with activist groups who – because of a shared grievance or common ideology or interest – have mobilized themselves against an organization, or even an entire industry sector. Activist groups may or may not be recognized as stakeholders by an organization, but nonetheless their actions may affect the reputation of an organization. This damage typically arises when the activist group raises an issue through media attention with the broader public and is able to mobilize other individuals and groups, including a firm's stakeholders, to position themselves against the organization. Examples of this process involve UK Uncut, an activist group against tax avoidance, mobilizing customers against Starbucks (Case Study 4.1), and Amnesty International raising awareness of Shell's environmental impact on the Niger Delta (Case Study 10.1). An activist group generally involves an organized group of politically active citizens who work on political or social issues and who, through their actions, might target governments or corporate organizations as a key antagonist. Their actions may consist of boycotts, street marches, demonstrations, media campaigns, letter writing and many other tactics aimed at raising awareness of the issue and influencing stakeholders, including government, to act in line with the proposed change.

In broad terms, activist groups or movements can be categorized as radical or reform-oriented in the way in which they target specific organizations or business in general. They may also differ in terms of whether they target, in the first instance, individual organizations to change their business practices, an entire class or industry of organizations, or whether they aim instead to instigate change by convincing others (such as customers or governments) who, as stakeholders, may have an effect on organizations. Reform-oriented groups are dedicated to changing specific norms, laws or practices. This may involve, for example, a labour movement trying to increase workers' rights, a human rights movement asking for a fair acknowledgement of the impact of a particular business on a community or an environmental group campaigning against a specific corporate decision that may harm the environment. Such reform-oriented groups typically campaign on a single issue, and use a range of tactics to exercise influence and strategically sway others to act on the issue. Radical groups or movements, on the other hand, are dedicated to changing deeper value systems within a society and as such have a much broader scope and orientation than reform movements.[11] Those activist groups that

> offer a more comprehensive version of the problem and more drastic change as a solution are normally called radical, whereas activist groups at the other end of the spectrum are considered moderate or reformative. In the context of corporate social change, reformative groups are taken to believe that although companies are part of the problem, they can also be part of the solution. In contrast, radical groups [generally] do not believe that companies can be part of the solution.[12]

Radical groups tend to argue for a drastic change to, or overhaul of, the entire social or economic system, such as a fundamental change to capitalism or an alternative way of organizing society. A recent example of a radical anti-establishment movement is the Occupy movement, which was started in September 2012 in New York City as a protest against the banks and corporations that have amassed great wealth, whilst many North Americans have grown poorer within the last two decades. Responding to a call to occupy Wall Street by *Adbusters*, the Canadian anti-consumerism maga-zine, the movement initially started with a small permanent encampment in New York City. This act instigated marches and demonstrations across the USA, and very quickly the movement spread around the world, with encampments being set up in major capitals and cities across the globe.

The movement's slogan of 'we are the 99 per cent' captures the main shared griev-ance around inequality and, as a deft framing, resonated with many others, including citizens and smaller activist groups, around the world. The movement has attracted people from all walks of life and across every segment of society. Perhaps reflect-ing the new media age, movements such as Occupy are both a real movement of thousands on the streets and a virtual movement with similar if not greater numbers online. Images of actions and campaigns are posted on websites, Facebook, YouTube, and shared via Twitter. On the streets, activists use smartphones or other electronic devices to coordinate campaigns and to broadcast to the world actions and events on the ground. Naomi Klein, a well-known cultural commentator, sees the use of social media as fundamentally changing activist groups and social movements:

> Rather than a single movement, what is emerging is thousands of movements intricately linked to one another, much as 'hotlinks' connect their websites on the Internet. This analogy is more than coincidental and is in fact key to understanding the changing nature of political organizing. Although many have observed that the recent mass protests would have been impossible without the Internet, what has been overlooked is how the communication technology that facilitates these campaigns is shaping the movement in its own image. Thanks to the Net, mobilizations are able to unfold with sparse bureaucracy and mini-mal hierarchy; forced consensus and labored manifestos are fading into the background, replaced instead by a culture of constant, loosely structured and sometimes compulsive information-swapping.[13]

The implication for corporate communication is that a movement may not involve a single organization, but a loose collection of groups. These groups may also quickly organize themselves and mobilize others, as part of their ongoing action. In addition, it is essential that corporate communication practitioners not only scan and monitor the environment for issues and activist groups, but also seek to actively communicate and engage with activist groups. This is particularly important in cases where activist groups are specifically targeting a particular organization, as in the case study of Shell (Case Study 10.1). A prolonged silence or continued dismissal of the claims of an activist group may, in those instances, come to harm rather than protect the reputation of the organization.

CASE STUDY 10.1

SHELL IN NIGERIA: ISSUES MANAGEMENT, ACTIVISM AND REPUTATIONAL DAMAGE

Shell is one of the first truly international corporations and has been one of the ten largest companies in the world for nearly a century. In the late 1980s, senior executives within Shell were particularly concerned about environmental issues and wished that the corporation would be seen by the general public as being more progressive and as making headway on these issues, rather than as operating under a 'business as usual' approach. They decided to use scenarios as one of the ways to communicate this aspiration to the rest of the company, which became known as the 'sustainable world' scenario. These executives were initially successful in influencing the internal culture of the corporation in some way, forcing every middle and top manager to think through how their investment proposals and projects would survive in an environmentally conscious world. However, the overall culture of the corporation was not significantly affected as became clear in 1995 when Shell found itself in heated debates with a whole range of critics (including the Movement for the Survival of the Ogoni People, Greenpeace, the Sierra Club, Amnesty International and the media) over the company's environmental impact on the Niger Delta in Nigeria. In that year, Shell failed to take a high-profile public stance against the Nigerian government, Shell's local business partner in Nigeria, when it executed nine environmentalists including Ken Saro-Wiwa, an internationally acclaimed journalist and writer who had spearheaded protest against Shell's environmentally destructive operations in the Niger Delta.

Nigeria and the Ogoni

Shell has been operating in the Niger Delta since the 1930s and is by far the largest operator in the area with an output of more than 1m barrels a day. But the company's 90 oil and gas fields have suffered spills and sabotage, damaging the livelihood of farmers and fishermen and threatening the half-million Ogoni people who live in the Niger Delta, in which the bulk of Shell's production is located. The ethnic minority communities such as the Ogoni people have also seen almost no return on Shell's revenues. Moreover, because of weak environmental regulation, these indigenous peoples who live traditionally by fishing and farming have suffered severe ecological and health impacts from oil spills. In Nigeria, much of the gas by-products from oil drilling was flared (i.e. burned off in the open air), which caused some of the worst local environmental pollution. Flaring is held responsible for acid rain in the Niger Delta which corrodes roofs, pollutes lakes and damages vegetation. Together, oil spills and gas flaring have threatened the Niger Delta, which is one of the largest and most ecologically sensitive wetlands in the world. In 1993, a nonviolent protest organized by the Movement for the Survival of the Ogoni People (MOSOP) against Shell and other oil companies led Shell to withdraw its staff and close operations in that part of the Niger Delta where the Ogoni lived. The Nigerian government, as Shell's business partner, blamed the MOSOP leadership for local resistance. The government tried Saro-Wiwa and others by a kangaroo court of the military tribunal. Nine Ogonis, including Saro-Wiwa, were executed on 10 November 1995.

From the early 1990s, Ogoni environmental activists and Delta tribal chiefs had documented the environmental degradation stemming from oil company activity.

Their accounts were taken up in the African media and in media around the world. Saro-Wiwa's high public profile within the worldwide environmental movement forced a communication response from Shell. Shell expressed 'shock' and 'sadness' over Saro-Wiwa's death. However, in the first instance, Shell also tried to minimize and displace blame for both the political and ecological problems in Nigeria. Shell Nigeria released a briefing statement which was mainly argumentative and defensive in nature. Overall, Shell characterized itself as a victim, arguing that the company had been 'unfairly used to raise the international profile' of the MOSOP campaign against the Nigerian government. Whilst the company acknowledged that there had been environmental problems, it downplayed the issue. Shell admitted that its facilities needed upgrading, but blamed sabotage rather than the corrosion of ageing pipes for the oil spills. It said that Ogoni claims of environmental 'devastation' were grossly exaggerated, citing conclusions of journalists who said that Shell's limited presence in the Delta area meant that the damage was only a tiny 'fraction' of that 'routinely claimed by campaigners'. Shell also cited a 1995 World Bank study that character-ized the problem of 'oil pollution ... only of moderate priority' in comparison to other poverty-related factors that contributed to environmental deterioration (i.e. popula-tion growth, deforestation, erosion and over-farming). It further relied on the World Bank study and a report by the World Health Organization to dispute the connection between gas flaring and health. Thus, it claimed lack of 'evidence' that such problems as asthma and skin rashes were due to its activities. Shell Nigeria also claimed that it had 'some influence' with the government but that 'force' was impossible: 'What force could we apply – leaving aside the question of whether it would be right for us to do so?' This mirrored the position of Shell Group chairman at the time, Cor Herkströter, who defined Shell's role as strictly economic and commercial and said that the com-pany lacked 'licence' to interfere in politics or the sovereign mandate of government.

Oil spills and environmental degradation

Since the initial issue emerged in 1995, Shell has continued to remain under fire over its environmental record in Nigeria. In January 2007, advertisements calling on Shell to 'clean up its mess' appeared in *The Guardian* and the Dutch newspaper *De Volkskrant*. The adverts were signed and financially supported by more than 7,000 people worldwide in an effort to encourage Shell to live up to the aims of its corpo-rate social responsibility (CSR) policies. Nnimmo Bassey, from Environmental Rights Action in Nigeria, said: 'Despite Shell's public commitment to CSR and specific promise it has made to communities, life on the fence line can too often be likened to hell. From Nigeria to Ireland, the Philippines to South Africa, Shell still too often fails to respect the environment or the needs of local communities.'

Shell's poor environmental record in Nigeria is given prominence in the adverts, which demand the company pay $10bn to clean up oil spills and compensate commu-nities in the Niger Delta. Environmental Rights Action, Friends of the Earth and others estimate that as much as 13m barrels of oil have been spilled into the Niger Delta eco-system over the past 50 years by Shell and its partners, an amount they say is 50 times more than that associated with the infamous *Exxon Valdez* tanker grounding off Alaska: 'The spills pollute the land and water of the communities. Drinking water is affected,

(Continued)

(Continued)

people get sick, fish populations die and farmers lose their income because the soil of the land is destroyed.' Shell has since responded to the adverts and has stated that the adverts 'neither reflect the realities of the situation and the very real progress made, nor represent the views of the wider communities around these locations. Shell is committed to being a good neighbour and maintains productive relationships with many local communities and their representatives.'

In recent years, the issue has not gone away and has in fact worsened. Although the news may not reach Western households, the frequent oil spills in the region have been described as the worst oil disaster in human history. In August and December 2008, two further major oil spills affected the livelihood of the 69,000 or so people living in Bodo, a town in Ogoniland in the Niger Delta. Shell Nigeria, the subsidiary of Shell, has so far not sufficiently cleaned up the effects of these oil spills. In June 2013, a fire also broke out near one ageing pipe. In all of these instances, Shell has blamed sabotage and the illegal tapping of oil from the pipes, rather than what the community and activist groups claim is the result of the corrosion of pipes and a lack of maintenance. A key difficulty here is that the company itself carries out investigations into the leaks, but there is no oversight by the industry or by the Nigerian government. With sabotage, Shell is also legally not entitled to pay compensation and has no direct obligation to clean up the environmental damage. Amnesty International has campaigned against Shell's constant tactic to externalize the responsibility to the local community, and has described it as a PR gimmick. Amnesty also believes that the company should be more transparent to the local community in disclosing information on investigations into the leaks. The continuing unrest in the region has led to militant terrorist groups, such as the Niger Delta Avengers, attacking the facilities and pipelines of Shell and of other petrol companies in the region. In May 2016, a major attack on central pipelines drove the output of Nigerian oil to a historic low.

In 2011, a United Nations report on the oil pollution in the Niger Delta concluded that a clean-up exercise would take 25 to 30 years, with the damage 'ranging from the "disastrous" impact on mangrove vegetation to the contamination of wells with potentially cancer-causing chemicals in a region that is home to some 1 million people'. The report also called directly on Shell to take responsibility and shoulder the financial cost of the clean-up exercise. Whilst the company may dispute the causes of the oil spills, there is a significant risk that continued inaction in restoring the area may, in the long run, damage its reputation with stakeholders around the world.

Questions for reflection

1   Describe the way in which this issue evolved into a crisis for Shell using the issue life-cycle models (Figures 10.1 and 10.3).
2   Discuss the way in which Shell has responded to the broader issue, using the concepts of buffering, bridging, advocacy and thought leadership. Should the company have opted for a different response?

Source: This case study is based on Macalister, Terry (2007) 'Campaigners urge Shell to put profits into clean-up', *The Guardian*, 31 January; Livesey, S.M. (2001) 'Ecoidentity as discursive struggle: Royal Dutch/Shell, Brent Spar and Nigeria', *Journal of Business Communication*, 38: 58–91; and www2.amnesty.org.uk/tags/niger-delta

10.6 CHAPTER SUMMARY

Issues management is an increasingly important specialist area of activity within corporate communication. Effectively, issues management starts with scanning the environment and identifying latent and emerging issues before they become salient in public debates and may potentially result in government legislation. However, when issues have become active and salient, it requires that communication practitioners decide on a response (buffering, bridging, advocacy or thought leadership) in line with the 'intensity' of the issue and its importance to the organization's stakeholder groups.

 DISCUSSION QUESTIONS

1. Describe the life cycle of issues and how they may develop into active and intense issues for organizations.

2. Consider the daily coverage on companies in *The Financial Times* – which of these news items reflect broader issues for the organization and its stakeholders, and which are simply reports of routine decisions with little broad public interest?

3. Reflect on the strategies of buffering, bridging, advocacy and thought leadership around issues. Using examples of organizations that you know, consider: when is the one or the other strategy more appropriate? What generally determines the feasibility of each of these options?

KEY TERMS

SWOT	DESTEP
Active issue	Environmental scanning
Advocacy	Intense issue
Public affairs	Issue
Bridging	Latent issue
Buffering	Crisis
Lobbying	Political action committee
Grassroots campaigning	Industry coalition
Material issue	Thought leadership

 FURTHER READING

Harris, Phil and Fleisher, Craig S. (2005) *The Handbook of Public Affairs*. London: Sage.
Heath, Robert L. and Palenchar, James Michael (2008) *Strategic Issues Management: Organizations and Public Policy Challenges*. London: Sage, 2nd edition.

Want to know more about this chapter? Visit the companion website at: https://study.sagepub.com/cornelissen5e to access videos, web links, a glossary and selected journal articles to further enhance your study.

NOTES

1. Giddens, A. (1990) *Consequences of Modernity*. Cambridge: Polity Press; Beck, U. (1992) *Risk Society: Towards a New Modernity*. London: Sage.
2. Chase, W.H. (1984) *Issue Management: Origins of the Future*. Stamford, CT: Issue Action Publishers.
3. Weick, K.E. (1988) 'Enacted sensemaking in crisis situations', *Journal of Management Studies*, 25: 305–17.
4. King, B.G. (2008) 'A political mediation model of corporate responses to social movement activism', *Administrative Science Quarterly*, 53: 395–421.
5. Nutt, P.C. and Backoff, R.W. (1992) *Strategic Management of Public and Third Sector Organizations: A Handbook for Leaders*. San Francisco: Jossey-Bass, p. 191; Bryson, J.M. (1995) *Strategic Planning for Public and Nonprofit Organizations: A Guide to Strengthening and Sustaining Organizational Achievement*. San Francisco: Jossey-Bass, revised edition, p. 284.
6. Nutt and Backoff (1992), pp. 196–98; Bryson (1995), pp. 285–86.
7. Dowling, J. and Pfeffer, J. (1975) 'Organizational legitimacy: Social values and organizational behavior', *Pacific Sociological Review*, 18: 122–36; Heugens, P.M.A.R., Van Riel, C.B.M. and Van den Bosch, F.A.J. (2004) 'Reputation management capabilities as decision rules', *Journal of Management Studies*, 41: 1349–77.
8. Monbiot, G. (2006) 'The denial industry', *The Guardian*, 19 September.
9. Entman, R.M. (1993) 'Framing: Toward clarification of a fractured paradigm', *Journal of Communication*, 43 (4): 51–58, quote on p. 52.
10. Nicholas, R. (1995) 'We'd like you to say yes, Minister', *Marketing*, 16 February, p. 16.
11. Karagianni, K.S. and Cornelissen, J. (2006) 'Anti-corporate movements and public relations', *Public Relations Review*, 32: 168–70.
12. Den Hond, F. and de Bakker, F.G.A. (2007) 'Ideologically motivated activism: How activist groups influence corporate social change activities', *Academy of Management Review*, 32: 901–24, quote on p. 903.
13. Klein, N. (2002) 'Farewell to "the end of history": Organization and vision in anti-corporate movements', *Socialist Register* [online]: 4.

Crisis Communication

11

CHAPTER OVERVIEW

Crises have the potential to damage an organization's reputation and the relationships with its stakeholders. It is therefore important that organizations anticipate and plan for probable crisis scenarios and prepare crisis communication plans. Drawing on frameworks and principles from theory and practice, the chapter discusses how organizations can prepare and plan for crises and can identify appropriate communication strategies that meet stakeholder expectations and protect the reputation of the organization.

11.1 INTRODUCTION

The current information age has created a challenging environment for many organizations. Because of modern communication and information technologies, people are increasingly aware of the issues and risks associated with organizations and their industries. These technologies also afford a way of voicing concerns on these issues, providing a direct challenge to organizations and their attempts to manage health, safety and environmental risks. These risks and issues may form the bedrock for crises. The public concern around the safety of airlines and flying in the aftermath of the 9/11 attacks on the twin towers in New York, for example, led to a crisis for the airline industry and contributed to the bankruptcy of airlines such as Sabena and Swissair.

The objective of crisis management and crisis communication is to exert control, insofar as possible, over events and organizational activities in ways that assure stakeholders that their interests are cared for and that the organization complies with social, safety and environmental standards. Such control requires that organizations develop contingency plans to prepare for possible crises as well as communication plans to effectively respond to crisis scenarios when they emerge. Whilst a lot of crises can be prepared for in advance, organizations may be confronted by natural accidents or terrorist attacks that, even when foreseen or planned for, cannot be prevented or avoided. But being prepared is half the battle. The other half is about having skills in communicating effectively and responsibly, and about taking action to contain the crisis and limit any negative consequences for stakeholders and for the company and its reputation.

This chapter defines crisis management, discusses crisis scenarios and presents principles for effective crisis communication. Before we outline these communication principles in greater detail, the chapter starts with a brief introduction to crises and crisis management.

11.2 DEFINING CRISES

Broadly speaking, a *crisis* is defined as an event or issue that requires decisive and immediate action from the organization. The necessity of immediate action may be triggered by, for example, mounting public pressure, intense media attention or the direct danger (in the case of an accident, product tampering or product fault) to employees, customers or members of the general public. Crises may involve accidents or natural disasters, but may also stem from actions and failures within the organization. A crisis may, for example, stem from a 'cultural' problem which escalates into a crisis. An example may illustrate how the internal culture of an organization may be a trigger for how a crisis may emerge and may potentially escalate.

In March 2015, one of the Dutch tabloids, the *Telegraaf*, reported on the planned additional bonus payments of 100,000 euro to six of the top executives of ABN AMRO. The Dutch bank had been bailed out at the height of the financial crisis and was still in the hands of the Dutch government, although at the time of these payments plans had been afoot for it to be privatized again. The bonus payments led to a broad discussion about the company in the media and in Dutch parliament, and became a real crisis for the bank when its senior management staunchly defended the payments as legitimate in the context of pay levels in the financial sector and as a reward for good performance. The Dutch finance minister had advised against these payments, realizing the effect that they would have on public opinion. Yet, the company still went ahead, believing that its payment and rewards committee had gone through the proper procedures and had made a fair and balanced decision. What senior management had not realized, because of its inward-looking focus, is that it was completely out of sync with public opinion, with its defensive comments fuelling the fire even further. Management had thus, on its watch, let an issue over pay escalate into a real crisis that questioned the overall governance of the bank (see Figure 10.1) and led the Dutch finance minister to delay the bank's privatization.

Besides culture as a potential triggering event, organizational crises may also stem from failures in managing the complex interplay between social, or interpersonal, processes and technology. Many industrial and organizational crises, such as the Bhopal and Chernobyl accidents and the Columbia and Challenger space-shuttle disasters, stem from human mistakes in miscategorizing early warning signals and from managerial processes of decision-making overruling expertise on the ground. Generally speaking, mistakes and managerial arrogance make companies blind to the onset of a crisis and create the almost perfect conditions for a significant crisis to take place.

11.3 CRISIS MANAGEMENT

Given the consequences of crises for stakeholders and for the continuity of an organization, an extensive body of literature explores how organizations can effectively deal with and even avoid crisis scenarios, including those that stem from badly managed issues as well as those involving large-scale human disasters.[1] A first step in this process is anticipation, which involves the capacity of organizations to predict and prevent potential crisis scenarios from arising before they have occurred. The second step is resilience or the ability to cope with a crisis once it occurs and confronts the organization. A resilient performance is, in effect, one where members of the organization improvise and act mindfully in real time to deal with the crisis and minimize its impact. A good example of resilience is how employees managed to save the lives of their guests during the terrorist attacks on the Taj Hotel in Mumbai (Case Study 11.1). Organizational resilience is generally enhanced by training employees for possible crises and by having management and operational systems in place that – rather than restricting and prescribing actions – allow for thinking and improvisation by employees in context.

Whilst organizations may not oversee every possible crisis that may affect them, they can develop crisis contingency plans in advance and in anticipation of major possible crises. Communication practitioners have an important role to play in working with others in the organization to identify probable crises and to develop contingency plans. Such identification may involve some kind of scenario planning and an organization-wide consultation of risks and issues surrounding company operations. Based on such planning and consultation, communication practitioners and other executives can identify the most probable crisis scenarios (rather than wasting time working through solutions to problems that have a low probability of occurring) for which they can develop contingency plans.

Crisis experts Mitroff and Pearson highlight five different levels of contingency plans.[2] Stage 1 involves minimal planning around a few contingency plans drawn up for an emergency response. This may involve a limited set of plans such as evacuating a building during fire or giving first aid to employees who suffer injury or sudden illness. Stage 2 involves more extensive planning but is limited to natural disasters and potential human errors. Planning at this stage involves measures for damage containment and business recovery. Stage 3 involves extensive contingency plans which include crisis procedures for probable natural disasters and human errors and the training of personnel so that employees can implement these crisis procedures. Stage 4 is similar to stage 3 but involves an organization-wide consultation of potential crises and their impact on stakeholders. The scope of stage 4 is wider than typical natural disasters and human errors and includes product defects, tampering and social issues regarding the company's supply chain, operations and contributions to society. Stage 5, finally, involves all of the previous stages but also incorporates environmental scanning and early warning systems to identify crises as early as possible.

The case example of Maclaren demonstrates the vulnerabilities of organizations when they have no crisis contingency plans in place. Company executives had not anticipated concerns about the safety of its products, nor had they prepared themselves in advance. As a result, executives did not communicate quickly enough and demonstrated a general lack of care and responsibility in the eyes of consumers.

 CASE EXAMPLE 11.1

BEING PREPARED: THE CRISIS SURROUNDING MACLAREN PUSHCHAIRS

Maclaren is a well-known global brand of children's pushchairs. The safety standard of its 'umbrella-fold' pushchairs has been one of its strengths, together with the durability of the product. Its folding frames and hinges are generally stronger than the pushchairs produced by its competitors. Nonetheless, the company was caught by surprise in November 2009 when it was widely reported that children's finger tops were being 'amputated' in the pushchair hinges. The company had known of the problems – there had been 15 incidents of fingertip laceration or amputation in the USA over a period of 10 years, and Maclaren executives had become particularly concerned when there were eight cases between 2007 and 2009. Maclaren engineers had been working tirelessly since the summer of 2009 on remedying the problem with the hinges. However, when the news was leaked, the company was caught unawares. It did not have any contingency plan in place. In a reactive way, Maclaren issued warnings to owners emphasizing that they should not let children stick their fingers in the folding mechanism as the pushchairs were opened. Maclaren also issued repair kits to cover the hinges but only to owners of the pushchairs in the USA. Where the company went wrong was to discriminate between US consumers and customers in other parts of the world. This decision had been made internally and had resulted from differences between safety regulators around the world; most countries had been happy with a simple warning, whereas the US Consumer Product Safety Commission insisted on a temporary fix. Eventually, and in response to a consumer backlash, Maclaren also offered the repair kits to consumers elsewhere. But by that point the damage to its image had already been done. Maclaren had also underestimated the power of the internet and social media for the news to spread. Executives had not anticipated the spread of the news, nor were they communicating through various channels about the problem and about the steps that the company was taking to address it.

Question for reflection

What are the more general lessons that you can draw from this case in relation to crisis management? In your view, what were consumer and legislator responses that the company could have anticipated versus those that they could not have foreseen? And what specific mistakes did the company make in terms of crisis communication?

Source: Rastegar, F. (2010) 'How I did it: Maclaren's CEO on learning from a recall', *Harvard Business Review*, Jan.-Feb.; Kirby, J. (2009) 'Maclaren's stroller recall: What would you do?', HBR online blog, 10 November (see http://blogs.hbr.org/2009/11/advice-to-maclaren-and-other-p/).

11.4 THE IMPACT OF A CRISIS ON CORPORATE REPUTATION

A crisis typically emerges as a sudden and unexpected event that disrupts an organization's operations and poses both a financial and a reputational threat. The financial threat stems from the fact that a disruption in the organization's operations may lead to a loss of income. A crisis may also damage the image or reputation of the organization more generally, which may also lead to a loss of earnings in the long run. If, as a result of the crisis, the company's reputation shifts from favourable to unfavourable, stakeholders are likely to change how they interact with an organization. Customers may walk away or boycott the firm and investors may decide to invest elsewhere. The roots to such a change in fortune lie in the way in which an organization deals with a crisis and demonstrates the appropriate level of care and responsibility to those stakeholders who are affected by and interested in the crisis. When an organization mishandles communication following a crisis, it may potentially lead to stakeholders severing their ties with the organization or spreading negative word-of-mouth about the company.

Whilst crisis communication affects the impact of the crisis on the company's overall reputation with stakeholders, any previously accumulated reputation capital may also buffer or shield the company from a crisis having a lasting negative impact. Reputational capital is an organization's 'stock of perceptual and social assets – the quality of the relationship it has established with stakeholders and the regard in which the company and brand is held'.[3] Based on past performance and communication, organizations accumulate such capital with their stakeholders over time. One way of looking at this is to liken the process to accumulating capital on a bank account: a crisis will inflict some reputational damage, and as such some capital is lost or spent. Yet, depending on the amount that was there in the first place, enough goodwill may remain. It has also been described in terms of a 'reservoir of goodwill', which means that, generally speaking, an organization with a more favourable reputation prior to a crisis is also likely to have a stronger post-crisis reputation because it has more reputational capital to spend than an organization with an unfavourable or neutral prior reputation. As a result, a favourable prior reputation means an organization suffers less and rebounds more quickly. It is also likely that, for these reputable organizations, stakeholders may regard the crisis event as a 'blip' or an isolated occurrence when judged against the company's track record over time, and prior to the crisis.[4]

As such, previously accumulated reputational capital may create a 'halo effect' that protects an organization during a crisis and negates any long-lasting reputational damage. At the other extreme, a company with a poor reputation may be stigmatized as a result of a crisis, and may struggle to recover from such a stigma. An organizational stigma is defined as a collective stakeholder group-specific perception that an organization possesses a fundamental, deep-seated flaw or quality which is demonstrated in repeated crises or failures, and which, in effect, leads stakeholders to single out and discredit the organization.[5] As such, different from the 'positive' notion of corporate reputation, an organizational stigma represents a negative social evaluation and a situation where, in effect, all reputational capital in the eyes of stakeholder groups has been spent. Stigma leads to negative stakeholder attributions and judgments of the organization, and leads stakeholders to 'disidentify' with the organization and act against the organization by, for instance, spreading negative word-of-mouth or boycotting a company.

One key objective for corporate communication practitioners is to protect the company's reputation following a crisis and to limit the damage to its image. However, with most crises, it would be irresponsible to focus crisis communication only on the perspective of the company's reputation with its most important stakeholders. Instead, the crisis situation demands that communication practitioners begin their efforts by releasing information to the media and by using communication to address the physical and psychological concerns of those directly affected by the crisis. It is only after this first crisis response has been realized that communicators may turn their attention to communicating more broadly with their stakeholders and focus on reputational capital. During and in the immediate aftermath of a crisis, those directly affected, such as victims and their families, need to be supplied with information on what happened, how the company is managing the crisis and what corrective actions are being taken to protect them from something similar happening again in the future. Providing such detailed information is not only crucial to meet the information needs of those affected and to possibly reduce their psychological stress, but it is also an expression of concern on behalf of the organization to those directly affected by the crisis. In other words, disseminating information openly and engaging with those affected in a dialogue on the crisis through direct meetings, newsfeeds and blogs is often seen as an important first step in an effective crisis response.[6]

The second crucial step is to determine the organization's responsibility for a crisis, and to communicate about its actions to a broad range of stakeholder groups. By identifying how much responsibility stakeholders attribute to the organization, corporate communication practitioners can 'frame' the crisis, explain the company's actions and aim to minimize the damage to its image or reputation. They may, for example, frame the company itself as a 'victim' when there is a weak perception of responsibility in the eyes of stakeholders, such as in the case of a natural disaster or product tampering. On the other hand, when the organization is perceived to have been in the wrong and directly to blame for a crisis, the appropriate communication strategy would be one of acknowledging responsibility and demonstrating how the company is taking immediate steps to resolve the crisis. In this way, by owning up to a crisis, a company may minimize feelings of anger and frustration amongst stakeholders, and may be seen to be doing something about it in a determined and potentially positive way.[7]

11.5 COMMUNICATING ABOUT A CRISIS

As we have discussed, when organizations do not deal with issues in a timely or responsible manner a crisis situation may emerge. But not all crises are self-inflicted by organizations or emerge from widely debated public issues. Crisis expert Timothy Coombs defines four types of crises based on two dimensions: internal–external and

	Unintentional	**Intentional**
External	*Faux pas*	Terrorism
Internal	Accident	Transgression

FIGURE 11.1   Crisis-type matrix

intentional–unintentional.[8] The internal–external dimension refers to whether the crisis resulted from something done by the organization itself (e.g. the actions of managers) or instead was caused by some person or group outside of the organization. The intentional–unintentional dimension relates to the controllability of the crisis. Intentional means that the crisis event was committed deliberately by some actor. Unintentional means that the crisis event was not committed deliberately by some actor. The two dimensions together give four mutually exclusive crisis types, as illustrated in Figure 11.1.

A *faux pas* is an unintentional action which is transformed into a crisis by an external actor (e.g. an NGO). A *faux pas* often begins as an issue between an organization and a particular external actor who challenges the appropriateness of the organization's actions. When an organization does not engage in debate with this actor or when public opinion and stakeholder expectations move against the organization, the issue may turn into a crisis. Social responsibility tends to be the focal point of most *faux pas*. The term *faux pas* comes from the French and literally means 'false step'. It generally refers to a violation of accepted, although unwritten, social rules and expectations.

Accidents are unintentional and happen during the course of normal organizational operations. Product defects, employee injuries and natural disasters are all examples of accidents. The unintentional and generally random nature of accidents often leads to attributions of minimal organizational responsibility, unless of course the organization was directly responsible for the accident. Accidents can be further divided into acts of nature (e.g. hurricanes, earthquakes, epidemics) and human-induced errors (e.g. industrial accidents). The rationale for this division is that stakeholders and publics are less likely to attribute blame and react negatively to acts of nature than to human-induced error.[9]

Transgressions are intentional acts taken by an organization that knowingly place stakeholders or publics at risk or harm. Knowingly selling defective or dangerous products, withholding safety information from authorities, violating laws, or 'creative' bookkeeping are all examples of transgressions.

Terrorism refers to intentional acts taken by external agents. These intentional actions are designed to harm the organization directly (e.g. hurt customers through product tampering) or indirectly (e.g. reduce sales or disrupt production). Product tampering, hostage taking, sabotage and workplace violence are all examples of terrorism.

Classifying crises into these four types (*faux pas*, accidents, transgressions and terrorism) is useful because it provides a basis for identifying the most appropriate crisis communication strategy.[10] The principle for choosing an appropriate communication strategy (Table 11.1) is the degree to which the organization is perceived by stakeholders and the general public to be responsible or culpable for the crisis. When the perception is that the organization is not directly responsible or culpable, the organization may attempt to distance itself from the crisis or deny that the crisis exists or is as serious as external actors make it out to be. On the other hand, when the organization is seen as directly responsible or culpable for the crisis, the organization will have to defend its position or may simply have to apologize for the crisis and change its behaviour.

The unintentional nature and external challenge of a *faux pas* may lead to an attribution of minimal organizational responsibility. However, an organization can often change in response to the challenge which means that the possibility of a perception of organizational responsibility for the crisis does exist. When the perception of organizational responsibility is low or weak, the organization may use a distance strategy to further weaken the linkage between the crisis and the organization (Table 11.1). For example, an organization may excuse itself by scapegoating a third party as responsible for the crisis or may downplay the actual seriousness and scale of the crisis. Exxon Mobil's denial of climate change is a good example of a strategy of downplaying the crisis. Alternatively, an organization may follow an association strategy to remind stakeholders and the general public of past good behaviour that may offset the negatives that the crisis brings to the organization. For example, an organization may associate an unfair dismissal with its past track record of fair worker treatment to put the incident in a wider context. However, when the perception of organizational responsibility for a *faux pas* is high or strong, an organization will have to follow an acceptance or accommodative strategy (Table 11.1). Besides apologizing for the crisis and openly accepting the blame, this may consist of remediation (giving compensation to victims) or rectification (taking corrective action to prevent the crisis from happening again).

Natural accidents are unintentional and outwit the control of organizations. Such accidents can therefore be easily responded to with a distancing strategy which serves to reinforce the organization's lack of direct responsibility for the crisis. For example, an organization may legitimately claim that it was not directly responsible for the crisis. *Human-error accidents* are more difficult to justify and will require an apology from the organization and an admission that it will take action to prevent a recurrence of the crisis in the future. Germanwings apologized for the loss of life following the deliberate downing of the plane by one of its pilots in 2015, who had been suffering from mental health problems. The company proposed as a rectification random checks of pilots' psychological fitness and has called for a relaxing of doctor–patient confidentially laws, to make sure that in cases of potentially grave bodily harm doctors would be able to come forward

TABLE 11.1   Crisis communication strategies

Perception of low level of responsibility	
Non-existence strategies	**Claim of denying the crisis**
1. denial	a simple statement denying that a crisis exists
2. clarification	an extension of the denial tactic with attempts to explain why there is no crisis
3. attack and intimidation	a tactic of confronting the person or group who claims that a crisis exists; may include a threat to use 'force' (e.g. a lawsuit) against the accuser
Distance strategies	**Claim of distancing the organization from direct responsibility for the crisis**
1. excuse	a tactic of denying intention or volition by scapegoating others for the crisis
2. downplay	a tactic of convincing stakeholders or the general public that the situation is not that bad in itself or compared to other crises
Association strategies	**Claim of connecting the organization to things positively valued by stakeholders and publics**
1. bolstering	a tactic of reminding stakeholders and the general public of existing positive aspects of the organization (e.g. reminders of past charitable donations or a history of fair worker treatment) in order to offset the negatives the crisis brings to the organization
2. transcendence	a tactic of associating the negatives and loss arising from a crisis with a desirable, higher order goal (e.g. animal testing to develop life-saving drugs)
Suffering strategy	**Claim that the organization suffers from the crisis**
1. victimization	a tactic of portraying the organization as a victim of the crisis in order to win public sympathy
Perception of high level of responsibility	
Acceptance strategy	**Claim accepting responsibility or culpability for the crisis**
1. full apology	a tactic of simply apologizing for the crisis and accepting the blame
2. remediation	a tactic of announcing some form of compensation or help to victims (money, goods, aid, etc.)
3. repentance	a tactic of asking for forgiveness; the organization apologizes for the crisis and asks stakeholders and the general public to forgive its misdeeds
Accommodative strategy	**Claim promising to prevent the crisis from recurring**
1. rectification	a tactic of taking corrective action to prevent a recurrence of the crisis in the future

and share this with the company. Germanwings also lobbied for new regulations that have now come into force and require two pilots to be present in the cockpit of large passenger aircraft at all times – again as a rectification tactic (Table 11.1).

Transgressions are intentional actions taken by organizations, making them directly responsible for the impact of those actions. A strategy of distancing the organization from the crisis or a non-existence strategy that denies the existence of the crisis is thus futile. Organizations instead need to follow an acceptance strategy where they admit their responsibility but work to atone for the crisis in some fashion. For example, an organization may remediate by willingly offering some form of compensation or help to victims, may repent by publicly asking for forgiveness, or may follow a rectification tactic of ensuring that the crisis will not recur in the future. After it came to light that Volkswagen (VW) had distorted the results of emissions tests of its cars to pass environmental protection laws, the company had no choice but to apologize and to take corrective action. Its CEO was fired, various executives issued apologies and VW set up an independent investigation to identify the root of the problem so as to ensure that it does not happen again. The company also agreed to offer compensation to US car owners in a variety of forms including car buybacks, repairs and financial recompense. The company said the potential agreement with US car owners is 'an important step on the road to making things right. Volkswagen intends to compensate its customers fully and to remediate any impact on the environment from excess diesel emissions'.[11]

Terrorist attacks are directed at the organization by external agents and often there is very little direct organizational responsibility or culpability. An organization may therefore adopt a suffering strategy which portrays the organization as an unfair victim of some malicious, outside actor. Johnson & Johnson's famous portrayal of itself as wounded by product tampering during the 1982 Tylenol crisis is a good example of the suffering strategy.

In short, depending on the degree to which organizations are seen as responsible or culpable for a crisis in the eyes of stakeholders, organizations can employ different communication strategies (Table 11.1). It is important to stress at this point that the *perception* of whether an organization is responsible or culpable matters as much as whether the organization is *factually* responsible or culpable. For example, Uber, the ride-hailing company, has been hit by a series of crises involving its drivers, including accusations of rape and a shooting in 2016 that left six people dead and wounded scores of others. In all of these cases, the company has highlighted its extensive background checks, suggesting that their internal procedures are in order and that they could not have foreseen the actions of particular individuals. With the rape allegations, the company responded to media reports and reported that the five official rape allegations that it received between December 2012 and August 2015 represent only '0.0000009% of customer journeys in the period covered', with 'legitimate' sexual assault claims accounting for one in every 3.3 million trips. In this manner, the company tries to deny, clarify and downplay the perception of a crisis.

Generally speaking, as perceptions of crisis responsibility strengthen – for example, when in the case of Uber background checks over time do not appear sufficient to rule out the possibility of its drivers harming and assaulting its customers – the threat of image damage becomes greater, which means that communication practitioners need to utilize acceptance and accommodative strategies. Acceptance and accommodative strategies emphasize image repair, which is what is needed as image damage worsens. Defensive strategies, such as denial or downplaying, logically become less effective as organizations are viewed as more responsible for a crisis.[12] It is also important to realize that a crisis may not be settled by adopting the 'right' strategy. When a crisis breaks, various actors and parties become involved in debating the issue and may remain more or less vocal over time. Crisis communication researchers Frandsen and Johansen describe such scenarios as an 'arena' where various actors and groups discuss and negotiate the crisis and its ramifications.[13]

Furthermore, once a strategy has been identified, the key to effective crisis management is to maintain effective control over the release of information and to ensure that no unauthorized information or potentially damaging rumours are allowed to circulate. Failure to respond effectively to the media's enquiries about a crisis will invariably lead to journalists seeking information from whatever sources they can (perhaps with only limited regard for the accuracy of the information obtained).

It is therefore important to develop communication plans for probable crisis scenarios and to establish key responsibilities for communication practitioners before a crisis actually happens. This includes:

- the identification of the organization's key spokespersons
- media training of the CEO, executive directors and key spokespersons
- the establishment of a crisis communication team and in major crises a press office to field media enquiries and to handle the release of information
- the establishment of safe crisis locations where the media can meet and be briefed in the event of hazardous situations
- the identification of contacts at relevant external agencies (e.g. police, fire services) who may need to be contacted in case of a crisis.

A good example of having a crisis communication plan in place is the way in which the toymaker Mattel handled communication between August and October 2007 following a recall of products that were found to contain dangerous levels of lead paint. The products were sourced from China, where their manufacturing had not been properly supervised. But Mattel was prepared for this eventuality. Nine years prior to the actual crisis, the Vice President for Corporate Communication and his team had developed a communication plan for this kind of scenario. This ensured that the company was able to hit the ground running when the crisis struck. The company's communication through multiple channels ensured that stakeholders were informed and kept abreast of developments, customers knew how to return their recalled products and Mattel was able to subtly shift the crisis into an example of the care and responsibility that it feels for its end-consumers. Following the plan, the team systematically targeted consumers, stakeholders and the media. Mattel also provided a constant stream of information on what the company was doing to improve the safety of its products (a rectification strategy). The company had widely spread the message of the toy recalls through full-page newspaper advertisements, a website, consumer hotlines, online ads and a recall website. Mattel's CEO, Robert

Eckert, used the media to his advantage by voicing his personal dedication to product safety and appealing to parents worried about their children. Eckert's most effective communication was the video message he posted online to 'emphasize his concern as a parent and his personal responsibility'. He apologized, publicly admitting responsibility and mentioned the steps taken to tighten quality assurance requirements on Mattel's suppliers. Mattel's response only fell short in its compensation to consumers. The company offered equivalent-value coupons for other Mattel products in exchange for any recalled products. Given the inconvenience caused to consumers and the need to motivate them to return the affected products, this remediation tactic was perhaps somewhat insufficient.

The proactive and immediate crisis response of Mattel stands in stark contrast to a series of crisis cases in China where companies communicated very little and often far too late, damaging their reputation and even trust in their businesses and Chinese exports as a whole. In 2008, for example, news broke that Sanlu had added melamine to its infant milk formula and other food materials, leading to kidney damage and at last six infant deaths. The company had already received reports about sick infants as far back as December 2007, but had not performed any tests until June 2008. It also did not actively report on the crisis when the news broke, hoping perhaps that in time media attention would die down. This case in China does not stand on its own, however. In 2010, the Zijin Mining Group experienced a leakage of acidic waste water from one of its plants following continuous heavy rainfall but the company did not report the incident until nine days later. The leak killed tonnes of fish in the nearby Ting River and has since raised cancer rates for people living in the area. The company tried to conceal the incident and apparently tried to bribe journalists to refrain from reporting on the issue.

CASE STUDY 11.1

TATA'S HANDLING OF THE MUMBAI TERRORIST ATTACKS

Tata, a global group of companies headquartered in India, operates in seven business sectors: communications and information technology, engineering, materials, services, energy, consumer products and chemicals. The group operates in more than 80 countries across six continents, with 58 per cent of its revenues coming from business outside of India. Well-known companies within the group include Tata Steel, Tata Motors, Tata Consultancy services, Tata Tea and Taj Hotels. Whilst Tata has been around for more than a century, it was only recently that its chairman, Ratan Tata, steered the company into international expansion. Using an aggressive strategy, it has invested over 3 billion dollars in 19 acquisitions worldwide. Ratan Tata explained his strategy as follows: 'what we are attempting is simply a greater internationalization of our business. Where this thrust is different from the past is that it goes beyond exports. We will want to be a part of the community in which we operate.'

Whilst its size, turnover and operations mark Tata as an international corporation, the company is still firmly rooted in its Indian heritage and culture. From the inception of the group, the Tata family has, through philanthropy and human resource practices, cared for the plight of Indian workers and their families. The company provides, for example, medical aid and social benefits to its employees. The emphasis on growth in recent years has also not come at the expense of the company's commitment to its employees. The company invests heavily in training and development programmes and in strong corporate communications to develop a distinctive, yet cohesive culture across its companies and the entire group.

The Mumbai terrorist attacks

The group's Indian heritage and commitment to its employees also shines through in the way in which the company dealt with one of the most difficult chapters in its history: the 26/11 terrorist attacks on Mumbai and the Taj Hotel in the city. They began on 26 November 2008 and lasted for more than 60 hours, killing 166 people and wounding at least 308. The Taj Hotel formed the scene for a number of explosions and the terrorists held a number of guests and hotel staff hostage on site. The choice of target was significant; besides being a place for the rich and famous in India, the hotel also formed the jewel in the crown of the Tata hotel chain. The Taj was also the worst hit of all the targeted locations. It was under siege for three days, with the terrorists indiscriminately shooting guests and taking them hostage on the premises. During the events, staff tried to evacuate as many guests as possible via the back entrance and via fire exits. However, as events were televised live around the world, the terrorists also got a direct news feed on the escape attempts of the hotel guests. When the security forces arrived and took over the handling of the hotel, one of the first things they did was to restrict access and news coverage by the media.

As the security operation went on, the group chairman, Ratan Tata, and the CEO of the Tata hotel chain, Raymond Bickson, openly communicated with the media. For example, on 27 November, following the initial attacks, the following message by Ratan Tata was issued to the media:

> The terrible wanton attacks last night on innocent people and the destruction of prominent landmarks in India deserve to be universally condemned. My sympathies and condolences go out to all those who have suffered, been injured, and those who have lost their loved ones in this terrible act of hatred and destruction. We cannot replace the lives that have been lost and we will never forget the terrifying events of last night, but we must stand together, shoulder to shoulder as citizens of India, and rebuild what has been destroyed. We must show that we cannot be disabled or destroyed, but that such [a] heinous act will only make us stronger. It is important that we do not allow divisive forces to weaken us. We need to overcome these forces as one strong unified nation.

Crisis communication

Both Ratan Tata and Raymond Bickson provided continuous updates to the media on the security operation, and responded to rumours about the terrorist motives and the targeting of the hotel. Questions were also raised in the media about the security measures of the hotel. Ratan Tata went on record saying that whilst security measures had been implemented, 'if I look at what we had ... it could not have stopped what took place'. He also singled out the courageous efforts of his staff, who helped

(Continued)

(Continued)

guests to evacuate and in doing so helped to avoid a much greater loss of life. Whilst over 700 guests were booked into the hotel, the number of deceased totalled 31. According to one employee, the main reason why they had been able to stay alert and calm during those 60 hours was their training and the endless fire drills that they had been forced to go through as part of hotel policy.

The entire security operation within the hotel and across Mumbai officially ended on 29 November and the hotel was handed back to the Tata group on 1 December. The decision was taken, and announced almost immediately, that the hotel would be restored to its former glory and re-opened a mere three weeks later on 21 December. To accomplish this, the management team initiated a clean-up and restoration of the hotel, but also realized that a significant part of the operation would be to pro- vide care to its employees and manage customer perceptions. Employees had to be rehabilitated and supported with counselling to deal with the traumatic events. Customers also had to be assured again that the hotel would be secure and safe, and would, in effect, be offering the same level of service as before.

One important step was that security was tightened at the hotel. The hotel restricted access to official guests, and X-ray scans and metal detectors were used by security personnel to check everyone coming into the building. Ratan Tata also told the media that new security measures were put in place as a way of thwarting any attacks. When the hotel re-opened, a select group of long-time supporters and guests booked in and a memorial service was held for hotel staff who had lost their lives in the tragedy. Key to the image restoration with customers were the Taj staff themselves and the way in which they had gone out of their way to save guests dur- ing the tragedy. The heartbreaking story of Karambir Singh Kang, the Taj Mumbai's general manager, touched the hearts of millions around the world. He was a key part of the evacuation effort and had worked tirelessly to get guests out of the building, even after realizing that the fire that had broken out on the sixth floor of the hotel had killed his own family. His story became a 'symbol' for the valour and customer focus of the hotel's employees.

The aftermath of the crisis

The Tata group arranged for counsellors to meet with staff and set up trauma camps to help staff get through their emotions and anxieties following the traumatic events. Families of the deceased members of staff were provided with compensation pack- ages and the last drawn salaries were paid out as a life-long pension of the company. Children of the deceased were provided with education allowances to ensure that they would be able to study wherever in the world they chose. Permanent jobs were also given to family members of five employees who had been the only breadwinners for their families.

The company furthermore set up a trust to provide direct aid to those affected by the terrorist attacks and to support those affected by similar events in the future. The trust initially provided direct relief to all those affected by the attacks, including its own employees but also police officers, fire fighters and security guards. It also got records of the 170 people killed in the attacks and the 400 who were injured. In turn, the trust contacted all the individuals directly affected, as well as their fami- lies, and conducted a needs assessment study to determine the psychological and financial requirements of those affected. Initially, it decided to cover all individuals in the city who were from the lowest strata of society and had received no support from the government. The support that the trust gave came in the form of a monthly subsistence allowance, depending on the number of children in the family; support towards the education of the 62 children of the terror victims; micro-finance support and sustenance to help victims set up businesses; and, finally, vocational and sustainable livelihood training for dependents and the injured. The vice-president for human resources for the Taj hotel chain explains the latter support as follows:

> The subsistence allowance is not meant to be a lifetime pension. We therefore identify one or two people in the family and train them in vocational skills such as tailoring, driving, baking and confectionery, and housekeeping. The Taj offers a three- to four-month course to impart these skills. Once the course ends, many of the trainees will be hired by the Taj on compassionate grounds. Others can easily find employment in Mumbai or the suburbs owing to the training they have received from the Taj. We want to ensure we are able to create and build sustainable livelihoods for these families before we stop the subsistence allowance.

In this way, the trust aims to help the victims of the Mumbai attacks and also pledges to help others who will be affected by similar events such as terrorist attacks and natural disasters in India in the future.

Question for reflection

Discuss the way in which the Tata group handled communication during and in the direct aftermath of the Mumbai terrorist attacks. What, in your opinion, did they do more or less well in this case? Relate your views to the available crisis communication strategies discussed in the chapter. Should the company have followed a different communication strategy or executed a particular strategy differently?

Source: Based on newspaper reports at the time, http://hbr.org/2011/12/the-ordinary-heroes-of-the-taj and material drawn from www.tata.com

11.6 CHAPTER SUMMARY

Crisis communication is an increasingly important specialist discipline within corporate communication. Managing crises typically starts with developing crisis contingency plans for the most probable crisis scenarios that an organization may encounter. Communication practitioners are involved in the development of these plans and are also responsible for working out the details of crisis communication. One important principle for crisis communication is the degree to which stakeholders and publics hold the organization responsible or culpable for a particular crisis. Based on the perception of organizational responsibility, practitioners can choose between different communication strategies, ranging from accommodative strategies to advocacy and defensive ones.

—————— DISCUSSION QUESTIONS ——————————

1. What are the main differences between an issue and a crisis? To put this in perspective, consider the daily reports on companies in *The Financial Times* – which of these news items in your view refer to issues and which refer to crises?

2. Select a number of recent crises such as the BP oil spill in the Mexican Gulf and reflect on how each of the relevant companies communicated about the crisis with the media and its stakeholders. Which of the crisis communication strategies did they follow? Was this successful in the end?

KEY TERMS

Acceptance strategy	Crisis communication plan
Accommodative strategy	Distance strategy
Crisis	Association strategy
Faux pas	Non-existence strategy
Crisis	Suffering strategy
Advocacy	Transgression
Accident	Terrorist attack

 —————— FURTHER READING ——————————————

Coombs, W. Timothy (2012) *Ongoing Crisis Communication: Planning, Managing and Responding.* London: Sage Series in Public Relations, 3rd edition.
Zaremba, Alan Jay (2010) *Crisis Communication: Theory and Practice.* New York: M.E. Sharpe.

Want to know more about this chapter? Visit the companion website at: https://study.sagepub.com/cornelissen5e to access videos, web links, a glossary and selected journal articles to further enhance your study.

NOTES

1. See, for example, Weick, K.E. and Sutcliffe, K.M. (2007) *Managing the Unexpected.* San Francisco: Jossey-Bass, 2nd edition; Weick, K.E., Sutcliffe, K.M. and Obstfeld, D. (1999) 'Organizing for high reliability: Processes of collective mindfulness', *Research in Organizational Behavior*, 21: 81–124.
2. Mitroff, I.I. and Pearson, C.M. (1993) *Crisis Management.* San Francisco: Jossey-Bass.
3. Fombrun, C.J. and Van Riel, C.B.M. (2004) *Fame and Fortune: How Successful Companies Build Winning Reputations.* Upper Saddle River, NJ: Prentice-Hall, quote on p. 32.
4. Dean, D.H. (2004) 'Consumer reaction to negative publicity: Effects of corporate reputation, response, and responsibility for a crisis event', *Journal of Business Communication*, 41: 192–211.
5. Devers, C.E., Dewett, T., Mishina, Y. and Belsito, C.A. (2009) 'A general theory of organizational stigma', *Organization Science*, 20: 154–71.

6. Yang, S., Kang, M. and Johnson, P. (2010) 'Effects of narratives, openness to dialogic communication, and credibility on engagement in crisis communication through organizational blogs', *Communication Research*, 37: 473–97.

7. Coombs, W.T. (2007) 'Protecting organization reputations during a crisis: The development and application of situational crisis communication theory', *Corporate Reputation Review*, 10: 163–76.

8. See, for example, Coombs, W. Timothy (2012) *Ongoing Crisis Communication: Planning, Managing, and Responding*. London: Sage.

9. Coombs, W.T. (1995) 'Choosing the right words: The development of guidelines for the selection of the "appropriate" crisis-response strategies', *Management Communication Quarterly*, 8: 447–76.

10. Coombs (2012).

11. *The Wall Street Journal* (2016) 'Volkswagen reaches deal with US over diesel emissions scandal', 21 April.

12. Benoit, W.L. (1995) *Accounts, Excuses and Apologies: A Theory of Image Restoration Discourse*. Albany, NY: SUNY Press.

13. Frandsen, F. and Johansen, W. (2013) 'Rhetorical arena (crisis theory)', in Heath, R.L. (ed.), *Encyclopedia of Public Relations*. Thousand Oaks, CA: Sage.

New Developments in Corporate Communication

5

Part 5 explores emerging areas of practice within corporate communication, including change and leadership communication and corporate social responsibility (CSR) programmes and community relations. In recent years, these areas have evolved into significant areas of activity, in part as a result of the recognized importance of effective communication around topics such as change and corporate social responsibility.

After reading Part 5, the reader will be familiar with these significant emerging areas of practice and developing trends, as well as with practical principles and frameworks for communicating around these topics in practice.

Leadership and Change Communication ## 12

┌─ CHAPTER OVERVIEW ┐

Managers need to demonstrate leadership skills and communicate effectively with stakeholders during major organizational changes. The chapter defines leadership communication and discusses various ways in which communication can be used effectively to initiate and realize organizational changes. These strategies range from narratives and stories promoting a change to informational and interactive strategies that allow employees to understand and help realize the change.

12.1 INTRODUCTION

Change is a constant within many organizations. At any one point, organizations initiate changes, ranging from a reformulation of their vision, brand or identity to the implementation of new customer management or software programs, to a restructuring of the organization. Change often implies a disruption of the status quo and previously established ways of working and doing things. As such, it may trigger controversy and confusion with employees and almost always presents a justification problem. It may also lead to resistance, particularly when managers do not sufficiently communicate about the change. Change per se may not necessarily be what worries employees but rather their expectation that they will no longer continue to work for the same organization. Denise Rousseau, an organizational psychologist, defined this expectation as a 'sense of continuity' and argued that it is essential for leaders to frame and emphasize a sense of continuity if employees are to maintain their identification with the organization in the wake of major organizational change.[1]

Organizational change requires the leadership of managers who articulate a rationale for why a change is needed and who also largely, through their communication,

drum up support from others ('followers') within the organization in order to implement and realize the change. The following section first defines the nature of leadership
in the context of organizational change. The subsequent sections then outline various
communication strategies during and after major organizational changes (e.g. organizational restructuring, lay-off of staff) to reduce employee resistance and to facilitate
the implementation and routinization of such changes. The chapter concludes with
general observations on the characteristics and skills associated with effective leadership communication.

12.2 DEFINING LEADERSHIP AND CHANGE

Leadership is one of those hard-to-define subjects. At one level, our understanding
of leadership builds on images of great leaders, including great historical and political leaders. However, most managers working in the more practical context of an
organization have relatively little in common with these historical figures.

Nonetheless, these images of great leaders, ranging from Roman emperors to figures
such as Churchill and Martin Luther King, have shaped how many people think about
leadership. The classic image of the leader is therefore often one of born-to-lead; leaders
have natural attributes and skills such as courage and charisma which are often seen as
'given'. This means that only some individuals are able to lead effectively from the very
top and motivate others in organizations. In fact, you often hear people make remarks
such as 'he is such a natural leader', with such remarks often being driven by classic and
often heroic images of what it means to be a leader.

An alternative, and increasingly popular, perspective on leadership is one which
suggests that leadership can be acquired and developed; including many of the
communication skills associated with leadership roles in organizations. It also recognizes that leadership may be situational, and that within organizations managers or
employees may demonstrate leadership in articulating changes or opportunities and
in getting others to follow them. The self-development perspective, in other words,
focuses on the ability of individuals to communicate and influence others, as well
as, of course, on simultaneously being influenced by others in the implementation
of a change or a specific task or project. Organizations require groups or teams of
people to work together, and effective leaders are those who can focus the efforts
of a group or team on a common goal and can enable individuals to work together.
When leading, individual managers influence and shape the interpretations of others
in the organization, but ideally are also sensible in not unduly burdening the process
with an overlarge ego.

The CEO and most senior executives in an organization naturally need to take
on leadership roles in articulating a vision for the organization and any overarching
corporate goals. They will also use various platforms, including management and
town-hall meetings, to communicate this directly to employees lower down the
organization. But middle managers and supervisors or managers of work teams also
need to demonstrate leadership skills in their interactions with employees around
them. Traditional images of organization and control suggested that managers

and supervisors should control and manage employees in strict ways, and from the top down on the basis of authority relationships. Since then, models of effective human resource management have highlighted that employees are not merely cogs in a machine or quantities of manpower, but in fact social beings who look for inspiration and want to be socially involved. Leaders in turn are those individuals who, in daily interactions with others, can articulate inspiring visions that marshal support.

Generally speaking, leaders may differ in terms of a 'leadership style', which is the way in which, in their communication and behaviour, they approach others and provide direction, implement plans and energize and motivate others in an organization.[2] Such a style may reflect their own leadership philosophy, personality and experience, but it may also stem from the organizational situations in which they work. For example, so-called 'transactional' leadership styles involve situations of leadership where the leader is concerned with maintaining and ensuring the completion of a specific set of tasks. These leaders use their designated authority and a range of incentives to motivate employees to perform to the best of their abilities in completing a set of tasks. The term 'transactional' refers here to the fact that the style of leadership is one where a leader essentially motivates subordinates by exchanging rewards for performance. Transactional leaders are, in doing so, focused on specific tasks and do not have a broad or long-term strategic vision for an organization. A different style – that of the 'transformational' leader – is one, however, where broad visions are mobilized by leaders to motivate employees and foster collaboration between them towards a set of higher-level ambitions. Transformational leaders set broad strategic goals and then use a range of influencing and motivational tactics to push and support their subordinates to higher performance levels, whilst, at the same time, providing opportunities for personal and professional growth for each employee. Compared to a transactional leadership style, the term 'transformational' refers to how, in this instance, leaders are not focused on specific operational goals or tasks per se, but instead are primarily aiming to empower employees and to support their growth and development, which in turn may translate into new strategic opportunities for an organization or a strengthening of its capabilities. Whilst these leadership styles are distinct, both are needed within an organization and at different levels. A transformational leadership style is key when, for example, a CEO wants to strategically move the organization in a different direction, whilst transactional leadership is central to supervising and supporting the day-to-day operations of an organization.

One important area where leadership is required involves the management of change. Change is a facet of many organizations. Organizational changes have often been classified in terms of degrees of change. For example, change can be major or radical (e.g. a complete restructuring of an organization) or more minor and convergent (e.g. an adjustment of customer service guidelines as a result of customer feedback). Radical change involves a complete re-orientation of an organization, whereas convergent change consists of fine-tuning the existing orientation and ways of working. Change can also be defined in terms of its time frame: evolutionary changes occur slowly and gradually, whereas revolutionary changes happen swiftly and affect virtually all of the organization.[3] Organizational changes can, of course, also be classified in terms of the primary focus of the change. The change may be the adoption of novel or updated *technology* to accomplish work; a *restructuring* and change in *policies* and routine *ways of working*; a change in the *products* and *services* of an organization; or a change in the *organizational identity* and *culture* of the organization.

One particularly helpful way to think about change is in terms of 'additive' versus 'substitutive' change. Change can be seen either as a departure from the old organization (a substitution) or as an addition to, or update of, the old organization (an addition). Substitutive change is a major strategic change that often involves a redefinition of the organization's mission and purpose or a substantial restructuring of the organization. Additive changes are less drastic and may involve, for example, improvements to ways of working. Substitutive changes are obviously more difficult to sell to employees and also more difficult to get support for (see Table 12.1). Such changes break down the current status quo and therefore require effective leadership communication (see Case Example 12.1). Managers, in their role as transformational leaders during such change, often craft a narrative for this purpose that provides an inspiring image of the new organization after the change that employees can transition to. For example, when Samuel Palmisano took over as CEO of IBM he set out

TABLE 12.1 Putting change in perspective: additive versus substitutive changes

	Additive change	Substitutive change
Definition	An incremental change at the level of work processes that enhances the productivity and performance of the organization	A redefinition of the organization's identity and purpose or a substantial restructuring of the organization
Nature of change	Small-scale	Large-scale
Reason for change	Productivity: specific operational problems or opportunities to change work processes to achieve superior economic performance	Continuity: the need for the organization to adapt or re-orient its overall structure and positioning in a particular industry or set of industries to secure its continuity
Term	Short-term and strict time frame with clear starting and end points	Long-term, start point clear but longer time horizon around realizing the change
Focus	Specific parts of the organization including structures, technologies or work processes	Strategic renewal of the entire organization, including its overall identity, structures, technologies and work processes
Leadership challenge	Getting support for changes to work processes that break with routines and conventions	Getting support for a drastic change that challenges the status quo and requires that employees embrace a new or revised identity

to change IBM from a profitable multinational corporation into a global integrated enterprise (Case Study 9.1). He managed to achieve the change with the support of his employees. A large part of his success was down to his skills as an effective communicator, his re-articulation of the IBM story and the way in which he involved employees in the transition.

 CASE EXAMPLE 12.1

STRATEGIC CHANGE AT BANK MANDIRI

In the aftermath of the Asian financial crisis, the Government of Indonesia decided to restructure all seven state-owned banks, with the aim of eventually selling and privatizing each of these banks. In 1998 the government announced that four state banks (Bank Bumi Daya (BBD), Bank Dagang Negara (BDN), Bank Exim and Bapindo) would be merged together into a single banking entity that would be named Bank Mandiri. This was initially criticized because of the costs associated with the merger but also because it would effectively involve 'bailing out' inefficient banks. The Indonesian government, however, argued that closing the four banks or allowing them to fail would have been far more costly. A few months after the official announcement, Robby Djohan was appointed Chief Executive Officer of Bank Mandiri. Djohan had a reputation for successfully turning businesses around including Garuda, the Indonesian state-owned airline, and Bank Niagara. His job was to restructure the new organization, improve the quality of its assets and increase efficiency by making improvements to the organization, systems and human resources of the four constituent banks. Djohan and his team embarked on a comprehensive process of consolidation. They closed 194 overlapping branches and reduced the combined workforce from 26,600 to 17,620. They also rolled out the single corporate brand throughout the network and started to actively advertise about the benefits and values of the new Bank Mandiri brand. The team also tried to establish professional standards for management across the organization, to ensure that the bank would operate under internationally recognized principles of corporate governance, control and compliance.

One of the key challenges facing the new bank was the legacy of a bureaucratic culture which stemmed from its former state-owned status. Djohan envisaged a clear break from this culture to improve the bank and to meet customer expectations in the private sector. His first move was to strategically place a number of managers as change agents in each of the constituent banks. These managers would bring new thinking and enthusiasm to the bank. Djohan himself was also open and direct in his management style and critical of bureaucracy and unclear communication. Despite Djohan's best efforts, for some time after the merger, Bank Mandiri still consisted of four distinct cultures associated with each of the constituent banks. In response, Djohan and his team started several communication initiatives to frame the common values of the new bank and strengthen the ties across the four constituent banks. Other start-up issues around liquidity however intervened, which resulted in progressively less time being spent on communicating to employees about the required transformation.

Robby Djohan was replaced overnight by the Indonesian government in May 2000 by E.C.W. Neloe, who was an astute manager but less challenging in his management style. Neloe set out to change the culture from the inside, spending his first six months in office to evaluate the structures and culture at the bank before taking steps to restructure and change the organizational design. He then set out to create a much flatter organization

(Continued)

(Continued)

with fewer layers of hierarchy between the head office and banking operations. Neloe also tried to change the culture within the bank, although during his tenure he admitted that 'we have not really been able to develop a culture as good as I would like to have [done]. I still hear employees referring to colleagues that are from this or that legacy bank.'

One additional step that the senior management took was to introduce new behavioural guidelines for employees within the bank. Dr Supomo, Executive Vice-President, explains:

> When we introduced the new organization structure, besides restating our vision, mission and shared values, we also introduced new daily behavioural guidelines for our employees. We call it [the] 'Three No's Behaviour': no delays, no errors, and no special payments. This aims to change the old perception of the state-owned banks as bureaucratic and poor at serving customers, even though it was not always true. The 'Three No's Behaviour' policy has been widely communicated both internally and externally.[4]

In addition to the introduction of these behavioural guidelines, Bank Mandiri has also run a series of corporate advertising campaigns extolling the virtues of its new cultural values including integrity, professionalism, customer focus and a commitment to service excellence. These campaigns have helped strengthen the brand image with customers and other external stakeholders, but importantly also influenced employees and strengthened the internal culture around these values.

Questions for reflection

1 Would you characterize the merger of the four banks and their distinct cultures into Bank Mandiri as an additive or substitutive change?
2 Given the nature of the change, do you feel that the initial leaders of the bank communicated in an effective manner to integrate the four cultures into one? What else could they have done?

Source: Information for this case was sourced from www.bankmandiri.co.id and from discussions with Bank Mandiri employees; quotes in the case are taken from Lasserre, P. (2003) 'Bank Mandiri: A case in strategic transformation', *Journal of Financial Transformation*, 9: 63-75.

12.3 COMMUNICATING DURING A CHANGE

An important area of corporate communication involves communicating to employees during and after a change. Large organizations are prone to initiate and implement many organizational changes ranging from, for example, a new performance initiative, the adoption of new technology or a new way of working, to the laying off of parts of the workforce. All of these changes affect employees in one way or another and their successful implementation often crucially depends on communication. Poorly managed change communication may result in rumours and resistance to change. Communication and change are related in a number of different ways. Communication is central to how a change is formulated, announced and explained to employees and also contributes to a successful implementation and

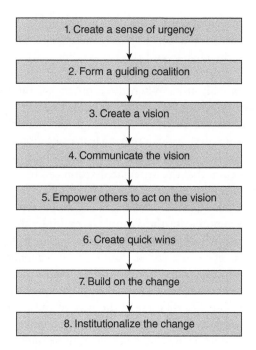

FIGURE 12.1 Managing change

Source: Based on Kotter, J. (2012) *Leading Change*. Boston, MA: HBS Press, first published in 1996.

institutionalization of the change. Kurt Lewin highlighted the importance of communication in his simple model of the change process.[5] Lewin likened the change process to the stages involved in water freezing. When snow melts as a result of heat from the sun and then refreezes when the temperature drops again, it takes on a different texture and becomes icy again. Lewin argued that change in an organization is a very similar process, involving an alteration of the organization (water) in terms of its structure or function (in the form of snow or ice) over time. Based on this metaphor, he argued that change involves four phases: (1) recognizing the need for change (*unfreezing*), (2) development of a change plan (*vision*), (3) implementation of the new change (*moving*), and (4) routinization of the change (*refreezing*). All of these phases (identification of the need for change, formulation of a change initiative, implementation of the change and institutionalization of the change) require communication between managers and employees.

The management guru and Harvard professor John Kotter provides a more specific breakdown of the change process.[6] His process model has eight steps, as displayed in Figure 12.1.

The first three steps involve the preparation in advance of a change initiative. In step 1, leaders, as change agents, need to have a firm grasp of what the reasons behind the organization's need to change are. They need to distil these key reasons, whether these are, for example, competitive or productivity-related, and have to convince others in the organization of the necessity for change. When they achieve this goal, it is likely that employees within the organization are more likely to see the rationale for the change and will buy into the change. Step 2 involves leaders continuing to promote the change and the reasons for it to key players within the organization. Such key players may be formal leaders or influential opinion leaders or experts across the organization. When these others are on board and, in effect, form a coalition, a key point for the change agent is to make sure that everyone is on the same page, so that the coalition as a whole can continue to build urgency for the change. Step 3 involves articulating a clear aspiration or vision around the change, which can be easily communicated and understood by employees across the organization. It is important that the articulated vision can be easily explained and is captured in a few short sentences. After the preparation phase, the implementation of the change initiative takes place in steps 4, 5 and 6. In step 4, change agents and the coalition openly communicate the vision via multiple channels to employees. Crucial to the success of their communication is the way in which they demonstrate passion when they speak about the vision, connect it to real behaviours and respond openly and honestly to feedback and questions from employees. In step 5, the focus is on empowering others to act on the vision and to change their behaviours. This may involve removing obstacles that get in the way of these changes in behaviour, and may also require positive reinforcements through incentives and reward systems. In step 6, when initial results of the change emerge, these 'quick wins' are communicated to everyone else in the organization. The purpose of doing so is that everyone is able to see the value of the change and that it is already happening. Steps 7 and 8, finally, involve the management and institutionalization of the change in the organization, so that, in effect, it becomes the new status quo. According to Kotter, step 7 is important in that many change agents think too quickly that they have already realized the change, whereas many changes require continuous effort, patience and a long time frame. Effective change agents realize this and constantly try to improve on the change effort, adjusting the change as it is implemented and as more feedback emerges as to what works and what does not. In step 8, the change is finally fully embedded in the organization's processes and practices. This involves, for example, incorporating the change ideals and values into practices including recruitment and training. It also requires that change agents keep talking about the progress resulting from the change and communicate success stories to everyone within the organization. The overall concept behind these eight steps is that it provides a systematic and 'proven' methodology for change management, and one that therefore may offset the potential for failing to realize a change.

In an important way, a change initiative can also be seen as a 'persuasion' process that is achieved in and through communication.[7] At first, and in preparation of the plan, leaders, as change agents, talk to other managers in the organization to convince them of the change and its urgency. This first step involves persuading key opinion leaders to gain a mandate for the change, and involves crucial negotiations before the change is actually announced and implemented. Garvin and Roberto, two Harvard Business School professors, see this first persuasion step as crucial to creating the context for change. This first step is followed in their model by a subsequent phase in which leaders have to craft a frame, or vision, of the strategic and economic issues motivating the change and of the change itself. As displayed in Figure 12.2, this second step involves deciding on a set of keywords and idioms that best capture the change, are easily understood and are likely to persuade employees. Where the Garvin and Roberto model complements the Kotter model (Figure 12.1) is in acknowledging the emotional distress and anxiety that a change may bring about. Step 3 of their model is thus about managing the moods of employees, which involves leaders engaging in continuous conversations with staff to glean feedback but also to keep persuading and motivating employees to make the change. The final step of their model is about reinforcing and institutionalizing the new behaviours. This involves leaders personally modelling the new ways of working, providing coaching and support, and positively reinforcing the desired behaviours of staff through rewards and incentives. This final phase is, in essence, about 'walking the talk'. In the words of Garvin and Roberto:

> effective leaders explicitly reinforce organizational values on a constant basis, using actions to back up their words. Their goal is to change behaviour, not just ways of thinking. For example a leader can talk about values such as openness, delegation, and direct communication in meetings and e-mails. But the message takes hold only if he or she also signals a dislike of disruptive, divisive behaviours by pointedly – and if necessary, publicly – criticizing them.[8]

These change management models highlight that once the change initiative has been defined and a vision articulated, leaders within an organization will have to identify an effective way of communicating the change to all of their employees. Obviously, when a change is radical or substitutive and involves the entire organization, managers would have to engage in a lot of conversations with employees across all levels of the organization to initiate the desired overhaul in thinking. Alternatively, when the change is more additive and involves, for example, an updating of technology (e.g. the introduction of a new intranet system) communication may consist of informing employees about the new technology and training them in their use of it.

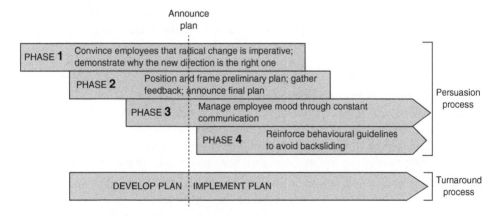

FIGURE 12.2   Change management as a persuasion process

Source: Based on Garvin, D.A. and Roberto, M.A. (2005) 'Change through persuasion', *Harvard Business Review*, February: 104–12.

The management scholar Clampitt and his colleagues observed five different communication strategies that managers use to communicate a change to employees in their organization:[9]

1. *'Spray and pray'* involves managers showering ('spray') employees with all kinds of information about the change. The idea with this strategy is that information is simply passed on to employees who, it is hoped ('pray'), will then themselves sort out the significant from the insignificant details and work out what the change means for their day-to-day job. Whilst this strategy may seem admirable, it is rarely effective. More information does not necessarily equate to better communication when it is not sufficiently focused on and tailored to the needs of employees.

2. *'Tell and sell'* involves managers communicating a more limited set of messages that they believe address the core issues about the change. In this strategy, managers first tell employees about the key issues and then try to sell employees a particular approach. This is a top-down strategy; employees are not engaged in a dialogue, but simply informed of a change. The danger with this strategy is that employees feel that they are not listened to and become sceptical, if not cynical, about the change.

3. *'Underscore and explore'* involves managers focusing on several fundamental issues most clearly linked to the organizational change, whilst allowing employees the creative freedom to explore the implications of the change in a disciplined way. When managers use this strategy, they often assume that communication is not complete and effective until they know how employees will react to the core ideas behind the change. In other words, managers are concerned not only with developing a few core messages but also with listening to employees, in order to identify potential misunderstandings and unrecognized obstacles to the change.

4. *'Identify and reply'* is different from the first three because it starts with the concerns of employees. The strategy involves employees setting the agenda to which managers reply. The assumption behind the strategy is that employees are in the best position to know the critical issues and the feasibility of a change. However, the danger is that employees do not have the wider picture of the entire organization and that managers use this strategy as a defensive posture in which they are seen to attend to employee concerns without actually using that feedback.

5. *'Withhold and uphold'* consists of managers withholding information until they can no longer do so because of rumours or employee revolt. When confronted by rumours or revolt, managers simply uphold the party line. Managers who use this strategy often assume that information is power and that employees are not sophisticated enough to grasp the big picture or simply do not need to know the rationale for a change.

Managers may use one or a combination of these five strategies. The underlying differences between these strategies involve the degree to which employees are provided with relevant information, are given guidance on the change and feel involved and

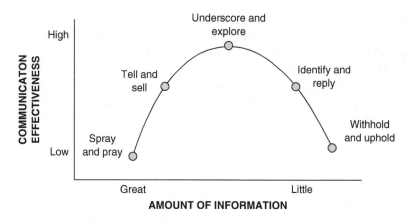

FIGURE 12.3 Change communication strategies

consulted in the change process. As demonstrated in Figure 12.3, the communication strategies towards the middle of the figure tend to offer employees more guidance by prioritizing communication and providing relevant and focused information on the change. These strategies are also more sensitive to employee concerns and needs, although of course they make different assumptions about the importance and nature of those concerns and needs. The 'underscore and explore' strategy, in particular, maximizes the likelihood of effective change by creatively synthesizing managers' change initiatives and employee concerns.

The 'underscore and explore' strategy is in line with what other research on organizational change has supported: organizational change is more successful when employees in non-management positions are able to exert influence over the change process by providing feedback on the change and its implementation. Managers may be tempted to impose changes on employees. However, joint involvement and collaboration between managers and employees in identifying the need for change and in formulating and implementing change programmes lead to greater employee commitment to a change. In a general sense, then, bottom-up involvement in change is generally more effective than a top-down or programmed implementation of change.

At the same time, many organizations do not or cannot always involve all of their employees in the formative stages of a change. Particularly in large, multinational corporations, top-down approaches are still common for practical reasons, because it will be impossible to involve all, if not most, of their employees in the development of a change initiative. British Airways (see Case Study 12.1), for example, has often opted for the top-down implementation of changes using a combination of 'tell and sell' and 'identify and reply' strategies. Issues in customer service, for example, have been 'sold' to all front-line staff through training programmes after being 'identified' by employees.

The choice of either a top-down or bottom-up approach to communicating change is coupled with the use of certain media.[10] When organizations opt for a top-down approach, they may involve employees only to a limited extent in the routinization of the change. Managers will not consult employees in the identification of the need for change and the formulation of a change initiative; instead, they will meet each other in management meetings and will consult external sources (e.g. management consultants), periodicals and formal documents. Once a change initiative is formulated, it will then be rolled out to employees through organization-wide media such as the intranet, announcement meetings and one-way audio or video messages. On the other hand, in a bottom-up approach, employees are involved to a greater degree in the entire change process. Managers speak to employees face-to-face and through e-mails and over the phone in the identification stage, will meet them in meetings and electronic conferences in the formulation stage and will engage with all employees through interactive meetings and technologies (video conference, e-mail) during the implementation and routinization stage.

The communication consultants Larkin and Larkin argue that for top-down change initiatives to be successful, they need to be communicated to employees in plain English and largely through face-to-face communication.[11] They argue that managers should only communicate the facts and essential information to employees and not refer to management speak. Face-to-face communication is also more successful, they argue, than videos and newsletters because of the involvement of employees and because it allows them to ask questions and talk back (see Chapter 9). Ideally, employees prefer news about the change to be given to them by their direct supervisors rather than more senior managers. Employees are more likely to trust their immediate supervisors, increasing the likelihood of the change being understood and accepted and decreasing the likelihood of resistance.[12] Face-to-face contact is also associated with an 'open' communication climate. Communication climate refers to the possibilities within an organization for employees to respond to and ask questions about the change. A more 'open' climate influences employees' trust, commitment and willingness to change.[13]

Managing change thus involves encouraging participation from as many employees as possible, addressing their concerns in the change programme and ensuring that managers act as role models for the change. However, as mentioned, managers cannot always involve all employees in the entire change process from formulation to routinization. In some change initiatives, the need for communication efficiency is higher than in others. Communication efficiency is defined as the accomplishment of change communication with a minimum expenditure of time, effort and resources.[14]

The need for communication efficiency is high in organizations where (a) it is physically impossible to communicate in a face-to-face or interactive manner with all employees, (b) resources devoted to change communication are scarce, and (c) there is an urgent need to progress through the change process and, thus, little time for interaction about it. Besides deciding how efficient the communication process should be, managers also need to decide how important a consensus with employees is for the success of the change. Consensus-building is defined as the effort in change communication to achieve commitment to a course of action as a result of joint decision-making. The need for consensus-building is high in organizations where (a) changes are perceived to be radical and/or controversial, (b) there is a history of resistance to similar change, (c) critical resources (e.g. expertise, approval) are controlled by employees, and (d) ongoing support and cooperation are needed to maintain the change. When these two dimensions of the change situation are combined, managers are provided with four different communication strategies. These communication

TABLE 12.2 Factors affecting the choice of change communication strategies

High need for communication efficiency	Need-to-know strategy	Quid pro quo strategy
Low need for communication efficiency	Equal dissemination strategy	Equal participation strategy
	Low need for consensus-building	High need for consensus-building

strategies provide an element of depth to the strategies discussed above (Figure 12.3) by highlighting the differential treatment of different groups of employees and the practical considerations of communication efficiency and consensus-building that will go into the decision for a change communication strategy. Table 12.2 shows the matrix of factors affecting the choice of communication strategies.

1. *Need-to-know strategy*: here, managers keep quiet about planned change except to those employees who really need to know or who explicitly express a desire for the information. This is done in part out of an efficiency motivation, in part to avoid giving rise to potential objections from some employees and in part to avoid overburdening employees with large amounts of information for which they have little time or use. The strategy's exclusive focus on a select group of employees may be useful when the change is more convergent or additive than radical or substitutive and when employees of the organization are themselves selective about which of the organization's activities are of interest to them.

2. *Quid pro quo strategy*: here, as the name implies, managers give more communicative attention to those employees who have something valuable (e.g. expertise, approval power, resources) for the change process. A franchise organization, for example, may only communicate to its franchisees and not to other hired staff about a change in governance. These employees are crucial to the change and thus need to be consulted and communicated with. The strategy combines a focus on consensus-building with efficiency as only certain groups of employees are communicated with. Because of cost considerations, managers focus their time and energy on those employees who are most crucial to the change's success. However, the risk of using this strategy is that it may anger other employees who feel left out of the change process.

3. *Equal dissemination strategy*: this strategy focuses on disseminating information to employees across the entire organization, early, often and, most importantly, on an equal basis. The strategy is one of blanket dissemination of information through newsletters, general meetings, listserv postings, individual meetings, phone calls, posters and banners. The purpose of this strategy is not to involve all employees in the change but simply to give everyone fair notice of the change and to keep them

informed of goings-on in the organization. The strategy is also often used to prevent the complaint by employees unfriendly to the proposed change that they were not told early enough or given enough details. The strategy is common in large organizations where communication channels are abundant and where extensive information dissemination thus adds little further cost.

4. *Equal participation strategy*: this final strategy involves two-way communication (i.e. both disseminating information and soliciting input) between managers and employees. This participative strategy is used when employees are crucial to the success of the change. However, the strategy is quite costly and may become overly political when opinions, support and advice from all sectors of the workforce are sought. This strategy is common in small and public sector organizations that embrace participative and democratic values and that have sufficient time, resources and communication channels available.

Organizational change often presents a challenge to employees. Employees usually do not resist the change itself, but rather the uncertainty associated with the change: uncertainty about job security, the fear of losing status and power within the organization, and uncertainty about whether they will fit in with the changed organization.[15] Uncertainty and fear may lead to stress, to a lack of trust between employees and managers and to low levels of commitment. It may even encourage people to leave the organization.[16] Effective change communication recognizes these uncertainties and, as far as is possible (based on the need for communication efficiency), tries to inform employees of the change and to engage with them to facilitate the implementation and routinization of the change.

12.4 EFFECTIVE LEADERSHIP COMMUNICATION

Given the significance of organizational change, managers, in their leadership roles, need to use communication to help employees understand and implement the change. Successful management communication can make a massive difference in realizing change, and requires that managers, as leaders, reflect on how they communicate with others and how they frame change to others to gain their support. A first attribute of successful management or leadership communication involves authenticity or a truthful and passionate commitment to a clear, inspiring change idea. Given the personal nature of leadership communication, it is important that communicating leaders are themselves committed to what they are saying. They know their commitments and convictions beyond the change idea, stay true to them in their advocacy and can communicate consistently in line with those commitments in order to drum up support. Authenticity gives a level of consistency and personal touch that is more likely to garner success. It also brings a personal passion that is more like to win people over. A good example of authenticity in leadership communication involves Al

Gore before and after the 2000 US presidential elections. In the televised presidential debates, Gore mentioned a number of government initiatives, but neither he nor his advisors had thought about a clear positioning of Gore as a candidate and person. In the end, he set out to project a persona of a competent statesman who would sustain the economy and bring about a more social democracy. But his delivery lacked something, as it was largely focused on the manufacture of an image, rather than being driven from within his own person. Yet in 2006, Gore toured the world and was able to sell out whole stadiums and movie theatres with people wanting to hear his message about climate change. This time, as shown in his movie *An Inconvenient Truth*, he conveyed a real and personal passion for a subject he cares deeply about. He does not speak any more in terms of political abstractions or technical language, but speaks from his own experiences and delivers the message with his own style and convictions.

Such authenticity assumes that managers or leaders are sufficiently reflective on their own commitments and of the ways in which they communicate. It also means that, as a leader, you have to learn to speak with passion and from experience, talk to your values and take a particular perspective or standpoint that is congruent with those values. This level of authenticity is often key in employees being able to trust a leader and believe that he or she has integrity. An additional strength of using values as a basis for leadership communication is that they may motivate and inspire employees. Whereas financial numbers and specific goals may be important to communicate, values and higher-level ambition may be what actually drives and motivates employees.

Besides speaking from the heart, passion is also conveyed through facial expressions and the use of gestures (natural movements of the arms and hands) by leaders. Gestures in particular are subtle, but important, means of communication and persuasion that are first and foremost seen to reflect a leader's emotions, or passion, about a subject. But gestures also do more – they have been proven to increase the attention to, and comprehension of, a message and they have been linked to persuasion. Skilfully using gestures to mark or convey a point in a speech or presentation leads to leaders being seen as persuasive and as far more persuasive than leaders who do not move their bodies or hands at all as they speak.[17]

Successful leadership communication also involves, as already mentioned, stories and frames to articulate a change initiative and motivate the workforce, as well as continuous conversations with employees.[18] In the context of change, stories can be useful to present in a single frame the rationale for the change, the steps needed to realize it and the overall beneficial outcomes that are likely to result. Crudely speaking, stories present a sequence of actions and events leading to a particular outcome (as the plot). The outcome in turn rationalizes any conscious actions taken by individuals to get there. Given that changes are uncertain and always about a future state, such stories provide a coherent structure and understanding of what the change may ultimately lead to. Skilful leaders are mindful of the words that they use, the narrative patterns or stories they form, and of how they use such stories in their communication with others around them. Sir Nicholas Young of the Red Cross, for example, uses aspirational stories within his organization to move people into taking the initiative and making a change:

Inside the Red Cross, stories are incredibly powerful change catalysts. People love to hear about the really heroic things that we do and those stories are very necessary and we tell them a lot, but the stories that work hardest are the ones that demonstrate what we still have to do, how much better we need to be. When I come back from a trip like Haiti, I can probably get more out of the organization by inspiring people with stories that illustrate what we still need to do than by telling them about things we have already done.[19]

Besides using stories that frame and rationalize a change, leaders also need conversational skills to tap into ongoing conversations about the change across the organization. If leaders are to succeed in inspiring enduring enthusiasm for change, they need to set aside any idea of imposing their will or moving their listeners to a predetermined position. The aim is rather one of mobilizing conversation at the interpersonal level to enable others in the organization to see possibilities that they may hitherto have missed. It means relating to the language of others in conversational settings so that they, for themselves, can view the organization and their relations with others in a new light. The very concept of conversation implies a dialogue in which two parties can relate to and elaborate on each other's points, rather than it being a straight monologue or a negotiation. Successful leaders are able to have open conversations. They are willing to say where they stand and what they think, at least provisionally, whilst showing themselves as being open to entertaining alternative viewpoints. They listen carefully to what others say, trying to make sense of their points and explore the implications. These conversations in turn may also trigger a reformulation in the definition or implementation of a change. Barge and Oliver comment on the importance of these conversations as follows:

Historically, managerial communication skills have been associated with encoding and decoding skills – a model of communication that is based on an approach to language in which it is assumed that meaning is fixed and that the point of communication is to clearly convey one's point to another ... viewing conversation as sites where various discourses intersect and meaning is continually unfolding requires managers to develop the ability to pick up the flow of conversation and to develop a sensibility for when and where to shape the conversation in new directions.[20]

The importance of conversations and conversational skills also emphasizes that a straightforward leadership presentation about change that is broadcast across the organization may not be sufficient. At most, it is simply a beginning. In order to continue and accelerate the enthusiasm for, and implementation of, a change, it requires that managers or leaders have regular, ongoing conversations with the people they are leading, about the things going on in their context and about how they can address any emerging issues. It is these detailed conversations that often matter the most and may be the deciding factor as to whether individuals in organizations are supportive of or resistant to a particular change. A good example of these principles of leadership communication is presented in the case study of British Airways (12.1).

CASE STUDY 12.1

BRITISH AIRWAYS: CHANGE AND LEADERSHIP COMMUNICATION AT 'THE WORLD'S FAVOURITE AIRLINE'

In a fiercely competitive industry, British Airways has, over the years, been forced to save costs and make, on occasion, large numbers of staff redundant. In 1999, for example, BA suffered as a result of the economic crisis in Asia and reported significant losses. The company then initiated cost reduction and efficiency pro- grammes in turn, which had an impact on staff morale. An internal survey at the time showed that many employees were unsure of management's ability to man- age costs effectively without sacrificing quality, their desire to communicate openly and honestly, and the extent to which they cared about employees. Informed by the survey findings, BA initiated a motivational programme for staff entitled *Putting People First* which was meant to train staff in customer service and to increase a sense of belonging.

In 2000, Rod Eddington took over as the CEO of BA and faced the challenge of further cutting costs by downsizing whilst sustaining an acceptable level of employee morale. When he took over, Eddington said:

> It is my job to empower the organization to be able to do that [compete]. People are the lifeblood of any airline and it is the people of British Airways, both as individuals and as a team, who will deliver its future success. I look forward to meeting as many as possible over the coming weeks and months and listening to what they have to tell me about how we can further improve our products and services.

In 2001, BA laid off 5,200 employees and saved £37 million. In 2002, BA launched its *Future Size and Shape* programme, which was designed to save costs by £650 million per annum. As part of the programme, 5,800 job cuts were announced at the head office. A year later, the airline introduced an electronic swiping card system in order to monitor employee absenteeism. BA wanted to reduce absenteeism from an average of 17 days per employee to 10 days within a year and save £30 million as a result. Because of these cost-cutting exercises and the ongoing pressures on staff to become more efficient in their work practices, BA recognized that it needed to look after employee morale. In late 2003, the company started the Industrial Relations Change programme, a joint initiative with the trade unions which was designed to develop better working relationships between BA and the unions. BA also announced an Employee Reward Plan, which provides employees with rewards when profit mar- gins of the airline move towards 10 per cent.

Cutting costs and leadership communication

Rod Eddington stepped down as CEO in September 2005 and was succeeded by Willie Walsh. Walsh had attracted the nickname of 'slasher' at his previous employer

(Continued)

(Continued)

Aer Lingus, where he was responsible for cutting a third of the workforce. In December 2005, as a result of high fuel costs and lower ticket prices, Walsh announced plans to cut a further 600 management jobs at BA but he insisted that the airline had long-term scope to grow. The job cuts involved a 50 per cent reduction in senior managers, from 414 jobs to 207, and a 30 per cent reduction in middle managers, from 1,301 jobs to 911. Walsh rationalized the job cuts as follows: 'We are restructuring the airline to remove duplication, simplify our core business and provide clearer account-ability. Managers will have greater accountability for making decisions, delivering results and leading the business.' On top of the cuts in management jobs, Walsh warned staff in March 2006 of further job cuts ahead. 'We're going to target every single aspect of the cost base', Walsh explained. 'Employee costs are an element of that but they're not the only part. We will continue to introduce new work practices and efficiencies, which will allow us to run the business with fewer people.' BA's cost-cutting target in 2006 was for £225m of savings and the same in 2007. The airline has put a squeeze on suppliers and has told every internal department to produce monthly reports on progress towards cuts.

In recent years, Walsh has faced further turmoil in an attempt to modernize the airline's labour agreements. In 2010, relations with trade unions culminated in pro-posed plans for a strike in March of that year. A strike by BA cabin crew looked certain to go ahead after Walsh refused to guarantee that he would not sack union officials of BASSA, the Unite trade union cabin crew branch at the heart of the indus-trial action. BA had also started disciplinary proceedings against 38 members of the trade union. Walsh appeared to harden his stance in subsequent communications with the union, a move that was criticized by employment analysts and academics as a blatant attempt to break the union's influence over cabin crew, and effectively over the company. As part of its communications offensive to explain its stance, BA launched a social media campaign, with a video of Willie Walsh talking of his disappointment at the forthcoming strike action and the negative consequences for customers. In the video, Walsh talks about how he is staking his own personal repu-tation on ensuring that the company does everything it can to limit the inconvenience to customers. Philip Allport from the BA corporate communications team explained the use of the video: 'This is the first time we've used YouTube to support our crisis communications', he said. 'We recognise how important social media is as a way to communicate directly to our customers.' The release of the video coincided with the start of industrial strike action and with a number of news stories backing British Airways in its actions.

Whilst BA announced a jump in profits in 2016, partly because of the low price of oil, Walsh made it clear that in the coming years more job cuts could be expected. Speaking to delegates at a conference for the airline industry, he referred to his short haircut and said 'Hence the reason for my haircut – that's the theme for 2016, it's all going to be about cutting costs'. No doubt this possibility of further job cuts, and the uncertainty that it creates for staff at BA, will put additional pressure on employee morale at the airline. On the other hand, industry insiders feel that Walsh has done a remarkable job at BA in making the company profitable again. A large part of his suc-cess, they feel, comes from his clear, consistent and no-nonsense leadership style, consistently encouraging a focus on financial results by telling staff to 'show me the money'. Walsh can be charming and diplomatic, but is, for the most part, transactional in his approach to dealing with staff, asking them to deliver on the basis of incentives and rewards. As one of his advisors says, 'He tends to eschew the pomp and ceremony of leadership and instead wears his no-nonsense approach to business with pride. He has zero time for titles'. Whilst this transactional style may come natural to Willie Walsh, and may also reflect the company's ongoing struggle to remain profitable, at the same time it may also make staff more transactional in their approach in return – that is, only be committed to the company for the short term, strictly work for pay and not going the extra mile in terms of customer service or any other behaviour supportive of the organization. In other words, a transactional leadership style may have predictable consequences; repeatedly asking staff to be incentivized by pay and financial rewards, they in fact will do just that and may in turn no longer identify with the broader organization or commit themselves to BA for the long term.

Questions for reflection

1 Reflect on leadership communication within BA from the perspective of employees. What in general can you say about the approach to communication with staff?
2 Is the leadership style of Willie Walsh the right one for this company? Would a more transformational style be possible in this scenario? What can Walsh do in terms of his communication to try and sustain morale whilst cutting jobs?
3 Identify the change communication strategy that BA used to communicate the cost reductions and job cuts. Was this the right strategy for the company or should another strategy have been used?

Source: This case study is based on newspaper articles drawn from *The Guardian* and Reuters.

12.5 CHAPTER SUMMARY

The chapter started by defining the importance of leadership and leadership communication in the context of organizational change. One important message in the chapter has been the importance of managers *as leaders* communicating with employees in such a way that they feel valued, listened to and involved in organizational change. This requires that managers are not only aware of and constantly reflect on their communication style but also use a range of tried and tested interactive strategies to inspire employees to commit to the change and to make the change happen.

 —————— DISCUSSION QUESTIONS ————————————

1. What defines successful communication around an organizational change? Use examples from cases that you know or from your own experience to motivate your answer.

2. Think about a manager or leader of an organization that you are familiar with or have worked for in the past. How successful was this manager or leader as a communicator? What in your view determined their degree (or lack) of success?

KEY TERMS

Need-to-know strategy	Organizational change
Conversation	Additive change
Substitutive change	Equal dissemination strategy
Quid pro quo strategy	Equal participation strategy
Tell and sell strategy	Identify and reply strategy
Underscore and explore strategy	Leadership communication
Withhold and uphold strategy	Leadership
Storytelling	Authenticity
Transformational leadership	Transactional leadership

 FURTHER READING

Fairhurst, Gail (2010) *The Power of Framing: Creating the Language of Leadership*. San Francisco: Jossey-Bass.

Lancaster, Simon (2015) *Winning Minds: Secrets from the Language of Leadership*. London: Palgrave.

Murray, Kevin (2012) *The Language of Leaders: How Top CEOs Communicate to Inspire, Influence and Achieve Results*. London: Kogan Page.

Want to know more about this chapter? Visit the companion website at: https://study.sagepub.com/cornelissen5e to access videos, web links, a glossary and selected journal articles to further enhance your study.

NOTES

1. Rousseau, D.M. (1998) 'Why workers still identify with organizations', *Journal of Organizational Behavior*, 19: 217–33.
2. Burns, James M. (1978/2010) *Leadership*. New York: HarperCollins.
3. See, for example, Corley, K.G. and Gioia, D.A. (2004) 'Identity ambiguity and change in the wake of a corporate spin-off', *Administrative Science Quarterly*, 49 (2): 173–208.
4. These quotes are taken from Lassere, P. (2004) 'Bank Mandiri: A case in strategic transformation', INSEAD case study.
5. Lewin, K. (1947) 'Frontiers in group dynamics 1', *Human Relations*, 1: 5–41.
6. Kotter, J. (2012) *Leading Change*. Boston, MA: HBS Press, first published in 1996.
7. Garvin, D.A., and Roberto, M.A. (2005) 'Change through persuasion', *Harvard Business Review*, February: 104–12.
8. Garvin and Roberto (2005), quote on p. 111.
9. Clampitt, P., DeKoch, R. and Cashman, T. (2000) 'A strategy for communicating about uncertainty', *Academy of Management Executive*, 14: 41–57.
10. Timmerman, C.E. (2003) 'Media selection during the implementation of planned organizational change', *Management Communication Quarterly*, 16: 301–40.
11. Larkin, T.J. and Larkin, S. (1994) *Communicating Change: Winning Employee Support for New Business Goals*. New York: McGraw-Hill.

12. See, for example, Llewellyn, N. and Harrison, A. (2006) 'Resisting corporate communications: Insights into folk linguistics', *Human Relations*, 59: 567–96.

13. See, for example, Poole, M.S. and McPhee, R.D. (1983) 'A structurational analysis of organizational climate', in Putnam, L.L. and Pacanowsky, M.E. (eds), *Communication and Organization: An Interpretive Approach*. Beverly Hills, CA: Sage; Smidts, A., Pruyn, A. Th. and Van Riel, C.B.M. (2001) 'The impact of employee communication and perceived external prestige on organizational identification', *Academy of Management Journal*, 44 (5): 1051–62.

14. Lewis, L.K., Hamel, S.A. and Richardson, B.K. (2001) 'Communicating change to nonprofit stakeholders', *Management Communication Quarterly*, 15: 5–41.

15. Dent, E.B. and Goldberg, S.G. (1999) 'Challenging a "resistance to change"', *Journal of Applied Behavioral Science*, 35: 25–41.

16. Schweiger, D. and Denisi, A. (1991) 'Communication with employees following a merger: A longitudinal experiment', *Academy of Management Journal*, 34: 110–35.

17. See, for example, Chen, X.P., Yao, X. and Kotha, S. (2009) 'Entrepreneur passion and preparedness in business plan presentations: A persuasion analysis of venture capitalists' funding decisions', *Academy of Management Journal*, 52 (1), 199–214; Antonakis, J., Fenley, M. and Liechti, S. (2011) 'Can charisma be taught? Tests of two interventions', *Academy of Management Learning and Education* 10, 374–96; Antonakis, J., Fenley, M. and Liechti, S. (2012) 'Learning charisma', *Harvard Business Review*, June, 127–30.

18. See, for example, Fairhurst, G. (2010) *The Power of Framing: Creating the Language of Leadership*. San Francisco: Jossey-Bass; Murray, K. (2012) *The Language of Leaders: How Top CEOs Communicate to Inspire, Influence and Achieve Results*. London: Kogan Page; and Lancaster, Simon (2015) *Winning Minds: Secrets from the Language of Leadership*. London: Palgrave.

19. Murray, K. (2012), quote on p. 141.

20. Barge, J.K. and Oliver, C. (2003) 'Working with appreciation in managerial practice', *Academy of Management Review*, 28 (1): 124–42, quote on p. 138.

Corporate Social Responsibility (CSR) and Community Relations

13

| CHAPTER OVERVIEW |

CSR and community relations has emerged as a specialized area of activity that involves CSR communication and integrated reporting as well as community engagement. The overall aim of these activities for an organization is to demonstrate its commitment to social and environmental issues and to build strong and lasting relationships with the local and global communities in which it resides and operates. The chapter discusses the concepts of corporate citizenship, CSR and community relations, and details various communication strategies and tactics, ranging from integrated CSR reports and charitable donations to partnerships that address pressing community issues.

13.1 INTRODUCTION

In other chapters of the book, we have discussed how stakeholder expectations of corporate and public organizations have changed, and how this affects how organizations operate. Traditionally, organizations were expected to behave as economic entities that are destined to make profits in their accountability to themselves and shareholders. The shift to issues of corporate social responsibility and corporate citizenship recasts traditional thinking and suggests instead that organizations are expected to demonstrate a level of accountability to the whole of society. Their licence to operate is not based on profit or dividends alone but on institutional legitimacy granted by each of the stakeholders with which they interact. British Petroleum (BP) is a good example of this principle. The corporation has for years been one of the most profitable in the world and admired for its bold attempts to combine an environmental agenda with its commercial operations. However, its social legitimacy has increasingly been questioned given BP's retreat from investments in alternative energies and the massive oil spill in the Gulf of Mexico in 2010, which has done excessive damage to the environment and affected local communities in the Gulf region. The company initially played down the size of the spill and its own role in the initial explosion that caused it, but because of the intervention of the US administration BP was forced to set up a fund of $20 billion to help compensate those living in the region whose livelihoods were directly affected by the spill.

Organizations like BP who do not align community relations – as an area of corporate communication – with their business operations, are likely to find their licence to operate questioned and possibly challenged by stakeholders, including local and national government officials. At the same time, of course, these changed expectations also present significant opportunities for organizations. Those organizations that enjoy positive relationships with the communities in which they operate are treated differently and respectfully. This leads to general goodwill and local support from the community and from local and national governments. A successful organization, in other words, is often one which has figured out the best ways of developing and nurturing community relations, of responding to community expectations and of taking advantage of such expectations in community involvement programmes that mutually support the community and the organization's business goals. In this chapter, we discuss the wider social remit of organizations – their corporate social responsibility (CSR) to stakeholders, including the communities in which they operate. We outline various ways in which that social responsibility can be realized in stakeholder engagement programmes and how organizations can best communicate about their CSR programmes. The chapter concludes with a closer look at community relations, an area of corporate communication that is closely aligned with the organization's CSR objectives and programmes. Good community relations can improve the community but can also directly add to a company's goals and reputation.

13.2 DEFINING CORPORATE SOCIAL RESPONSIBILITY

In previous chapters, we have described how an organization is increasingly seen as part of a larger social system that includes commercial parties as well as, for example, communities, NGOs and government agencies in society, and as dependent on that system's support for its continued existence. In this sense, organizational goals and activities must be found legitimate and valued by a range of stakeholder groups in the larger social system of society. This stakeholder-based model has significant implications for organizations, both public and private. Even private organizations that do not necessarily protect a public good in society have realized that they need to listen to and communicate with a whole range of stakeholder groups for their own as well as for society's sake, and in order to avoid certain stakeholder groups raising issues that are potentially damaging to their reputations.

In a fully developed stakeholder model, a manager's key objective is basically to coordinate the conflicting interests and values of stakeholders rather than controlling them. The logic would not be one of containing stakeholder interests, but the aim would be to try and accomplish them through corporate activity. Management would work across all stakeholders, thus seeking the most creative co-determination for the benefit of all stakeholders. Thus far, versions of such a model have been developed in quasi-public enterprises and in a few countries. In Germany, for example, trade union involvement at the level of corporate boards (the famous practice of *Mitbestimmung* or 'co-determination') is seen by many Germans, including Angela Merkel, the country's Chancellor, as 'an essential part of Germany's economy'. In such a strong model, stakeholder participation and inclusion are not meant to balance or trade off social and economic interests, but are essential for the process of creative decision-making that can advance both. As we know from collaborative decision-making contexts, creativity and mutual satisfaction are based on a commitment to a co-determinative or democratic process rather than just arguing out self-interests.[1]

These democratic models of representation and participation in society also form the foundation for recent ideas on 'corporate citizenship'. Organizations are 'legal entities with rights and duties, in effect, "citizens" of states within which they operate'.[2] 'Corporate citizenship' refers to the portfolio of activities that organizations undertake to fulfil their perceived duties as members of society. The underlying idea is that individual citizens have certain rights and responsibilities in society. Equally, when organizations are granted the legal and political rights of individual citizens through incorporation, they are also ascribed, explicitly and implicitly, a set of rights and responsibilities. Examples of corporate citizenship include pro bono activities, corporate volunteerism, charitable contributions, support for community education and healthcare initiatives, and environmental programmes – few of which are legally mandated, but many of which have come to be expected as corporate citizen responsibilities. The World Economic Forum defines corporate citizenship as:

> the contribution a company makes to society through its core business activities, its social investment and philanthropy programmes, and its engagement in public policy. The manner in which a company manages its economic, social and environmental relationships, as well as those with different stakeholders, in particular shareholders, employees, customers, business partners, governments and communities determines its impact.[3]

The idea of corporate citizenship rests on a long and respected tradition of thinking on citizenship in political theory. Corporate citizenship, however, differs in one crucial respect from individual citizenship in society. State-based citizenship is typically conceived of as being, more or less, symmetrical. There is a symmetry or balance in the exchange between a government that grants and administers certain fundamental rights, on the one hand, and the citizens who enjoy them, on the other, with taxes and political responsibilities (e.g. voting in elections) serving as the currency of the exchange. This symmetry between rights and obligations in the exchange between governments and citizens is central to citizenship; the advantages that an individual derives from citizenship are mirrored by at least an obligation to contribute whatever is necessary to realize the same for others in the cooperative venture of the state. The citizenship of organizations often seems less symmetrical in this sense. Organizations tend to focus on making positive contributions to their stakeholders as opposed to, as 'citizens', being locked into a mutually beneficial exchange that protects fundamental human rights and responsibilities. The asymmetry is clear in the numerous instances where big corporations, besides their charitable donations and community initiatives, still negatively affect the health and wellbeing of certain communities by paying below 'living' wages or through environmentally damaging production or supply chain practices.[4]

Some academics and industry analysts have therefore argued that corporate citizenship may not have much currency as a concept given the business reality on the ground.[5] Instead, they favour the more specific and descriptive concept of corporate social responsibility (CSR). In a general sense, the drive for CSR came with the appeal to business organizations to deliver wider societal value beyond shareholder and market value alone. According to the World Business Council for Sustainable Development, in its 2002 publication *Making Good Business Sense* by Lord Holme and Richard Watts, the term CSR can be broadly defined as 'the continuing commitment by business to contribute to economic development while improving the quality of life of the workforce and their families as well as of the community and society at large'. Strictly speaking, it implies the adoption by an organization of 'the responsibilities for actions which do not have purely financial implications and which are demanded of an organization under some (implicit or explicit) identifiable contract'[6] with stakeholders in society. This contract is largely a moral 'contract' in the sense that organizations are expected to meet the social and environmental expectations of stakeholders, as a good corporate citizen, which not only creates goodwill but also provides a licence to operate. In addition, organizations often also consider CSR in an effort to boost their reputations. With the media constantly reporting on their affairs, and because of greater product homogeneity and competition in many markets, many organizations realize that doing business in a responsible and just manner offers strategic and reputational advantages. As with stakeholder management, CSR initiatives may, in the first instance, be started for either moral or instrumental reputational reasons. However, the actual reasons for CSR are often difficult to separate given the 'significant difficulties in distinguishing whether business behaviour is truly moral conduct or instrumental adoption of an appearance of moral conduct as reputational strategy'.[7] However, regardless of the underlying motives, CSR initiatives, including community outreach and charitable donations, often appear to be of direct instrumental value to an organization. Research has found that these initiatives are related to reputational returns and an overall better financial performance.[8]

CSR is often defined in terms of the notion of a 'triple bottom line' that includes people, planet and profits.[9] John Elkington introduced the term and suggested that CSR can be broken down into activities that include social ('people') and ecological ('planet') initiatives alongside the generation of profits and healthy financial accounts ('profit'). 'People' stands for all social and labour issues both inside and outside the organization, including employee support and compensation, gender and ethnic diversity of the workforce, the reduction of corruption and fraud in business transactions and health and safety codes. 'Planet' refers to the responsibility of organizations to integrate environmental care into its business operations, such as the reduction of harmful waste and residues and the development of environmentally friendly production processes. 'Profit' involves the conventional bottom-line of manufacturing and selling products so as to generate financial returns for the organization and its shareholders. This latter category of responsibilities ('profit') is often considered as a baseline or requisite before an organization can even start considering meeting its social ('people') and ecological ('planet') responsibilities. That is, these other responsibilities cannot be achieved in the absence of economic performance (i.e. goods and services, jobs, profitability) – namely, a bankrupt organization will cease to operate.[10]

Over the years, the general approach of organizations to CSR has changed (see Table 13.1). Stakeholder expectations regarding CSR have changed as well. These changes can be captured by classifying the various approaches to CSR as 'defensive', 'charitable', 'promotional' and 'strategic' CSR and by a final 'transformative' stage in which CSR becomes integral to the organization.[11] The latter, transformative approach, is considered the ideal for our current day and age. This approach is sometimes labelled as CSR 2.0 to distinguish it from the more narrow tactical and promotional versions of CSR (CSR 1.0) that went before.

Defensive CSR involves ad hoc investments in social and environmental practices when they pay off for the bottom line and for the organization's primary shareholders. For example, an organization may try to reduce its waste as a way of fending off regulation or to avoid paying a fine. Charitable CSR, in turn, involves an organization supporting various social and environmental causes through donations and sponsorships, aimed at empowering community groups or civil sector organizations. Whilst beneficial to the community (see section 13.4), CSR is limited in this approach

TABLE 13.1 Approaches to corporate social responsibility (CSR)

Approach to CSR	Main vehicle	Managerial responsibility	Primary stakeholder audience
Defensive	Ad hoc interventions	Public affairs team (as part of corporate communication)	Primary stakeholders: shareholders and governments
Charitable	Charitable donations	Community relations officer/ team (as part of corporate communication)	Secondary stakeholders: communities
Promotional	Public relations campaigns and events	PR and events managers (as part of corporate communication)	Primary stakeholders (including customers) and the general public
Strategic	Management systems	Spread across the organization (including involvement from corporate communication)	Primary stakeholders (including customers) and the general public
Transformational	Business models	Spread across the organization (including involvement from corporate communication)	Primary stakeholders, including current and future generations

to local, charitable investments. Promotional CSR involves a largely rhetorical or symbolic use of CSR through public relations programmes and campaigns to bolster the organization's brand or reputation. This approach may, when it is not adequately matched with substantial change, be seen as 'PR spin' and 'greenwashing'. Strategic CSR breaks with more tactical and local approaches to CSR and involves the organization identifying the social and environmental issues that connect to its strategy and core business operations. With this approach, an organization actively identifies issues that matter to its business and to its long-term performance, implements CSR codes and social and environmental management systems and routinely reports on its progress to stakeholders.

The approach of transformative CSR goes even one step further in that it involves organizations focusing their activities on the root causes of environmental sustainability and social responsibility, and trying to invent business models and revolutionary products and services that allow them to address these foundations in society. Unilever (Case Example 5.1) is an example of an organization that has put CSR at the centre of its operation, changing its business model and transforming its strategy. Its Sustainable Living plan sets the company on an ambitious course of transformational change through which it aims to change the world, in environmental and social terms, for the better. The key difference is that where strategic CSR is still focused on the micro-level – supporting social or environmental issues that align with a given strategy – transformative CSR is broader in scope. It involves managers focusing on the foundations of our macro-level society and on the ecosystem of our planet in the first place and then reasoning backwards to their organizations to identify how knowledge about society or the environment may transform their business strategies in radical ways. The underlying intent of doing so is to find ways in which business operations can fundamentally improve our society and the planet for the better. This transformative CSR approach is closely allied with notions such as corporate sustainability and sustainable development goals in business. Sustainability stresses the importance of organizations adopting a global and 'outside-in' view of CSR, as opposed to a local, firm-centric ('inside-out') perspective on their environmental and social responsibilities. The idea is that when organizations adopt such a global view, they are more likely to realize, and potentially own up to, the fundamental responsibility that they have to current and future generations in terms of adopting socially responsible and environmentally sustainable practices. In line with increasingly strategic and, in some cases, transformative approaches to CSR, there has, in recent years, been an explosion of codes of conduct, principles and standards related to CSR.[12] Broader in scope than earlier codes of conduct that tended to focus on specific issues such as bribery or corruption, today's CSR codes tend to have a much broader remit to multiple stakeholders and include both social and environmental performance. Many of these codes were developed by business associations, industry groups or multi-stakeholder coalitions involving public and governmental institutions. Well-known codes include the OECD guidelines for multinational enterprises, which include recommendations for voluntary principles and standards of ethical business conduct for companies operating across the globe; and the UN Global Compact principles, which involve ten principles that focus on human rights, working conditions, the environment and anti-corruption. The adoption of these and other kinds of codes by organizations has in turn led to an assurance and reporting industry, which supports and consults organizations on the way in which they report their CSR and assures stakeholders of true progress in their social and environmental performance. One of the most well-known frameworks for such reporting is the Global Reporting Initiative, which is a corporate reporting framework that is tuned to the specifics of each industry and is internationally seen as one of the standards for integrated reporting on environmental, social and economic performance.

13.3 COMMUNICATING ABOUT CORPORATE SOCIAL RESPONSIBILITY

Generally speaking, most approaches to communicating with stakeholders about CSR traditionally tended to be those based on a model of strategic persuasion rather than 'democratic' communication or 'dialogue' (see Figure 4.6). Managers are often hesitant to include stakeholders in crucial CSR decisions by disclosing information, sharing power or granting autonomy. They often also lack the right model and skills of democratic communication necessary for coordinating the divergent interests of their stakeholders. Stanley Deetz, a communication scholar, has argued that most models of stakeholder communication and 'dialogue' are borrowed from liberal democratic communication models used in state processes of governance.[13] These models stress commitment to representation and consensus, which contrasts with participatory models committed to diversity, conflict and creativity. Deetz also argues that the widespread use of these models in corporate organizations may partly account for the poor regard people have for processes of corporate decision-making and the cynicism of the use of terms such as 'stakeholder dialogue' and stakeholder 'participation' in areas such as CSR. Instead, other models of communication, drawn from models of participatory democracy, may better meet the challenge of a 'democratic' and actual stakeholder dialogue about CSR. These models specify the conditions for stakeholder involvement in corporate decision-making discussions. The conditions include, for example, a reciprocity of opportunity for expression; an equality in skills for expression; the setting aside of authority relations, organizational positions and other external sources of power; the open investigation of stakeholders' positions to more freely ascertain their interests; an open sharing of information and transparency of decision processes; and the testing of alternative claims in the discussion. Many of these conditions are directly applicable to corporate organizations. However, it is often difficult for managers (as it is for politicians) to meet these conditions, giving up some of their own power and influence in the process.

These difficulties are reflected in how most organizations traditionally communicated about CSR to their stakeholders. Many organizations, for example, put out glossy social and environmental reports that are often more about style than substance, according to Sustainability, a consultancy that evaluates the CSR reporting of organizations worldwide. Organizations may also view social responsibility as a PR exercise instead of as a refocusing and reshuffling of their business operations. Studies that scrutinize the integration of CSR into business practices show that whilst many large organizations communicate quite extensively about their CSR, the actual implementation of CSR in their organizations often lags behind.[14] Surveys by the consultancy firm McKinsey also report that organizations often simply focus on the media and on public relations tactics to manage their CSR initiatives without considering other ways to embed CSR within their organizations. What these examples indicate is that organizations often struggle to engage in a real dialogue about CSR with stakeholders, which would require that they fully and openly respond to stakeholder expectations and fully embed CSR in their business practices. Instead, many organizations may still approach the subject from a more limited symbolic or rhetorical perspective where they communicate about CSR for image- and reputation-building purposes only. The gap between the rhetoric and the implementation of CSR has, at times, been described as 'greenwashing', which involves companies declaring and framing themselves as promoting environmentally friendly policies whereas, in reality, the actual implementation is out of step with the rhetoric. The term may be somewhat misleading, as the problem does not only relate to environmental aspects of CSR but also to social responsibilities. However, the general point is clear: if companies put too much spin on their CSR or communicate aggressively or excessively about their CSR, they may achieve the opposite of what they intended and be negatively perceived and evaluated by stakeholders.[15]

To put this in perspective, it is useful to think of three basic communication strategies for CSR (see Figure 4.6).[16] The first strategy, which is an informational strategy, is one where there is not necessarily a persuasive intent, but companies instead aim to inform the public as objectively as possible about their CSR activities. Companies produce information and news for the media, as well as a variety of brochures, societal reports, pamphlets, magazines, facts and figures to inform the general public. The second strategy is a stakeholder response strategy where stakeholders are asked for feedback on CSR activities, or more generally in response to organizational decisions and actions. The communication model with this strategy is 'two-way' in that stakeholders are asked about their opinions and expectations, but it is ultimately the company that decides what the focus of CSR activities should be, and then engages with stakeholders to promote these activities. As such, the stakeholder response strategy may turn out to be pretty one-sided, with companies putting out glossy society reports or running campaigns that are intended to convince stakeholders of their CSR credentials. The risk here is that CSR is perceived as largely a marketing or PR ploy, rather than as a steadfast commitment to stakeholders and society. The third and, in some senses, preferred strategy is the stakeholder involvement strategy where there is a real mutual dialogue between a company and its stakeholders. Stakeholders have a genuine say in the CSR commitments of a company, with the company trying to meet, if not exceed, the expectations of various stakeholder groups on social and environmental issues. With this strategy, companies would not only influence but also seek to be influenced by stakeholders, and therefore change and evolve in their CSR commitments when necessary. The advantage is that by engaging in a dialogue, a company ensures that it keeps abreast not only of its stakeholders' expectations, and any shifts in expectations, but also of its potential influence on those expectations, as well as letting those expectations influence and change the company itself.

This strategy assumes that companies not only publish reports or launch CSR campaigns but set up public consultation forums with their stakeholders and conduct ongoing surveys on stakeholder opinions to inform their CSR objectives. On balance, companies may be better off involving stakeholders in their CSR versus largely setting their own targets and then trying to convince stakeholders of their efforts.

Besides processes of stakeholder communication around CSR, many of the largest and most visible corporations also routinely publish CSR reports. For example, more than 90 per cent of the FTSE 100 largest listed corporations in the UK issue such reports. In recent years, the quality of such reports has also steadily increased, with CSR information being more transparently and objectively documented by organizations. Yet, as reporting is done by individual organizations themselves, this often makes comparison across organizations difficult. For example, although almost all of the largest 250 companies worldwide disclose a code of governance or ethics, typically only half of them report on incidents of compliance with the code. Similarly, nearly all large corporations have a supply chain code of conduct, but only half disclose the details of how it is implemented and monitored. Approximately half of the largest corporations worldwide disclose some level of information about climate risks, but roughly the same number report very little, if anything.[17]

However, in recent years standards and frameworks for 'integrated' social and environmental reporting have become more commonplace, such as the Global Reporting Initiative and the more recent Integrated Reporting Framework supported by the UN Global Compact. Both prescribe clear standards in specific areas such as working conditions, environmental performance and the promotion of human rights, which are assessed by a professional corps of social auditors (independent of corporate control and accountable to the public) and include safe harbours that limit legal liability (so as to encourage companies to open their businesses to social audits). Increasingly, these reporting frameworks are used on a worldwide scale, giving greater levels of transparency and comparability between companies. Formal third-party assurance of CSR reports has also jumped in recent years with greater use being made of major accountancy firms, as auditors, and third-party stakeholder voices and expert statements. In both reporting frameworks, corporate communicators play an important role in involving stakeholders, in gathering information across the organization and in disclosing and reporting this information in an integrated manner. Increasingly, companies are also opting, for various reasons, to publish a single 'integrated' report that includes their CSR alongside their financial performance over the year. The reasons for this are that it makes more sense to present financial, social and environmental information together, including their possible interconnections as part of the company's strategy or business model, and the company's ability to sustain value in the long term. Many companies also feel that publishing a separate CSR report makes it somewhat of a stand-alone exercise. A lot of these 'integrated' reports are also increasingly written from the perspective of multiple stakeholders, rather than shareholders or investors alone.

Over the years, it has also become clear that those companies that are rated highly by their stakeholders for their CSR reporting generally appear to adhere to the following guidelines:

Set clear objectives: the company shows that it is serious about CSR by setting clear objectives for social and environmental performance annually, and by systematically reporting on the results achieved afterwards.

Set progressive objectives: objectives are progressive in bringing new aspirations and standards to bear upon business operations instead of a regurgitating of existing practices that may be seen as socially and environmentally viable.

Involve stakeholders: objectives and targets include issues that are relevant to stakeholders (or 'material' in integrated reporting terms) and are linked to clear benchmarks and standards (at the industry and policy levels).

Report transparently: reporting is an honest, transparent and full-scale self-assessment instead of a polishing of performance data.

Be accountable: performance data are rigorously assessed and verified by credible auditors (accountants or consultants).

13.4 COMMUNITY RELATIONS

Corporate citizenship and CSR have, in principle, quite a broad scope in that these activities involve multiple stakeholders and both social and environmental responsibilities. Community relations form a specific part of a company's CSR and relate primarily to communications and engagement with residents of the local communities in which the company resides with its facilities. Whilst it is a rather specialized area of activity within corporate communication, it can, if badly managed, have significant consequences for the reputation of an organization. Consider, for example, Wal-Mart, which is a retail corporation that has excelled in a very effective market expansion and low-cost growth strategy. However, the company recently has received much more criticism than before for its strategy and for the way in which it engages with, and cares for, important stakeholder groups such as employees and members of the local communities in which the company operates. Its recent store openings have attracted organized opposition from a broad coalition of labour, small business, local government and community groups. Wal-Mart is not the only target of such opposition; large corporations such as Disney, Shell, BP and Monsanto have been similarly affected. Why has this been the case? One reason, as social movement scholars have argued, is that anti-corporate community activism has increased in scope and frequency because of the fact that corporations themselves have become larger and more powerful and have increased their hold over individuals.[18] Through mergers and acquisitions, corporations have grown in size and now control a bigger share of the overall assets in an economy than they used to do. This concentration of assets means that relatively few large corporations control many aspects of our individual lives. This control ranges from economic power in influencing what products are available to political power in lobbying governments and shaping legislation. A second reason is the so-called psychological contract between companies and communities in society, which refers to the implicit expectations that community members have of companies. People generally want to live in communities that are clean, environmentally safe, friendly and socially cohesive. Within communities, individuals, including local councillors, shopkeepers and social services, work together towards these shared ends. Hence, when a company enters a community, different individuals and groups may appreciate its economic and competitive objectives but will also expect a fair and supportive contribution to that community.

It is this implicit 'psychological contract'[19] that defines the expectations between companies and communities, a feat that often influences how community support and involvement programmes are given shape (by companies) and evaluated (by communities). Such support and involvement programmes may meet, exceed or fall short of community expectations. For companies, it is important to gauge such expectations at the level of each community affected by the company's operations as well as how such expectations may change over time. For example, in the past many communities expected companies to provide lifetime employment to residents, to support important community projects, to be involved in civic and business organizations and to respect the community's values and way of life. Presently, many communities expect employment opportunities (but not necessarily for life anymore) and that companies should generally be more responsive to the concerns and issues of a community. This may involve partnering in improving public education, being environmentally responsible and correcting past mistakes and problems. In other words, companies are now more than ever assumed to act as responsible and proactive 'citizens'. In fact, such changing attitudes to, expectations of and behaviours towards companies impact on a company's licence to operate. The freedom that companies once had in making business decisions has become constrained and challenged by local communities who expect ever greater forms of socially responsible behaviour and community involvement. As such, community involvement needs to be managed by companies as part of their corporate communication. If not, companies may see a further challenge to their licence to operate and may no longer have the support of the community that they need for survival.

Prior to the 1980s, the contribution of many companies to communities consisted of charitable donations, often to high-profile charities. The community relations expert Edmund Burke refers to this as the 'balloon and T-shirts era',[20] to make the point that community relations in those days consisted of giving freebies to non-controversial non-profit organizations such as hospitals, museums and community centres. The relationship was often one of purely making donations, rather than taking an active part in community issues or causes. The decision-making around those donations was also often ad hoc, triggered by approaches from community leaders or by senior executives' networks and family ties. The overall objective with such donations was to create some goodwill on the part of the community towards the company.

The 1980s saw a marked change in community relations programmes. One change involved the greater emphasis on employee volunteer programmes. Because of the harsher economic climate, many governments had introduced drastic cuts in social welfare programmes. There was a real pressing need for such programmes to continue and many governments called on business organizations for their contributions. In the USA, for example, Reagan called on businesses to double their charitable donations and to become involved in alleviating social problems. It is essentially in this era, with the growing pressures from governments and charities placed on business organizations, that community relations emerged as an important sub-field of corporate communication. As a result of this development, companies themselves also started to redefine their expectations of the community. They were looking for a motivated workforce, backed up by a strong and thriving community that would essentially help businesses secure a competitive edge. At the same time, employees themselves were looking for companies with a strong reputation in the communities in which they operate.

The third and final stage of community relations took place in the 1990s onwards. It suggests a further shift beyond a company's charitable donations and employee volunteer programmes. It encompasses more broadly how a company acts, as a citizen, and what it does for the community, besides any charitable donations. This 'citizenship' approach is driven by wider expectations and the rise of community stakeholders. A company, it is argued, needs to behave in ways that promote and build trust between it and the community, and that provide it with legitimacy to operate in that community. Legitimacy refers to some kind of social acceptance resulting from the adherence of a company to regulations but also to community norms and expectations. In contrast, goodwill and reputation refer to an evaluation of an organization and its ability to deliver a particular good. Reputation does not necessarily capture the same normative dimension of civic and morally sound behaviour which communities, as well as many other stakeholders, now expect of businesses.

This shift of course implies that organizations are pressured to build sustainable and ongoing relationships in a community in order to gain trust and legitimacy. The development of trust depends on respectful relationships which are hard earned over time. Such trusting relationships are, however, helpful to companies in keeping track of changing expectations in the psychological contract with communities. The social acceptance that it implies also means that when things go wrong, companies are more likely to be given the benefit of the doubt.

The overall changes in how companies have approached community relations are summarized in Table 13.2. These approaches also suggest a number of different community relations programmes. When he was vice president for public affairs at the Honeywell Corporation, Ronald Speed defined three different programme elements: philanthropy, volunteers and partnerships.[21] These elements can be combined in a model to demonstrate the greater levels of commitment and support that are implied by a combination of these elements or by simply emphasizing partnerships over charitable donations, the latter being less taxing (see Figure 13.1):

Philanthropy: at the bottom of the figure are the company's charitable donations, or philanthropy. These are cash or in-kind contributions to local community causes or charities. Whilst they may be seen as indicating a minor involvement in community affairs, they do provide a strong symbolic signal that the company cares about the community.

Volunteers: at the next level up are employee volunteering programmes. Employee volunteers are the most important resource of a company; they can help build relationships with local communities. When employees are working on local causes or public programmes, they act as ambassadors for the company, enhancing its reputation in the community.

Partnerships: the third and final element, partnerships, assumes an even higher level of commitment and community involvement. Here, companies engage in partnerships with community agencies, and may form alliances with other organizations, to address public or community issues around education, infrastructure and welfare. Doing so may not only allow a company to help address pressing community needs, but may also mean that it can leverage and enhance the entire community relations programme. For example, Toyota partnered with the Japan Alliance for Humanitarian De-mining Support (JAHDS) in Thailand and Cambodia to provide landmine-detection technologies and backup systems to international NGOs. In Britain, Toyota has joined with the British Red Cross to hold interactive road shows to raise awareness levels regarding road accidents amongst kids. In both cases, Toyota makes its expertise and technology available to address issues that affect local communities. Similarly, FedEx provides transportation and logistics support for emergency and disaster relief. The company has partnerships with several relief agencies, including the American Red Cross, United Way International and Heart to Heart International, to help ensure that aid reaches people quickly and efficiently in such crises. In these examples, the partnerships not only connect with the expertise or technology of these companies, but the larger causes or issues (road accidents, logistics for disaster relief) are owned up to by these companies in the name of community support.

As suggested in Figure 13.1, partnerships imply a greater involvement with community causes. Companies that are known for good community relations intimately connect and internalize such programmes into the values of the company. The point then is to align external commitments with the internal values and responsibilities of a company. Companies that have not aligned these programme elements risk losing

TABLE 13.2   Characteristics of the 'old' and 'new' approaches to community relations

	Charitable donations (prior to 1980)	Community involvement (1980–1990)	Citizenship approach (1990–present)
Objectives	Goodwill (with local community leaders and resident employees)	Reputation as employer of choice (with resident employees)	Trust and legitimacy (across stakeholders in the community)
Scope of community programmes	Charitable donations to local charities and causes	Employee volunteer programmes, growing involvement in social welfare programmes	Partnerships with local public institutions in improving the community and increasing welfare
General approach	Idiosyncratic implementation dependent on requests from community leaders or managers' personal networks	Specific approach of fostering productive workplaces, linked to competitive goals	Wide-ranging approach driven by mission, values and multiple stakeholders

FIGURE 13.1 Elements of a community relations programme

their reputation or goodwill in the community. Shell, for example, has not partnered with local community leaders and movements in the Niger Delta to address the environmental problems in the region (see Case Study 10.1). Whilst the company has increased its charitable donations, it has not involved itself in making real changes to the welfare of the community. Nnimmo Bassey, from Environmental Rights Action in Nigeria, for example, has said: 'Despite Shell's public commitment to CSR and specific promise it has made to communities, life on the fence line can too often be likened to hell. From Nigeria to Ireland, the Philippines to South Africa, Shell still too often fails to respect the environment or the needs of local communities.' Shell's poor environmental record in Nigeria is perhaps an indication of its lack of community involvement, which would imply compensating communities such as the people living in the Niger Delta and helping them in addressing sanitary and health issues arising from the degradation of the land.

CASE STUDY 13.1

KRAFT'S TAKEOVER OF CADBURY: FORGETTING THE COMMUNITY?

Kraft Foods, the second largest food company in the world, managed to take over Cadbury, a strong player in the confectionery market, in January 2010. The key motivation for Kraft was to expand its global presence and to gain a foothold in emerging markets such as India, where Cadbury has a strong presence. The acquisition would also bring certain brand portfolio and cross-selling opportunities with it, as it brought many famous brands such as Kraft's Oreo cookies and Cadbury's chocolate bars under one roof. For Kraft, the idea was that the acquisition would expand its market reach and also increase the margin potential of the combined business. Kraft believed that the acquisition would give meaningful revenue synergies and, at the same time, yield pre-tax cost savings of at least $625 million annually to boost its growth targets. The bidding process started in August 2009. Before the final deal was announced, Kraft Foods had repeatedly approached Cadbury. Initial offers were rejected and Kraft was pressured to increase the offer value a number of times. The background to this drawn-out process was that Cadbury was a very profitable and successful company in its own right, with, for example, a market share of 70 per cent in the Indian chocolate market and 1.2 million retail outlets in that country. On the whole,

(Continued)

(Continued)

Cadbury occupied a leadership position in 20 of the world's top 50 emerging confectionery markets. In 2008, with a market share of 10.5 per cent, Cadbury was also effectively ranked as the number two worldwide in confectionery.

Cadbury and the community

The Cadbury company has a long tradition of caring for the communities in which manufacturing facilities were set up and Cadbury products were sold. A good example of this commitment is the development of the Bournville manufacturing site. In 1893 George Cadbury bought some land around Birmingham where he planned a model village which would 'alleviate the evils of modern more cramped living conditions'. Cottages and houses were built for workers in the village. The houses had large gardens and modern interiors. The Cadbury brothers were particularly concerned about the health and fitness of their workforce, creating park and recreation areas, and stimulating their workers to take up sports or other leisurely exercise. Sports playing fields were developed, as well as several bowling greens, a fishing lake and indoor and outdoor swimming pools. Workers and their families could use these facilities free of charge. The Cadbury brothers cared deeply about their employees; they believed in the social rights of workers and, after his brother died, George opened a works committee for each gender which discussed proposals for improving the company. He also advanced other ideas, like an annuity, a deposit account and education facilities for every employee.

Throughout its expansion over the years, the company remained a family business. Members of the Cadbury family occupied management positions in the company and the vast majority of its stock belonged to family members or trusts. In line with its social and family values, Cadbury also maintained a strong commitment to local communities. The company has, for example, been credited with good community relations in India. Cadbury partnered with farmers in Kerala to cultivate cacao and has transparently reported on its efforts to reduce excess packaging, and to cut water and energy use. In addition, when the company was confronted with two crisis scenarios – the first around worms in Cadbury products and the second about an ill-judged ad about Kashmir – it directly responded by improving on the retailing and distribution set-up and by apologizing publicly. Regardless of whether the worms had entered the product at the manufacturing stage or within a retailing setting, Cadbury addressed the crisis head-on and consumers judged it to be an incident rather than a breach of trust and of the brand equity that Cadbury had built up.

Controversy around the takeover

Within the months that Kraft was making bids for Cadbury, the senior management of Cadbury was seriously concerned about the takeover and what it would imply for the Cadbury business and workers. Cadbury repeatedly insisted that Kraft's offers were far too low. Roger Carr, chairman of Cadbury, for example, urged shareholders not to sell themselves short: 'Kraft is trying to buy Cadbury on the cheap to provide much needed growth to their unattractive low-growth conglomerate business model. Don't let Kraft steal your company with its derisory offer.' Politicians and union officials also weighed in, protesting against the takeover. The trade union

Unite estimated that a takeover by Kraft would saddle the company with £22 billion worth of debt and could put some 30,000 jobs at risk, including around 7,000 jobs at Cadbury itself. Gordon Brown, the then Prime Minister, sought assurances from Kraft that 'Cadbury workers – the 5,500 – can retain their jobs and make sure that new investment goes into a product that is distinctly British and is sold throughout the world'. Carr also criticized the role of shareholders in the takeover bidding, many of whom secured some profits by selling Cadbury shares, a process known as 'top-slicing'. These shares were snapped up by short-term investors such as hedge funds, which gambled that Kraft or another bidder would prevail. 'At the end of the day, there were simply not enough shareholders prepared to take a long-term view of Cadbury and prepared to forgo short-term gain for longer-term prosperity', Carr said. Felicity Loudon, George Cadbury's great-granddaughter, said her ancestors would be 'turning in their graves', knowing that Cadbury had been sold to a company that 'makes cheese to go on hamburgers'. Peter Cadbury, a great-grandson, said: 'It is regrettable that a company which took 186 years to build up has had its future decided by investors whose aims are short term.'

Promises to communities

In the bidding process, Kraft had assured the British government that UK jobs would be protected. However, on 9 February 2010, Kraft announced that it was planning to close the Somerdale factory, with a loss of 400 jobs. Kraft had initially promised to keep the factory open, but then decided that plans to move production to Poland were already too advanced to be realistically reversed. Employees from the factory felt betrayed and demoralized. The government's business secretary Lord Mandelson had met with Kraft chief executive Irene Rosenfeld, who had given no hint of the closure. Mandelson expressed his frustration and said:

> When I met the chief executive of Kraft last week, I made it clear that she had not given me any specific commitment or reassurance about any plant in Britain. What I do think, however, is that a week ago, she would have known what announcement was going to be made, barely six days later, and I think it would have been more honest, more straightforward and straight-dealing with the company and its workforce, and also with the Government, if she had told me what their intentions were.

Shadow business secretary Kenneth Clarke was similarly dismayed: 'Kraft gave me reassurances last week that they expected to be able to keep the factory open, despite Cadbury's announcement in 2007 that it would have to close.' The local Cadbury management at the facility has since been partnering with regional development and job agencies to minimize the impact of the closure on the workforce and local economy. Kraft was initially reluctant to engage with any local communities of Cadbury, but has since gone on the PR offensive. Kraft was renamed as the Mondelēz International group in 2012 and has since been regularly meeting with community groups. Despite the promises that were made, 200 jobs were cut in 2015 and workers in Bournville continue to be apprehensive about their jobs and about job security at the site.

(Continued)

(Continued)

Questions for reflection

1 Describe and evaluate the approach to community relations within Cadbury, before and after the takeover by Kraft.
2 What, in your view, should be the approach to community relations within Kraft, as part of its wider stakeholder management?

Source: This case study is based on BBC news (2010) 'Clegg attacks Brown over RBS funding for Cadbury bid', 20 January (see http://news.bbc.co.uk/1/hi/8470776.stm); Skapinker, M. (2010) 'Staff ownership can save a company's soul', *Financial Times*, 8 February; Dixon, L. (2010) 'Mandelson attacks Kraft on Cadbury job losses', *The Times*, 10 February; 'Rock-bottom morale putting Cadbury production at risk', *Daily Mail*, 10 February.

13.5 CHAPTER SUMMARY

Corporate social responsibility and community relations together form an increasingly important area of activity within corporate communication. As an emerging and specialized area, the subject is, however, not often documented in books or in training and educational programmes. This chapter has therefore discussed the basic concepts of corporate citizenship, corporate social responsibility and community relations, and has documented principles and approaches for how companies can communicate about their CSR and engage with communities in different ways and with varying degrees of commitment.

 —— DISCUSSION QUESTIONS ——

1. What is the difference between corporate citizenship and corporate social responsibility?

2. Describe in your own words the idea of a triple bottom line.

3. What would be important motives and objectives for an organization to engage in community relations?

KEY TERMS

Corporate social responsibility
Triple bottom line
CSR reporting
Greenwashing
Community relations
Charitable donation
Volunteering
Anti-corporate activism

Corporate citizenship
Democracy
Integrated reporting
CSR communication
Partnership
Philanthropy
Transparency
Materiality

── 📖 ── FURTHER READING ────────────────

Coombs, W. Timothy and Holladay, Sherry J. (2011) *Managing Corporate Social Responsibility: A Communication Approach*. Oxford: Wiley-Blackwell.
Moon, Jeremy, Rasche, Andreas and Morsing, Mette (2016) *Corporate Social Responsibility: Strategy, Communication, Governance*. Cambridge: Cambridge University Press.

Want to know more about this chapter? Visit the companion website at: https://study.sagepub.com/cornelissen5e to access videos, web links, a glossary and selected journal articles to further enhance your study.

NOTES

1. Crilly, D. and Sloan, P. (2012) 'Enterprise logic: Explaining corporate attention to stakeholders from the "inside-out"', *Strategic Management Journal*, 33: 1174–93.
2. Marsden, C. (2000) 'The new corporate citizenship of big business: Part of the solution to sustainability', *Business and Society Review*, 105: 9–25, quote on p. 11.
3. World Economic Forum (2003–4) Global competitiveness reports, quote on p. 4.
4. Matten, D. and Crane, A. (2005) 'Corporate citizenship: Towards an extended theoretical conceptualization', *Academy of Management Review*, 30 (1).
5. Van Oosterhout, J. (2005) 'Corporate citizenship: An idea whose time has not yet come', *Academy of Management Review*, 30 (4): 677–81; Moon, J., Crane, A. and Matten, D. (2005) 'Can corporations be citizens? Corporate citizenship as a metaphor for business participation in society', *Business Ethics Quarterly*, 15 (3): 429–53.
6. Gray, R., Owen, D. and Maunders, K. (1987) *Corporate Social Reporting: Accounting and Accountability*. Hempel Hampstead: Prentice-Hall, quote on p. 4.
7. Windsor, D. (2001) 'The future of corporate social responsibility', *The International Journal of Organizational Analysis*, 9 (3): 225–56, quote on p. 226; see also Pavelin, S., Brammer, S.J. and Porter, L.A. (2009) 'Corporate charitable giving, multinational companies and countries of concern', *Journal of Management Studies*, 46: 575–96.
8. See, for example, Margolis, J.D. and Walsh, J.P. (2003) 'Misery loves companies: Rethinking social initiatives by business', *Administrative Science Quarterly*, 48: 268–305; Orlitzky, M., Schmidt, F.L. and Rynes, S.L. (2003) 'Corporate social and financial performance: A meta-analysis', *Organization Studies*, 24: 403–41; Porter, M.E. and Kramer, M.R. (2006) 'Strategy and society: The link between competitive advantage and corporate social responsibility', *Harvard Business Review*, December: 78–92; Porter, M.E. and Kramer, M.R. (2011) 'Creating shared value', *Harvard Business Review*, Jan./Feb., 89 (1/2): 62–77.
9. Elkington, J. (1997) *Cannibals with Forks: The Triple Bottom Line of 21st Century Business*. London: Capstone Publishing.
10. Carroll, A.B. (1991) 'The pyramid of corporate social responsibility: Toward the moral management of organizational stakeholders', *Business Horizons*, 34 (4): 39–48.
11. Visser, W. (2013) *The Age of Responsibility: CSR 2.0 and the New DNA of Business*. London: Wiley.
12. Waddock, S. (2008) 'Building a new institutional infrastructure for corporate responsibility', *Academy of Management Perspectives* (August): 87–108.
13. Deetz, S. (2007) 'Corporate governance, corporate social responsibility, and communication', in May, S., Cheney, G. and Roper, J. (eds), *The Debate Over Corporate Social Responsibility*. Oxford: Oxford University Press, 267–78.
14. Christmann, P. and Taylor, G. (2006) 'Firm self-regulation through international certifiable standards: Determinants of symbolic versus substantive implementation', *Journal of*

International Business Studies, 37: 863–78; Crilly, D., Zollo, M. and Hansen, M.T. (2012) 'Faking it or muddling through? Understanding decoupling in response to stakeholder pressures', *Academy of Management Journal*, 55: 1429–48.

15. Ilia, L., Zyglidopoulos, S., Romenti, S., Rodriguez, B. and Del Valle, A. (2013) 'Communicating corporate social responsibility to a cynical public', *MIT Sloan Management Review*, 45 (3): 16–19; Wickert, C. and Cornelissen, J.P. (2016) 'CSR and reputation: Too much of a good thing?', in Moon, J., Rasche, A. and Morsing, M. (eds), *Corporate Social Responsibility: Strategy, Communication, Governance*. Cambridge: Cambridge University Press.

16. Morsing, M. and Schultz, M. (2006) 'Corporate social responsibility communication: Stakeholder information, response and involvement strategies', *Business Ethics: A European Review*, 15: 323–33.

17. KPMG (2015) Currents of change: The KPMG survey of corporate responsibility reporting in 2015. Downloaded from www.kpmg.com/crreporting

18. Soule, Sarah A. (2009) *Contention and Corporate Social Responsibility*. Cambridge: Cambridge University Press.

19. See, for example, Rousseau, D.M. (1995) *Psychological Contract in Organizations: Understanding Written and Unwritten Agreements*. London: Sage.

20. Burke, Edmund M. (1999) *Corporate Community Relations: The Principle of the Neighbor of Choice*. London: Praeger, quote on p. 15.

21. Burke (1999), pp. 130–3.

Glossary of Corporate Communication and Other Communication Terms

4 Ps
: Product, Price, Promotion (marketing communications) and Place (distribution)

Above the line
: All media that remunerate agencies on the basis of commission (e.g. advertising)

Acceptance strategy
: Organizational claim accepting responsibility or culpability for a crisis

Accommodative strategy
: Organizational claim accepting responsibility for a crisis and preventing it from happening again

Account management
: The process by which a communications (PR, advertising) or marketing agency or supplier manages the needs of a client (corporation)

Accountability
: An evaluation of the contribution of functions or activities against their costs

Added value
: The increase in worth of an organization's product or services as a result of a particular activity – in the context of communications, the activity might be effective stakeholder dialogue

Additive change
: A change that is an incremental addition to the existing strategies, routines and procedures within an organization (*see also* Substitutive change)

Advertisement
: A paid-for dedicated space or time in which only the advertiser is represented

Advertising
: The process of gaining the public's attention through paid media announcements

Advertising agency
: An agency specializing in advertising and other marketing communications on behalf of a client organization

Advertising campaign	A planned use and scheduling of advertising over a defined period of time
Advertising media	Paid-for communications channels such as newspaper (print) or television
Advertising value equivalent (AVE)	A measure of evaluating press publicity by counting the column inches of press publicity and seconds of air time gained and then multiplying the total by the advertising rate of the media in which the coverage appeared
Advertorial	An editorial feature paid for or sponsored by an advertiser
Advocacy	An attempt to try to change stakeholder expectations and public opinions on an issue through issue campaigns and lobbying
Advocacy advertising	Advocacy advertising expresses a viewpoint on a given issue, often on behalf of an institution or organization
Agenda building	The process by which corporate communication professionals feed corporate news to journalists to build awareness of a topic, or set of topics, as a potential news item
Agenda setting	Media reporting on organizations that primes awareness of an organization and certain content about that organization
Ambient media	Originally known as 'fringe media', ambient media are communication platforms that surround us in everyday life – from petrol pump advertising to advertising projected onto buildings to advertising on theatre tickets, cricket pitches or even pay slips
Ansoff matrix	A model relating marketing strategy to general strategic direction. It maps product–market strategies – e.g. market penetration, product development, market development and diversification – on a matrix showing new versus existing products along one axis and new versus existing markets along the other
Anti-corporate activism	Political activism directed at specific organizations, industry sectors or general issues associated with corporations and capitalism

Association strategy	Claim of connecting the organization to things positively valued by stakeholders and publics
Attention	The act or faculty of a stakeholder attending to a corporate message or activity
Attitude	A learned predisposition towards an object (e.g. organization, product), person or idea
Audience fragmentation	The process or trend whereby audience segments become more heterogeneous and divided (and therefore more difficult to reach in one)
Audit	*See* Communication audit
Authenticity	The quality or condition of communication (e.g. leadership communication) being authentic, trustworthy or genuine
Awareness	Measure of a proportion of the target audience who have heard of the organization, product or service
BCG matrix	Boston Consulting Group matrix based on market share and market growth rate
Below the line	Non-media advertising or promotion where no commission has been paid to the advertising agency; includes direct mail, point of sale displays and giveaways
Benchmark studies	Studies comparing organizations in a particular sector or industry, used to create yardstick comparisons for improvement and allowing outsiders to evaluate the relative performance of organizations
Blog	A blog (short for weblog) is a personal online journal that is frequently updated and intended for general public consumption
Boundary spanning	The role of corporate communication to act as an intermediary between an organization and external stakeholder groups
Brand	The set of physical attributes of a product or service, together with the beliefs and expectations surrounding it – a unique combination which the name or logo of the product or service should evoke in the mind of the audience

Brand acceptance	The condition wherein an individual, usually a customer, is well disposed towards a brand and will accept credible messages
Brand awareness	The condition wherein an individual, usually a customer, is aware of the brand
Brand equity	The notion that a respected brand name adds to the value of a product (and therefore generates returns to an organization upon customer purchase)
Brand image	The perception of a brand in the eyes of an individual, usually a customer
Brand loyalty	The extent to which individuals, usually customers, repurchase (or utilize) a particular branded product or service
Brand management	The process by which marketers attempt to optimize the 'marketing mix' for a specific brand
Brand portfolio	The total collection of branded trademarks that a company owns and applies to its products or services
Brand positioning	The way in which a brand is communicated to its target market, describing the attributes and values of the brand and its added value/appeal relative to its customers and the competition
Branded content	The generation of content on a marketed online platform that features both product-related content as well as general interest content that speaks favourably to the corporation or brand in question; typically involves PR techniques being used for marketing purposes
Branded identity	A structure whereby businesses and product brands of an organization each carry their own name (without endorsement by the parent company) and are seemingly unrelated to each other
Bridging	Organizations adapting their activities so that they conform with external expectations and claims of important stakeholder groups
Budgeting	The costing of communication activities against a specified amount of money
Buffering	Organizations trying to ignore the claims and interests of stakeholders or stop them from interfering with internal operations

Business communication	The (vocational) discipline of writing, presenting and communicating in a professional context
Business plan	A strategic document showing cash flow, forecasts and the direction of a company
Business strategy	The means by which a business works towards achieving its stated aims
Business-to-business (B2B)	Relating to the sale of a product for any use other than personal consumption; the buyer may be a manufacturer, a reseller, a government body, a non-profit-making institution or any organization other than an ultimate consumer
Business-to-consumer	Relating to the sale of a product for personal consumption; the buyer may be an individual, family or other group, buying to use the product themselves or for end use by another individual
Buzz	Media and public attention given to a company, its products or services
Centralization	Bringing tasks and/or activities together as the responsibility of one person or department in an organization
Change communication	Communication activities to support the formulation, implementation and routinization of a change (e.g. restructuring) within an organization
Channel	The method(s) and media used by a company to communicate and interact with its stakeholders
Channel noise	Confusion caused by too many messages trying to be delivered at one time
Charitable donation	A gift made by an individual or an organization to a non-profit organization, charity or private foundation
Clutter	The total number of messages competing for attention of the audience; usually mentioned in the context of excessive amounts of communication
Cobweb method	A technique whereby individuals rate an organization on a number of selected attributes, which is then visually represented in the form of a wheel or web with eight or more scaled dimensions
Collaborative project	Technology that allows individuals to jointly and simultaneously work together in an online setting

Communication audit	A systematic survey of members of a target audience (often members of the media or potential customers) to determine awareness of or reaction to a message about a product, service or company
Communication climate	The ease with which information flows freely between managers and employees through an organization's formal and informal networks
Communication effects	The impact of communication programmes or campaigns on the awareness, opinions, reputations and behaviours of stakeholder groups
Communication efficiency	The accomplishment of communication with a minimum expenditure of time, effort and resources
Communication facilitator	A role in which practitioners act as liaisons, interpreters, information brokers and mediators between the organization and its stakeholders
Communication strategy	The general set of communication objectives and related communication programmes or tactics chosen by an organization in order to support the corporate strategy of the organization
Community of practice	A group of people who share common interest in a particular domain or area, often created specifically with the goal of gaining knowledge and advancing ideas and technologies related to their field
Community relations	The various forms of activity and communications companies use to establish and maintain mutually beneficial relationships with the communities in which they operate
Competence	Knowledge of a certain (professional) area that is difficult to emulate/a domain of knowledge or specific expertise that an individual needs to properly perform a specific job
Competitive advantage	The product, proposition or benefit that puts a company ahead of its competitors
Competitor	A company that sells products or services in the same market as another
Consumer	An individual who buys and uses a product or service

Consumer behaviour	The buying habits and patterns of consumers in the acquisition and usage of goods and services
Consumer research	Research into the characteristics, changes, usage and attitudes of consumers
Content community	An internet site through which users share media content such as text, photos, videos or PowerPoint presentations
Continuous research	Research conducted constantly to pick up trends, issues, market fluctuations, etc.
Conversational voice	An engaging and natural style of communicating through social media as perceived by the organization's stakeholders and as based on their direct communication with the organization
Copy	The written words (storyline, formatting etc.) to appear in a communications medium (press release, commercial etc.)
Copy date	The date by which a publication or medium requires copy
Copy testing	Research into reactions and responses to written copy
Copywriting	The creative process by which written content is prepared for communication material
Corporate advertising	Advertising by a firm where the corporate entity, rather than solely its products or services, is emphasized
Corporate brand	*See* Monolithic identity
Corporate citizenship	Expressions of involvement of an organization in matters concerning society as a whole
Corporate communication	The function and process of managing communications between an organization and important stakeholder groups (including markets and publics) in its environment
Corporate identity	The profile and values communicated by an organization/the character a company seeks to establish for itself in the mind of its stakeholders, reinforced by consistent use of logos, colors, typefaces and so on

Corporate image	The way a company is perceived, based on a certain message and at a certain point in time/the immediate set of meanings inferred by an individual in confrontation or response to one or more signals from or about a particular organization at a single point in time
Corporate information and communication system	Technology (e.g. intranet) used to disseminate information about the organization to employees across all ranks and functions within the organization in order to keep them informed on corporate matters
Corporate personality	The core values of an organization as shared by its members (*see also* Organizational identity)
Corporate public relations	Public relations activities aimed at 'corporate' stakeholders, which exclude customers and prospects in a market but include issues management, community relations, investor relations, media relations, internal communication and public affairs
Corporate reputation	The general evaluation of an organization (compared to its nearest rivals), leading to likeability and preference
Corporate social responsibility (CSR)	Actions which do not have purely financial implications and which are demanded or expected of an organization by society at large, often concerning ecological and social issues
Corporate strategy	The general direction taken by a company with regard to its choice of businesses and markets and the approach of its stakeholder groups
Coverage	The percentage of the target audience who have the opportunity to be confronted with the communications message at least once
Crisis	A point of great difficulty or danger to the organization, possibly threatening its existence and continuity, and that requires decisive change
Crisis management	The reactive response to a crisis in order to pre-empt or limit damage to the organization's reputation
Crowd-casting	The ability of members of the public to generate content on organizations and to organize themselves with others online into communities or 'crowds'

Culture	The general values and beliefs held and shared by members of an organization
Customer	A person or company who purchases goods or services (not necessarily the end-consumer)
DAGMAR	Defining Advertising Goals for Measured Advertising Response – a model for planning advertising in such a way that its success can be quantitatively monitored
Database marketing	Whereby customer information, stored in an electronic database, is utilized for targeting marketing activities; information can be a mixture of what is gleaned from previous interactions with the customer and what is available from outside sources
Decoding	A process where the receiver converts the symbolic forms transmitted by the sender
Demographics	Information describing and segmenting a population in terms of age, sex, income and so on, which can be used to target communication campaigns
Departmental arrangement	The administrative act of grouping or arranging disciplines, activities and people into departments
Depth interview	An interview, usually one-to-one, exploring deeper motivations and beliefs
Desk research	Using publicly available and previous data (e.g. on certain issues, markets)
DESTEP	Demographic, Economic, Social, Technological, Ecological and Political analysis – a broad analysis of macro factors that may impinge on an organization's business and operations
Dialogue strategy	A process of communication in which both parties (organizations and stakeholders) mutually engage in an exchange of ideas and opinions
Differentiation (competitive strategy)	A competitive strategy whereby the unique and added value of a product or service is emphasized (which then warrants a premium price)
Direct mail	Delivery of an advertising or promotional message to customers or potential customers by mail

Direct marketing   All activities which make it possible to offer goods or services or to transmit other messages to a segment of the population by post, telephone, e-mail or other direct means

Direct response   Communications (e.g. advertising) incorporating a contact method such as a phone number, address and enquiry form, website identifier or e-mail address, with the intention of encouraging the recipient to respond directly to the advertiser by requesting more information, placing an order and so on

Distance strategy   A claim of distancing the organization from direct responsibility for a crisis

Distribution channel   The process and way of getting the goods from the manufacturer or supplier to the user

Dominant coalition   The group of people, usually the executive or senior management team, within an organization making the important decisions (concerning the direction and focus of the firm etc.)

Downward communication   Electronic and verbal methods of informing employees about their organization, its performance and their own performance in terms they can comprehend

Elaboration likelihood model   A theoretical model of how attitudes are formed and changed based on an 'elaboration continuum', which ranges from low elaboration (low involvement and attention) to high elaboration (high involvement and attention)

Emotional message style   This attempts to provoke involvement and positive reactions through a reference to positive (or negative) emotions

Employee voice   A state in which employees are able to speak up, express opinions and are listened to by managers

Encoding   The process of putting information into a symbolic form of words, pictures or images

Endorsed identity   A structure whereby businesses and product brands of an organization are endorsed or badged in communications with the parent company name

Environmental scanning	The process whereby the environment of an organization is continuously scanned for issues and trends, usually in relation to important stakeholder groups
Equal dissemination strategy	A process of communication in which managers disseminate information to all stakeholders early, often and, most importantly, on an equal basis
Equal participation strategy	Two-way communication (i.e. both disseminating information and soliciting input) between managers and stakeholders
Evaluation	An assessment of the effects of a communication programme or campaign
Exchange	The process by which two or more parties give up a desired resource to one another
Execution	The act of carrying something out (usually a set of planned-for communications programmes)
Executive team	The senior management team of an organization, typically led by the chief executive officer, responsible for the overall management and strategic direction of the firm
Expert prescriber	A role in which a communication practitioner acts as a specialist on communication problems but largely independently of senior management
Exposure	The condition of being exposed to a company-related message or activity
External analysis	A study of the external environment of an organization, including factors such as customers, competition and social change
Faux pas	A claim made by an external agent (e.g. NGO) that the organization violates accepted, although unwritten, social rules and expectations
FMCG	Fast Moving Consumer Goods – such as packaged food, beverages, toiletries and tobacco
Focus group	A tool for market, communications and opinion research where small groups of people are invited to participate in guided discussions on the topic being researched

Forecasting	A calculation of future events and performance
Formal research technique	*See* Informal research technique
Formative evaluation	A type of evaluation which has the purpose of improving communication programmes or campaigns
Frame alignment	A situation where an organization's explanation of a decision, issue or event coincides with the way in which journalists think about the same decision, issue or event
Frame contest	The negotiation between communication practitioners and journalists about the preferred angle to a story about an organization
Framing	Presenting a story about an organization from a particular angle
Frequency	The average number of times a target audience will have the opportunity to be exposed to (see) a certain message
Full service agency	An agency that specializes in a whole range of communications disciplines and can assist the client in the full process of communications planning and execution
Gatekeeping research	An analysis of the characteristics of a press release or video news release that allow them to 'pass through the gate' and appear in a news medium
Generic message style	A straight claim about an industry or cause with no assertion of superiority
Geodemographics	A method of analysis combining geographic and demographic variables
Global brand	A brand which has worldwide recognition (e.g. Coca-Cola)
Goal	The primary and direct result a company is attempting to achieve through its communications efforts
Grassroots campaigning	People or society at a local level (e.g. citizens), rather than at the centre of major political activity, who campaign on political or corporate issues
Greenwashing	Instances where organizations communicate excessively about their CSR compared to real achievements

Hierarchy of effects	The sequence of effects that an audience may go through from exposure to a message to, ultimately, behavioural change
Image	An individual's perceptions of an organization, product or service at a certain point in time
Industrial goods	Products/resources required by industrial companies
Industry coalition	A collation of corporate organizations and interests representing a corporate voice to government and politicians
Infomercial	An advertising commercial that provides extensive information
Informal research technique	Casual observations on audiences, markets or industries acquired through informal contacts and communication (*see also* Formal research technique)
Informational strategy	The process of making information about an organization available to its stakeholders
Integrated reporting	A concise representation of a company's performance in terms of both financial value and social and environmental value
Integration (integrated communication)	The act of coordinating all communications so that the corporate identity is effectively and consistently communicated both to internal and external groups
Intentional communication	A message that an organization intends to convey
Intermediary	Any individual/company in the distribution channel between the supplier and the final consumer
Internal analysis	The study of a company's internal resources in order to assess the opportunities, strengths and weaknesses
Internal communication	All methods (internal newsletter, intranet) used by a firm to communicate with its employees
Issue	An unsettled matter (which is ready for a decision) or a point of conflict between an organization and one or more publics
Issues management	The proactive attempt to identify and control issues in order to pre-empt or limit damage to the organization's reputation
Kelly grid	*See* Repertory grid

Laddering	A research technique whereby people's opinions are represented as a means–end chain; used to infer the basic values and motivations that drive people
Leadership	The skill and activity of leading others within an organization
Legitimacy	The assessment of an organization against the norms, values and expectations of its stakeholders, in terms of what those stakeholders deem acceptable and favoured by the organization
Licensing	The act of formally accrediting an agency or professional, often done by a professional association or legal body
Life cycle	The stages through which a product or brand develops (*see* PLC)
Lifestyle	A research classification based on shared values, attitude and personality
Likert scale	A research scale which uses statements to indicate agreement or disagreement
Line extension	Extending existing brands to other products in the same product category
Line function	An organizational function that is directly involved in the core and operational business process (i.e. the 'line') of producing products and bringing them to market (i.e. marketing)
Lobbying	A form of corporate advocacy with the intention of influencing decisions made by legislators and officials in the government
Logo	A graphic, usually consisting of a symbol and/or group of letters, which identifies a company or brand
Low-cost (competitive strategy)	A competitive strategy where the low cost of a product or service is emphasized
Macro environment	The external factors which affect a company's planning and performance, and are beyond its control: for example, socio-economic, legal and technological change
Management communication	Communication between managers and employees; restricted to dyads and small groups

Manager (communications manager)	A practitioner who makes strategy or programme decisions concerning communications and is held accountable for programme success or failure; engages in research, strategic planning and management of communications
Market	A defined group for whom a product is or may be in demand (and for whom an organization creates and maintains products and service offerings)
Market development	The process of growing sales by offering existing products (or new versions of them) to new customer groups (as opposed to simply attempting to increase the company's share of current markets)
Market orientation	Steadfast adherence to the marketing concept: an approach in which customer needs and wants are the underlying determinants of an organization's direction and its marketing programmes
Market penetration	The attempt to grow one's business by obtaining a larger market share in an existing market
Market research	The gathering and analysis of data relating to marketplaces or customers; any research which leads to more market knowledge and better-informed decision-making
Market segmentation	A division of the marketplace into distinct subgroups or segments, each characterized by particular tastes and requiring a specific marketing mix
Market share	A company's sales of a given product or set of products to a given set of customers, expressed as a percentage of total sales of all such products to such customers
Market structure	The character of an industry, based on number of firms, barriers to entry, the extent of product differentiation, control over price and the importance of non-price competition
Marketing	The management process responsible for identifying, anticipating and satisfying customer requirements profitably
Marketing audit	A comprehensive and systematic review and appraisal of every aspect of a firm's marketing programme, its organization, activities, strategies and people

Marketing communications	All methods (advertising, direct marketing, sales promotion, personal selling and marketing public relations) used by an organization to communicate with its customers and prospective customers
Marketing concept	The process by which the marketer responds to the needs and wants of the consumer
Marketing mix	The combination of marketing inputs that affect customer motivation and behaviour; these inputs traditionally encompass four controllable variables known as 'the 4 Ps': product, price, promotion and place
Marketing objective	A market target to be achieved reflecting corporate strategy
Marketing public relations	The use of what are traditionally seen as public relations tools (media, free publicity) within marketing programmes; used to reach marketing objectives
Marketing strategy	The set of objectives which an organization allocates to its marketing function in order to support the overall corporate strategy, together with the broad methods chosen to achieve these objectives
Materiality	The environmental and social issues that are defined as being at the core of an organization and its integrated reporting; these issues are of 'material consequence' for the organization, its stakeholders and society
Matrix structure	A structure where a professional has a dual reporting relationship; this structure aims to foster both functional expertise and coordination at the same time
Media	1. Members or tools for disseminating the news; unbiased third parties (press representatives); 2. Communication channels for a certain campaign
Media coverage	Mention of a company, its products or services in the media
Media favourability	Positive news coverage of an organization in which the organization is praised for its actions or is associated with activities that should raise its reputation

Media logic	The dominant or overriding frame of reference adopted by a news organization that influences how they cover and report news on organizations
Media plan	Recommendation for a media schedule including dates, publications, TV regions, etc.
Media relations	The function or process of gaining positive media attention and coverage
Media richness	The ability of a medium to allow for immediate feedback between the two parties and for expressing and articulating the message in different ways
Media schedule	Records of campaign bookings made or a proposal (with dates, costs etc.) for a campaign
Merchandising	Traditionally, in-store promotion and displays
Message style	The way in which a message is given form and delivered to a target audience
Metrics	Operational measures of online behaviours (such as click-throughs) that can be tracked over time
Microblogging	The practice by which an individual quickly posts and comments on messages online (e.g. through Twitter)
Micro environment	The immediate context of a company's operations, including such elements as suppliers, customers and competitors
MIIS	Management Intelligence and Information System – a system for collecting and examining environmental and/or market data
Mission	A company's overriding purpose in line with the values or expectations of stakeholders
Mission statement	A company's summary of its business philosophy and direction
Monolithic identity	A structure whereby businesses and product brands of an organization all carry the same corporate name
Multinational	A corporation whose operational and marketing activities cover multiple countries across the world

Need-to-know strategy	A process of communication in which managers keep quiet about decisions or changes except to those stakeholders who really need to know or who explicitly express a desire for the information
Net promoter score	A measure reflecting the willingness of customers to recommend a company's products or services to others; it is used as a proxy for gauging the customer's overall satisfaction with a company's product or service and the customer's loyalty to the brand
Network ties	The connections that individuals form between them as a result of communication
News routine	The way in which news is produced in a particular media organization, starting with the journalist consulting sources and ending with the editor making the final decisions about an article or feature
Niche marketing	The marketing of a product to a small and well-defined segment of the marketplace
Noise	*See* Channel noise
Non-existence strategy	A claim made by an organization denying an issue or crisis
Non-verbal communication	Transmission of a message without the use of words or language
Objective	A company's defined and measurable aims for a given period
Omnichannel approach	A tactic of linking on- and off-line media and contact points with customers and other stakeholders, and in such a way that it stimulates and drives their behaviour and optimizes media spending
One-time studies	Studies focused on measuring effects at a single instant in time – for example, after a corporate advertising campaign
Online newsroom	An online facility, often on the corporate website, archiving press releases, video materials and company reports

Organizational identification	The perception of oneness with or belongingness to an organization, where the individual defines him- or herself in terms of the organization(s) of which they are a member
Organizational identity	The set of values shared by members of an organization (*see also* Corporate personality)
Organizational silence	A state in which employees refrain from speaking up and withhold information about potential problems or issues
OTH	Opportunities To Hear – the number of opportunities a target consumer has of hearing an advertisement
OTS	Opportunities To See – the number of opportunities a target consumer has of seeing an advertisement
Output analysis	A measurement of the amount of exposure or attention that an organization receives in the media; often done by collecting press clippings (copies of stories or articles in the press) and by recording the degree of exposure in terms of column inches in print media, the number of minutes of air time in the electronic media or the number of citations on the web
Partnership	A collaborative relationship between a private organization and public sector or community organizations to address local or global societal and community issues
Partnership promotion	A joint promotion aiming to achieve additional exposure
Perception	The way a corporation/product/event/stimulus is received and evaluated by an individual
Personal selling	One-to-one communication between seller and prospective purchaser
Persuasion	A means by which a person or organization tries to influence and convince another person to believe something or do something, using reasoning and coaxing in a compelling and convincing way

Persuasive strategy	A process of communication in which an organization, through campaigns, meetings and discussions with stakeholders, tries to change and tune the knowledge, attitude and behaviours of stakeholders in a way that is favourable to the organization
Philanthropy	The act and effort of increasing the wellbeing and welfare of communities through charitable aid or donations
Pitch	A prepared sales presentation by an agency to a client organization, usually one-on-one
Planning	Setting communication activities and campaigns on the basis of communication objectives and against a timeline
PLC	Product life cycle – supposed stages of a product, e.g. birth, growth, maturity and decline
Political action committee	A committee formed by business, labour or other special interest groups to raise money and make contributions to the campaigns of political candidates whom they support
Porter's five forces	An analytic model developed by Michael E. Porter which analyses businesses and industries; the five forces are: Buyers, Suppliers, Substitutes, New Entrants and Rivals
Portfolio (and portfolio analysis)	The set of products or services which a company decides to develop and market; portfolio analysis is the process of comparing the contents of the portfolio to see which products or services are the most promising and deserving of further investment, and which should be discontinued
POS	Point Of Sale – The location, usually within a retail outlet, where the customer decides whether to make a purchase
Position–importance matrix	A tool to categorize stakeholders and publics according to their position on a particular issue and according to their importance to the organization
Positioning	The creation of an image for a company, product or service in the minds of stakeholders, both specifically to that entity and in relation to competitive organizations and offerings

Power–interest matrix	A tool to categorize stakeholders on the basis of the power that they have and the extent to which they are likely to have or show an interest in the organization's activities
PR	*See* Public relations
Pre-emptive message style	A generic claim about an organization with a suggestion of superiority
Press agentry	The use of press agents, promoters and publicists to promote and publicize an organization and its products or services through the media; often used to describe communications during the early decades of the twentieth century
Press conference	An organized gathering or event where an organization announces decisions or fiscal results to journalists
Press kit	Several press deliverables combined in one package (usually a folder)
Press release	A paper or electronic document submitted to the media with the intent of gaining media coverage
Prestige	The level of respect or status associated with an organization, and which may reflect on its members
Problem-solving process facilitator	A role in which communication practitioners collaborate with other managers to define and solve organizational problems
Process effects	Evaluation of the cost-effective manner in which a communication programme or campaign has been planned and executed
Projective technique	A qualitative research technique by which an individual is asked to respond to ambiguous stimuli such as vague statements or objects; designed to measure feelings, opinions, attitudes and motivations
Proposition	The message that the advertiser wants the customer to focus on
Psychographics	A base for segmentation derived from attitude and behavioural variables
Public	A population of individuals (say, within a society), often defined in broader terms as specific groups such as stakeholders or audiences

Public affairs	The public policy aspect of corporate communication
Public information	The use of writers and publicists to inform and reassure the general public of corporate practices; often used to describe communications before the Second World War
Public relations	The function or activity that aims to establish and protect the reputation of a company or brand, and to create mutual understanding between the organization and the segments of the public with whom it needs to communicate
Publicity	Media coverage
Pull strategy	Pull communications, in contrast to push communications, address the customer directly with a view to getting them to demand the product, and hence 'pull' it down through the distribution chain; it focuses on advertising and above-the-line activities
Push strategy	Push communications rely on the next link in the distribution chain – e.g. a wholesaler or retailer – to 'push' out products to the customer; it revolves around sales promotions – such as price reductions and point-of-sale displays – and other below-the-line activities
Qualitative research	Research that does not use numerical data but relies on interviews, 'focus groups', 'repertory grid', and the like, usually resulting in findings which are more detailed but also more subjective than those of 'quantitative research'
Quantitative research	Research that concentrates on statistics and other numerical data, gathered through opinion polls, customer satisfaction surveys etc.
Quid pro quo strategy	A process of communication in which managers give more communicative attention to those stakeholders who have something valuable (e.g. expertise, approval power, resources) to offer a decision or change process
Rational message style	A superiority claim based on actual accomplishments or delivered benefits by the organization

Reach	The percentage or number of people exposed to a media vehicle at least once
Recall	Used by researchers to establish how memorable a certain communications message was
Receiver	In communications theory, the party receiving the message
Repertory grid	A technique for representing the attitudes and perceptions of individuals; also called Personal Construct Technique, this technique can be useful in developing market research (and other) questionnaires
Reputation	*See* Corporate reputation
Return on investment (ROI)	The value that an organization derives from investing in a project
Sales promotion	A range of techniques used to engage the purchaser; these may include discounting, coupons, guarantees, free gifts, competitions, vouchers, demonstrations, bonus commission and sponsorship
Sampling	The use of a statistically representative subset as a proxy for an entire population, for example in order to facilitate quantitative market research
Secondary research	*See* Desk research
Segmentation	*See* Market segmentation
Selective attention	Where receivers only notice some of the message presented
Selective distortion	Seeing and hearing differently from the message presented
Selective exposure	The idea that individuals only expose themselves to certain messages
Selective perception	The process of screening out information that is not of interest and retaining information of use
Sender	In communications theory, the party sending the message
Share of voice	Calculation of a brand's share of media expenditure in a particular category

Shareholder value	The worth of a company from the point of view of its shareholders
Skill (communication skill)	The ability to produce or craft communication materials (e.g. a written document by way of a skill in writing)
Slogan	A frequently repeated phrase that provides continuity in messages and campaigns of a certain corporation, its products or services
SMART objectives	Objectives which are Specific, Measurable, Achievable, Realistic and Timely
SME	A small to medium-sized enterprise – variously defined: according to one EU definition, it must employ under 250 people, have either a turnover of less than EUR 40 million or net balance sheet assets of less than EUR 27 million, and not be more than 25 per cent owned by a larger company
Social identity	The degree to which individuals describe and define themselves, as individuals or in terms of their membership of a certain social group
Social networking site	An internet site that allows users to present personal information and create profiles of themselves, and to share these in turn with others
Social reporting	The social and environmental issues and achievements declared by an organization and as assessed and written down in a formal report
Spin	An attempt to manipulate the depiction of news or events in the media through artful public relations; often used with derogatory connotations
Spokesblogger	An official spokesperson for an organization who, whilst publishing an independent blog, often does not speak only for themselves, but also on behalf of their employer or the organization that they represent
Spokesperson	An official representative of the organization who deals with journalists and the media
Sponsorship	A specialized form of sales promotion where a company will help fund an event or support a business venture in return for publicity

Staff function	An organizational function (e.g. communications) carrying no direct executive power over the primary operational process or responsibility for it, but fulfilling an advisory role for other functions within the organization
Stakeholder	Any group or individual who can affect or is affected by the achievement of an organization's objectives
Stakeholder advocacy	The process by which stakeholders actively argue in favour of and support a particular organization
Stakeholder audit	A systematic survey of stakeholders to determine the nature of the relationship and any issues around and possible reactions to corporate actions
Stakeholder collaboration	A situation where an organization builds long-term relationships through working together with stakeholders on issues of common concern
Stakeholder engagement	The process of actively involving stakeholders in communication, listening to them and allowing them to have a say in corporate decision-making
Stakeholder mapping	An analytical tool whereby stakeholder groups are identified and their relationship to the organization becomes visually represented in a map
Stakeholder salience	The visibility or importance of a stakeholder based on their possession of one or more of three attributes: power, legitimacy and urgency
Storytelling	The act of telling stories or narratives in an organization to persuade employees or other stakeholders into certain ways of thinking about an organization
Strategic intent	The general direction of an organization, often articulated in objectives, together with the general patterns of actions that will be taken to achieve these objectives
Strategy	General broad patterns of actions to accomplish corporate, market and/or communications objectives
Substitutive change	A drastic change within an organization that changes the very status quo and previous ways of working

Suffering strategy   A claim that an organization is suffering from a crisis or a public policy decision

Supportive behaviour   Behaviour of stakeholders that is positive and supportive of an organization (e.g. investing in shares, buying products and services), often in a way that is desired by the organization

SWOT   A method of analysis which examines a company's Strengths, Weaknesses, Opportunities and Threats; often used as part of the development process for a corporate or marketing plan

Symbolic association   A claim of associating an organization with general
message style   (culturally shared and recognized) moral values, symbols and sentiments

Tactics   Specific action items to support strategies and objectives

Tagline   A short and memorable phrase at the end of an advert or other corporate message that aims to either sum up a company's claims or to reinforce and strengthen the recall of those claims

Target audience   The key groups or individuals that a company wants to reach with its communications messages

Target market   The segment of a market at which marketing efforts are directed

Targeting   The use of market segmentation to select and address a key group of potential purchasers

Technician (communication   A practitioner who in their day-to-day work
technician)   focuses primarily on programmatic and tactical communication activities such as writing, editing, producing brochures, etc.; a technician thus tactically implements decisions made by others

Telemarketing   The marketing of a product or service over the telephone

Themed message   A message that is identified as central to the organization's reputation and that is designed to change or reinforce perceptions in line with a vision of how the organization wants to be known

Thought leadership	The decision of an organization to take up a proactive position on issues that matter to its stakeholders and society and are connected to its business strategy (e.g. environmental issues for petrol firms)
Through the line	A mixture of below- and above-the-line communications
Tracking	The surveying of individuals' attitudes to and perceptions (images and reputations) of an organization, products or services on a continuous basis
Trademark	A sign or device, often with distinctive lettering, that symbolizes a brand
Transactional leadership	A leadership style that is based on motivating employees through (financial) incentives and rewards
Transformational leadership	A leadership style that is based on motivating employees through visions and involvement
Transgression	An intentional act taken by an organization that knowingly places stakeholders or publics at risk or harm
Transparency	A state where the image or reputation of an organization held by stakeholder groups is similar to the actual and/or projected identity of an organization
Triple bottom line	The idea that organizations have social ('people') and ecological ('planet') responsibilities besides their economic imperative of generating profits and healthy financial accounts
Unintentional communication	A message that an organization does not intend to convey
Upward communication	Information from employees that is cast up to managers within the organization; it involves information about the employee themselves, about co-workers, about organizational practices and policies, and about what needs to be done and how
USP	Unique Selling Proposition (or Point) – the benefit that a product or service can deliver to customers that is not offered by any competitor: one of the fundamentals of effective marketing and business

Vision	The long-term aims and aspirations of the company for itself
Volunteering	The act of people working on behalf of others or a particular cause without payment for their time and services
Web 2.0	Web applications that facilitate interactive information sharing, interoperability, user-centred design and collaboration on the World Wide Web
Word-of-mouth	The spreading of information through human interaction alone
Zero-based planning	A review of media options during communications planning based on research, analysis and insight, and not on habit and preference

Index